DATE			

PALAEOPATHOLOGY OF ABORIGINAL AUSTRALIANS

For Beata

PALAEOPATHOLOGY OF ABORIGINAL AUSTRALIANS

health and disease across a hunter-gatherer continent

Stephen Webb

CAMBRIDGE
UNIVERSITY PRESS

Published by the Press Syndicate of the University of Cambridge
The Pitt Building, Trumpington Street, Cambridge CB2 1RP, UK
40 West 20th Street, New York, NY 10011–4211, USA
10 Stamford Road, Oakleigh, Melbourne 3166, Australia

Printed in Hong Kong by Colorcraft

National Library of Australia cataloguing-in-publication data

Webb, Stephen G.
Palaeopathology of Aboriginal Australians.
Bibliography.
Includes index.
1. Paleopathology – Australia. [2.] Aborigines, Australian –
Diseases – History. [3.] Aborigines, Australian – Health and
hygiene – History. I. Title.
616.00899915

Library of Congress cataloguing-in-publication data

Webb, Stephen.
Palaeopathology of Aboriginal Australians: health and disease
across a hunter–gatherer continent / Stephen Webb.
Includes bibliographical references and index.
1. Paleopathology – Australia. 2. Australian aborigines – Health
and hygiene. I. Title.
R134.8.W427 1994   94–15247
616.07'0994–dc20   CIP

A catalogue record for this book is available from the British Library.

ISBN 0 521 46044 1 Hardback

Contents

List of illustrations

Maps

Figures

List of tables

Acknowledgements

There are a number of people and organisations which helped me prepare and write this book. The South Australian Museum, Queensland Museum, Western Australian Museum and the Prehistory Department of the Research School of Pacific Studies, Australian National University, provided the photographs. In particular, I want to thank Dragi Markovic whose extraordinary photographic skills produced many of the photographs. The recent reburial of some items required reproduction of certain plates from colour slides taken by me, often cursorily and in poor lighting many years ago, when I could never have realised that they would one day be the only photographic record. I am indebted to Dragi for his attempts to enhance these photographs, as well as for other work he has done for me over the years. I wish to thank the Prehistory Department of the Research School of Pacific Studies, Australian National University, for the financial support for the photographic work and the Australian Academy of Humanities.

Without the co-operation of museums and their staff throughout Australia the gathering of data and the re-examination of many pathological examples would not have been possible. These include the Queensland Museum, the Australian Museum, the National Museum of Australia, the Victorian Museum, the South Australian Museum, the Western Australian Museum and the Tasmanian Museum and Art Gallery. Professor Jim Allen carried out the excavations at Motupore Island and I am grateful to him for access to the skeletal remains described in Chapter 11 as well as for his editorial comments. Many physicians and specialists have allowed me to pick their brains, albeit that one or two pathological examples have foxed them, and I thank them for their time.

Much has been said with regard to the reburial issue that has arisen in Australia as well as in North America. I can only say that I have spoken with Aboriginal people from many parts of the continent and while they have expressed general reservations concerning palaeobiological research on the remains of their ancestors, I have received understanding from them for what I was trying to do. I hope, therefore, that in some small way that community will find this book useful for the information it contains and that they may appreciate the testament of unwritten knowledge that their ancestors left for us all to 'read'. An elder of the Mutti Mutti people of New South Wales once told me that she believed research was important because the fossil humans that emerged from the sand dunes in her country were coming back to tell us something. They tell us who they were, where and how they lived and provide proof to both Aboriginal and non-Aboriginal people of how long the first Australians have been living here. I have to say that without the co-operation, friendship and understanding that I have received from many Aboriginal people this book may not have been possible.

Lastly, but most sincerely, I want to thank Beata Malczewska whose tireless strength, unfailing support and sincere interest largely kept me writing. This is for her and she has earned every comma.

Chapter 1

Introduction

The history of mankind is the history of its diseases.
(Henschen 1966:25)

No one would argue that the health of Australian Aboriginal people suffered disastrously following European settlement here in 1788. In addition, it is a commonly-held belief that Aboriginal health before the coming of Whites was probably very good. There is one problem with the latter belief, however, and that is there is little empirical data upon which to base it. In any case, it is not good enough to make such statements, we need to be able to identify and quantify what we mean by them. Until now, any comparisons that have been made between the pre- and post-contact health status of Aboriginal people have relied on ethnographic and ethnohistorical sources. It is these sources, largely unrepresentative and often unreliable respectively, that have been used to construct the non-Aboriginal perspective of what Aboriginal health was like prior to colonisation. It was this uncertainty that originally made me ask: how healthy were Aboriginal people? Other questions naturally followed. Who were the sickest people in Australia, someone had to be? What kinds of disease were here before Europeans arrived? Did Aboriginal people really murder the sick and malformed (another commonly held belief)? Did they suffer from stress, and if so why and in what form? What is the earliest evidence for disease in Australia and what is the disease? What was the health of Australians like during the last Ice Age? and what might the wider interpretations of the patterns of health on this continent tell us about the people themselves and their various lifestyles?

This book has been written to try and answer some of these and many similar questions. They are, I believe, not merely academic but questions that apply not only to Aboriginal people but to us all. Answers to them can help us understand more about the pathology we all suffered at one time or another in the past. They also teach us something about ourselves, the ecology of our species and the origins of our diseases. To answer them, however, we have to take a broad, generalised approach to the subject rather than concentrate on one particular area of Australia or on one or two pathologies.

Until the early 1980s no systematic palaeopathological study had been undertaken in Australia. Nothing was known about what kinds of disease might have been introduced here by numerous human migrations to the continent or about the health of more recent Aboriginal people. It is surprising that this situation continued in Australia while in Europe and North America the formal study of palaeopathology was celebrating its centenary. It is even more surprising if we remember that Johann Friedrich Esper, acknowledged by some as the father of palaeopathology, made his now famous but erroneous pronouncement on the pathological status of a fossilised cave bear femur some fourteen years before the first Europeans arrived to settle in Australia in 1788. It is not difficult to understand, therefore, that the main reason for writing this text is to help redress an enormous gap in our knowledge of the pre-contact health of Aboriginal Australians and the story of human health in this part of the world over the last 50,000 years or more.

The continuing return of whole skeletal collections to Aboriginal communities for reburial has added further impetus to the production of this book. Because of these events many of the remains used in this survey are no longer available for study. Under these circumstances I felt that it was important to make available much of the palaeopathological data that I have gathered from all Australian collections for over a decade. Unfortunately, the sudden demise of such scientifically important collections has prevented further and much needed study of many pathologies, including rare and unique examples; it has also meant the loss of other important palaeobiological information. Moratoria prevented many collections from being studied for several years before burials took place. Reassessment and further study of certain pathological conditions which I would like to have undertaken has not, therefore, been possible in the interim. This has resulted in a more cursory description and diagnosis of some pathologies than I would have liked. These have been based of necessity on sparse notes taken under the misapprehension that I could have returned to study them further.

Internationally, the 1960s marked a turning point in the study of palaeopathology, following the rather staid and narrow 'medicine at work' approach of the first half of this century. The revival emerged from a dynamism derived from improved methods and analytical techniques which, in themselves, borrowed from the huge advances being made at that time in the fields of physics, chemistry and medicine. Later, data analysis began to focus on systematic assessment and the need to understand patterns of human disease in their wider palaeo-epidemiological context. The pathology of earlier societies was beginning to be seen not just as a product of pathological processes but as a phenomenon closely related to the interplay between demography and social, economic and cultural behaviour on the one hand and the environment on the other. Angel's (1964, 1967) Mediterranean work is a fine example of this new approach. His work emerged soon after palaeopathology 'took off' for a second time in the latter half of the twentieth century. The post-1960s renaissance was born out of a renewed vigour for understanding palaeoepidemiological problems as well as major improvements in investigative techniques. New techniques were as important an incentive as they had been at the turn of the century when Ruffer (1909) applied histological techniques and Dedekind (1896) added radiography to palaeopathological analysis. The publication of Jarcho's (1966) and Brothwell and Sandison's (1967) edited volumes, however, inspired new ideas and approaches from within the discipline itself. These volumes also gave incentive to many new devotees, they certainly did to me when I read them fifteen years after their publication. They also played an important role in documenting the frontiers of palaeopathology at that time. For these reasons alone their influence cannot be underestimated and they will always remain cornerstones of the palaeopathological literature. During the 1970s 'non-specific' stress markers, such as Harris lines, cribra orbitalia and dental hypoplasia, became more widely used in a mutually supportive way to understand diet, demography and social structure in past societies. With an upsurge in bone composition analysis, palaeonutrition became an inseparable adjunct to palaeopathology as the popularity of the subject grew through volumes such as Wing and Brown (1980).

In the last 10 years palaeopathology has begun to change as a discipline so that now its philosophy and emphasis has altered radically from its Virchowian beginnings. Rather than its major theme being the discovery of past diseases, or the publication of 'interesting' or 'unusual' conditions, its focus is now directed towards the origins and ecology of disease, particularly disease as a function of human demography and adaptation to an ever-changing social and biological environment. We have now entered the era of palaeoepidemiological study in its widest sense.

The combined use of various pathologies and pathological stress markers, together with studies of bone-remodelling dynamics and trace element analysis, now enables us to come to grips with the history of human society in a way never before possible. Ancient communities can be shown more as the living populations they once were, reflecting their particular environments and the constantly changing dynamics of human populations. Interpretations made by the palaeopathologist often add unique, rather sophisticated and vital data to our knowledge of our past and biological history. In this way palaeopathology now plays a part as important to the understanding of the evolution and development of human society as any branch of traditional anthropology and archaeology; in some respects it contributes more. In other words, it strongly underpins our ability to piece together the complex, fascinating and extremely important jigsaw of who we are and where we have come from.

We now know that Australia's slowly emerging human story is very long, although we do not know how long that may turn out to be. It is also enormous in its breadth and extremely complex in its composition. Certainly no single text can do justice to all the information we now have concerning this story as was possible when D. J. Mulvaney first published his *Prehistory of Australia* in 1969. Our knowledge and understanding of the culture and diversity of the first Australians has grown at such an astonishing rate since then that many volumes would be needed if we wanted to include all the basic information we have. I have to say that biological anthropology has contributed a respectable slice of that knowledge, adding to the study of prehistory by focussing on the people themselves rather than on the consequences of their behaviour in the rather disembodied way that often characterises archaeological interpretations. It is hoped that this book can add a fresh set of data to the study of the human prehistory of this continent by opening up an area which has been almost completely ignored. In so doing I believe it extends also our knowledge of the wily tenacity and adaptive strengths of the myriads of people who lived on and wandered across the Sahulian (Tasmania, Australia and Papua New Guinea) and then Australian landscape for at least 3000 generations.

Chapter 2

Australian palaeopathology, survey methods, samples and ethnohistoric sources

A brief history of Australian palaeopathological study

This chapter briefly outlines the few major papers that have discussed Australian palaeopathology. I will confine my remarks largely to those publications of substance and will not be referring to every remark made about a pathological bone from Australia, although I assure the reader that there are few of these.

The first palaeopathological survey of Aboriginal skeletal remains undertaken in Australia was made by Cecil Hackett (1933a,b,c, 1963, 1968, 1974, 1976). His data focussed on treponemal lesion morphology, particularly cranial vault lesions. He hoped that through analysis of a series of discrete and unique pathological changes in the appearance of these lesions he would be able to distinguish and document the differences between endemic forms of treponemal infection and those resulting from syphilis. The diagnostic criteria he established helped him achieve these ends so that the palaeoepidemiology of treponemal disease in Australia as well as its spread and distribution around the world could be understood more fully. Hackett extended his research to include a study of the tibial distortion known as 'boomerang leg' and I discuss this more fully in Chapter 6. His work in Australia, however, was part of a lifelong study of the treponematoses, particularly endemic forms, which he had pursued in many parts of the world, including Africa and the Middle East. He did not set out to document the status of Aboriginal health in the past, nor was his work considered strictly of a palaeopathological nature. His main aim was to understand the history of treponematoses and in many ways he achieved this.

Apart from Hackett's publications and a brief description of five scaphocephalic crania by Fenner (1938), only one paper describing pathological lesions in Aboriginal skeletal remains was published in Australia before 1970. This was largely descriptive, however, and detailed particular observations made on 325 pathological bones only from the Murray Valley (MacKay 1938). The material was part of the Murray Black collection, named after George Murray Black, who gathered it from what are believed to be a series of discrete traditional burial places adjacent to the Murray River and elsewhere in the region. By the early 1950s the collection amounted to over 1700 individuals and was held jointly by the Anatomy Department of the University of Melbourne and the Australian Institute of Anatomy in Canberra. Until 1938 they were housed only in the latter institution where Charles V. MacKay was acting director at the time his paper was published in the *Australian Medical Journal.* Various pathologies were noted by MacKay, including fractures, osteoarthritis, osteomyelitis, periostitis, osteitis and tibial bowing. His differential diagnosis made brief mention also of the part that 'syphilis' may have played in the formation of some of the infectious lesions he noted. It is interesting to see that MacKay disagreed with Hackett's belief that 'yaws' was present in parts of Australia other than the tropics and that all evidence for treponemal disease in southeastern Australia, particularly in the Murray Black collection, was due to introduced European syphilis. I will take up these arguments again in Chapter 6. In his paper MacKay stated that he would 'embody the detailed result of this work in a special monograph' (MacKay 1938:3). Unfortunately, no monograph ever emerged and although I have attempted to trace a manuscript, all efforts have proved fruitless. MacKay died in 1939.

I must point out that I am largely ignoring references to dental disease. A number of papers referring to these conditions as well as non-metrical and general morphological characteristics of Aboriginal dentition and palate were published by T. D. Campbell and his colleagues in the 1920s and 30s. It is worth pointing out, however, that many of these concern observations on contemporary traditional Aboriginal people as well as those living on missions, and cannot be considered under the category of palaeopathology. By this time Aboriginal dental health was also beginning to suffer from a diet that included large amounts of white sugar and refined flour. For references to this work see the *Bibliography of Anthropology and Genetics* 1991, published by the Department of Dentistry, University of Adelaide.

Between 1938 and the late 1960s no further palaeopathological papers were published in Australia with the exceptions of Dinning's trauma paper (1949) and Macintosh's 1967 contribution describing the Green Gully remains. But between 1973 and 1980 six emerged (Sandison 1973a,b, 1980; Zaino and Zaino 1975; Prokopec 1976; Jurisich and Davies 1976). Two others describe pathology observed during a wider examination and general biological description of remains from Queensland (Wood 1969, 1976)

Sandison's 1973a and 1980 publications are almost identical. The enormous contributions that he made to palaeopathological study, particularly in Britain and Europe, are, unfortunately, not reflected in these papers which are marked by their brevity. Several papers have emerged from the twenty-year study of the Roonka population of South Australia (see Pretty and Kricun 1989). For this reason I have chosen to ignore this collection except for one individual.

Zaino and Zaino's (1975) article concentrated on cribra orbitalia and is the only contribution which takes a quantitative approach. Unfortunately, it, again, is very brief and lacks a differential diagnosis and discussion of the palaeoepidemiological implications of the findings. Oddly, the sample also contained many more individuals from New South Wales, where the study was centred, than were in collections at that time.

It was the singular lack of information about pre-contact Aboriginal health and the paucity of palaeopathological information about Australia that provided the main stimulus for my work. This study began with a small survey of cribra orbitalia carried out as part of my honours thesis (Webb 1981, 1982). The bulk of the data described here were gathered during 1982–84 and some were used as the basis for my doctoral thesis (Webb 1984). A briefly edited version of the thesis was published in 1989 along with several papers dealing with individual pathologies (1988, 1990a,b; Webb and Thorne 1985). Since then I have made a number of observations and reconsidered some of my earlier conclusions and interpretations. I wanted to take the opportunity to include these, report a number of pathologies of a more rare as well as interesting nature, and draw together the data in a continental synthesis. Thus, this book has emerged. To make the text more complete and to present as wide a picture as possible in a single volume I have included some data which also appear elsewhere. In some chapters I have decided to retain sections dealing with methods and results although these are an abbreviated version of those appearing in the 1989 publication.

The reasons for the survey

This survey is primarily concerned with the Australian mainland. Tasmania was originally included but the sample has a number of problems concerning size and provenance. Therefore, the results will be published in a separate report. Some reference is made also to limited data from neighbouring regions. For example, I include a report on the palaeopathology of a coastal village community from Papua New Guinea because of its fairly close position to Australia, across Torres Strait, and for general comparative purposes (Chapter 11).

The main aim of this work has been to study a selection of pathologies in order to provide some measure of the health status of late Holocene Aboriginal people living in different parts of the continent. Late Pleistocene remains were also surveyed not only to record the earliest indications of disease on this continent, but to contrast those results with others obtained from the later populations. It is hoped that this study will provide also a picture of pre-contact Aboriginal health, palaeoepidemiology, adaptation and the relationship between all these and the environment in a way that may not be possible for us to construct again. Many of the examples described here are no longer available for study but the value of the data necessitates its publication even, at times, in a cursory form. I ask the reader to bear with this.

The philosophy behind this survey

The health of past societies can only be known by making population surveys using optimum samples from many regions. When planning the survey there was a need to present a broad, generalised study rather than concentrate either on one particular area or region of Australia or one or two pathological conditions. Because this is the first survey of its kind from this continent, I thought it essential also to highlight the range of pathology that existed. By comparing results on an inter-regional or area basis, this range could be shown. If there were vast differences in the pattern of health, how big were they? Were there differences between male and female patterns, for example? What might these mean? Were there radical differences between different groups of people? And, where did the healthiest and sickest people live? Once these patterns were established then, it was hoped, reasons for any observed differences might become clear or understood a little better. A survey of only one or two pathologies would not provide these answers, neither could a broad assessment of traditional health be made. At that level one area might have a higher frequency of one particular pathology than another, but how would we know? Using a range of pathologies and an integrated approach, however, it is possible to gauge the overall pattern in an indirect but substantial manner. By using pathologies with different aetiologies the most likely reasons for the manifestation of that particular combination of pathological frequencies can be shown. This approach also provides a better understanding of what the data may reflect in terms of natural and human environments as well as providing a basic template of pathological variation across the continent and defining subtle differences in the sort of stress or pathology affecting one group over another. A healthy group cannot be determined as such until it has been compared with all others. It is for these reasons also that a continental survey is essential, although sample sizes for some areas are so small they have been rendered almost useless for representative interpretation.

Stress indicators, such as cribra orbitalia, dental hypoplasia and Harris lines, are useful in this sort of exercise but not all of them mean the same thing. Some indicate long-term, persistent or chronic forms of stress and others short-term or acute types. The application of these two categories for interpreting skeletal biology of hunter-gatherer society is extremely valuable. For example, some forms of stress might be largely nutritional, caused by seasonal food shortages.

Whereas, a long-term or chronic stress may reflect population size, sedentism, a poor environment or variation in settlement patterns. Similarly, variation in osteoarthritic patterns may not have the same behavioural connotations in all populations.

The present volume seeks to do two things, then. Firstly, it documents a range of pathologies from all over the continent. Secondly, it also provides a temporal as well as a spatial contrast to the health of the first Australians and ties this in with the people's natural and social environments. In so doing I hope it also lays to rest some of the myths surrounding Aboriginal health and that society's toleration and treatment of the sick and injured.

A study with caution

Palaeopathological work is generally but not solely concerned with the identification of diseases suffered by peoples who have no written records. Data obtained in this way are then translated into information that we hope will tell us more about the general living conditions of past societies. Taken one step further, these results, when measured against a background of social, cultural, demographic and environmental factors, allow us to compare and contrast the palaeoepidemiology of ancient human populations from different parts of the world so that we learn more about the history, origins and distribution of our diseases.

The palaeopathologist seeks to identify and interpret past diseases largely from lesions and other pathological indicators left on osteoarchaeological remains. Further information is gained from the soft tissues of mummified remains. Although there are quite a number of the latter remains in Australia, they are not dealt with in this work. Naturally, palaeopathology is limited in what it can tell us about ancient health because it concentrates on those diseases that affect the skeleton only and also those that can be readily identified. Hence, a number of cautionary statements have been raised concerning the equivocal nature of skeletal pathology, the difficulties of accurate lesion identification and the classification of disease from this source (Sandison 1968; Dastugue 1980). Dastugue remarks, for example:

> At every step of his work, the paleopathologist must be
> cautious and aware of his own limitations ... In short ...
> many paleopathological diagnoses are mere
> approximations ... Each of us must be aware that his
> duty is not to give a solution at all costs but to assemble
> honestly the data of the problem. (5-6)

The possibility arises also that osteological lesions may not be readily classifiable. This can come about because they derive from diseases that may have been unique to a particular era; or have no modern counterpart to compare them with, or those that are ancestral to a contemporary disease but manifest different symptoms (Klepinger

1983). The cautious worker, therefore, always has to admit that without the benefit of the living patient, a palaeopathological diagnosis can often fall short in its findings.

Certain pathological bone markers, such as cribra orbitalia, Harris lines, dental hypoplasia, non-specific infection and osteoarthritis, are far more useful when used in concert than studied separately. They are particularly rewarding as indicators of the environmental, pathological, nutritional, biomechanical and demographic circumstances of past human communities. Even so, caution is still being expressed over interpretation of some of these. Generally, however, it is felt that more confidence can be placed in them if they are used in a mutually supportive manner, particularly when conclusions are sprinkled with a moderate degree of scepticism. The best palaeopathological studies are probably those that speak in generalities rather than rigid specifics. Moreover, when reasonable sample sizes are used certain pathological trends are hard to ignore and should not be explained away just because an extremely conservative approach may be thought to be more acceptable to colleagues or the wider audience. To me this is as bad as falsifying data: both ignore the *status quo*. Palaeopathological data provide us with more information about human palaeobiology and ecology than any other archaeological evidence I can think of and when studying hunter-gatherer societies such data are probably the most valuable information of all.

General methodology

A section on methodology is not usual in a volume of this type. Nevertheless, I have decided to include a basic outline of the general methods used for three main reasons. First, it is useful for those interested in how the data was gathered and wish to make comparisons with other studies. Second, it helps standardise palaeopathological surveys elsewhere by offering a consistency of methodological approach, which is necessary for comparing the results of various studies of similar pathologies. This can only result in the eventual enhancement of all our diagnoses. Third, fellow workers are, quite naturally, interested in how certain pathologies have been defined, data compiled and results obtained and thus benefit from comparing methods.

Osteology

Much of the data in this book was gathered during research for my doctoral thesis so there were constraints on time and data handling which restricted the survey to the major long bones (humerus, radius, ulna, femur, tibia and fibula) (Table 2–1), and the cranium (Table 2–2). Other parts of the post-cranial skeleton were also studied in a less systematic way. Standards required all long bones to be complete and included broken bones, providing the break was simple and it constituted a complete specimen. Exceptions to this were made with

Table 2–1 *Post-cranial samples.*

SUB-ADULTS

Bone Code		Left							Right						
		10	11	12	20	21	22	T	10	11	12	20	21	22	T
CM		17	7	9	12	12	11	68	20	7	10	12	9	10	68
R		5	1	3	4	5	4	22	5	1	4	6	5	2	23
SC		12	3	6	2	3	–	26	9	3	5	3	5	–	25
DES		2	2	2	–	3	2	11	2	1	1	1	2	1	8
CTL		12	13	13	11	11	7	67	12	13	13	8	10	7	63

ADULTS

Bone Code		10	11	12	20	21	22	T	10	11	12	20	21	22	T
CM	M	100	57	46	124	78	56	464	111	60	56	98	77	56	458
	F	54	36	40	58	50	34	272	55	28	36	66	49	31	265
	U	22	34	39	34	133	61	323	23	42	39	38	128	56	326
	T	176	127	125	216	261	151	1059	189	130	131	202	254	143	1049
R	M	34	44	64	52	52	44	290	35	48	62	54	52	44	295
	F	21	22	30	33	26	31	163	23	23	32	29	25	29	161
	U	73	13	16	9	20	12	143	76	15	19	5	24	14	153
	T	128	79	110	94	98	87	596	134	86	113	88	101	87	609
SC	M	32	21	25	34	55	25	192	36	28	25	33	64	24	210
	F	31	21	21	35	41	16	165	23	19	20	32	41	12	147
	U	89	66	74	75	42	–	346	88	70	47	75	40	–	320
	T	152	108	120	144	138	41	703	147	117	92	140	144	36	677
DES	M	23	19	21	18	24	18	123	21	21	18	19	29	16	124
	F	4	5	4	4	4	4	25	6	5	6	5	6	3	31
	U	1	–		–	–	–	1	–	–	–	–	1	–	1
	T	28	24	25	22	28	22	149	27	26	24	24	36	19	156
TRO	M	4	1	2	3	3	2	15	4	3	2	4	5	1	19
	F	4	3	3	4	4	3	21	3	3	3	4	3	3	19
	U	2	2	2	1	2	3	12	1	2	1	1	3	3	11
	T	10	6	7	8	9	8	48	8	8	6	9	11	7	49
CTL	M	56	53	59	56	49	49	322	64	60	56	65	69	41	355
	F	27	26	20	25	24	17	139	26	25	22	28	26	23	150
	U	16	14	14	19	17	9	89	16	15	15	18	19	8	91
	T	99	93	93	100	90	75	550	106	100	93	111	114	72	596

Bone Code:
10–Humerus, 11–Ulna, 12–Radius, 20–Femur, 21–Tibia, 22–Fibula
M–Male, F–Female, U–Unsexed, T–Total

Area Codes:
CM–Central Murray, R–Rufus River, SC–South Coast, DES–Desert, TRP–Tropics, CTL–East Coast

fossil material and individuals from under-represented areas. Crania were selected in a similar way so that incomplete, badly eroded and fragmented individuals were generally rejected. Unfortunately these standards effectively reduced samples from areas such as the desert because of both the comparative rarity of bone from arid regions and its often poor condition. The latter is due to the extremes of desiccating heat and sub-zero cold of desert environments which, when combined with wind-blown sand, causes rapid surface erosion and cracking of bone after exposure. This is closely followed by fragmentation in the

Table 2–2 *Cranial samples.*

	Sub-adults				Adults					
					Male			Female		
	1	*2*	*3*	*T*	*6*	*7*	*T*	*6*	*7*	*T*
CM	7	19	29	55	92	152	244	98	51	149
R	4	5	7	16	48	74	122	53	30	83
SC	6	12	21	33	42	96	138	57	66	123
DES	5	7	9	21	24	106	130	23	28	51
TRO	2	4	10	16	36	56	92	27	34	61
CTL	9	13	10	32	30	103	133	45	38	83

Age Code:
1–6 years, 2–6-11 years, 3–12-20 years, 6–Young Adult (35-40 years), 7–Old Adult (>40 years),
T–Total

Area Codes:
CM–Central Murray, R–Rufus River, SC–South Coast, DES–Desert, TRO–Tropics, CTL–East Coast

extremely dry conditions. Post-mortem tooth loss, broken zygomatic arches and basi-cranial damage were ignored in all crania because the loss of these did not interfere with the observations being made. Any individuals of mixed genetic origin, named individuals and those with dubious provenance or who had died in hospital, prison or from any European disease, were excluded.

The poor condition of late Pleistocene and early Holocene remains was ignored because of their obvious scientific value and these were included in the survey if at all possible. Cremated, highly fragmented, badly eroded and calcified Pleistocene bone, however, was left out.

All the material used for this survey was or still is stored in museum collections in capital cities throughout Australia. Remains in overseas collections have not been included. In most museum collections cranial and post-cranial material are separated and kept in trays representing various bone types. Complete skeletons are few, rarely complete and often articulated with wires preventing proper access for examination.

Age assessment

The sub-adult crania have been roughly divided into three age groups: 0–5 years, 6–11 years and 12–20 years using tooth eruption sequences (Table 2–2) (Barrett and Brown 1966; Scott and Symonds 1977). The presence of fully-erupted third molars and fused spheno-occipital synchondroses were used to define adult individuals. The variability in Australian Aboriginal tooth wear, both regionally and between males and females, precludes its use for dividing adults into multiple age groups. So, a gross categorisation has been employed to divide adults into young and old age groups, using a combination of tooth wear, edentulism and ectocranial suture fusion. Even though the latter is problematic for any accurate ageing of skeletal remains, it can be used to provide a division at 35–40 years of age (Abbie 1950; Krogman 1962; Powers 1962; Perizonius 1984).

There are no suitable techniques available for sexing the Australian Aboriginal tibia, fibula, ulna or radius. These were sexed only when they accompanied crania, pelves, or when large rugose or small, very gracile bones were encountered, representing male and female individuals, respectively. Femora were sexed using Davivong's (1963) technique but van Dongen's (1963) method for sexing humeri was found to be unacceptable because of the limited numbers of bones that can be sexed this way. Moreover, the samples he used to develop his technique were limited in both size and provenance. When the morphological variety of male and female Aboriginal post-cranial remains is considered, the value of the technique is reduced further. The sexing of crania has been discussed elsewhere (Webb 1989).

The samples

This study contains only three collections of archaeologically recovered and dated remains. These are: Broadbeach, excavated in southeastern Queensland (Haglund-Calley 1968a, 1968b; Wood 1968; Haglund 1976), Roonka, on the lower Murray in South Australia (Pretty 1977; Prokopec 1979) and Kow Swamp, from the Victorian side of the Murray River (Thorne 1969, 1971a,b, 1972, 1975, 1976, 1981) (Map 2–1). For some reason there has been a lack of enthusiasm to date collections such as the Murray Black collection as well as many other individuals and groups of individuals held in museum collections around the country even though some are clearly of considerable antiquity. Unfortunately, the bulk of individuals dealt with in this study lack formal dating and with the recent reburial of the dated Broadbeach and Kow Swamp collections these have been reduced even further.

Much of the data used in this study, particularly for the large grouping known as the 'central Murray' (CM), were gathered from the Murray Black collection. The collection, as already noted, is named after George Murray Black and has nothing to do with the geographical origin or racial affinity of the remains themselves (Mulvaney 1989). The Murray Black collection formed Australia's largest single sample of Aboriginal skeletal remains but in 1984 it became the main focus of Aboriginal concerns over the storage, curation and continued study of ancestral remains (Webb 1987a). Moves by the Aboriginal community to have the collection reburied have been largely successful following legislative support from both state and federal governments. The bulk of this collection has now been reburied.

While archaeological methods were not employed in the retrieval of the Murray Black collection, certain inferences can be made about its age. The nature of the burials suggests traditional interment in the fashion of discrete cemeteries (Sunderland and Ray 1959). When land along the Murray River was divided into 'runs' by European settlers, its continued use by Aborigines became restricted and, no doubt,

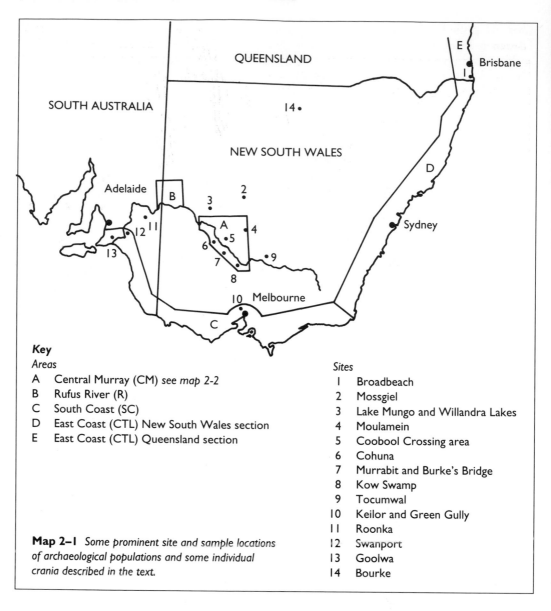

Key

Areas

A   Central Murray (CM) *see map 2-2*
B   Rufus River (R)
C   South Coast (SC)
D   East Coast (CTL) New South Wales section
E   East Coast (CTL) Queensland section

Sites

1   Broadbeach
2   Mossgiel
3   Lake Mungo and Willandra Lakes
4   Moulamein
5   Coobool Crossing area
6   Cohuna
7   Murrabit and Burke's Bridge
8   Kow Swamp
9   Tocumwal
10   Keilor and Green Gully
11   Roonka
12   Swanport
13   Goolwa
14   Bourke

Map 2–1 *Some prominent site and sample locations of archaeological populations and some individual crania described in the text.*

Aboriginal people themselves probably would not have wished to continue burying their dead near European settlements. The Murray Valley Aboriginal population was devastated by smallpox and other introduced diseases before actual European settlement of the area and it is possible that a portion of some of these remains originate from that time (?circa 1790 and 1828-31) (see Chapter 12). Moreover, although most of the pathologies that I discuss are observed on adults, some began during childhood, 20–50 years before.

The boundary I have chosen for the central Murray grouping encloses an area of about 26,000 km², extending from Echuca in the east to Euston and Robinvale in the west (Map 2–2). This includes about 700 km of riverbank (350 km on either side) and encloses an

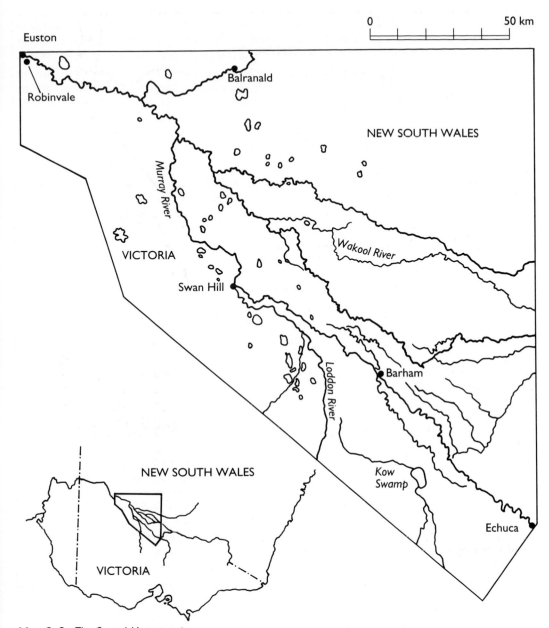

Map 2–2 *The Central Murray region.*

area on the northern side of the river, bounded by lines running east from Euston and north from Echuca. The southern boundary runs parallel with the river and extends 30 km south of it. By defining an exact boundary in this way one could be criticised for applying such artificial limits to or even over-extending the size of the area. The continuum of Aboriginal occupation which extended from the Murray River north to the Murrumbidgee and Lachlan Rivers and south into Victoria makes it impossible to envisage any 'central Murray border' that means very much, but this definition is suitable for this study.

Another large collection from Swanport, on the South Australian lower Murray, was also used in this survey (Map 2–1, 12). Like the Murray Black collection, the Swanport collection is not dated but is derived from a discrete burial complex accidentally exposed during levee building at the turn of the century (Stirling 1911). One advantage of this population is that it represents a single unit of people, originating from one tribe or closely associated grouping. The uniformity of preservation of Swanport and its excellent condition suggests that it is not very old, the majority of individuals probably span the four hundred years prior to European settlement. This collection has also been set aside for reburial. It should be noted that both the Murray Black and Swanport collections have been the mainstay of osteological and physical anthropological research in Australia for a number of years.

While the Roonka collection, also from the lower Murray River north of Swanport, is dated, unfortunately most of it is very fragmentary, poorly preserved and severely eroded (Map 2–1, 11). Moreover, the results of a long-term study on this population have been presented elsewhere (see Pretty and Kricun 1989). Much of the Broadbeach collection from southeastern Queensland was in a similar condition to that of Roonka so far as erosion, fragmentation and preservation are concerned (Map 2–1, 1). Also, the sample was heavily biased towards males and sub-adults (Haglund 1976). These factors imposed limitations on its usefulness for the sort of study undertaken here. Nevertheless, the frequency of various pathological conditions was noted and used in a limited way. The Broadbeach collection was reburied in 1985.

Most of the other material used in this work comprises individuals as well as some multiple burials acquired by museums from the late nineteenth century to the early 1970s. Occasionally individual crania or an isolated post-cranial bone is handed in by the police, usually through coronial offices. Others come from urban development projects, natural erosion and from farming activities in rural areas while others are occasionally handed in by private citizens. Active collection by most museum authorities has not taken place for over half a century and many have not received Aboriginal skeletal remains from any source for more than twenty years.

The lack of archaeologically derived, properly dated remains is unfortunate and imposes limitations on interpretations made by biological anthropologists and others on many Australian collections. Nevertheless, most of the collections remained unstudied for decades because of the paucity of properly trained physical anthropologists here. With the exception of a few researchers from overseas and one or two local 'interested anatomists', systematic assessment of museum collections did not begin until the mid-1960s.

'Areas' and other samples

An 'area' is based on common environmental, geographical and, in some cases, cultural factors. In some regions good samples can be

located to a particular town, and this is especially true for much of
the Murray Valley (Sunderland and Ray 1959; Pietrusewsky 1979;
Webb 1981, 1982; Green 1982). Others may come from closely associated geographical features. The Rufus River (R) sample consists, for
example, of material recovered from Lake Victoria, Lindsay Creek,
Chowilla and Rufus River itself (Map 2–1, B). These form a discrete
area around the junction of the Murray and Darling Rivers which
represents an intermediate zone between the central Murray area to
the east and Swanport near the mouth of the Murray River. Sometimes it was difficult deciding how material was best combined to
form areas. Western Australia posed a particular problem. Originally
remains from here were divided into northwest, central and southwestern samples, but their individual size made them too small for
any results to mean anything. Combining them was no answer because
this would bring together individuals from totally different ecological
zones which, presumably, included some social, cultural and nutritional differences also. Eventually Western Australia was merged into
the desert (DES) and east coastal (CTL) groups, largely on environmental grounds (Map 2–3).

Some samples are large enough to allow a close comparative analysis
of adjacent groups, which helps define pathological differences
between outwardly very similar people. Normally, however, we are
unable to do this because of inadequate sample size. 'Areas' have been
formed largely to overcome this problem and are based upon wider

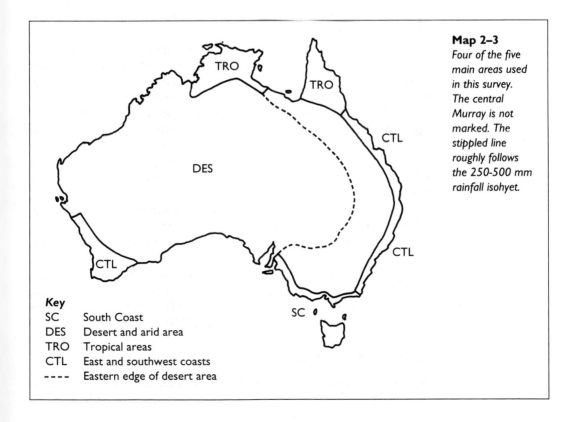

Map 2–3
Four of the five main areas used in this survey. The central Murray is not marked. The stippled line roughly follows the 250-500 mm rainfall isohyet.

Key
SC   South Coast
DES   Desert and arid area
TRO   Tropical areas
CTL   East and southwest coasts
----   Eastern edge of desert area

geographical and environmental considerations or both. This level of analysis reduces also the complexity of comparing many smaller occasions and allows for easier interpretation. Six 'areas' have been formed representing all the basic ecological zones in Australia. These are: the central Murray (CM), Rufus River (R), south coast (SC), the desert (DES), the tropics (TRO) and the eastern coast (CTL) and this is the order in which they appear in the tables (Map 2–3).

The use of ethnohistorical sources

There is a vast amount of Australian ethnohistorical literature relating to almost every aspect of Aboriginal life in all corners of the continent. It has been a valuable and plentiful source of information for the archaeologist, prehistorian, anthropologist and others trying to understand how Aboriginal people lived before Europeans arrived. For those wishing to understand traditional health patterns as well as the types of diseases that existed among Aboriginal groups, particularly in the southern half of the continent, their value is limited, however. My use of this literature has depended on a number of factors which assess the reliability of reports. For example, the closer an account is to the time of first contact the more reliable it is likely to be. Then, one must take into account the writer's qualifications for describing accurately what is seen. Medically trained people were better able to describe disease although not all were clear and accurate writers. Another factor to consider is the time of contact between Aboriginal and non-Aboriginal people, which varied greatly from one part of the continent to another. In remote desert regions reports of disease are fairly reliable up to the late 1950s and early 1960s because of the fairly recent first contact with some groups in this area. This situation often presented the opportunity for modern, medically trained personnel to examine people living traditionally and record accurate and well informed medical reports about them.

Unfortunately, early ethnohistoric accounts are not always helpful because they were generally not written by people with medical training. Any description of disease, therefore, is likely to be very general, misleading, inaccurate or, even worse, mistaking a post-contact health pattern with a pre-contact one or vice versa. A common theme in these reports is that Aboriginal men were 'muscular', 'well built', 'strong' and 'fit looking' (Bennett 1832:119; Eyre 1845:206; Leichhardt 1847:166; Sturt 1849:137; Bonwick 1857:67; Lang 1861: 50). This presents basic evidence for the well-being of males, although quite often the opposite picture is presented for females and descriptions of them being ill-treated and inferior in stature and appearance are common (Bennett 1834:250; Mitchell 1839:259, Eyre 1845:206; Sturt 1849:77; Westgarth 1848:78; Lang 1861:51; Chauncy cited in Smyth 1878 II:259). At this level such reports can be of some value, albeit that they often reek of nineteenth-century European social and cultural standards and values. Some reports clearly contain distortion of facts, rumour, anecdotes (Smyth 1878), wrong diagnoses (Howitt cited in Smyth 1878 II:302; Mackillop 1892), confusing euphemisms, as a form of Victorian moral censorship (Eyre 1845 II:379; Sturt 1833 II:96), and bias (Cunningham 1827 II:45). Moreover, most accounts were written long after contact had taken place. Others described a situation that existed after European disease had reached Aboriginal communities but before settlers had arrived. The deterioration in Aboriginal health that usually followed contact is a major reason why it is difficult to use some of these sources as accurate records.

Aboriginal health declined rapidly in the face of highly infectious diseases such as influenza, measles and smallpox, the latter occurring as early as 1789 at Sydney Cove (see Chapter 12). In one way, smallpox was a major catalyst for the decline of traditional Aboriginal society during the nineteenth century. In southeastern and southwestern Australia, Aboriginal health never had a chance to recover as colonisation relentlessly pushed further and further inland and along the major river systems as, one after another, exotic diseases assailed traditional communities. This situation was naturally compounded following the confinement of many Aboriginal people on crowded missions and in work camps on rural properties. The attraction of Aborigines to the new settlements, frontier towns and gold mining centres encouraged the growth of fringe dwelling communities in which alcoholism, nutritional deficiency, parasitism and infection from a range of highly contagious diseases was rife. In this way they rapidly became enmeshed in a European health pattern in some places even before the middle of the nineteenth century. The result was not only devastating on their society, with the breakdown of traditional laws and lifestyle, but they were affected physically. The pathological impact of European migration has stayed with them to this day in many places. Certainly, Aboriginal people living in many rural and urban centres today suffer from a range of diseases that should not be seen in such frequencies in a notionally healthy and advanced western society. Aboriginal health in parts of Australia today matches closely that of a Third World community.

It is against this background that many ethnohistoric accounts were written and because of it they are often of little value in assessing traditional Aboriginal health. Consequently, the only recourse we have is that of palaeopathology as an interpretative tool for understanding the health status of Aboriginal Australians at the time of contact. On the other hand, there is no need to throw the baby out with the bathwater. Not all historical accounts of a medical nature are untrustworthy. The assessment of the accuracy or value of a particular report must be made by the researcher in full knowledge of the circumstances of the account as outlined above. The subjectivity of this approach can be modified if a number of factors are taken into consideration. These include: the known competence of the observer; the type of description given; the pathology being dealt with; the region involved; the date of writing; the amount of previous European influence or contact experience (or both) of the group or person described and how long introduced diseases might have been present in that particular area. Since there is no universal rule for this type of assessment each source must be judged using these criteria as well as those peculiar to the source itself. As can be imagined, experience makes one a little wiser a judge in this work. From time to time I will return to this subject in the following chapters.

Chapter 3

Upper Pleistocene pathology of Sunda and Sahul: some possibilities

It is not too much to hope that Australian archaeology will shed light on disease introduction to this continent and how far back in time that first occurred. (Macintosh et al. 1970:94)

Introduction

The time is the Upper Pleistocene and the world's human population is about to embark on a growth spiral that will continue until it becomes the single most important problem that it will ever face. At the same time, human exploration of the Old World is drawing to a close and many distinctive cultures are beginning to emerge. Unfortunately, it is a time also that marks a latter stage in the 'dark age' of our understanding of the health of those cultures and, unfortunately, the origins of many of today's diseases lie buried in this darkness.

The will to overcome suffering and illness and to carry on regardless on the part of those living in the past is testament to the tenacity and toughness of our human ancestors. It reflects the same spirit that enabled them to carry out their continental explorations and voyages in small craft across unknown seas. What kinds of disease might have been suffered by those early explorers largely remains a mystery, but what we can be sure of is that a variety of conditions have been with us for a long time. Disease has been as great a force in the process of natural selection for our species as any other and at times it may have contributed more than its fair share. There is little doubt also that this kind of selective force has not only played an active role in the formation of our biological adaptability but also in our demographic, social and belief systems. Of course, the degree to which disease has brought its influence to bear on these processes has varied both through time and across continents. Our ability to live successfully within the whole gamut of environments found on this planet, something achieved by no other species, is probably the best demonstration of our determination, however, not to let the disease process influence us too much.

There is no doubt that we brought some of our diseases with us when we moved from the comparative safety of the forests out onto the African savannahs, some time between five and ten million years ago. Although we left our ape and other primate cousins behind we continued to share with them many pathogens. Today, we can only guess at the kind of new and exotic forms of infectious, parasitic, zoonotic and environmentally-determined diseases that were encountered by groups of early hominids, particularly when they began to explore other parts of the world. What kinds of pathology did *Homo erectus* (or *Homo sapiens* as some prefer) suffer when, between one and a half and two million years ago, they moved out of Africa to explore the millions of square kilometres of Europe, the Middle East and Asia?

The trouble is, we know very little about the health of humans in the Pleistocene, even the late Pleistocene. Indeed, our knowledge of human health does not improve significantly until we consider middle and late Holocene peoples. In Australia's case, what kind of disease was carried or encountered by the seafaring bands of *Homo sapiens* that roamed island southeast Asia and settled here perhaps as far back as 100 or 200,000 years ago? It is worth considering that illness may have had a devastating effect on such people: striking down individuals without notice; imposing sudden and drastic reductions in population size; forcing people out of some areas and into others; dictating movement across the landscape and even preventing entry to some places. Perhaps new belief systems, rituals and ceremonies arose, deliberately contrived to explain illness. Such systems were meant to appease or ward off malevolent spirits, demons or other creatures believed responsible for an unseen phenomenon that attacked people completely without warning and laid them low. It seems only reasonable that anyone might find perplexing why someone who is a healthy and strong person one day should suddenly be reduced to a shivering yet sweating and very useless wreck the next. It seems reasonable to suggest that it was this kind of incident that helped form human concepts of disease, its cause, what it was, how it might be avoided or cured and generally how to deal with it. We can be certain, for example, that early migratory bands of human beings journeyed through areas where malaria was endemic. People may or may not have been familiar with this fever, but either way their reaction to such places and whether they occupied or avoided them must have been tempered to a certain extent by the manner in which disease was viewed and whether they believed it was linked to evil spirits and the areas where it occurred were places they should not go. Thus the demography of some of the early explorers may have been fashioned by the presence of endemic disease which either provided barriers to occupation or an incentive to move on quickly.

Australia's human beginnings

Modern Australia covers over seven and a half million square kilometres (Williams 1979). Within that immense area lies an environmental diversity incorporating most of the major ecosystems found on our planet. It also houses two unique orders of animals, the marsupials and monotremes, and some special floral populations that have withstood the vagaries of time for the last fifty million years or so. Australia also boasts the world's oldest rocks, algae, simple life forms, invertebrate fauna, quadruped footprints and flower fossils. Because this vast continental raft has been cut off from the rest of the world for more than fifty million years it has become an enigma and a source of intrigue for many branches of science (Cook 1981). With the exception of Antarctica, Australia was the only continent not to become part of the vast bridging system that joined all the other continents during the Quaternary Ice Ages. In fact, this situation has been the predominant geographical setting for human migrations for over one million years: if humans wanted to come here then they had to cross open ocean. The interglacial that we are now experiencing is but a short interlude in this setting. During the major Ice Ages hominid bands could have walked from present-day Dublin to New York and on to Tierra Del Fuego. Vast distances were travelled by them without their having to cross large expanses of water or 'invent' the ocean-going boat. Indeed, lowered sea levels during a glacial event some time between one and two million years ago enabled *Homo erectus* to reach the Indonesian archipelago without the need for sea-faring skills.

Sea levels around the Australian continent fluctuated several times during the last glaciation (between 8–60,000 years ago), at times enlarging the continent to around ten million square kilometres (White and O'Connell 1982). This was partly due to incorporation of Papua New Guinea and Tasmania as part of its landmass. Even then Australia, as part of the super-continent of Sahul, remained isolated. With lowered sea levels, large and small island chains were joined throughout the Indonesian and Malaysia archipelagos, forming another huge land mass, Sunda. During these times it was possible for hominids to travel south as far as Java without getting their feet wet. Some time during the Upper Pleistocene the people inhabiting the southern fringes of Sunda began to use watercraft on the open ocean and when they did Sahul became a target for their eastward migrations. This event not only marked the beginning of the story of Australia's human habitation, it was also the beginning of the story of human health and disease here.

Possibilities for assessing the health of Upper Pleistocene migrants to Sahul

This section is not an exhaustive study of all the possibilities for early human disease in the region. Clearly, this is impossible in a text of this kind, neither does it serve any useful purpose. Australia and its early human story pose some interesting questions and possibilities in terms of palaeoepidemiology, but any contemporary assessment of the health status of the first migrants has to rely more on theory and supposition than empirical data. We can, therefore, only make suggestions concerning the range and variety of potential pathogens which might have existed among the Upper Pleistocene people of Sunda and the later sailors that pushed east towards Sahul. Nevertheless, when using a theoretical approach in dealing with the subject of very ancient human disease we might seriously consider the following statement:

> We need to take new and more general theoretical positions. The ones we take may be totally wrong, but science learns a great deal from the process of disproof. Strong inference may lead to erroneous conclusions, but it invariably leads to new knowledge, new problems, and new theoretical positions. It would seem that as a discipline, skeletal biology has, as of the past decade, completed its first phase as a descriptive enterprise, and it is clearly time for the analysis and construction of general theory to begin. (Lovejoy *et al.* 1982: 336)

Several papers have described ancient hominid pathology from the Australasian region and possibly the best known of these is the Trinil femur (?700,000BP) from Java (Day and Molleson 1973). Cranial trauma has been noted in the Ngandong series (?250–100,000BP) as it has for remains from both the Upper and Lower Caves at Choukoutien (Weidenreich 1939a, 1951). The trauma on these individuals, however, tells us more about behaviour than epidemiology or the systemic disease these people suffered. Aside from these examples nothing is known of the health of the hominid bands who occupied Australia's closest island neighbours throughout the Pleistocene (Weidenreich 1939). Scratches and abrasions from weapons tipped with natural poisons, such as rotting flesh or faeces, would have been a constant hazard for the introduction of infection. These as well as severe wounds derived from acts of aggression may even have caused the occasional case of osteitis or osteomyelitis, although we have no evidence for this among the fossils recovered so far.

We have no idea why or when the first migrations to Sahul took place, nor do we know where they left from or anything about the type and size of the watercraft that were used. These factors may seem irrelevant to our story but they do play a part in understanding the palaeoepidemiology of that time and the types of disease that could have accompanied the explorers. For example, the earlier migrations began the less likely it is that extreme population pressure was the reason for them. With small populations in the southern extremities of Sundaland we can eliminate most, if not all, of the crowd diseases such as measles, smallpox, chickenpox, herpes, influenza and cholera. It is probably safe to say that infections of this kind were unheard of among the world's hunter-gatherer populations in the Upper Pleistocene.

Even if such disease did exist at the time of Australia's first migrations, the isolation of a single raft containing a few family members or several carrying a small band would have prevented the transmission of acute infections transmittable for only twelve to fourteen days (Hare 1967). No doubt the permanent water gap between Sunda and Sahul would have acted in a similar manner to the 'cold screen' proposed for the Bering Bridge: '... serving ... to prevent the flow of many pathological germs along with the movements of their human hosts' (Stewart 1960:265; Cockburn 1971, see also Newman 1976). Moreover, it is unlikely that the first crossings took less than fifteen days and that the voyagers made straight for the Sahul coast. We must consider also that the first complete crossing may have taken more than one generation. The most parsimonious view of these early migrations, however, is one of well separated and small populations being gradually dispersed across thousands of square kilometres of island-dotted ocean and empty coastline, with occasional additions of fresh migrants to these founder populations as time went on. Such populations would have been far too small to allow infectious disease to thrive, and the lack of susceptibles on Sahul itself would have underpinned this process. For infection to survive, particularly that having a short incubation period, transportation by a more rapid and direct route would have been necessary. Under these circumstances highly contagious infection is not likely to have bothered the first Australians even if it was present on Sunda. What are the other possibilities for poor health and disease among early hominid sailors?

There are three likely sources: bacterial infection, parasitism and secondary host infections. Many of these are intimately associated with animal hosts of one kind or another and come under the category of zoonoses. Virchow used 'zoonosis' to describe disease which was naturally transmitted from animals to man, although the word seems to have entered the medical vocabularies of France and Germany somewhat earlier, by the middle of the last century (Fiennes 1978). Over 150 diseases defined under this broad category are now known and more than half cause major health problems throughout the world (Muul 1970:1275). Added to these are a whole range of protozoan and helminthic diseases contracted by humans through parasite infestation from vertebrate animal sources (Sprent 1967; Fiennes 1978; Reinhard 1990). Transmission of infection can be direct, through an arthropod vector, or indirect, from a similar source or vertebrate reservoir (Mims 1977).

> ... man started off by inheriting a mass of infections
> from his forbearers [*sic*], and these were modified and
> added to by changes in climate, customs, agriculture, the
> domestication of animals, natural selection and an
> increasing population. (Cockburn 1967:106, cited in
> Goldstein 1969:286)

Bacterial infection among humans is no doubt very ancient and many were probably caused by organisms such as *Clostridia* (Hare 1967). Infection arises when these organisms enter an open wound from their natural environment in soil or faeces. Occasionally gas gangrene can result when devitalised tissues are invaded by *C. welchii*, leading to a potentially fatal outcome for a hunter or anyone without access to modern facilities. Amputation of the infected limb may have been used to prevent its spread, as it often is today, but even when we find ancient evidence for this type of surgery we cannot be sure that it was carried out because of this kind of infection (see Chapter 8). Tetanus (*C. tetani*) may have caused similar complicating problems for the injured from time to time and it is well to remember that without proper treatment it has a fifty per cent mortality rate. It seems likely that these infections may well have played a part in maintaining a brake on human population growth. As unlikely as this sounds, the death of a young female, particularly in small scattered groups such as those under discussion, could effectively reduce the rate of population growth at a time when that growth was almost negligible over many generations.

For those consuming the meat of scavenged animals or animals that had been hunted and killed some days before, there was always the danger of food poisoning. Botulism (*C. botulinum*) could have been another serious health hazard, with the growth of organisms arising in suitable conditions during decomposition of large amounts of animal or fish flesh. Other types of food poisoning may also have resulted from infection by other bacteria such as *Salmonella* sp. and *Staphylococcus* sp. (Mims 1977). *Salmonella paratyphosa* has been isolated in primates, which may tell us something about the zoonotic origins of paratyphoid and the possibility for the ancient hunters of these animals to contract it. Others have pointed out that a number of organisms which live in the intestinal tract, including those causing dysentery (*Shigella dysentariae*), may well have existed in early hunter-gatherer societies (Hare 1967). We may remember that both *Shigella* and *Salmonella* are organisms known to cause infectious or septic arthritis among these societies (Ortner and Putschar 1981). *Escherichia coli* and *Staphylococcus aureus* are other bacterial strains that behave in a similar manner to *Shigella* sp. These intestinal forms can cause diarrhoea and vomiting leading to the loss of body fluids and dehydration which, in the young child, as well as others with a weakened constitution, can often be fatal. It is interesting to note also that *S. aureus* is one of the major bacterial infections causing haematogenous osteomyelitis, which may continue as a suppurating infection for a number of years (see Chapter 6).

Cockburn (1971) has suggested that anthrax (*Bacillus anthracis*) and some zoonotic forms of tuberculosis may have been a problem to humans on occasion, with the more well-known pulmonary tuberculosis occurring much later during the agricultural revolution of the Holocene. Many of the above conditions have probably plagued human populations from the time of the Australopithecines, but none would have been transmitted to Australia as a new disease.

Parasitism is probably another very ancient source of poor health in humans and must have been with us from our earliest beginnings.

A variety of parasites infest wild primate populations and we still share a number of these with them. It has been suggested that parasitism would have increased among humans as we dwelt longer on the ground and adopted a more omnivorous diet (Watson, cited in Sandison 1967). The gradual increase of uncooked meat and fish in our menu during the formative stages of our evolution would have certainly encouraged further infestation with intestinal worms. These would have come both from the accidental swallowing of animal commensals and from parasites in the rotting flesh that humans probably consumed from time to time. Although not necessarily life-threatening, tapeworms (*Taenia* sp.), threadworms or pinworms (*Enterobius* sp.) and roundworms (*Ascaris* sp.), are likely to have been fairly common among human populations everywhere from a very early period. Large worm loads in small children can severely affect their general health and, in some cases, cause more serious secondary conditions leading to gastrointestinal upset, dehydration, anaemia, malnutrition and occasionally death. There is ample evidence, of course, for widespread parasitism among Holocene human populations, something which is documented in an exhaustive literature (see Brothwell and Sandison 1967, Section II, and Reinhard 1990). Infection with the tropical hookworms (*Necator americanus* and *Ancylostoma duodenale*) has more serious effects on human health, however, causing minor haemorrhages in the small intestine and malabsorption of nutrients across the gut wall (Cilento 1942). In a chronic form hookworm infestation becomes debilitating and, in particular, has dire consequences for the young. Hookworm are contracted from the soil which is a constant hazard for those living close to the environment. Both *Necator* and *Ancylostomata* are endemic to the equatorial and sub-equatorial regions of Indonesia and Melanesia today as well as the tropical regions of Papua New Guinea and Australia and are common among contemporary, traditionally-living peoples inhabiting these areas. It is not unlikely that this state of affairs goes back a very long time.

There is a whole range of fevers caused by secondary host infections normally transmitted via the parasites, ticks and fleas of animals, birds and fish. For example, lice, mites, ticks and fleas carry a range of rickettsia (*Rickettsia* sp.) which cause scrub and murine typhus as well as other conditions (Cilento 1942; Manson-Bahr 1961). The invertebrates are themselves parasites of rats, voles, pheasants and bandicoots with which hunter-gatherers living on both Sunda and Sahul would have come into fairly regular contact. Another similar condition to typhus is amoebic dysentery (*Amoebiasis*), caused through infection by *Entamoeba histolytica*, which is often transmitted by rats. A similar entamoeba to *E. histolytica* and carried by snakes may cause similar symptoms.

As usual, nothing is known of the history of these pathologies, how long they have been around in this region or whether their various epidemiologies have changed over time. We do know, however, that they exist in southeast Asia, Indonesia and island Melanesia today and, because most of them are not dependent upon man as a natural host, it is possible that they were about in southern Sundaland during the Upper Pleistocene. We know there was little environmental change in these regions during the Pleistocene, so conditions have not changed much even at the height of the glaciations. Most of these diseases are not dependent on changes to human ecological conditions, the main feature of which is the enormous growth and spread of human populations in southeast Asia during the last few thousand years or so. If anything, this has only acted to enhance the growth and spread of such diseases. What did change, however, were sea levels.

The sea acts as a natural barrier, separating vertebrate host species and thus providing a natural barrier also to the spread of any disease or infection that is carried by them. The reverse would have happened in Sunda during times of low sea levels, however. There, previously separated land would have been blended to form a larger single landmass which provided an excellent opportunity for the spread of a particular disease from one 'island' to others. In this way introduced pathogens or those arising spontaneously on a particular island during an interglacial, could be spread far and wide as physiogeographical barriers were lowered by falling sea levels. Thus, geographical extension of various diseases could have come about in southeast Asia as Sundaland was formed. Pathogenic dispersal may have taken place by means of two vectors: by dropping sea levels and by the bands of roving hunters that opportunistically moved through Sunda during the Upper Pleistocene. These processes would have provided also a natural passage for many diseases from the higher latitude areas of southeast Asia, across the equator and towards Sahul.

Imagine, then, a group of humans who had lived for thousands of years on a particular island, irrespective of its size, who were suddenly exposed to a disease quite unfamiliar to them as it spread to their island when it became part of a new land mass. This process might have had devastating effects for them, particularly if the disease was brought by others already adapted to it. Is it possible that replacement, migration and dominance of certain gene pools over others may have been determined to some extent by these sorts of processes? It is possible that rather than spontaneously arising in certain areas, genetic variants such as thalassaemia, or an ancient equivalent, may have spread in this way. Of course, some diseases may not have survived through lack of a suitable host or vector. Humans provide admirable hosts and their presence in Sunda for over one and a half million years would have facilitated transmission of diseases like malaria for much of the Pleistocene, in theory at least.

We must not forget in our discussion, the environmental changes that took place within continents during glaciations. These brought a series of internal alterations to the distribution of various ecosystems, changing forests to savannahs, swamps to woodland as well as enlarging continents. During this time some zoonoses may have adapted and evolved to cope with the environmental reversal, while others did not fare so well. So, with the dynamism of constant physical and environmental change occurring during the Quaternary, one can appreciate that it is a formidable job to try and envisage the kinds of disease that may have been encountered by those moving through Sundaland and crossing to Sahul.

Sahul: environment and diseases

Having discussed some of the pathologies that could have affected people living on Sunda, what sort of diseases, if any, might these people have faced on their arrival in Sahul? Apart from an occasional difficult childbirth, snake or carnivore bite, wounds from fighting, and old age, what did people living here in the Upper Pleistocene suffer and die from? Were there pathological conditions for which there are no modern equivalents? If so we will probably never know what they were.

With hominid neighbours for at least one and a half million years, Sahul must have experienced literally hundreds of migrations. Even if we choose to ignore the first half million years for reasons of limited human intellectual development, it seems unlikely that these would have begun before 500,000 years ago. Many of the earliest crossings were probably accidental, unsuccessful, ill-fated, involved single or few individuals and were widely separated in time. There may have been a steady increase in their frequency during the Upper Pleistocene, a process which, over the last 100,000 years, finally provided enough people to constitute a viable population on Sahul. Crossings may have increasingly varied, from solitary, lost craft with several people on board to small flotillas carrying oceanic bands. In fact, Australia continues to witness the most recent manifestation of this phenomenon with the arrival of refugee 'boat people' from Vietnam and Cambodia over the last twenty years. Unlike these people, however, the early migrants were not met by quarantine authorities armed with a battery of health checks and eager to know whether highly infectious or exotic diseases accompany the seafarers.

We know now that the first migrations arrived at least 60,000 years ago (Roberts *et al.* 1990). Whether voyages were initiated by curiosity, natural or environmental catastrophe, a simple need to explore or social or demographic pressure of some kind may never be known. Whatever it was, the journey necessitated open ocean travel which, even at the time of lowest sea level, required a journey of around 75 kilometres. There is little doubt that the people themselves came from somewhere to the northwest; from among the islands (or land mass) of the greater Indonesian archipelago, a place where a variety of tropical diseases are found today. On their arrival the first colonists would have discovered Australia's environmental diversity, but we can only guess how quickly this discovery process unfolded. Such diversity would not have been part of the experience of the migrants, since the nearest regions with a similar geography are found on the Indian sub-continent or central parts of China and Asia; unless, of course, the migrants came directly from there! For people to notice the diversity exploration would have had to be speedy. A slow, gradual movement of people, taking several generations to cover several hundred kilometres or less, would eliminate the element of surprise at discovering different ecological settings.

Today, Australia's environmental diversity varies from humid tropical rainforests in the north to sub-alpine heaths and meadows and temperate rainforests in the south, with many deserts, savannahs, open woodland and riverine plains between. During most of the Holocene desert environments with chenopod shrublands took up forty-four per cent of the land surface with semi-arid tussock and grasslands contributing another thirty-three per cent (Williams 1979). Although rainfall averages close to 4000 mm in parts of the north, much of the central portion of the continent receives less than 120 mm with 45°C plus summer temperatures and annual evaporation rates of 3000 mm or more. As winter snows lash the southeast, balmy breezes temper 30°C midday temperatures on the northern coasts, and droughts and widespread flooding can occur simultaneously in different parts of the country. At present seventy per cent of Australia does not receive enough rain to grow crops and probably never did during the Pleistocene. This has earned it the dubious title of the driest continent on earth. Dust storms, bush fires, cyclones, torrential rains, parched landscapes and snow drifts have been, therefore, constant companions of the people who have lived here for well over fifty millennia. Their success as one of humanity's outliers can be measured directly not only by their survival in the many contrasting environments in which they lived but also by the fact that they thrived in them, using a whole battery of social and biological adaptations to survive. Their lifestyle was strongly marked by a wily flexibility which came into play in response to the vagaries of the environment rather than meeting them head on. This strategy helps to avoid clashes between humans and their environment which are injurious to health, but even with this flexibility people still became sick.

The last Ice Age probably had the effect of imposing an even bigger need for humans to adapt and be flexible in the face of the additional environmental changes associated with the period. The eventual blossoming of Aboriginal society from earlier biological and cultural foundations laid down by the original hominid populations, is testimony to the strong and very ancient link that developed between Aboriginal people and the Australian environment. With the flooding of the Arafura Plain and the reformation of Torres Strait around 7000 years ago, the separate cultural identities of Aboriginal Australians and the Melanesian people of Papua New Guinea began to develop in their separate spheres as did the Tasmanians, who became isolated with the sundering of the Bassian land bridge at roughly the same time. During the Ice Age, however, the humans of Sahul inhabited a complex environmental cline that stretched north from a latitude of about 43°S to the equator, that contained almost as many variations in culture and lifestyle as could be found anywhere in the world at that time.

To put this into a northern hemisphere geographical perspective, it is an equivalent distance from Yugoslavia to Tanzania or from just south of New England in the United States to the Amazon River. Obviously, the epidemiological picture over such a vast distance has the potential to be very different with opposite ends that contrast enormously. Since the last glacial the epidemiological histories of Australia and Papua New Guinea have developed quite differently. This has been due largely to their individual demographic and environmental situations, notwithstanding their oceanic separation which has played an important part in the prevention and spread of certain pathogenic organisms and conditions, mainly from north to south (see Chapter 11).

The demographic structure of the two countries plays a particularly important role in their respective epidemiological and pathogenic profiles. Australia probably had between 750,000 and one million people in 1788. The distribution and structure of this population has always been very different from that of its Papua New Guinea neighbour, however. The latter, for example, has villages based on extended families sharing large permanent, often rather crowded dwellings. Melanesians also cultivate gardens and have large regional aggregations of people, as in the Highlands where a pre-contact population of almost one million people lived in less than 150,000 square kilometres with densities as high as 200 people per square kilometre (Riley 1983). No real equivalent of these conditions has ever been a feature of Australian Aboriginal society with a population which was scattered over 7.5 million square kilometres and no crowded villages.

Infectious disease becomes a serious problem and a permanent feature of societies with high population densities. Papua New Guinea is renowned for its tropical diseases, particularly highly infectious varieties. Its equatorial and sub-equatorial environments have encouraged also the mosquito vector, which works synergistically with the human demography to play an important role in the transmission of malaria along with a whole range of other equally infectious and debilitating diseases. With the exception of a 1500-metre depression of the tree line in the New Guinea Highlands during the last Ice Age, there has been little environmental change in this region throughout the Quaternary (Dodson 1989). Subsequently, there would have been little change in terms of its epidemiological environment for tropical diseases to thrive during that time. Presumably, then, the only epidemiological factor that changed during this time was when humans moved into the area providing a new pool of susceptibles and fresh avenues for disease introduction and transmission: 'Early man migrating into New Guinea, would have carried malaria with him and found new and efficient vectors on arrival' (Riley 1983:130). In contrast, Australia does not have an environment which supports the variety of tropical diseases found across the Timor Sea and Torres Strait. Although scattered outbreaks of malaria have occurred in northern Australia from the earliest times of European settlement, the comparatively sparse population and humid, sub-tropical climate has not encouraged its spread nor has it facilitated the spread of other tropical diseases (Breinl 1912; Breinl and Holmes 1915). We can be fairly sure that Australia's original migrants, then, would not have contracted malaria here, even if some brought it with them in a direct or single generation crossing (Webb 1990a). It is possible also that when Australia and Papua New Guinea were joined the southern boundary of malaria would have extended south of the Arafura land bridge and into parts of what is today northern Australia. Changed environmental conditions at the end of the last glaciation, probably blocked that spread and confined malaria to the latitudes in which it is found today.

So, there were no infections and few or no tropical diseases to meet the first people that stepped onto Australia's shores. But what kinds of disease were here? Leaving aside, for the moment, injury and death resulting from encounters with animals, and poisonous plants, only one other avenue for disease was possible and that was from the faunal assemblage.

As we have already seen, zoonoses are distributed and controlled by physical and environmental barriers to a large extent. The mere fact that another animal (humans) joined others on Sahul tens of thousands of years ago may have changed the pathological environment of the continent. Even more important in this type of discussion are the changes that we have to consider since the arrival of non-Aboriginal people, just over two hundred years ago. Besides the enormous population increase that has taken place, the whole natural environment has been altered to some extent by development, the effects of domesticated animals, rural industry, agriculture and the introduction of various exotic pests and plants. All these have helped change Australia's original palaeoepidemiological status to such an extent that an increasingly thick veil of confusion has descended, confounding those wishing to understand what that status might have been like.

Today, Australia has no natural endemic diseases that may have proven overly detrimental to the health of the first or subsequent people to arrive here. If the occasional outbreak of malaria is discounted, we also seem to have escaped the worst of the tropical zoonotic diseases. Whether this was always the case, however, remains unknown. Is it possible that the first people had little to fear in terms of disease? It is often the case that, following transmission to humans, many zoonoses become more severe, particularly among those lacking previous experience of them. One can imagine that a group of exploring humans arriving in a new country might have been highly susceptible to any zoonoses found there. New and unknown infections could, therefore, have caused an unexpected morbidity and, possibly, high rates of mortality (Muul 1970). Of course, this would have had drastic repercussions for small founding bands who depended on maintaining minimal numbers (particularly females) for their continued survival. One group of infections that may have had such effects are the vector-borne diseases such as the rickettsias and arthropod-borne viruses (arboviruses). Arboviruses infect both animals and man and some of the more well-known types in Australia are Murray Valley encephalitis, Ross River and dengue fever, and Sindbis (Benenson

1975). The vector for all these is probably the Culcine mosquito and in some cases ticks but none are communicable from one human to another. Without the need for a human host they are the kinds of disease to which sparse populations of hunter-gatherers may have been very susceptible and the sort of condition present when the first migrants reached these shores. Today, dengue fever is largely endemic to New Guinea although sporadic outbreaks are not unknown and are, in fact, becoming more common in northern Australia, particularly north Queensland. It is possible, however, that it became fully endemic to large sections of what is now northern Australia during the glaciation, spreading south to its environmental limits, unhindered by an ocean barrier. If this was the case then it may have stretched in an endemic belt from Cape York, across the Arafura Plain, down into Queensland's Gulf Country, across Arnhem Land and even as far as the northern Kimberley region. These are regions, of course, through which any migrations would have to pass and no doubt where the earliest people dwelt for some time before moving into more southerly parts of the continent. Deaths from dengue are few but those from Murray Valley encephalitis range from five to sixty per cent depending on the strain or type of virus involved (Benenson 1975). Mosquitos usually acquire the virus from other animals, particularly wild birds or rodents, but the pig (*Sus scrofa*) is important in the transmission of the most virulent types of encephalitis: the Japanese and eastern equine forms. It is worth noting that these strains might have been much less frequent or non-existent until the introduction of the pig into New Guinea at the end of the late Pleistocene.

A closer examination of such introductions during the long prehistory of the region may teach us more about its palaeoepidemiology over thousands of years. Although the pig did not enter Australia before Cook's men put them overboard, it is, nevertheless, worth considering that Aboriginal Australians might have suffered from arboviral conditions in the more recent past. Diseases like these, together with others carried by birds and bats, can be transmitted across vast distances without the need for a human host or the advent of ice ages. They have a potential to be found in many regions separated by hundreds or even thousands of kilometres and must have always posed a potential problem in disease transmission for humans who also hunted and consumed them.

Another disease which is contracted directly from birds is psittacosis or ornithosis. It is caused by chlamydia (*C. psittaci*), found especially in parrots, parakeets, cockatoos, budgerigars, canaries, chickens, pigeons as well as a variety of other tropical, sub-tropical and sea birds (Manson-Bahr 1960; Mims 1977; Robbins and Cotran 1979). It is highly contagious, transmitted through infected faeces, blood or emulsions of the liver or spleen but rarely passed between humans. Less serious in young people, it usually proves fatal in the elderly with a twenty per cent mortality rate overall (Manson-Bahr 1960). Interestingly, *C. psittaci* has been isolated also in the conjunctival sacs of koalas with conjunctivitis and keratitis (Cockram and Jackson 1974, in Arundel *et al.* 1977).

As a centre for the distribution of many of the above bird species, Australia is likely to have always been a place where psittacosis has been endemic and, therefore, a possible hazard for humans. With continent-wide distribution of almost all the bird species mentioned above, as well as the koala in eastern Australia, the reservoir for *C. psittaci* would have been potentially quite large. The hunting of both the birds and koalas was the most likely way in which the disease could have been contracted. Preparation, cooking and consuming partly cooked meat would have acted only to enhance the chances of contagion. Like most of the conditions described here psittacosis was most likely confined to isolated outbreaks and, in terms of the unique incidence among koalas, it is interesting to speculate if any of the extinct megafauna species carried this disease. Nevertheless, it is almost certain that another chlamydial species (*C. trachomatis*) existed in Australia at least 12,000 years ago. The evidence for this has been described elsewhere but manifests itself as scarring in the orbits of fossil human crania from southeastern Australia dated to that time (Webb 1990a). These scars occur in most recent crania from all parts of the continent, with the highest frequencies in older people and those who inhabit the hot, arid and dusty regions. The only explanation for the age and spatial distribution of these bony scars is a long-term, chronic infection with trachoma which is prevalent in these areas today. With such conditions conducive to the spread of trachoma, there is little reason to doubt its presence among groups living here during the glacial maximum, particularly in central Australia, where very dry and windy conditions began around 60,000 years ago.

In Australia leptospirosis is caused by infection with *Leptospira australis A* and *B* and occasionally *L. icterohaemorrhagiae* via water contaminated by the urine of the carrier animal (Cilento 1942; Robbins and Cotran 1979). The reservoir for the leptospirae is a wide range of wild and domestic animals of which the rat is probably the most common. Although the introduced rat species (*Rattus norvegicus* and *R. rattus*) as well as foxes, cattle, dogs and swine, are known to transmit leptospirosis, the Australian native canefield rat (*R. sordidus* or *conatus*), as well as some other native species, also carry the disease in the northeast. The question that naturally springs to mind is: was this disease found among native fauna before the arrival of introduced species or did they become natural carriers after contact with the latter? All that can be said is that marsupials have been a potential host-carrier during the time people have been here. In that case, hunters could have come into contact with this disease through still or stagnant water in isolated water-holes or soaks being frequented by carriers. This was most likely during a prolonged dry period when the two might share fewer and fewer sources of water. Although trypanosoma are known to occur in the platypus (*Ornithorhynchus anatinus*) (Owen 1934; Mackerras 1958) and the bandicoot (Mackerras *et al.* 1953), trypanosomiasis, endemic to Central and South America and Africa, is essentially a disease foreign to Australia. There is no record of human infection from Australia's native animals.

The first men to arrive in Australia would have
encountered a completely new fauna, the marsupials.
The infections of these marsupials would have differed
considerably from those of the animals of the Asian area,
although unfortunately there is little data on this point.
(Cockburn 1971:48)

Even twenty years later we still know little more than Aiden Cockburn did about the zoonoses of Australia's marsupial fauna. It must
be said, however, that those trying to unravel Australia's palaeoepidemiological zoonotic history face an extremely difficult task. To
begin with there is a total lack of empirical data made worse by a
commensurate lack of knowledge about the biology and physiology of
over fifty species of the marsupial fauna which became extinct at the
end of the last Ice Age. These extinctions not only eliminated many
possible host–carriers, the natural ecological balance in which the
animals lived was changed also by their demise. It has become exceed-
ingly difficult, therefore, to get the kind of information we need when
the vector–host relationships and possible co-extinction of certain
pathogenic organisms and transmission pathways have disappeared.

A more direct method of finding out about the variety of palaeo-
faunal disease is to turn to the palaeopathology of the animals concerned. During the last two hundred years the palaeopathology of
Quaternary extinct fauna has been studied at some length elsewhere
(Esper 1774; Goldfuss 1810; Schmerling 1835; Mayor 1854; Moodie
1917, 1923; Pales 1930). In fact, it is widely recognised that the
formative period of palaeopathological investigation, from 1774 until
the 1870s, largely concentrated on the disease of animals (Pales 1930;
Roney 1966; Armelagos *et al.* 1971; Chaplin 1971; Siegel 1976; Wells
and Lawrance 1976; Ubelaker 1982).

Unfortunately, we know almost nothing about the palaeopathology
of Australia's Pleistocene megafauna. Most species disappeared at the
height of the last glaciation, around 18,000 years ago (Flood 1989).
In central Australia, they disappeared much earlier, probably around
60,000 years ago. Unlike other continents Australia lost *all* of its
largest animals at that time leaving only the medium-sized grey
(*Macropus giganteus*) and red (*M. rufus*) kangaroos as the largest ter-
restrials still living. Many theories have been put forward to explain
the demise of these animals but at present none seem strong enough
to push the others from the field (Merrilees 1968, 1984; Gillespie *et
al.* 1978; Horton 1979, 1980, 1984; Murray 1984; Flannery 1990).
While environmental change, the use of fire by hunters, direct hunting
itself and a combination of all these (the most likely reason) have been
proposed, nobody has seriously suggested that disease was the cause
of this faunal collapse and neither will this author. Nevertheless, these
animals did suffer from disease because traces have been found in
remains of *Macropus titan* and *Protemnodon* sp. dated to around
26,000 years at Lancefield in Victoria (Horton and Samuel 1978).
The conditions included cases of infection (periostitis), possibly some
examples of 'lumpy jaw' (necrobacillosis) a periodontal disease caused

by *Fusobacterium necrophorum* and, not uncommon in kangaroos today, osteoarthritis and minor trauma. These are not unexpected pathologies in active and aged animals and as such do not tell us much more than we could have guessed concerning disease in macropod populations in the past. It has been suggested that even these conditions may have been caused by drought and subsequent clustering of animals around a dwindling water source where they were also attacked by a carnivore. It is doubtful whether any of the minor infections would have caused health problems for humans even if the flesh from these animals was consumed. But were there any diseases carried by these animals harmful to humans? If there were then there was ample time for transmission because the two lived together for over thirty thousand years in some places.

What impact (if any) the zoonotic or helminthic diseases of the marsupial fauna had on the first people to enter this continent may never be known. In theory, Australia's fifty-million-year isolation provided ample opportunity for a unique pattern of zoonotic diseases to evolve, although if there were any there seems to be little evidence for it now. Alternatively, this isolation may have encouraged comparative pathogenic sterility in which the evolution and breeding of pathogens was minimal. The situation would depend somewhat on the kind of pathogens that existed at the time of the Gondwanaland break-up and how many of these remained and survived on the Australian section of the land mass before its final separation from Antarctica. Many unique organisms evolved following isolation; the plethora of marsupial species is an example. We can only guess at what pathogens arose in a similar fashion from observing those present among Australia's extant fauna. During examination of many megafaunal skeletal remains I have found little evidence for infectious disease, suggesting, against the incidence cited above, that while it did exist its frequency may have been quite low. Similarly, the frequency of healed trauma is low also, but it is likely a broken leg for a *Diprotodon*, as well as other large animals, meant certain death. Whether the common occurrence of sub-adult animals in fossil populations I have examined in central Australia has a pathological origin is unknown. If this was the case then it is possible that the disease, whatever it was, may have been acute, only affected soft-tissues, always proved fatal in younger animals or left little osteological scarring for later identification. I suspect, however, that predation is a more natural and non-pathological explanation for this phenomenon.

Evidence for the hunting of megafauna is largely circumstantial although there are some instances where an association is strongly indicated (Tindale 1955; Gillespie *et al.* 1978; Archer *et al.* 1980). It seems to me only reasonable that these creatures were hunted from time to time along with all the others. The argument that the megafauna was never hunted seems untenable in the face of what we know about the generalist type of hunting strategies that humans commonly employed in the late Pleistocene. We, the scientists, are the ones that subdivide the small from the larger varieties and label them as special sorts of creatures because they are no longer living. 'Megafauna' is a term of the palaeontologist and prehistorian, not the Ice Age hunter to whom they were as common as cats are to us. Bone from these animals, displaying blue-black colouration and white calcination typical of high temperature burning, has been found in the Willandra Lakes region of western New South Wales and central Australia, indicating burning in a high temperature camp fire not a transient bush fire. When these animals were hunted or scavenged for food, it was likely that their parasites and any other communicable diseases were transferred during consumption. While nothing is known about their parasites and other diseases, we do know that there is an extensive range of diseases that affect Australia's modern marsupial and monotreme species (Mackerras 1958; Arundel *et al.* 1977; Beveridge 1986; Butler 1986; Finnie 1986). Most of these occur in two major categories: parasitic and bacterial. A third, viral, is not thought to be important to humans and will not be discussed here.

Probably, the only pathogens that we can safely assume were transmitted between the giant animals and humans were those of a parasitic nature. A large variety of parasites are found in Australia's contemporary marsupial species which makes them a potential source of poor health for hunter-gatherers. With the introduction of domestic animals over the last 200 years, however, we can no longer accurately know what the list of endemic species was or what their geographical distribution was like before 1788, let alone as far back as the last Ice Age. Also, there is still some doubt about how many parasites carried by today's marsupials directly affect humans. Nevertheless, there is no reason why many of those found among modern animal populations were not shared by the larger species of the late Pleistocene. Perhaps some parasites were specific to certain species of marsupial megafauna as well as harmful to humans. With the demise of these animals came the concomitant demise of their parasites and the elimination of one source of pathogenic organism. We can only assume that as a general statement, parasites contracted by the hunters of these animals must have caused cases of vomiting, diarrhoea, anaemia and occasional death, as they often do today. Conversations with colleagues working in traditional Aboriginal communities continue to highlight the debilitating and often severe and chronic parasitic conditions that can be contracted from the ingestion of partly-cooked game, although these seem to affect Aboriginal people less severely than non-Aboriginal people. In the past, parasites would certainly have been contracted through eating raw or partially-cooked flesh, intestines and/or partly-digested stomach contents of animals. Other infection pathways would also have included handling, skinning and butchering. As bigger animals, it is likely that the megafauna had bigger parasite loads and one might speculate as to whether people quickly learned to avoid these by leaving the large animals alone or if they developed a general immunity against the effects of parasite ingestion.

The bacterial diseases of marsupials are not likely to have caused any major health problems among the earliest people although occasional infections would be expected. Adult marsupials and monotremes are believed to be asymptomatic carriers of the typhoid producing *Salmonella typhimurium*, with pouch young often dying from infection (Butler 1986). Kangaroos carry tetanus (*Clostridium tetani*) also as well as the *Fusobacterium necrophorum* and *Actinomycetes* spp. and *Bacteroides* spp. implicated in 'lumpy jaw', an infection of bone and soft tissue in the periodontal regions of the mandible and maxilla (see above). There is no evidence that humans suffer from the latter, but occasional outbreaks of melioidosis (*Pseudomonas pseudomallei*), which is found in the soil and carried by macropods, are reported among people living in tropical regions of Australia, particularly northeast Queensland and Torres Strait islands. *Mycobacterium ulcerans* also lives in soil and is thought to be a common source of infection for the rare 'Bairnsdale ulcer' confined to temperate southeastern Victoria.

Other hazards for the newly-arrived explorer, although not strictly zoonotic, would have been those resulting from the poisons of unfamiliar snakes, fish, jellyfish, plants, spiders, scorpions, ticks and centipedes as well as a whole range of other insects. It is not possible to cover all these in this volume but some are worth brief discussion. Australia is well endowed with deadly creatures. For example, of the 140 or so species of snake here over one hundred are venomous to some extent, many are extremely so and rank among the deadliest snakes in the world. Today the annual death rate from snake bite in Australia is between one to five per cent (Hennessy 1979). If untreated, however, the story is different. Snake bite was not rare among Aboriginal people and many deaths took place (Dawson 1881; Meston 1895; Macpherson 1902; Bennett 1927; Cleland 1928; 1958; 1962; Webb 1933). This must have been one of the most common and long-standing natural hazards among all peoples who closely shared the environment with these creatures.

The stone fish (*Synanceja trachynis*), blue-ringed octopus (*Hapalochlaena maculosa*) and sea snakes of the northern tropical waters would have been another source of severe sickness and death, but one assumes that these, together with the blue-bottle (*Physalia physalis*), box jelly or sea-wasp (*Chironex fleckeri*) and Carybdeid jellyfish (*Carukia barnesi*) would have been familiar to those living by and off the warm waters of the region. Various species of sea shell and urchins would also have caused painful if not serious injury from time to time.

I am not the first to be puzzled by the question of how people originally discovered what plants were safe to eat and what were not. The trial-and-error process of '… eat, die and learn' seems the most likely answer although it must have been a rather slow and hazardous way to learn (Webb 1973). Perhaps at one time our combined senses of smell and taste were so finely honed that lethal fruits, nuts and berries were quickly identified. The question is particularly interesting when we consider the first people entering this continent. Some plants must have been familiar to the new arrivals while others probably reminded them of related species or resembled some they knew to be dangerous. Most poisonous species are confined to tropical rainforest environments, which may be one of the reasons for the general lateness of human exploitation of these very special and complex ecosystems in Australia. We should not forget, however, that people have been living close to such environments in Indonesia for hundreds of thousands of years and I would have thought that the equatorial and tropical origins of the first arrivals would have served them well in coping with these environments as well as in recognising what sort of edible foodstuffs were provided by them. In terms of human health there are two main types of poisonous plant to consider: those that are dangerous but can be processed to make them edible and others that remain dangerous no matter how they are prepared. The best known example of the first type in Australia is the *Macrozamia*. This is a species of the ancient cycad family, their nuts are highly nutritious and also highly prized by Aboriginal people who used them to support large gatherings during ceremonies (Beaton 1982; Flood 1989). The nut kernels were ground into flour to make a kind of bread, but in their natural state they are very poisonous, containing a powerful carcinogenic substance. To neutralise this Aboriginal people learned to make them edible by soaking them in running water for days at a time to leach out the toxins. The cycad nut was used in a similar way in the Northern Territory and eastern parts of Queensland, but the oldest evidence for their use comes from the extreme southwest of Western Australia where they were being processed in the late Pleistocene (Smith 1982). This behaviour is a good example of learning to process food in order to make it safe for eating at a very early time. Surely, the long-term effects of the poison of the cycad and its carcinogenic properties cannot have been clearly understood by early peoples, or were they? We may often underestimate our ancestors.

There are many examples of the second type of poisonous plant, far too many to describe here. One of these, however, is the fruit of the finger cherry or native loquat (*Rhodomyrtus macrocarpa*), which grows in Australia's northeastern rainforest. It is not literally deadly but will cause blindness, which is just as bad for a hunter-gatherer (Cilento 1942). Not all dangerous species are confined to the tropics and many do not need to be ingested to cause serious health problems. Stinging Trees (*Laportea* sp.) are found in a 3000 kilometre-long band that stretches from the south coast of New South Wales to Cape York. The sharp stinging hairs of the leaves contain a lethal mixture of formic and acetic acid which produce a very potent sting, intense and agonising to those unfortunate enough to brush against them. The leaves of the arum lily (*Colocasia macrorrhiza*) can, if ingested, cause death in children and this is only one example of a range of similar plants that while having very unpleasant side-effects for the adult will actually kill a child.

Other dangers lurking among Australia's foliage come from spiders, in particular the 'funnel-web' (*Atrax* sp.) and 'red-back' (*Latrodectus hasseltii*) varieties. The bite from the female funnel-web and to some extent the red-back, can cause death in children and others who have poor general health or are suffering heart problems. Serious pain, fever and/or paralysis are other side effects and death from the funnel-web bite usually ensues in one to 11 hours. This spider is confined to the east coast, from Sydney to southeast Queensland, but the red-back is widely distributed throughout Australia as well as neighbouring regions of the Pacific and southeast Asia. There is some dispute concerning the presence of this spider in Australia before 1788. It may, in fact, have arrived from the south Pacific in the middle of the nineteenth century, as there seems to be no record of the insect in Australia before that time (MacKay, pers. comm.). The Australian bush or scrub tick (*Ixodes holocyclus*) is not nearly so dangerous as the funnel-web but it can have fatal consequences, particularly for the infant (Cleland 1924, 1932, 1942, 1966). This usually follows respiratory paralysis if the insect is not detected and burrows into the skin. Ticks are common to the eastern seaboard, live in rainforest, scrub and long grass and are easy to acquire during a day's walk. The usual symptom is persistent inflammation in those that do not discover the burrowed insect and receive treatment. The effect is similar to the untreated bite from a large centipede (*Ethmostigmus rubripes*) which produces a lesion that often becomes badly infected and takes some time to heal. The scorpion is another creature that is 'greatly respected by bushmen' and with good reason (Cilento 1942:393). It is not unknown for cardiac failure to follow a bite from one of these and, again, the young child is most vulnerable. Other side-effects include swelling around the wound, elevated respiration, vomiting and convulsions. Persistent inflammation is the usual symptom in untreated cases similar to the untreated centipede bite. The result is a lesion that often becomes badly infected and may take some time to heal.

I have mentioned only a few of the known hazards of the Australian bush, but it is obvious that these come from a wide variety of sources that hunter-gatherers must have encountered constantly. The long-standing familiarity that Australia's Aboriginal people have with their bush would have made them acutely aware of the everyday dangers that constantly challenged them. For the first arrivals, however, that awareness had yet to grow from the wide range of experience which was gradually to build up over the next 60,000 years. They probably did not enter the continent completely unaware of the dangers from plants, shellfish, insects and animals, however, and probably possessed a large baggage of bush-craft and cultural experience concerning these. This experience would have been as important to them as their weapons. Yet the dangers of being a hunter-gatherer on a strange continent must have constantly caught out the unwary. Those that let the vast inverted pyramid of ancestral experience teeter risked serious illness, injury and death. Most of these cannot be detected by the palaeopathologist, yet the enormous pharmacopoeia that Aboriginal people possess must testify to the everyday hazards of those living this original way of life. One thing of which we can be sure is that it was obviously not compiled for nothing.

Chapter 4

Pathology in late Pleistocene and early Holocene Australian Hominids

Introduction

The paucity of information about late Pleistocene palaeopathology from the region is a severe handicap to those trying to put together a picture of the health of the first Australians. Therefore, I want to present this chapter as a beginning in our effort to change that situation and develop an understanding of ancient health in this part of the world. I do this by introducing some solid palaeopathological evidence from the earliest human skeletal remains discovered so far on this continent. That evidence comes to us in the form of a series of osteological lesions observed on skeletal remains of people who lived in Australia roughly between 8,000 and 50,000 years ago. It is derived mainly from southeastern Australia where most late Pleistocene and early Holocene archaeological sites have been found. The Murray River corridor and western New South Wales are particularly well represented (Map 2–1).

As meagre as they are, the pathologies described below are the only empirical data we have for the health of people living at that time. They are also the oldest for anatomically modern humans living anywhere in Australasia and certainly the oldest yet discovered for ancient Australians. The descriptions are presented as a series of case studies which contrasts with the population studies of Holocene remains featured in later chapters. This is done because of the lack of population samples from the late Pleistocene. An epidemiological approach will be taken whenever possible, but the nature of the data does not lend itself to any significant in-depth study. Nevertheless, some tentative indications of what the early palaeoepidemiology of the region might have been like do emerge from the reporting of these data.

The Willandra Lakes hominid series

The Willandra Lakes hominid (WLH) series consists of human skeletal remains recovered from the Willandra Lakes system in western New South Wales (Webb 1989) (Map 2–1, 3). The archaeological significance of this fossil-rich area was recognised in 1982 with its successful nomination to the World Heritage listing. The lake system lies in the Murray Basin and straddles the Willandra Creek, a defunct distributary of the Lachlan River. The system itself is a fossil relict which began its final drying phase shortly after the glacial maximum (about 16–18,000BP), remaining dry ever since. (For a detailed bibliography of research carried out in the area I refer the reader to Webb 1989.)

The WLH series of fossil hominids consists of 135 individuals many of which are represented by a few fragments or even single pieces of bone. These remains have been exposed by natural erosion which has continued intermittently in the region for over 2000 years (J. Magee pers. comm.). This process has removed metres of soil from extensive sand dunes (lunettes) that formed around the lakes during the late Pleistocene, burying the ancient shoreline and its beaches. Erosion has exposed these beaches together with the camps, shell middens and stone artifacts of the inhabitants who lived and foraged along these shorelines between about 14,000 and at least 40,000 years ago. The erosion processes have also uncovered the remains of the people themselves.

The Willandra hominid series was assembled between 1969 and the early 1980s. Collection was carried out not only because of concern for the loss of extremely valuable palaeobiological data but also because the remains represented the earliest evidence for modern humans in this part of the world. Bone quickly disappears in the Willandra Lakes system through the natural destruction of the lunettes caused by weathering and erosion and this has been exacerbated by grazing over the last one hundred years and tourism in the last fifteen years.

The value of the collection has been recognised internationally and this attention has been particularly focussed by the discoveries of WLH1 and 3 in 1969 and 1974, respectively. These display different forms of burial practice as well as other cultural and morphological traits which shed much light on the social, ceremonial and human evolutionary history of ancient Australia. WLH1, for example, represents the oldest evidence for human cremation in the world and it has now been handed back to regional Aboriginal custodians. There are others, such as WLH69, which also bear the signs of having been cremated but they have yet to be formally dated.

WLH 3

Although a general description of WLH3 has been excluded from this survey, the severe osteoarthritic condition in its right elbow needs to be described within the context of other pathologies evident in the Willandra Lakes hominid series.

WLH3 was found in February 1974 on the southern end of the Lake Mungo lunette (Bowler and Thorne 1976). The lunette is a curved sand dune composed of beach-derived aeolian sands largely accumulated between 14–40,000 years ago. WLH3 was an extended burial within a stratum of the lower deposits known as the lower Mungo stratigraphic unit. Subsequent excavation revealed an almost

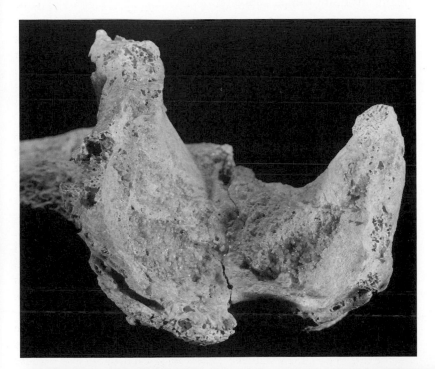

Plate 4–1a
Prominent pitting on the articular surface of the WLH3 right ulna together with osteophytes around the margin of the trochlear notch.

Plate 4–1b
The lateral view of the WLH3 ulna has an osteophytic scroll (centre) which originally formed part of an ankylosis between this bone and the head of the radius.

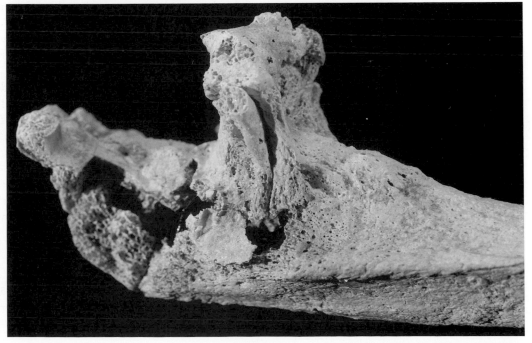

complete and extremely friable male skeleton, lying partially on its right side, with knees slightly flexed, hands in the lap and a layer of red ochre sprinkled over the body. It was dated by stratigraphic association to between 28,000–32,000 years BP (Bowler and Thorne 1976). Almost all cranial sutures have fused both ectocranially and endocranially suggesting an age for this man of over 50 years at the time of his death (Abbie 1950).

Osteoarthritic lipping on the thoracic and lumbar vertebrae has already been described elsewhere (Bowler and Thorne 1976), but it consists of osteophytes on both the superior and inferior borders of the centra of the second and third lumbar and ninth thoracic vertebrae. Such outgrowths are not uncommon, particularly in an active male, and probably caused little if any discomfort. The right elbow of WLH3 shows extreme osteoarthritic involvement of all bones, however. Severe osteophytic lipping is present around the trochlear notch of the ulna, together with erosion of its articular surface (Plates 4–1a and b). Similar changes occur on the coronoid process but these have developed into a bulky proliferation of bone nearly nine millimetres high in some places. A large mass of exostotic bone is present at the origins of the head of the *flexor digitorum superficialis* and *pronator teres* muscles and the attachments of the anterior part of the ulna collateral ligament. Osteophytosis occurs around the radial notch in which lie remnant osteophytes originating from the head of the radius (Plate 4–2). The latter formation suggests that the ulna and radius were ankylosed at their proximal ends. Extreme proliferative osteophytosis is present also around the head of the ulna. Advanced erosion and minor eburnation on the articular surface has produced a very rough and pitted surface that slopes anteriorly (Plates 4–3a and b). The distal end of the radius is missing.

Plate 4–2
The head of the right radius is severely eroded with pitting and eburnation.

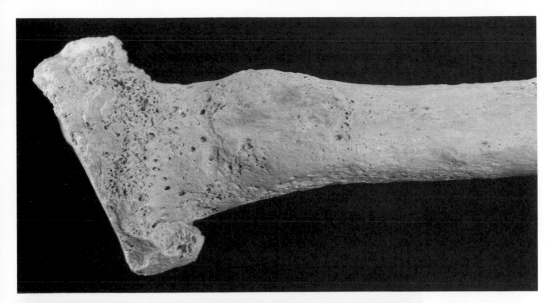

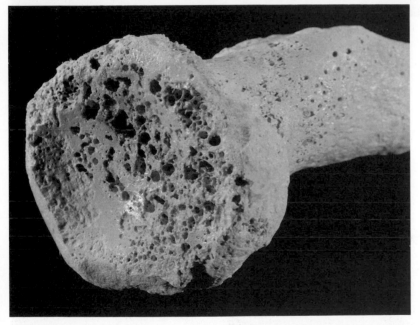

Plate 4–3a
Lateral view of the head of the right radius. Remnant osteophytes appear around the inferior margin.

Plate 4–3b
The surface of the head of the right radius with extensive confluent pitting. Almost the whole surface has been polished following loss of the articular cartilage.

Osteophytosis is so well developed around the medial side of the distal humerus that it has produced a scroll-like lip of bone measuring up to eight millimetres deep in some places (Plate 4–4a). It has proliferated around the attachment of the articular joint capsule, forming subsynovial osteophytes that trace the capsule's outline. The articular surface of the capitulum has been heavily eroded with patches of shiny eburnation. An oval wear pattern has been worn into its surface reflecting the continuing rotation of the head of the radius after the articular cartilage was lost (Plate 4–4b). These features suggest that osteoarthritic processes were taking place on all joint surfaces simultaneously and over some considerable time. The radius and ulna

Plate 4–4a
The distal end of the right humerus has a massive scroll-like osteophytic proliferation on the medial margin.

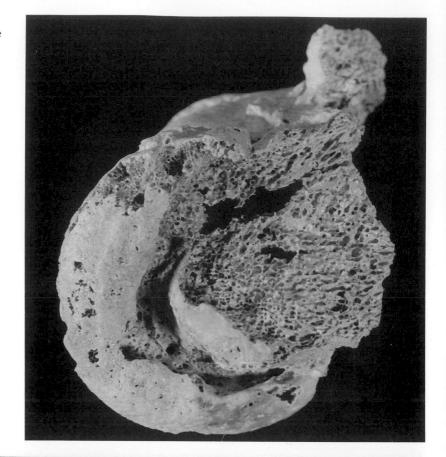

Plate 4–4b
The anterior surface of the distal humerus bears the distinctive pattern of the head of the radius etched into its surface (left).

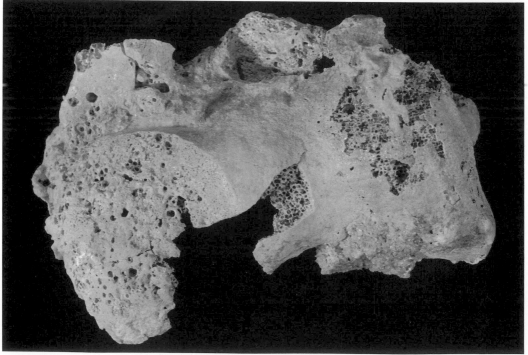

became ankylosed following the loss of articular cartilage which prevented complete destruction of the articular surfaces by immobilising the joint.

The coronoid fossa of the humerus is filled with proliferative hypertrophic bone and from the presence of similar exostoses in areas adjacent to the olecranon fossa they too were also affected. This helped preserve the joint by limiting extension and flexion at the elbow. It is likely that the pain from this deterred use of the elbow for anything but essential movement. With the bones of the lower arm ankylosed, rotation of the lower arm would have been impossible. Moreover, the massive accumulation of hypertrophic bone in the distal humeral fossae and on the coronoid and olecranon processes probably limited movement at the elbow to less than 40 per cent of normal bend. Collectively, these limitations would have curbed many everyday tasks associated with hunting activities ⟨...⟩, would have been im⟨...⟩ and use weaponry wo⟨...⟩y, from the degree of ⟨...⟩derable time before h⟨...⟩ many years.

Initially, th⟨...⟩antial, repetitive stre⟨...⟩ wear often occurs a ⟨...⟩cating the handednes⟨...⟩nown, however, that ⟨...⟩ing a spear thrower, ⟨...⟩oduce certain wear pa⟨...⟩966; Ortner 1968). T⟨...⟩joint associated with s⟨...⟩ a distinctive set of degenerative featur⟨...⟩ together have been termed 'atlatl elbow' (Angel 1966:3). These include erosion of the capitulum which, together with the head of the radius, undergoes a double stress action when the spear thrower is used. It is precisely these parts of the bone that have been worst affected in WLH3, together with the head of the ulna which bears the most stress during rotation. Moreover, the large exostosis formed at the origin of the *pronator teres* could indicate that large mechanical forces were applied during rotation of the lower arm. It has been suggested that certain types of degenerative features around the shoulder joint help define osteoarthritis caused by using a spear thrower (Angel 1966; Ortner 1968). Except for a small fragment of the right humeral head, however, little remains of the shoulder joint to check these in WLH3.

The pattern of osteoarthritis in WLH3 may not be solely a product of spear thrower use. The condition is unusual in both its degenerative morphology and distribution across the joint. Initially, this condition was thought to have been caused by the same form of arthritic disease common to any synovial joint subjected to long-term strenuous and repetitive activity. Generally speaking, this extreme form of osteoarthritis is not common in more recent Aboriginal skeletal remains, which is unexpected considering the widespread use of the spear

Plate 4–5

Internal build up of new trabecular in the vicinity of this hole in the right humerus of WLH3 suggests an infection. How large the original hole was is difficult to determine but it has been considerably enlarged during interment.

thrower in many parts of the continent. Another possible cause, however, is infection. The proximal half of the right humeral shaft has a large oval, medially-facing hole, exposing the medullary cavity (Plate 4–5). This may have been caused by the same erosive processes that brought about the extensive damage to other parts of the skeleton. There is no obvious sign of pathology around the margin of the hole, but some small patches of fine, cancellous bone situated posteriorly on the upper section of the deltoid tuberosity might be periostitic in origin. Whether this opening began with a small or medium-sized cloaca, which then became enlarged by natural processes after interment, is not known. It is possible that any evidence of infection may have been removed by erosion of the bone surface. The cortex around the hole is very thin and mainly consists of trabecular bone. Inferiorly, the shaft has much thicker walls but at the expense of a marked narrowing of the medullary cavity. Cortical bone thickness at the distal end ranges from 4.3 mm to 8.5 mm, whereas higher up the shaft it is less than two millimetres. Part of this thickening consists of trabecular bone in the form of an involucrum of a type normally associated with chronic localised infection (Steinbock 1976). Periostitis can be seen around the distal end of the left humerus, particularly within the olecranon fossa and the posterior surface of the lateral epicondyle. This could signal a more generalised infection of the skeleton affecting both arms, at least.

There seems to be little evidence for acute or chronic suppurative osteomyelitis which is normally accompanied by cloaca, sequestra of dead bone, extensive new bone formation and remodelling of external bone surfaces (Steinbock 1976; Ortner and Putschar 1981). Alternatively, non-suppurative osteomyelitis lacks pus formation and, consequently, the associated scarring and alterations to bone architecture. This condition normally affects the diaphysis and is characterised by new bone formation, increasing cortical width and narrowing the medullary cavity (Steinbock 1976: 76–77). Chronic non-suppurative osteomyelitis, however, is rare and it may have been even rarer 30,000 years ago.

There is enough evidence from alteration to both internal and external bone structures to firmly support the existence of a generalised infection of the right, upper arm of WLH3. It affected cortical and trabecular bone but cannot be immediately associated with the periostitis which occurs on parts of other long bones of this individual.

The infection in the right arm seems to have progressed to a non-specific cortical osteitis altering internal structures, effectively thickening the cortex and imposing an irregularity on the external surface. Infectious osteoarthritis is caused when the synovial joint becomes infected from a site usually situated superior to that joint. Pus forms and rapidly destroys articular cartilage at contact surfaces. The process becomes chronic, sequestra formation is rare but arthritic bone changes occur, including frequent bony ankylosis (Steinbock 1976: 79). The lack of evidence for pus production within the WLH3 humerus is at odds with a diagnosis following the above description. Nevertheless, such a process cannot be ruled out as a cause of these arthritic changes.

WLH106

Almost all the articular ends of the major long bones in the Willandra Lakes hominid series are missing. It is probably for this reason that only one other individual in the collection has enough articular surface to show any arthritic change. This occurs on the distal end of the right humerus of WLH106. Unlike WLH3 the changes are not severe and take the form of minor osteophytic lipping and surface erosion of the mid-trochlear ridge. In the latter, the normally sharp border has been removed leaving a worn, granulated surface. Articular surfaces either side have not been affected but minor osteophytosis has formed around the rims of the coronoid and radial fossae. The lateral crest of the olecranon fossae has been accentuated by this process which extends anterolaterally as the lateral border of the capitulum. Post-mortem damage has removed bone along the entire length of this ridge but the base of the outgrowth is still present.

There is nothing remarkable about the condition of this male individual. He displays a primary stage in the onset of a wear process typical among those engaged in strenuous use of the upper limb, particularly the elbow joint. The involvement of the right arm probably reflects handedness or use-bias or both, albeit that the missing left arm cannot be checked. Arthritis involving the right elbow only is typical of skeletal remains of more recent hunter-gatherer groups (Jurmain 1977b, 1980).

More intriguing than the arthritis is the moderate, medially-directed bow in the shaft of this bone (Plate 4–6). A large section of the well developed deltoid tuberosity indicates that the arm was used in a normal manner and that, despite its shape, no particular favouring of the arm took place. Bowing can be caused by a congenital deformation of some kind; nutritional inadequacy; a metabolic disorder (such as rickets); 'endemic' non-specific bowing of the limb, or a developmental response by the bone to an accident or injury.

Rachitic bones are normally light and rather brittle, these are not. Also, rickets usually occurs during childhood, bowing is bilateral and is more common in the weight-bearing bones of the legs, which are weakened by demineralisation. Upper limb deformity normally only occurs in those suffering a severe form of the disease, where

Plate 4–6

The general robust appearance of this bone suggests that the bow does not have a metabolic or nutritional origin.

support of the upper trunk is needed following a weakening of spinal support. All the other long bones of WLH106 look normal and robust. No other bone from this individual has changes similar to these, although the left humerus is missing. Neither do they reflect the substantial nutritional inadequacy normally associated with this kind of architectural change. In fact, the cortical bone is dense, quite normal and shows none of the osteoporotic resorption and lack of mineralisation typical of rickets and other nutritional disorders, such as osteomalacia (Steinbock 1976; Ortner and Putschar 1981). It is possible that this individual may have fully recovered from rickets, with only the bowed diaphysis left as a permanent reminder. But I doubt this is the case.

Congenital deformities of the skeleton are usually very distinct, often involve a number of skeletal elements and do not change even into adulthood if that is attained by the sufferer. Radiographic examination of this humerus shows that except for its shape, its gross and internal structures are normal in every way. The cortex is thick, although not overly so, and rather uniform (Plate 4–6). An accident causing a deformity at the shoulder or to the arm itself is not likely to have caused humeral bowing of this type. Atrophy of the bone can result from fracturing, particularly if malunion or some sort of localised paralysis ensues. This bone shows no sign of such atrophy.

Finally, there is the possibility of 'endemic' or non-specific bowing. Topinard (1894) noted bowing in the shafts of ancient long bones and more recently Trinkaus (1982, 1984) has described a similar condition found among the remains of the Shanidar Neanderthal groups. Bowing of human long bones has, therefore, a rather long history and has been noted in groups from many parts of the world (see Chapter 6). In Australia, this deformation normally takes the form of an anteroposterior bend in the tibia, often accompanying platycnemia or lateral flattening of the shaft. It has been associated with endemic treponematosis but is more commonly seen, at least in skeletal collections, without any form of associated infection of the bone itself (Hackett 1936; Webb 1984). This intriguing pathology has been observed in recent Aboriginal skeletal remains from most parts of Australia. The greatest frequencies are found in the tropical north and the Murray River region, with 4.8 per cent and 3.7 per cent affected, respectively (see Chapter 6). As well as the tibia, diaphyseal bowing has been observed in fibulae, femora, ulnae, radii and humeri.

Although bilateral involvement is most common, asymmetrical bowing is not rare. Except in the few cases that have accompanying infection, no other changes to the general appearance of these bones are encountered. Normally in the tibia, sub-cortical bone apposition is observed thickening both the anterior and posterior walls of the middle one-third of the shaft, narrowing the medullary cavity but reinforcing the bone at its weakest point. This possibly occurs as a secondary response, to prevent weight-bearing bones from breaking as the continued bowing encourages an increasing weakness mid-way along the diaphysis. The process may be, in turn, a response to a primary pathology associated with some form of decalcification due to a nutritional or metabolic imbalance or both, affecting bone mineral production.

The cause of the bowing in WLH106 is unknown, but I suggest that it could be an ancient example of a similar condition observed in recent Aboriginal populations. If this is so, the late Pleistocene age of the individual (?>15,000BP) extends the known geographical range of this type of malformation from Ice Age European hunters and others in the Middle East to hunter-gatherers living beside a freshwater lake on the opposite side of the world. It is likely also that the arthritic condition seen on the distal articular surface of this bone may be closely linked to a discontinuity of the upper arm originating in its bent form. The dysfunction at the elbow joint caused by the mis-shapen humerus has resulted in a chronic joint malfunction that during movement has caused a slow degeneration of the articular tissues.

Arthritis – temporomandibular joint

Five individuals have arthritic degeneration of the glenoid fossa. They are WLH27, 44, 67, 72 and 101. The condition varies in degree and involves different parts of the bone or the mandibular condyle or both.

WLH27

This robust male individual was found in 1977. It is highly miner-alised and its surface is covered with a thin silica wash. As with WLH106, no accurate date is available for these remains but, as with many other individuals described from this series, it can be placed within the general time of lunette building which terminated around 14,000BP.

The only section of the temporomandibular joint remaining is the left mandibular condyle. It has most of its articular surface missing but osteophytic lipping is evident on the anterior margin. The extent of the lipping conforms to the advanced form of joint degeneration (category 2) as defined for late Holocene Aboriginal skeletal remains (see Chapter 7). Normally osteophytosis of this kind accompanies erosion of the articular surfaces, often with preceding eburnation.

WLH44

Found in 1978, the blue-black colour of the bone of WLH44 suggests that this female individual was cremated and, perhaps, deliberately smashed in the same manner as WLH1. An accelerator mass spectrometer date has given a minimum age of $18,635 \pm 335$BP (NZA-159) although its true date is believed to be closer to 25,300BP (Webb 1989:6–7).

The anterior half of the left glenoid fossa has been almost completely destroyed (Plate 4–7). The fossa itself is small, very shallow, with little development of the articular tubercle, a feature contrasting sharply with the normally deep glenoid fossae often seen in modern Aboriginal crania. Destruction of this kind hampers proper function of the temporomandibular joint and compounds an increasingly poor contiguous relationship between the mandibular condyle and the fossa, thus aggravating the condition. This small fossa would seem to have been maladapted to the kinds of strong, constant and repetitive stresses that recent Aboriginal people put on this joint. Is it possible that the larger and deeper glenoid fossae, typical of those seen among skeletal remains dating to the last 10,000 years or so, may have been selected for as a *better* joint, in terms of a more secure construction, in order to cope with the increased stresses put on it in the recent past. Dietary and behavioural factors arising in the Holocene almost certainly must have selected for a deeper and less delicate structure in order to maintain the integrity of the joint. I return to this topic again in Chapter 7.

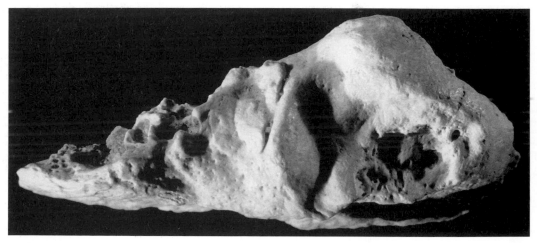

Plate 4–7
Severe arthritic degeneration in the glenoid fossa and on the articular tubercle (right) of WLH44.

WLH67

WLH67 was found in 1978 and is represented by bone from most parts of the skeleton. This generally gracile male has all its cranial sutures fused and obliterated indicating an age probably greater than 50 years. These remains are undated but fossilised in the normal manner associated with other late Pleistocene remains from the region.

The whole of the articular surface of the left glenoid fossa and the articular tubercle has been worn away. The fossa itself is large but shallow, although its exact depth cannot be measured or even estimated due to the deposition of new bone within it. The deposition of this bone has been caused, no doubt, by a reaction to bone-on-bone contact between the mandibular condyle and the surface of the glenoid fossa after the loss of articular cartilage from both surfaces, as well as the articular disc that acted as a buffer between them. The new bone itself has been scoured out by hard bony spicules on the simultaneously degenerating surface of the mandibular condyle, leaving deep anteroposteriorly directed grooves etched into the surface. The condition of the bone makes it difficult to determine whether there was any eburnation but its severity suggests that there might well have been. Well-emphasised muscular markings on both the medial and lateral surfaces of the gonial angle, as well as gonial eversion, suggest a robust masticatory apparatus that applied strong chewing forces. Such stress on the temporomandibular joint can quite easily instigate degeneration of this kind.

WLH72

Also found in 1978, WLH72 is a very robust male. The bone is completely fossilised but no accurate date is available.

The right glenoid fossa has only minor pitting of the posterior surface of the articular tubercle (category 1). The pitting takes the form of a small cluster of tiny holes, some confluent, situated on the medial half of the fossa. The morphology of the fossa itself differs considerably from those already discussed. It is much deeper (12.5 mm) and narrower in the coronal plane which gives it a distinct oval appearance. The general shape is close to that expected for the mandibular condyle, which would probably fit very snugly. Biomechanically, the shape of this fossa seems far more adaptive than the shallow fossae of WLH44 and WLH67 (see above). The shape would more readily have prevented anteroposterior excursion by the condyle, for example, than the fossae of WLH67. It was probably such a movement in the fossae of WLH44 and 67 that caused their complete degeneration in these individuals. Incisal chewing, or using the anterior tooth complex for gripping objects, encourages the condyle, through an anteroinferior movement, to override the articular tubercle (Shipman *et al.* 1985). The use of the jaws in this manner almost certainly took place in these individuals, adding to the degeneration of their respective joints. The adaptive morphology of the fossa of WLH72 would, therefore, be highly beneficial for maintaining joint contiguity and helping prevent its destruction by arthritic degeneration even under similar behavioural circumstances.

WLH101

This undated, highly mineralised and robust male was also found in 1978.

The floor of both glenoid fossae and their articular tubercles have been extensively eroded together with the inferior surface of the root of the zygomatic processes (category 2). The latter indicates a lateral excursion of the mandibular condyle during chewing. The depth of the fossae is not great, although its measurement (8 mm) would suggest it was not particularly shallow either. This contradiction is due to its shape, which is triangular in the horizontal plane, and the roof, which ends in an apex. Bone remodelling has deposited new bone in the fossa, but while this is a natural process which protects the joint it effectively reduces the overall depth, although it continues to allow natural movement and articulation with the mandibular condyle. Thus, the process of scouring continues and the new bone deposition itself becomes eroded in a similar way to that already observed in WLH67. Although minor erosion in the area of the articular tubercle has damaged this feature, it is likely that it was never very well developed in the first place. Subsequent natural erosion of many of these remains has tended to 'soften' the profile of pathological features preventing a more detailed description.

Trauma – cranial

The only form of cranial trauma encountered among the Willandra series is small depressed fractures on the vaults of WLH22 and WLH63. In both these cases the trauma is minor and affects only the outer cranial table.

WLH22

This male was found in 1977 but is not dated. There is a shallow, slightly oval depression situated posteriorly on the left parietal close to the sagittal suture. It is about 20.4 mm at its greatest width and conforms to the usual type of depressed fracture commonly encountered in archaeological populations.

WLH63

WLH63 consists of a single large piece of frontal bone. The robust morphology, however, is strongly suggestive of maleness and, as is the case with all the specimens described so far, it is completely fossilised. There are two elongated oval dents on this section of bone, one 36 mm long and the other 21.3 mm long (Plate 4–8). They are orientated sagittally and would have been positioned well forward on the frontal squama. Both dents are larger than the depression on WLH22, but they have probably not penetrated further than the outer cranial table, which is 7.5 mm thick. The overall vault thickness is 12.5 mm. Some remodelling of the bone has taken place in the central portions of both fractures leaving uneven scar tissue. These fractures may have involved scalp wounds. We cannot be certain, however, because this minor pitting could indicate either a transient periostitis or just erosion of the bone surface.

Trauma – post-cranial

The pattern of long bone trauma among late Holocene Australian populations is biased towards the upper limb (Chapter 8). The majority of upper limb fractures are, however, 'parrying' fractures of the distal one-third of the ulna and occasionally involve the associated radius. Five individuals in the WLH series have some form of post-cranial trauma. These are: WLH27, 72, 106, 117 and 127.

WLH27

The right third metacarpal of WLH27 has suffered a complete mid-diaphyseal fracture. The form of the break is oblique in an infero-superior direction and the shaft has telescoped, resulting in a shorter diaphysis. The bone has healed well with very little callus formation around the break. A fracture of this sort usually stems from an awkward fall onto outstretched hands or from a blow to the knuckles (Adams 1979).

WLH72

A section of the left fibula of WLH72 has a completely healed fracture of the diaphysis. No misalignment of the shaft is apparent indicating that the fracture may not have been complete. Often the strong inter-osseous membrane between the fibula and the tibia and the unbroken tibia itself acts as a form of splint in the case of fibula fracture alone, thus preventing complete discontinuity of the shaft.

WLH106

The left fibula of WLH106 has suffered a complete break. The edges of the bone at the site of the break are quite jagged, lack any sign of healing and show only a minimum amount of new bone formation distal to the break. The bone itself is in two pieces and the broken ends are covered in the same calcium carbonate deposit as other surfaces of this individual. This condition, together with the new bone, suggests that the fracture was present when the individual died.

WLH117 and 127

Plate 4–9
Radiography reveals how well a parrying fracture in the left ulna of WLH117 has healed (top) after a complete break in the shaft.

Both WLH117 and WLH127 have parrying fractures of their ulnae. Such fractures normally occur on the left or 'shield' arm which is used to block a blow from a weapon held in the right hand of an opponent. The arm is usually raised in front or above the head, and the lower two-thirds of the ulna is exposed to the blow, hence the distinctive position of the break.

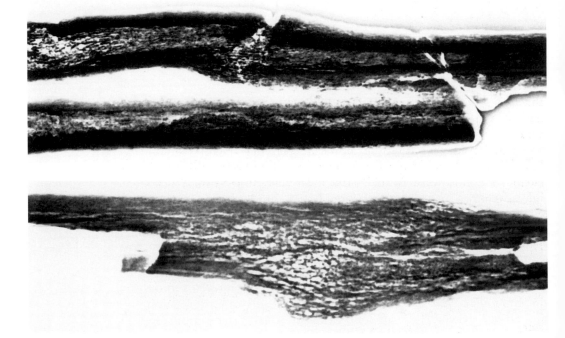

Plate 4–10
The parrying fracture in WLH127 has produced a large callus formation.

In WLH117 the break is complete and lies in a transverse direction roughly between the distal and middle third of the diaphysis (Plate 4–9). Both ends of the bone are jagged, slightly misaligned and bear no visible sign of uniting. The bone either side of the break is slightly swollen, indicating that a callus did begin to form prior to death. It is clear from this primary stage of unification that this individual probably died soon after the injury was sustained. No other injuries are apparent on the rest of the skeleton.

In contrast, the ulna fracture in WLH127 has completely healed. The break was long and oblique but the fractured ends seem to have united in almost the correct anatomical position (Plate 4–10). Normally, few parrying fractures result in misalignment of the shaft for similar reasons to those outlined above for the fibula. These include the strong interosseous attachment between the ulna and radius which together with the radius brace the fractured bone and prevent excursion of the broken ends. There is substantial callus formation around the shaft in WLH127 but this might indicate only that the arm was used before it healed. Nevertheless, the bone has healed well without any secondary infection, perhaps attesting to the individual's good health also.

Infection

Besides WLH3, only two other individuals in the Willandra Lakes hominid series, WLH25 and WLH107, have distinct lesions caused by bone infection.

The undated WLH25 female has a localised periostitis on a small section of the right clavicle. Changes to internal cancellous structures suggest that this bone may have been fractured and localised periostitis followed. There is also a patch of periostitis on the upper medial surface of the right tibia. This consists of a very thin layer of new bone, extending about 5 cm down the diaphysis and causing minor thickening of the cortex. An infection of this kind is more likely to have resulted from a blow to the leg rather than any generalised or systemic infection.

An anteroproximal section of the left tibia of the unsexed WLH117 has a long (7.2 cm) strip of new bone formation (periostitis) on its lateral surface. As with WLH25, this individual probably derived the infection from a blow but the structure of the new bone is distinct. The woven architecture of the cancellous-like formation is different from that of WLH25 and conforms to a more extensive and virulent type of infection.

It has been suggested that in hot, arid regions the sun acts as a form of cleansing agent or disinfectant on soils, preventing infectious agents from taking hold (Abbie 1960). The demography of the hunter-gatherer also plays a part in prevention of infection. The constant movement in small groups, together with the continuous formation of new and simple camps, would have helped prevent the build-up of human and other wastes that normally support infectious organisms and bacteria. The use of faecal and similar materials for hunting and warfare could have been one way, however, that serious infections arose. Introduction of such material into a wound through an accidental scratch or being struck by a spear tipped with these natural poisons may always have been one avenue of such infection among humans living in the late Pleistocene and Holocene.

The evidence from the WLH series strongly supports the presence of infection among people living in Australia 30,000 years ago.

Whether this reflects demographic factors, such as a localised semi-sedentary behaviour, based on close occupation of resource-rich lake edges, is interesting to speculate upon. A more likely explanation may lie in the one offered above regarding the use of natural poisons to tip weapons. The likelihood of infection in the arm of WLH3 is certainly significant for its age, 30,000 years, although Neanderthal populations had similar infections over 40,000 years ago (Trinkaus and Zimmerman 1982; Trinkaus 1983, 1985), the lesions described here are the earliest known for people living in this part of the world at a similar time.

Harris lines

Only a trace of one Harris line was found in any of the long bones. It lies on the posterior wall at the proximal end of the right tibia of the robust male individual WLH69. Its position corresponds to a personal age of about 3–4 years in the growing bone. From previous observations, a line at this position is common in tibia of recent Aboriginal groups (see Chapter 5). It has been proposed that the presence of a line in this position may be an indication of 'weaning shock' caused by the first real reliance of the weaning infant on unsuitable adult foods. The recording of this single incidence of Harris lines more likely reflects the broken and poor condition of the long bones in the Willandra Lakes hominid collection rather than their almost total absence among this late Pleistocene population.

Dental hypoplasia

Only one tooth, an upper central incisor of WLH133, in the whole collection shows any evidence of dental hypoplasia. These unsexed, undated but highly fossilised remains consist of a few mandibular fragments and one tooth. Hypoplastic lines like the one recorded here are normally formed by disturbance of ameloblastic activity during enamel formation on the growing tooth (Sarnat and Schour 1941, 1942; Acheson 1960; Park 1964; Garn *et al.* 1968). The condition is caused by any stress or metabolic disturbance that interferes with the body's natural growth processes (see Chapter 5). The most likely cause in a hunter-gatherer group is a systemic illness or nutritional deprivation, perhaps during winter. The result is the formation of a transverse line, groove or, in severe cases, a row of pits across the tooth. The position of this line indicates, to some degree, the age at which the metabolic insult took place (Green 1982). In WLH133 this stress indicator takes the form of a line 1.7 mm from the cemento-enamel junction, which indicates formation some time between 2.0 to 2.5 years. Normally weaning does not take place among hunter-gatherers at this early stage of development so the cause is more likely to have been a moderately severe illness or period of nutritional inadequacy before weaning.

Cyst

A small oval dent lies just below the left temporal line on the vault of WLH55. The internal surface is smooth and lacks any sign of infection, stellate fracturing or healing. It appears to be too deep in relation to its small diameter to be a depressed fracture and because of its almost perfect circular symmetry and smooth interior surface there is some suggestion that it may be a scar left by some form of benign dermal cyst.

Pre-mortem tooth loss

Although this volume avoids dental disease, tooth loss and edentulism, some interesting features noted in the dentition of WLH3 and 22 require description because of their late Pleistocene age.

WLH3

WLH3 has lost both lower canines (Plate 4–11). The upper dentition is missing so these teeth cannot be checked, but as it stands the loss of only the lower canine teeth is a very unusual occurrence. Resorption of the alveolar bone around the sockets indicates that they were lost some considerable time before death and the degree of resorption around each socket suggests also that they were lost at about the same time. The resorptive processes have reduced both the thickness and height of the bone around the area of the socket, forming a sharp ridge which runs between the interproximal surfaces of the lateral incisors and the first premolars which are still firmly held in the jaw. The loss has caused both lateral incisors to lean distally into the adjacent gap. Canine teeth are not normally missing among more

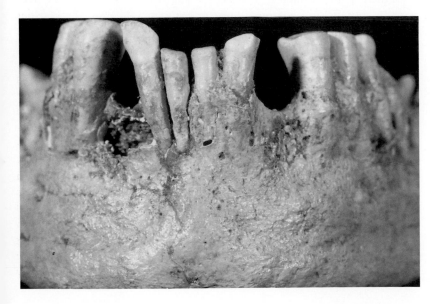

Plate 4–11
The lower jaw of WLH3 has both canines missing. Extensive resorption of the alveolar bone around the gingival margin and the angular set of the teeth on either side indicates that both canines were lost some considerable time before the man died. The bilateral loss is very unusual and suggests deliberate avulsion.

recent Aboriginal dentitions unless most of the other teeth on either side have been lost also. Natural tooth loss among traditional Aboriginal people has a number of causes, principally old age and extreme forms of occlusal attrition. Although there is an uneven wear pattern on the whole mandibular dentition of WLH3, there is nothing to suggest this was extensive enough to have caused both canines to fall out. The teeth on either side are not unduly worn which suggests that the canines may have been deliberately removed or lost through an accident of some kind. It is worth noting that beside this example there are no ethnohistorical or ethnological references to deliberate canine avulsion, as there are for the deliberate removal of upper central and lateral incisors. Neither are there any examples of canine avulsion among collections of Holocene skeletal remains (Campbell 1981). Nevertheless, deliberate avulsion seems a more logical explanation than a freak accident resulting in bilateral loss without damage to adjacent teeth.

In the light of this finding it is worth describing briefly the pattern of dental attrition on the other teeth in the mandible of WLH3. Attrition of the anterior tooth complex has reduced the height of the central incisors, leaving the lateral incisors with higher crowns and a medially directed slope on their occlusal surface. This form of wear pattern is typical of that resulting from the use of the mouth to hold material while it is manipulated or to shred fibre by drawing it from the mouth, forward and across the surfaces of the central incisors.

In the rear complex the right, first and second molars are missing but this probably occurred post-mortem. Loss of alveolar bone around the base of these teeth, however, prevents this being verified. The roots of the left, first and second molars have been exposed through loss of bone from the lateral wall of the mandible. Periostitis is evident around the edge of the hole through which the distobuccal root of the first molar has been exposed. This sort of exposure is commonly associated with periapical disease among more recent Aboriginal remains, but WLH3 has no sign of apical root infection. Resorption of alveolar bone extends back to the third molar. Heavy attrition on the buccal half of the left first and second molars has produced a steep helicoidal pattern on their occlusal surfaces. Continued downward pressure on these oblique surfaces has caused lingual tilting and the forcing outward and subsequent exposure of their roots through the thin lateral wall of the mandibular corpus.

The whole tooth wear pattern of WLH3 is unusual and quite unlike that of other teeth in the Willandra Lakes collection. I have observed similar patterns in more recent skeletal remains from the Murray River region of southeastern Australia, but, in general, this sort of wear contrasts with the more even pattern generally found in Holocene people. This is due mainly to the later introduction of a larger vegetable component into the diet and the use of the grindstone in food preparation which brought with it greater quantities of dental abrasives. The wear on the buccal side of the first and second molars of WLH3 reaches almost to the alveolar bone. It is an unusual pattern and one more in keeping with the deliberate drawing of an extremely abrasive material, perhaps a tough plant fibre, in a transverse and downward movement across the tooth, similar, perhaps, to the activity suggested for the wear on the incisors. A close examination of molar surfaces using a binocular microscope reveals a series of thin but distinct parallel grooves or striations cut into both the exposed dentine and the remaining enamel (Plate 4–12a and b). These striae run parallel to the slope of the wear (buccolingually) and their presence does appear to support the suggestion that stripping of some sort of plant fibre with sharp inclusions (quartzitic grains or phytoliths) may have been responsible for them (T. Loy, pers. comm.). Could it be that these fibres were used to construct fishing nets, baskets or dilly bags?

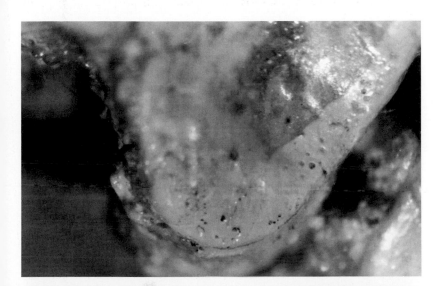

Plate 4–12a
A close-up (x3) of scratches across the molar enamel of WLH3 (lower and centre).

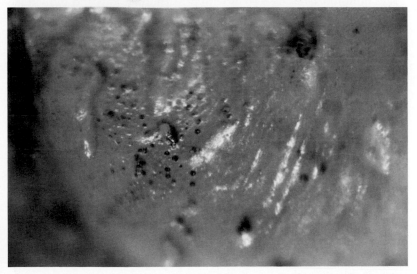

Plate 4–12b
At a higher magnification (x15) the scratches noted in Plate 4–12a appear as a series of parallel grooves in the enamel.

WLH22

The lower central incisors of WLH22 are missing. From the extent of bone resorption around the gingivae it appears that these teeth were lost some considerable time before death. Nothing is left of the sockets themselves, which have been completely filled with new, spongy bone. The breadth of the mandible at this point has been reduced by resorption of the alveolar area which highlights further the length of time elapsed since the incisors were removed. The loss of central incisors through accident or attrition is very rare. The loss of these teeth is, therefore, more consistent with deliberate avulsion, as in the case of WLH3. A study of this practice among late Holocene Aboriginal people has shown that removal of the lower dentition is rare (Campbell 1981). Either way, extrapolation of the manner and frequency of this practice from modern populations back to the late Pleistocene is difficult to make. All that can be said is that the loss of upper or lower central incisors in skeletal remains of this age suggests a cultural practice that goes back a very long time.

Cranial thickening in WLH50

> It is a well-known fact, and one often reported, that the skull caps of fossil hominids appear considerably thicker than those of modern man. But as yet … no one has provided actual figures or deemed the entire phenomenon worth consideration. (Weidenreich 1943:161)

This section discusses the extraordinary cranial thickening of the male individual WLH50 (Plate 4–13). This phenomenon has been discussed elsewhere (Webb 1990b), but for the purposes of bringing together all known pathology from late Pleistocene Australia I want to include it in a brief form here.

Even a cursory comparison of WLH50 with others in the Willandra Lakes hominid series, as well as with other populations and individuals around the world, quickly establishes that it has an unusually thick vault (Webb 1990b). Vault thickness is fairly uniform and ranges from 15 mm at obelion and lambda to 19 mm on the frontal squama at a point just posterior to the frontal boss (Plate 4–14). Certain individuals in the Willandra series do come close to matching WLH50's cranial thickness at one point or another, as do one or two from the Kow Swamp and Coobool Crossing populations. Both WLH19 and WLH28 have an inion measurement, for example, which exceeds that of WLH50. Considering the variability of vault development at this particular point and the influence of muscular insertion, it is not considered worthwhile pursuing comparisons using this particular morphometrical point or, for similar reasons, that of asterion. More recent Australian crania are thickened somewhere on the vault, usually at lambda, asterion as well as inion, with a range in the order of 13–16 mm. Late Holocene Murray Valley crania are among those particularly noted for this trait. None of these, however, are uniformly thick, neither do they reach the stage of development displayed by

Plate 4–13
The robust calvarium of WLH50.

Plate 4–14
Radiography reveals the extensive cancellous formation of internal structures throughout the vault.

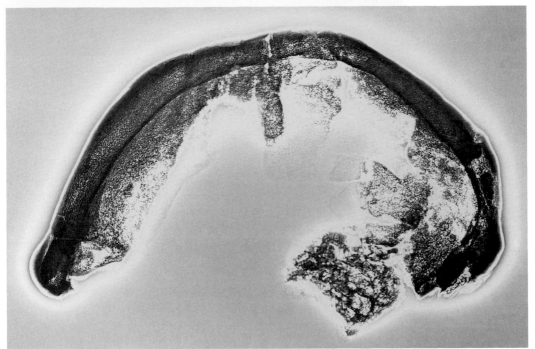

WLH50 or, indeed, WLH19, another individual with thick cranial walls. My observations of vault thickness in Melanesian crania confirm that vault thickening, particularly in the regions of asterion and lambda, often results in measurements close to those noted for Murray crania, thus demonstrating that vault thickening at these points is a shared trait in this region.

While substantial thickening of the vault can occur in one or two places among both late Pleistocene and Holocene individuals, the uniformity of thickness observed in WLH50 has no equal. Uniform thickening has been noted among the late Pleistocene Kow Swamp population from the Murray River although details have not been made available (Thorne and Macumber 1972). Nevertheless, the largest known measurements from Kow Swamp are rather ordinary compared to those of WLH50, for example 13.5 mm at mid-frontal (Thorne and Macumber 1972:318). The uniformity of the cranial thickness among Coobool Crossing individuals has not been demonstrated either, thus preventing direct comparisons between this group and WLH50. For example, while a maximum of 16.3 mm has been claimed for the mid-frontal region of one individual, it is not explained whether this cranium has been subjected to head binding (Brown 1981).

Artificial deformation imposes changes to vault structures that result in the thickening of posterior areas of the frontal squama, particularly around bregma. The massiveness of *H. erectus* cranial bones from China, Java and in the archaic *H. sapiens* population from Ngandong has been discussed by Weidenreich (1943, 1951). His general conclusion was that massive walls were associated with middle Pleistocene hominids and although every so often a thick cranium can be seen among modern humans, the calvarium has become thinner as modern humans emerged. Even in earlier hominids from China and Java, uniformity of thickening is lacking. Weidenreich has shown that a 5 –7 mm difference can occur between various points (e.g. mid-frontal and bregma) on early crania from these regions (1943:162, Table 35). Again, some of the measurements taken by him approach those of WLH50 at some point on the calvarium, but the *uniformity* of thickness is lacking. It is worth noting also that no individual from the Chinese and Javan series actually achieves the thickness of WLH50 in *any* of the vault areas discussed here.

The composition or construction of the WLH50 cranial wall is another area for examination. The proposition that thick walls are indicative of a 'primitive' or archaic hominid has been used often by the physical anthropologist. The way in which this massiveness is constructed in both the Choukoutien and Javan *H. erectus* remains, however, follows a pattern whereby: 'all three constituents of the bone take equal part in the thickening, the two tables slightly more than the diploe' (Weidenreich 1943:164). This pattern is typical of vault construction in other middle and upper Pleistocene crania, as well as those individuals from the Ngandong series. The pattern in WLH50 is quite the reverse, however, with very thin inner and outer cranial tables (1–2 mm each) (Plate 4–15). The rest of the thickness, up to 16 mm or 87.5 per cent, consisting of diploeic or cancellous bone (Plate 4–16).

So what has caused the extraordinary thickening in the WLH50 cranial vault?

General cranial thickness in late Pleistocene Australia is a phenomenon that cannot be addressed here. WLH50 seems to be a 'thickened' version of other individuals in the WLH series, such as WLH18, WLH19 or WLH27. But with its high ratio of cancellous to tabular

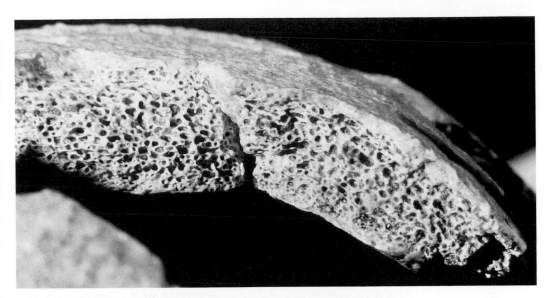

Plate 4–15
A cross-section of the left parietal of WLH50 shows that it consists almost entirely of cancellous tissue. The thickness of the compact bone of the cranial tables varies from about one millimetre to almost zero.

Plate 4–16
The complex and tightly woven structures of the diploeic bone in the vault of WLH50. Note also the very thin outer cranial table (bottom).

bone, as well as its enormous overall thickness, WLH50's vault composition does not conform to *H. erectus* or early *sapiens* populations in the Australasian region (or elsewhere). The difference between the thickness of WLH50 and earlier hominid groups can be described, then, as a thicker cranium and a replacement of compact tabular bone with diploeic cancellous bone. This may be a local adaptation which occurred either before or after people entered Australia. The reason for such a change is unknown, but an alternative explanation for such a thickening is a pathological one.

Cranial thickening among modern human populations, involving expansion of diploeic tissues, is usually indicative of pathology.

Diploeic hyperostosis can result from a number of pathologies, including Paget's disease, *hyperostosis frontalis interna*, leontiasis ossea and the haemoglobinopathies (Jaffe 1975). The latter include the genetically-determined balanced polymorphisms of sickle cell anaemia, other haemoglobin (Hb) variants and the thalassaemias (Britton *et al.* 1960; Aksoy *et al.* 1966; Jaffe 1975). Both the rarity and the distinctive nature of the first three conditions almost certainly precludes their implication in this case. For example, the changes to the cancellous bone structure in Paget's disease sharply distinguishes it from the diploeic structure of WLH50. Also, changes to internal vault structures are very distinctive in Paget's sufferers with areas of rarefaction and new bone formation (Hamdy *et al.* 1981). *Hyperostosis frontalis interna* largely affects the anterior sections of the calvarium and 'Leontiasis ossea ... was only occasionally encountered in the past and is very rarely encountered now' (Jaffe 1975:278). Both these conditions are characterised also by substantial alteration of both external and tabular bone surfaces, but they do not occur uniformly and, more often than not, grossly alter the appearance of the whole skull in a very obvious and distinctive manner.

On the other hand, skeletal changes due to genetically-determined anaemias are more common and have been observed in various ancient populations for over half a century (Cooley and Lee 1925; Williams 1929). Accompanying gross morphological changes include a thickened diploe and symmetrical osteoporosis, which usually appears on the frontal and parietal squamae (Hrdlicka 1914; Cooley and Lee 1925; Williams 1929; Hooton 1930; Angel 1964; 1967). These structural alterations are normally due to haemopoietic hyperostosis triggered by genetically-determined blood dyscrasias such as thalassaemia and sickle cell anaemia. The result is enlargement of the marrow tissues between the cranial tables and elsewhere as the body attempts to counter the disease by producing more red blood cells. The hyperostosis causes pressure atrophy, particularly of the outer table, which results in the resorption, thinning and, occasionally, the complete destruction of compact bone. The condition can affect all major cranial bones but usually not the whole bone and never the complete cranial vault. Radiologically the affected bone presents a brush or 'hair-on-end' appearance, caused by the formation of bone spicules within the diploe which pile up at right angles to the table as a result of osteoclastic and osteoblastic activity during the proliferation process (Jaffe 1975). In their heterozygous form, the balanced polymorphisms are highly adaptive, presenting an effective partial immunity against malaria, so they are normally encountered in areas where malaria is endemic (Bodmer and Cavalli-Sforza, 1976). Few osteological changes take place in heterozygous sufferers. Enlargement of the vault and asymmetrical osteoporosis is normally associated with the homozygous condition. If left untreated, these people rarely live beyond adolescence.

WLH50 is neither adolescent nor overtly suffering from symmetrical hyperostosis. Around bregma, however, radiographic examination reveals a hint of the diploeic hair-on-end morphology often associated with severe non-genetic anaemia. It seems reasonable to suggest that if WLH50's thick vault is due to some form of haemoglobinopathy, using both contemporary diagnostic criteria and the known aetiology of the disease, he must have been heterozygous for the condition in order to have reached adulthood. As far as we know, malaria, as the primary selective agent for haemoglobin polymorphisms, was not endemic in prehistoric Australia. Sporadic outbreaks have been reported in Australia's north from time to time but these have been mainly due to changes to the environment brought about by non-Aboriginal settlement patterns following colonisation and the influx of foreign malaria sufferers during the past 200 years (Breinl 1912; Breinl and Holmes 1915; Cilento 1942). The low population density and nomadic lifestyle of the traditional Aboriginal population in this area presented an unsuitable human ecology for the transmission and spread of malaria. Support for the idea that malaria was not a problem to pre-contact Aboriginal people, comes from the complete absence of abnormal haemoglobins among recent Aboriginal groups (Horsfall and Lehmann 1953, 1956; Kirk 1981). Nevertheless, could malaria and its associated pathologies have existed in Australia or Sahul more than thirty thousand years ago and subsequently died out?

From the less than meagre evidence we have to go on it would seem that endemic malaria, as opposed to sporadic outbreaks, is unlikely to have been a problem in Australia at any time in the past. This strongly contrasts with nearly all Australia's northerly neighbours who are heavily affected by it as far as about 170 degrees east (Manson-Bahr 1961). In southeast Asia the dominant adaptive polymorphism is represented by the HbE variant, while in our immediate neighbourhood, Java and Melanesia, thalassaemia is the dominant form. These genetic blood disorders, which include the African sickle cell anaemia, have arisen among many human populations around the world and are now believed by some researchers to be the most common human hereditary defect in the world (Williamson 1977). In southeast Asia these conditions are associated with and are a defence mechanism against the very dangerous Malignant Subtertian malaria which causes 15 per cent mortality annually among those living in endemic areas. It is 'almost universally fatal … for those unfamiliar with it and … *P. falciparum* is evidently a recently acquired pathogen of man' (Fiennes 1978:108). At this point, of course, many questions have to be asked, such as: how recent is recent? Obviously the polymorphisms had to begin at some stage; is it possible that some sort of genetic precursor arose very early, selected as general defence against malaria? If it did, when did it do so and what form might it have taken? And so on. Before we become too embroiled in these largely unanswerable questions, however, I want to propose that both southeast Asia and particularly Java are almost sure to have had malaria for a very long time. As a likely stepping-off point for Australia's progenitor populations the latter becomes especially important in the following discussion. Going one step further, is it also likely that northern

Sahul (present-day Papua New Guinea and Irian Jaya) supported endemic malaria before the arrival of humans?

The zoonotic origins of malaria are not well established but it seems likely that it was contracted by our early ancestors from other suitable reservoirs such as primates (Bruce-Chwatt 1965; Fiennes 1967, 1978; Toft 1986). Moreover:

> ... it has been found out that of the 65 species of
> Anopheles recognised as vectors of human malaria, not
> less than 21 were natural or experimental vectors of
> simian malaria. (Bruce-Chwatt 1965:369)

Four species of plasmodium (*Plasmodium* sp.) produce quartan malaria in East Indian gibbons (*Hylobates* sp.), which are natural hosts for the disease (Toft 1986). We have already noted that malaria was almost unknown in Australia, not because there was an unsuitable vector or natural environment but because of the demographic status of the susceptible group – the Aboriginal population. Java is different. It seems likely that it has always been an area, at least in the course of its human history, where malaria was endemic. This was so primarily because of its primate populations which acted as a suitable pool for continual or at least regular, sporadic infections to occur. There is little doubt that initial endemicity of the disease in certain areas began with simian malarias. It is not inconceivable, therefore, that during the one-and-a-half-million years or more of human habitation in Java, humans became infected (Franzen 1985). On the subject of adaptive genetic blood disorders or dyscrasias that have arisen in human groups, I return to Fiennes:

> These genetic changes and the severity of malarial
> infections show that the pathogenic malarias of man
> have arisen in remote times from some animal source;
> one may be reasonably sure that the original source must
> have been simian. (1978:109)

Certainly, the less deleterious benign tertian and quartan malarias had plenty of opportunity to emerge among the many varieties of primate species in the far east. How and when the earliest forms of the adaptive balanced polymorphisms of humans arose in response is not known. Nevertheless, they must have occurred in places like Java where environmental conditions remained fairly constant during the last few million years, even in the face of the Quaternary glaciations, and where primate populations acted as a natural reservoir for transmission. Could the excessive thickening displayed by WLH50 be symptomatic of the emergence or, at least, presence of these polymorphisms in this region? If so, this question begs the others I raised before. When did they first appear? Moreover, could they have emerged via a common precursor which gave rise to the many variants known today, and what effect would such a precursor have had on Upper Pleistocene human osteology, particularly that of the pre-existing thick cranial vault?

The only other example of a similar type of cranial thickening in a fossil human is that of the Upper Pleistocene Singa skull from the Sudan (Stringer *et al.* 1985). Cranial vault thickness in this individual is 14 mm on the parietal (WLH50 is 16 mm), 15 mm at asterion (WLH50 is 17 mm) and 80 per cent of its width consists of diploe (WLH50 is 87.5 per cent). Except for its thickened vault, others found no evidence of osteological changes which could be firmly associated with anaemia but further study was suggested (Stringer *et al.* 1985).

While WLH50 does not display skeletal changes that conform exactly to those found in recent populations suffering hereditary anaemias, the thickened vault strongly indicates a need for haemopoietic 'reinforcement', otherwise so much haemopoietic tissue would not be required. Some thickening of the human cranial vault occurs with age (Adeloye *et al.* 1975). But the thickness of WLH50 has no equal and it cannot be accepted as normal development at any age. It can only be assumed, therefore, albeit tentatively, that the vault thickness is a product of a pathological condition and probably derives from some form of haemoglobinopathy. But what is it doing in Australia where there has never been selective pressure for such a condition?

It is possible that the condition was brought to Sahul, as part of the genetic baggage of human migrations from Java where it developed. WLH50 may have been personally part of that movement or, more likely, an unwitting recipient of genes passed down from his ancestors. In the absence of a selective agent for the maintenance of this condition in Sahul, the genes could have disappeared quite quickly, within the continent, perhaps within a few thousand years (R. L. Kirk, pers. comm.). With the post-glacial division of Sahul into New Guinea and Australia and extensive increases in New Guinea's Holocene population, a firm selective pressure encouraged the adoption from outside or selection from within for the dominant thalassaemia variant found there today. If this can be taken as a likely palaeoepidemiological mechanism that took place, and there is no reason to suspect that it did not, how far south might the southern limit of this disease have extended, considering Australia and Papua New Guinea were joined for tens of thousands of years at a time?

Australia probably maintained very small late Pleistocene populations, of a wider and more isolated geographical distribution than those of our northern neighbour, and comparatively more isolated from later migrations into the continent. They would have also been more firmly under the influence of a pattern of internal population growth from an earlier period than those of Papua New Guinea which, as the nearest point on Sahul to southeast Asia, have always been in the forefront, able to receive any polymorphic genes from the north and northwest. For this reason we cannot expect to find many other fossils with a vault construction similar to WLH50, unless our osteoarchaeological evidence for the particular time at which the genes were moving into Australia (whenever that was) becomes extensive enough to reveal another sufferer.

Other late Pleistocene/early Holocene remains

Kow Swamp and Coobool Crossing

A full anatomical description of the Kow Swamp remains, which includes pathology has already been made but not published (Thorne 1975) (Map 2–1, 8). A description of the Coobool Crossing population, believed to be contemporary with Kow Swamp, has been published elsewhere (Brown 1989) (Map 2–1, 5). For these reasons I will refer to them here only where I have made personal observation.

Murrabit

This male individual from near the southern side of the Murray River is undated and has now been returned for reburial (Map 2–1, 7). Few details of its discovery are available. Its state of fossilisation together with the distinctive manganese staining of the bone; general robust morphology and its close geographical association with the Kow Swamp and Coobool populations strongly suggests, however, that it is part of this population complex. (For an extended discussion of the manganese staining of late Pleistocene Australian skeletal remains, see Webb 1989.)

Large osteophytes occur around the distal joint of the right humerus but there is no sign of accompanying erosion or eburnation. No arthritic changes are visible on the associated ulna and the right radius is missing. The right humerus is more robust than the left, which implies handedness and probably a greater susceptibility to arthritic conditions. The left humerus has slight osteophytosis around the distal joint and on the distal end of the left radius, which is probably due to a severe break near the wrist.

The Murrabit skeleton has fractures to both its lower arms and lower right leg. The left radius is broken nine centimetres above its distal end and delayed union has caused a diarthrodial pseudoarthrosis to form (Plate 4–17). The only other example of this type of malunion that I have observed in late Pleistocene Australian skeletal remains is a fracture close to the distal end of a left ulna from Kow Swamp (K.S.1) (Plate 4–18). This has formed a ball and socket joint, with the socket on the distal section of the ulna. It originates from a Colles' fracture, probably resulting from a fall onto outstretched hands. Besides occurring on different bones, the major difference between these two united fractures is that the articular surfaces of the Murrabit bone are rather flat and similar to examples of pseudoarthrosis described by others (Stewart 1974; Ubelaker 1980). The pseudoarticular surfaces are smooth, although undulating, with patches of porosity quite unlike the polished inner surface of the socket from Kow Swamp. The associated ulna from Murrabit has a

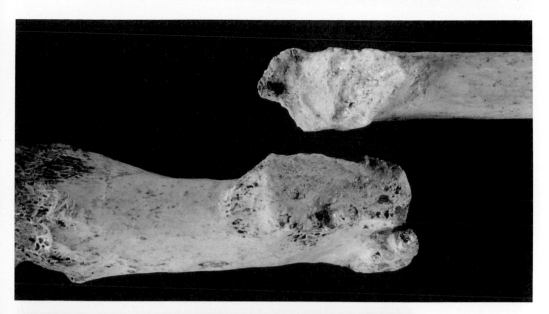

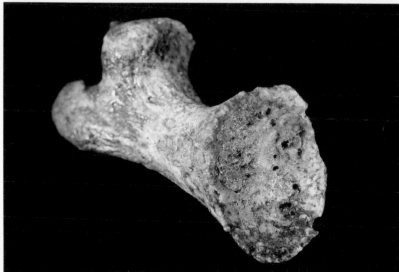

Plate 4–17
The fractured radius of the Murrabit individual showing the healed surfaces of the broken shaft forming a pseudoarthrosis.

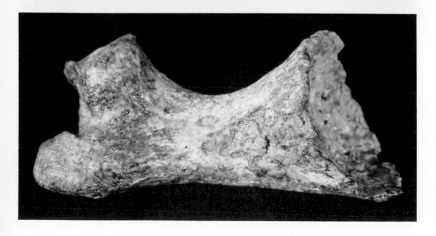

Plates 4–18a, b
A pseudoarthrosis in the distal portion of the left ulna of Kow Swamp 1 has formed a deep socket for the resultant ball and socket joint.

healed parrying fracture with small callus about 3.5 mm above its distal end. The bone has mended well but it has left a slight misalignment of the shaft.

These fractures are too high on the arm for a typical Colles' fracture, often sustained when falling onto outstretched arms, but conform more to the unhealed parrying fracture sustained during combat. A severe blow on the partially pronated left wrist of the upstretched shield arm caused both bones to be broken at approximately the same place. Continued use of the arm resulted in the pseudoarthrosis. It is likely that the radius did not sustain a complete break but rather a partial comminuted or greenstick fracture, thus maintaining its general alignment during the healing process.

Both the right radius and ulna have been fractured in approximately the same position as that observed on the left arm (Plate 4–19). There is a strong callus formation around both these breaks but this is not excessive. The right arm has continued to be used following the fracture causing the misalignment of the shaft, but not used so much as to form a pseudoarthrosis. As a result of the injury there would have been a reorientation of the wrist limiting extension and pronation at the joint. Overlap of the broken ends of the right ulna would have shortened the lower arm. Another fracture is apparent in the distal one-third of the right tibia and fibula. This has caused ossification of the interosseous membrane in the immediate area of the break, resulting in strong well formed ankylosis between the two bones (Plate 4–20).

It is difficult to know whether all these injuries happened at the same time or on different occasions. In the case of the lower arm, the pattern of injury suggests use of the right arm to fend off an attack at the time when the left was incapacitated. Once healed, the left would have been used again as the parrying arm. It can only be said, therefore, that these injuries probably occurred at the same time or during the time at which the left arm was still mending. The act of pronation would have tended to twist the bone, thus forcing the two ends to pivot, one on another. These injuries could have been caused

Plate 4–19

Fighting probably caused these fractures of the right ulna and radius in the Murrabit individual. The medial angulation of the distal portion and lipping along one side of the callus suggests ossification of the interosseous membrane at one point.

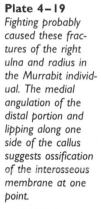

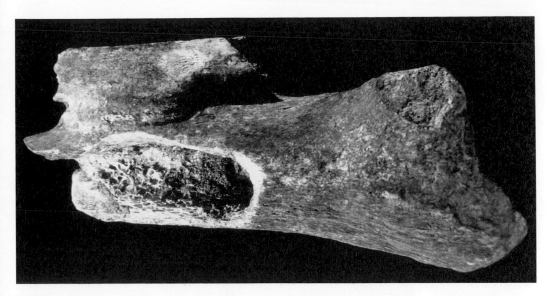

Plate 4–20
The tibia and fibula are ankylosed 5.5 cm above the ankle.

by a bad fall, but the nature of the fractures and their position point to aggression as the most likely cause. The fact that this man lived some considerable time after sustaining them suggests that he must have received some nutritional and nursing care. After all, a man with two broken arms and a broken leg is not able to go hunting or provide for himself.

There is vertebral osteophytosis on the inferior margins of the L4 and L5 of the Murrabit skeleton, but this may be caused by the combined factors of age and an active lifestyle in a similar fashion to those already mentioned for WLH3.

Keilor

Found in a quarry near Melbourne, Victoria in 1940, the male Keilor cranium is believed to be around 13,000 years old (Macintosh 1965; Macintosh and Larnach 1976) (Map 2–1, 10). (For detailed and comparative descriptions of this cranium see Adam 1943; Mahoney 1943a and b; Wunderly 1943 and Weidenreich 1945.)

There is severe arthritic degeneration of the left glenoid fossa which has obliterated and filled it with proliferative bone. This has formed a 'plate' upon which the mandibular condyle would have pivoted. Moderate osteophytosis is evident around the periphery of the plate. Unfortunately the mandible and the right fossa are missing so we are unable to determine whether the condition was bilateral or not.

The Keilor cranium also has a supernumerary tooth embedded centrally in the palate (Adam 1943). It lies in the sagittal plane, just to the left of the interpalatine suture, with the tip of the root pointing anteriorly (Plate 4–21). As Adam observed, the tooth type is difficult to ascertain but appears to be one of the anterior complex; perhaps a canine or lateral incisor. The crown lies in a depression in the anterior section of a well-developed palatine torus, situated in the midline of

Plate 4–21
A supernumerary tooth embedded in the palate of the Keilor cranium. Note also the large palatal torus.

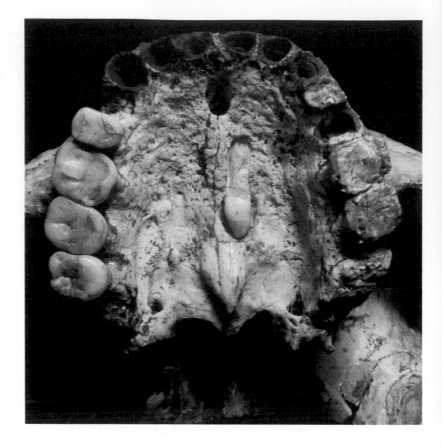

the horizontal palatine bone. This condition is very rare among more recent examples of Australian and Tasmanian crania. Other variations of supernumerary teeth do occur in people from the Murray River although none have been noted embedded in the palate in the same way as this example.

Burke's Bridge

The Burke's Bridge skull represents a large mature male individual who stood over 180 cm tall and was very well built. The cranium is part of an almost whole skeleton recovered on the south side of the Murray River in extremely hard calcareous soils (Map 2–1, 7). The calcium carbonate proved extremely difficult to remove. So much so that many bones of the hands and feet were still embedded in this matrix at the time they, along with the rest of the skeleton, were put under scientific moratorium in the Museum of Victoria. Their fate is unknown. The bone is completely mineralised and covered with small patches of dark blue-black manganese staining. No accurate date exists for these remains but from their fossilised condition and inspection of the area from which they came, their age has been estimated to be around 15–17,000 years (Alan Thorne, pers. comm.)

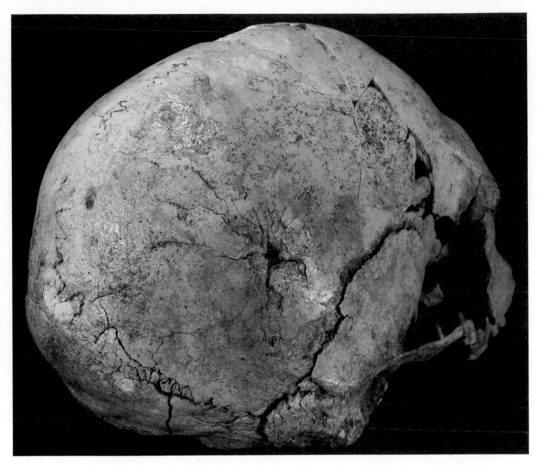

Plate 4–22
The large stellate fracture on the left parietal of the Burke's Bridge individual.

The cranial vault displays an obvious trauma just below the right parietal tuberosity (Plate 4–22). The wound appears as a stellate fracture radiating from a central hole which completely penetrates the vault wall. Damage to the outer table has removed a patch of bone roughly 7 mm in diameter. This has left a ragged edge caused by chipping around the margin and it is from this that the stellate fractures radiate in all directions. The central hole is only 2 mm wide and emerges on the endocranial surface very close to the impression for the posterior branch of the meningeal artery.

The wound appears to have been caused by a sharp, pointed object, perhaps a spear tip. Complete penetration of the cranial vault indicates that some considerable force was used in the blow. Any perforation or severing of the internal meningeal vessels would almost surely have resulted in cerebral haemorrhage and death. It is uncertain whether this was, in fact, the case, but the lack of any sign of bone healing or new bone formation around the hole suggests that death probably occurred immediately or quite soon after the injury occurred. Apart from this trauma the skeleton is completely free from other signs of pathology.

Museum of Victoria No. 31837

Although this individual is not accurately dated, its complete mineralisation and original cover of calcium carbonate (now removed) suggests that it may be contemporary with other late Pleistocene hominids, such as Coobool Creek and Kow Swamp that bear similar preservational features. Thus, a late Pleistocene to early Holocene date is possible for this individual.

Number 31837 is a robust male cranium found in the Riverina district of central southern New South Wales. Like other individuals mentioned in this volume, details of when and how it was discovered are not known. The head is high and extremely dolichocephalic, with prominent sagittal keeling further emphasised in *norma frontalis* by strongly flared malars (Plates 4–23 and 4–24). Fenner (1938) first described this individual over 50 years ago, together with four other morphologically similar crania (see below and Chapter 10). He concluded that the complete fusion of all cranial sutures, plus the elongated, narrow and high vault, were consistent with scaphocephaly (Plate 4–25). Some relevant measurements include a maximum length of 213 mm, maximum breadth of 134 mm, and a height of 149 mm. There is little doubt that it shows a close morphological similarity to other scaphocephalics from the Americas (Eiseley and Asling 1944; Bennet 1967; Ortner and Putschar 1981). Fenner noted also that the '… glenoid fossae show advanced arthritic wear' (1938:153). The wear is extreme and is morphologically similar to that described previously for the Keilor cranium. Both glenoid fossae are filled with new bone and display marginal osteophytosis (Plate 4–26). The mandibular condyles have a 'mushroom' morphology resulting from erosion of the articular surfaces, which is typical in cases where extreme arthritic degeneration has taken place.

Plate 4–23
The norma lateralis view of the heavily mineralised 31837 cranium shows its prominent dolichocephalic morphology, a well developed temporal crest and angular torus.

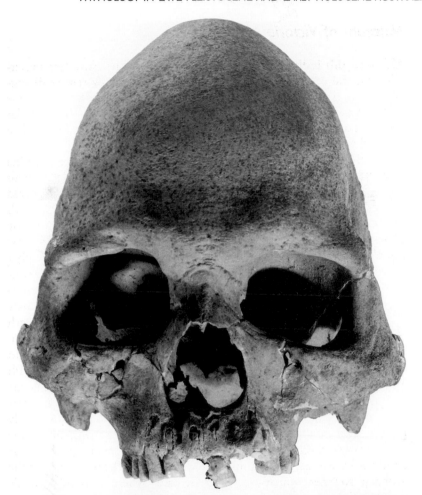

Plate 4–24
In norma frontalis the high, narrow vault with prominent keeling of 31837 contrasts with its wide rather robust face.

Plate 4–25
31837 in norma verticalis.

Plate 4–26
Heavy use of the
TMJ has flattened
both glenoid fossae
into plates. Both sur-
faces are worn by
arthritic degenera-
tion, producing a
well developed mar-
ginal osteophytosis.

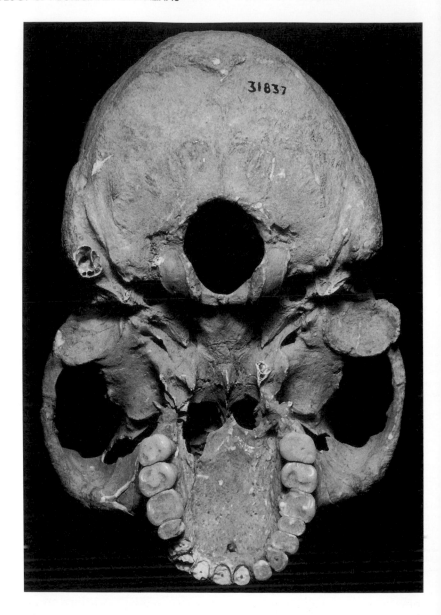

Museum of Victoria No. 38586

Introduction

In my opinion 38586, housed in the Museum of Victoria, displays the most unusual morphology of any cranium yet discovered on the Australian continent (Plate 4–27). It has already been noted by Fenner, but his 'short description [was] intended to do no more than bring the skull [*sic*] under scientific notice' (Fenner 1938:155). It was found near Moulamein in the Riverina district of central, southern New South Wales (Map 2–1, 4). As with so many individuals in

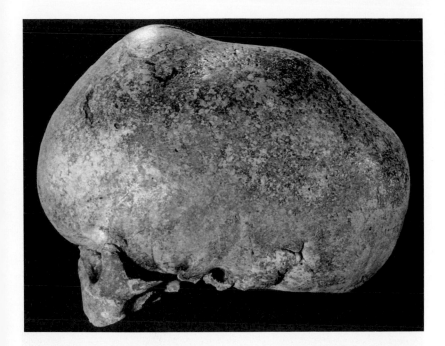

Plate 4–27
*The unusual profile
of the 38586
cranium emphasises
the extraordinary
bony development
throughout the head.*

Australian collections, details of its discovery have not been recorded and there is no mandible or other associated post-cranial remains.

When I first saw this individual it was covered in a thick coating of calcium carbonate (something noted by Fenner). Although most of this has been removed, some remains in and around the nasal area. The first thing one notices about this sub-adult individual is its distorted appearance; the second is its weight, which Fenner put at 1.5kg. The main reason for the latter is that the cranium is completely fossilised and all the interstitial spaces of the trabecular, diploic bone are filled with a matrix of grey calcium carbonate. Because of the extraordinary thickness of all the cranial bones it has become very heavy in proportion to its size. Both the fossilisation and the widespread occurrence of dark blue-black manganese staining suggest a late Pleistocene origin for this individual.

The stage of dental eruption is not clear from these remains because only half the maxilla is present and the remaining teeth have either been broken at their cemento-enamel junctions or almost buried by the massive proliferation of bone in the maxilla. Because of the considerable distortion of normal morphological features, the usual methods for determining personal age are useless. I have, therefore, relied solely on the stage of fusion of various parts of the occipital squamae as a basic age indicator. The two lateral squamous portions of the occipital have completely fused but residual notches can still be seen on the rim of the foramen magnum. The basilar portion of the occipital has not fused and so an age of around four years has been assigned to this individual. Because of the obvious premature fusion of many cranial bones, however, three to four years is a more parsimonious estimation of age.

Description

Fenner (1938) provided an extensive range of measurements for this cranium which include a maximum length of 196 mm, a maximum breadth of 134 mm and a height of 137 mm. I have measured the maximum height from basion to the top of the bulge near bregma at 157 mm. There is a fairly uniform thickening of all the cranial walls which averages around 25 mm. All cranial sutures have fused and become obliterated, with the single exception of the sphenoidal border of the temporal squama. Overall the bone is quite smooth with few of the normal features usually visible at various points across the vault. The outer bone table is missing in some places but this is due to post-mortem damage.

In *norma lateralis*, the face is tucked under a very pronounced forehead which bulges forward over the orbits (Plate 4–27). The rounded contour of the frontal then continues in a posteriorly directed upward sweep to end at a peculiar bulge or 'clown's chaplet' at bregma. This

Plate 4–28
In norma frontalis *the small face of 38586 is almost lost under the prominent forehead and high vault which is accentuated by an enormous and very unusual bregmatic swelling.*

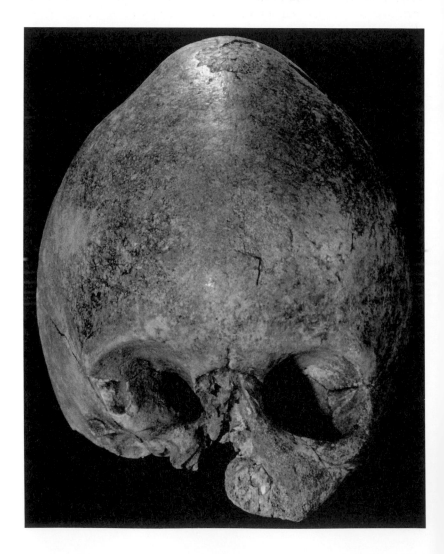

is the single most dominant feature of the cranium. A long but shallow post-bregmatic saddle lies between this feature and another well-defined bulge that lies in the midline, roughly midway along the normal line of the sagittal suture. The profile continues with another shallow depression ending around the region of the obliterated lambdoid suture. Of course, the overall distortion of the cranium and complete lack of normal morphological features make the accurate assessment of the position of these features rather arbitrary. The contour at the back of the cranium promptly changes direction below lambda, dropping sharply and presenting a full, square profile with the inferior section of the occipital contour falling away in an anterior direction. This tends to give the back of the cranium a rather bun-like appearance.

The sub-occipital region is notably flat with little of the normal roundness normally associated with this part of a child's cranium. This flatness extends as far as basion on the anterior border of the foramen magnum. The distance from the position of the superior nuchal line forward to the external auditory meatus emphasises the elongated shape which has accompanied the distortion in the occipital region. Almost one-third of the length of the cranium lies posterior to the foramen magnum.

In *norma frontalis* the face occupies slightly less than one third of the total area of the frontal aspect which is dominated by the height of the vault (Plate 4–28). This may be due in part to the incomplete face which lacks the right maxilla, malar and zygomatic arch. On the left side, a mass of proliferative bone has formed a bridge between the inferior border of the malar and the alveolar process of the maxilla. The swelling is due to the thickened walls of the maxillary sinus and the alveolar process of the maxilla. This feature gives an added emphasis to the oval shape of the cranium. The inter-orbital region is wide, but post-mortem damage of structures here as well as around and within the nasal orifice prevents an accurate and detailed description of any pathological changes. The orbits give the appearance of having been scooped out of a solid piece of bone rather than constructed from many different and slender bony parts. Their internal surfaces are very smooth and firm due to internal bony reinforcement.

From a superior position in *norma verticalis* the cranium appears as an elongated oval (Plate 4–29). At several places across the external vault surface there is a porosity which consists of foraminae of varying diameters. The largest of these occurs in the region of the post-bregmatic saddle and in the shallow depression posterior to this (Plate 4–30). Some post-mortem damage has produced eroded patches on the vault surface in a number of places particularly across a large area on the left side of the head. Tabular bone has been removed, leaving a rather jagged edge, but the process does not penetrate very far into the internal structures of the cranial walls. From the superior view, both the large bregmatic and smaller posterior swellings so prominent in *norma lateralis* spread laterally. In the case of the former the line of this swelling follows roughly that of the coronal suture.

Plate 4–29
The extreme dolicho-cephalic morphology of 38587 is very obvious in norma verticalis.

In *norma basalis* the effects of the abnormal thickening can be seen in many areas. Hyperostosis of the maxillary bone has caused expansion in and around the alveolar region so that the deciduous dentition has become partially embedded in the jaw (Plate 4–31). (I use the term 'hyperostosis' here purely in its descriptive form to refer to a pathological expansion of the cancellous bone and not in regard to bone reaction in anaemic disease.) The surface of the bone is porous with a coral-like appearance but there is no sign of the reactive processes of infection. The bones making up the basi-cranium are not the delicate structures normally associated with a child's skeleton but are thick and bulky in all areas. As with other parts of the cranium, this area displays a bilateral thickening, particularly of the wings of the sphenoid, around the mastoid and the lateral fontanelles. A deep cleft has resulted between them, emphasising their respective changes and demarcating the natural unfused division between these bones

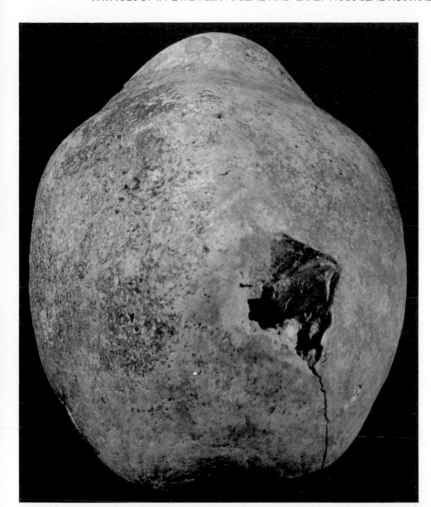

Plate 4–30
38587 in norma occipitalis. The large opening was made during investigation of cranial wall thickness.

Plate 4–31
The teeth are embedded within the bony proliferation typical of a fibrous dysplasia around the maxilla. Normally sharp basi-cranial features have developed a rounded, bulbous appearance because of these processes.

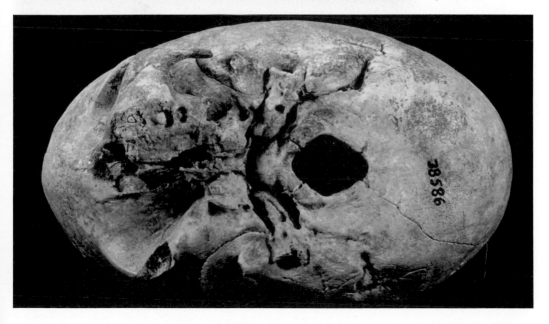

which would normally exist in a non-pathological cranium. In this case, however, the bone in the cleft is completely fused as is the whole of the lambdoid suture of which this is the most inferolateral section.

There is an unusual uniform thickening of the cranial vault. It is made up almost entirely of cancellous tissue with very thin inner and outer cranial tables. The thickening extends from the roof of the sphenoid sinus forward in the floor of the anterior cranial fossa then around the vault structures as far as the foramen magnum. Localised thickening has also taken place in almost all of the other regions of the cranium including the petrous portion of the temporal. A large piece of bone was removed to examine the thickness and composition of the cranium in the occipito-temporal region (Plate 4–32). The wall of the vault in this region was measured at just over 21 mm. The maximum thickness that can be discerned from radiographic analysis is around 30 mm, which occurs towards the back of the cranium in the midline. Radiography also showed the endocranial morphology of this individual to be as distorted as that of the ectocranial outline, with the inner cranial table following the contour of its external counterpart and presenting a brain shape not unlike the form of a crouching wombat (Plate 4–33). The internal contour shows a scooped-out feature within the large swelling at bregma but a second, midway along the sagittal line, seems to have been caused by damage to internal structures. I can only assume that in the case of the frontal depres-

Plate 4–32
The vault of 38587 is variable in thickness but averages around 20–25 mm. The bone is thoroughly mineralised and the interstices of the cancellous tissues have become filled with calcium carbonate.

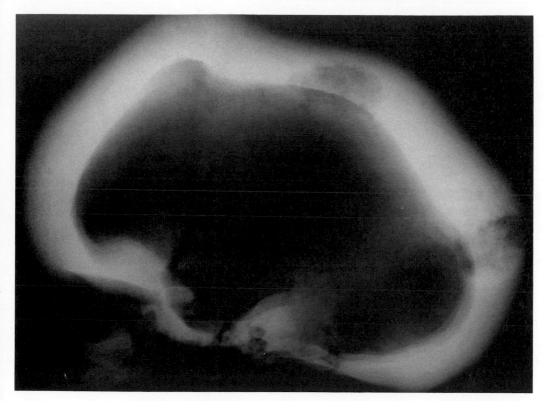

Plate 4–33
The extremely thick and dense cranial morphology of 38587 prevents a detailed radiographic examination of vault structures.

sion, medial sections of the superior frontal or precentral gyri were pushed into it in an abnormal manner. The altered internal architecture suggests that the whole shape of the brain was distorted to some degree, which probably caused mental retardation.

Differential diagnosis and discussion

This distorted and enlarged child's cranium, with its elongated head form and synostosis of all cranial sutures, strongly suggests a case of extreme scaphocephaly (see Chapter 10). But it is more than this. The scaphocephaly is only a secondary manifestation of a primary pathology which has caused the massive thickening of the cranial walls as well as other bones around the head. I can only assume that a condition as advanced as this in a three-to-four-year-old child must be related to some form of congenital pathology. There is no sign of non-specific infection, osteomyelitis, treponemal infection or bone changes associated with neoplastic disease. In any case, none of these conditions caused the morphological changes seen in this individual. There is an excessive production of bone, the like of which I have not encountered before in Australia or in the literature. There are few pathologies that spring to mind that might cause such excessive osteogenic proliferation and malfunction of the bone remodelling system. These include some forms of chronic or hereditary anaemia, endocrine or pituitary disturbances, Paget's disease and leontiasis ossea.

Although some porosity is evident on the superior surfaces of the cranium these areas are not as extensive as might normally be expected from genetically-determined and chronic anaemias. Neither is there any sign of the cribra orbitalia that almost always appears in the superior portions of the orbits of anaemia sufferers. Moreover, even in their most extreme form these changes in modern populations do not bring about the massive and widespread changes to bone structure that we see here. I suspect also that the surface erosion on 38586 is almost certainly post-mortem in origin.

The same can be said for many of the metabolic disorders, such as infantile rickets or osteomalacia (Ortner and Putschar 1981). Changes accompanying these conditions are more evident on the post-cranial skeleton which, of course, we lack for this child. Gigantism and acromegaly are often associated with increased bone production, but these are diseases of adulthood and would not normally be expected in a child of four years, in an advanced stage, such as displayed here. The osteological manifestations of these diseases are also different in that they produce an exaggerated supraorbital region and enlarged mandible as well as a posterior occipital protuberance. *Osteitis deformans* or Paget's disease is another condition that enlarges and distorts cranial and post-cranial bones (Jaffe 1975; Ortner and Putschar 1981; Manchester 1983). Again, this is an adult disorder, particularly one of middle age onwards. It also affects slightly more males than females and from 0.1 to 3 per cent of the population in the USA and Great Britain (Robbins and Cotran 1979). The aetiology of Paget's disease is unknown but prominent among its effects is thickening of the cranial walls. This can become extreme in some patients but cases are usually confined to people over 60 years of age. Even among these few reach the dimensions observed in this child. Moreover, sufferers of Paget's disease do not normally display the uniform thickening or marked changes to the external morphology manifest in this case. Further discussion is not needed: the age of onset and appearance of Paget's disease eliminate it from the list of possible causes.

Although leontiasis ossea is said to be an extreme manifestation of Paget's disease (Manchester 1983), most authors treat it as a separate condition (Jaffe 1975; Robbins and Cotran 1979). Like Paget's disease its aetiology remains unknown but it is believed to develop over a long period of time, perhaps during childhood, from a 'creeping osteitis' (Jaffe 1975:278). It is extremely rare and seems to occur with even less frequency now than in the historical past. Typical changes result from subperiosteal new bone apposition which normally begins in the nasal region and spreads throughout the cranium from bone to bone. Examples show a random thickening although there are exceptions to this. One presented by Jaffe (1975, Figs. 96C and D) shows thickened facial and vault bones, complete synostosis, as well as some degree of scaphocephaly. While these features are similar to those described for 38586, periorbital expansion in the Jaffe example has not occurred in this child. Also, Jaffe's example was 65 years old at the time of her death, which is the normal age when extreme forms of leontiasis ossea emerge. No two cases seem to manifest the same changes, however, so it remains hard to identify the disease in accurate and regular gross morphological symptoms.

Another disease causing skeletal enlargement is infantile cortical hyperostosis or Caffey's disease. As its name implies, however, it usually affects infants less than two years of age and males more than females. Again, its cause is obscure although it is thought to be of a fairly recent origin (Jaffe 1975). In some cases osteological changes caused by subperiosteal new bone formation manifest themselves in infants only a few weeks old, which suggests a congenital component is probably involved in its aetiology. Lesions occur mainly in the post-cranial skeleton, causing swelling of one or both arms and legs, but the mandible can also be involved and changes are sometimes limited to this bone. The swelling is normally transitory with seriated involve-ment of bones, each recovering after a given period of time. Chronic cases have been recorded in which repeated swelling takes place and secondary infections may occur causing death in some sufferers.

Infantile cortical hyperostosis may have produced the 'unknown' pathology in the mandibular corpus in a six-month-old Nubian child (Alexandersen 1967b, Fig. 5). Even in the unlikely event that that mystery is solved, ours is not. With minimal involvement of the cranial bones and regression of swelling in affected areas, there seems little likelihood that infantile cortical hyporostosis is the cause of the pathology in 38586. Moreover, it occurs too early in childhood to be seriously implicated here. Lcontiasis ossea in conjunction with or ini-tiating scaphocephaly seems to be the only condition(s) which fits the massive alterations to the cranium of this late Pleistocene Australian child. I am not completely convinced about this diagnosis, however, on the grounds of age. There is no evidence for an advanced form of leontiasis ossea occurring in children as young as 38586. Nevertheless, I look forward to receiving some suggestions as to other possible causes from those reading this book.

Mossgiel and Green Gully

For descriptions of pathology occurring on the mid-Holocene Green Gully (6,500BP) and Mossgiel (>4,600BP) individuals see Macintosh 1967 and Freedman 1985, respectively (Map 2–1, 2 and 10).

Harris lines in Pleistocene and early mid-Holocene material

Because of the incomplete and often extremely fragmented nature of many of Australia's late Pleistocene and early Holocene human remains, few are in a suitable condition for examining Harris lines. Of these only two, the male from Burke's Bridge and an adolescent female from Kow Swamp (KS16) have lines. There may be some faint lines in the distal tibia of KS5, but these are too indistinct to be positively identified.

There are at least two Harris lines in the distal left femur of the Burke's Bridge man. Other faint lines are present but too indistinct to be positively identified as Harris lines. KS16 displays a number of lines in various long bones, 14 in the distal left tibia, four in the distal right tibia and seven in the distal left femur. The regular 'step ladder' pattern in the distal left tibia suggests a seasonal shortage rather than a regular annual bout of disease. I outline my reasons for thinking this in more detail in Chapter 5. Recent individuals from the central Murray do not display large numbers of lines, but this may not mean that nutritional stress has not been a problem for people living in this area for thousands of years. As I explain in the next chapter, the fact that this number of lines occurs in people from this period may indicate that at least there was ample opportunity to recover from the stress that caused them. I strongly suggest, however, that the most logical reason for multiple line formation among people living in late Pleistocene Australia lies in an annual nutritional deprivation, or a regime of feast and famine.

Chapter 5

Stress

Cribra orbitalia
Dental enamel hypoplasia
Harris lines

General introduction

One of the few tenets of palaeopathological and palaeoepidemiological study is that there is an intimate relationship between the lifestyle of humans and the frequency and types of disease from which they suffer. That relationship has been demonstrated repeatedly in numerous studies of ancient and more recent skeletal populations from many parts of the world. They have shown, for example, that there is an increase in the frequency of certain types of stress and infectious disease with socio-economic, cultural and demographic change. This association has provided archaeologists with an important interpretive tool for unravelling the time at which socio-economic as well as demographic changes in ancient populations took place. Moreover, palaeopathology has helped to identify when some hunter-gatherer groups began to lead a more sedentary existence, that transitional stage before taking up farming and developing permanent towns and villages. This has been a particularly difficult stage of cultural development to detect in the archaeology using more traditional methods of investigation. Of equal importance is the fact that this same research has enabled us to study the temporal and spatial origin of disease. In turn we have gained a better understanding of the ecology of certain pathogens and the environmental changes which affect them. In this way palaeopathology and palaeoepidemiology have contributed enormously to our understanding of present-day disease.

The presence of certain skeletal stress indicators has been correlated with subsistence and dietary change, population growth and the degree of sedentism and crowding. In other words, the study of stress patterns among various prehistoric peoples helps anthropologists and others understand life in the past in a way that cannot be achieved using any other single form of archaeological data. People reflect their environment and the stresses that come from the lifestyle that they follow.

These are stamped into their skeletal remains, not on their artifacts, but when these two sources of evidence are used concurrently a stronger interpretation of what a particular society was doing at a certain time can be made. This leads to a better understanding of prehistoric social variation, adaptive capability, diet, ecology, behaviour, palaeoepidemiology and palaeobiology and, in the wider sense, the breadth and diversity of humans.

From a palaeopathological standpoint, stronger conclusions are possible if a number of pathologies or stress indicators are used in combination. The results of such an approach are now presented in this chapter. It is the first chapter of this book which deals with the more recent remains of Aboriginal Australians as well as examining the evidence for stress among them prior to 1788. Three stress indicators are used: cribra orbitalia, dental hypoplasia and Harris lines and they are discussed in that order. By using these singly and in combination it is hoped that more can be said about the general health and biology of pre-contact Australians than at any time before. Integral to this exercise is the comparison of skeletal samples from very different environmental settings across the continent. It is hoped that by tackling such a large amount of data from widely-separated groups a better overall picture can be obtained of the diversity of health and stress among Aboriginal people in the past.

Cribra orbitalia (anaemia)

Introduction

For the size of the skeletal samples used in this and all subsequent chapters, I refer the reader to Tables 2–1 and 2–2. Cribra orbitalia is the only stress indicator used here that is believed to have a singular cause: anaemia. The other two, dental hypoplasia and Harris lines, are more idiopathic, although recent research has shown that the former, like cribra orbitalia, probably indicates a longer stress episode than Harris lines, which are an indication of a more acute or short-term condition. Cribra orbitalia or cribra, as it will be termed here, consists of one or several clusters of small holes that appear on the upper surface of the orbit and occasionally on the frontal bone. Because of the wide variation in the amount of these perforations, I initially divided the lesion into three categories: porotic, cribrotic and trabecular (Plates 5–1a, b and c). In this volume I have combined these form a single category to which all frequencies refer. A 'recovery' category consisting of medium-to-large foramina filled with new bone will be discussed later (Plate 5–2). Bone remodelling is believed to be responsible for these changes as the orbital plate forms a new surface in response to the relief of the anaemic condition, thus terminating the processes of diploeic hyperplasticity (Webb 1989).

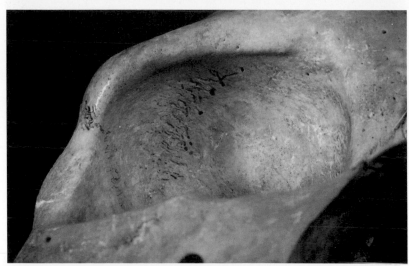

Plates 5–1a, b and c
Three categories of cribra orbitalia: porotic (a), cribrotic (b) and trabecular (c).

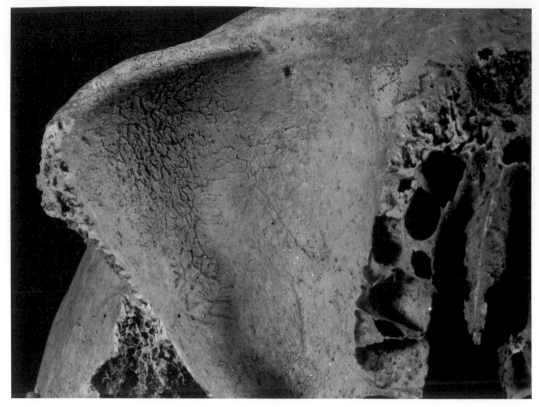

Plate 5-2
The recovery scar from remodelling of a cribra orbitalia lesion.

Cribra was first mentioned by Welcker (1885, 1887, 1888), but since then it has only rarely been referred to in texts dealing with anatomy (Wolff 1954; Duke-Elder *et al.* 1961) and pathology (Hogan and Zimmerman 1962). Only those dealing with skeletal populations, like the palaeopathologist and physical anthropologist, have noted its frequency in spatially and temporally disparate people. Originally it was suggested that cribra was a racial characteristic originating as an embryological phenomenon (Toldt 1886; Welcker 1887, 1888; Adachi 1904; Oetteking 1909). Others thought a pathological aetiology more likely and nobody has seriously challenged this idea since (Koganei 1912). Other causal conditions proposed have included compression or infection, specifically leprotic infection, of the lachrymal gland (Møller-Christensen 1961; Hogan and Zimmerman 1962; Blumberg and Kerley 1966), mumps (Møller-Christensen 1978), trachoma or localised periostitis (Blumberg and Kerley 1966), poor nutrition (Henschen 1961; Nathan and Haas 1966), infantile scurvy and genetically-determined blood dyscrasias (Angel 1964, 1967). The latter, which include thalassaemia and sickle cell anaemia, also form distinctive lesions on the outer cranial table due to hyperplastic activity by haemopoietic tissue in the diploe (Britton *et al.* 1960; Aksoy *et al.* 1966) (see also Chapter 4). These usually form on the frontal and parietal bones and have been variously termed symmetrical osteoporosis, porotic hyperostosis and cribra cranii. In some individuals these lesions can also be caused by severe iron deficiency anaemia of a non-genetic form (Henschen 1961; Steinbock 1976). These cases are almost always associated with the most extensive cribra lesion which, in some cases, extends beyond the orbit to involve the brow ridge (Stuart-Macadam 1989). It is the link between cribra and anaemia that has prompted a consensus of opinion to regard it as a sign of anaemia and a common link between all those in whom it has been observed (Mosely 1966; Hengen 1971; Saul 1972; Carlson *et al.* 1974; El-Najjar 1976, El-Najjar *et al.* 1976; Steinbock 1976; Cockburn 1977; Cybulski 1977; Lallo *et al.* 1977; Trinkaus 1977; Hartney 1978; Mensforth *et al.* 1978; Huss-Ashmore 1982; Goodman *et al.* 1983; Sandford *et al.* 1983; Stuart-Macadam 1989).

Studies of Australian remains have used cribra as a genetically-based non-metrical trait rather than a pathology (Brothwell 1963b; Larnach and Macintosh 1966, 1970; Milne *et al.* 1983). Nevertheless, Brothwell published a frequency of 5.26 per cent for Australia and suggested that cribra might be of 'some value as an environmental "indicator"' (1963:95). Larnach and Macintosh (1966) recorded only 1.1 per cent in crania from Queensland and none at all in a similar non-metrical survey of New South Wales crania. Milne's (1982) figures, derived from a Western Australian sample, are not comparable with those presented here because of differences in methodology and definition. Sandison acknowledged cribra as a pathological indicator but thought it 'extremely rare [in Aboriginal people] except in children' (1980:46). In a survey of 544 crania purported to be from New South Wales, Zaino and Zaino (1975) found 26.6 per cent in sub-adults and 2.4 per cent in adults. No other subdivisions for age, sex or provenance were made.

Distribution of cribra orbitalia

There is great variation in the adult frequency of cribra across Australia. It ranges from a high of 33.7 per cent in the central Murray (CM) people to 8.3 per cent in desert dwellers (DES) (Table 5–1). The central Murray has been defined here as that part of the Murray valley between Euston in the west and Kerang in the east (Map 2–2). The frequency pattern across this large area is variable, however, but the major difference is that between inhabitants of this section of the river and those living farther downstream (R), west of the Murray–Darling junction, where it reaches a maximum of 24.4 per cent. Decreasing amounts occur along the east (CTL) and south (SC) coasts, 19.4 per cent and 18.4 per cent respectively, and the tropical regions (TRO) of northern Australia, 13.7 per cent. These figures leave little doubt that people living in arid areas of the continent suffered much less stress of this type than those living elsewhere. The central Murray, on the other hand, displays a frequency which needs some explanation.

Table 5–1 shows plainly that the distribution of this stress disadvantages females, their frequencies being always higher than those of males in all areas. The continental pattern follows the trend seen for

Table 5–1 *Frequencies of cribra orbitalia for adults.*

		n	*n̄*	%
CM	M	246	7	29.7
	F	149	60	40.3
	T	395	133	33.7
R	M	122	29	23.7
	F	83	21	25.3
	T	205	50	24.4
SC	M	138	21	15.2
	F	123	27	22.0
	T	261	48	18.4
DES	M	130	10	7.7
	F	51	5	9.8
	T	181	15	8.3
TRO	M	92	10	10.9
	F	61	11	18.0
	T	153	21	13.7
CTL	M	13	21	15.8
	F	83	21	25.3
	T	216	42	19.4

Key:
M–Male, F–Female, T–Total

Area Codes:
CM–Central Murray, R–Rufus River, SC–South Coast, DES–Desert,
TRO–Tropics, CTL–East Coast

combined adult frequencies whereby the highest incidence (40.3 per cent) is among women in the central Murray and the lowest in those living in the desert region (9.8 per cent). It is worth noting that female frequencies among some discrete samples within the central Murray do go as high as 46.6 per cent. Most other areas have frequencies of between 18 per cent and 25 per cent. Male frequencies are, in every area, lower than those for females, but they trend in the same manner with the highest in the central Murray and the lowest in the desert.

The highest frequency of cribra in sub-adults is just under 60 per cent in central Murray children (Table 5.2). This is not unexpected given adult trends, but is significantly higher than the next highest figure of 40.6 per cent from the east coast and a frequency of 39.6 per cent for all other areas combined. Rufus River is also high with 62.5 per cent, but both this and the sample from the tropics (TRO) contains only 16 individuals which is below the standard minimum sample size of 25. Continental trends for sub-adults are similar to the adult distribution. I have shown elsewhere that by using three sub-adult age groups and three different categories of cribra it is possible to trace the dynamics of anaemia through childhood and into adulthood (Webb 1989). This study showed the highest frequencies of cribra occurring among the youngest age group (0-5 years) with gradual reduction as the child reached maturity. Moreover, the category of cribra changes so that the more severe forms (cribrotic and

trabecular) occur more frequently with age. Frequencies drop significantly when adulthood is attained, so that, for example, in the central
Murray a combined sub-adult frequency of around 60 per cent drops
to 34.2 per cent among young adults (21–35 years) and to 33.5 per
cent in old adults (>35 years). This trend is repeated for other areas
but with generally lower frequencies in the oldest adult age group
(Table 5–2). On the east coast there is a marked increase in frequency
from the under fives to the 6–11 age group; but what is noticeable
is the enormous frequency reduction when young people reach adulthood. Among adults this trend continues so that older adults suffer
less than younger adults. Both the coastal groups show dramatic
reductions as adults become older. In complete contrast, the Rufus

Table 5–2 *Frequency of cribra orbitalia for five age groups.*

	Age	n	$\bar{n}$	%
CM	1	7	5	71.4
	2	19	14	73.7
	3	28	13	46.4
	6	190	65	34.2
	7	203	68	33.5
R	1	4	4	100.0
	2	5	4	80.0
	3	7	2	28.6
	6	91	22	24.2
	7	97	18	20.7
SC	1	6	3	50.0
	2	12	4	33.3
	3	20	8	40.0
	6	92	33	35.9
	7	141	15	10.6
DES	1	5	1	20.0
	2	7	4	57.1
	3	8	1	12.5
	6	43	6	14.0
	7	118	10	8.5
TRO	1	2	2	100.0
	2	4	4	100.0
	3	10	2	20.0
	6	58	13	22.4
	7	82	8	9.8
CTL	1	9	2	22.2
	2	13	7	53.8
	3	10	4	40.0
	6	72	23	31.9
	7	122	19	15.6

Age Codes:
1–0-5 years, 2–6-11 years, 3–12-20 years, 6–Young adults (<35-40),
7–Old adults (>40)

Area Codes:
CM–Central Murray, R–Rufus River, SC–South Coast, DES–Desert,
TRO–Tropics, CTL–East Coast

River people and those living in the Euston and Swan Hill areas of the central Murray, show opposite trends with a distinctive increase in the frequency of cribra among the old compared to young adults.

Aetiology of anaemia in Australian Aborigines

Sub-adults

As far as we know no endemic forms of genetically-derived blood disease have been found in Australian Aboriginal populations (Horsfall and Lehmann 1953, 1956; Moodie 1971; Kirk 1981). Moreover, the classic form of symmetrical osteoporosis, often associated with chronic or genetically derived anaemia, is not seen on Aboriginal remains from the mainland or Tasmania. These conditions can, therefore, be discounted as a contributory cause of the cribra described here.

We have seen that there is a major difference in the incidence of cribra between children below and above 11 years, the younger ones suffering the highest frequencies (Table 5–2). Most of the youngest group have the mildest form of the lesion, with only a few individuals showing intermediate and severe forms. Chronic anaemia often persists through the first two age groups, as demonstrated by a shift of greatest frequency from porotic to the intermediate cribrotic forms. This is caused by continuing bone resorption within lesion foramina and enlargement of the lesion itself, hence a category change. Infants do not have this condition in their first six months but acquire it with increasing frequency as they get older (Mensforth *et al.* 1978; Goodman *et al.* 1983). One likely reason for this is that after six months of age there is rapid loss of natural iron reserves, leaving the child less to draw on during stressful periods, such as weaning and growth spurts. A natural ability to overcome these physiological difficulties with age could also account for the clear reduction in all forms of cribra among the 12–20 year olds. Nevertheless, chronic anaemia persists in some, as the presence of the most severe trabecular form of cribra lesion in some individuals testifies. The pattern here suggests that while nutritional or pathological stresses continue throughout childhood, the capacity for recovery increases with age. The small size of sub-adult samples from other parts of Australia prevents me confirming whether the central Murray pattern is common to all Aboriginal children, although from the data available it would seem that might be the case.

Palaeopathological studies have shown that children generally suffer more anaemia than adults (Nathan and Haas 1966; Carlson *et al.* 1974; El-Najjar *et al.* 1976; Cybulski 1977; Lallo *et al.* 1977; Mensforth *et al.* 1978; Stuart-Macadam 1989) (Table 5–3). The basic reason for this is that they reflect more readily the effects of social and environmental pressures and economic change. Results of a study of skeletal remains from the Dickson Mound sites in Illinois exemplify this link. In that study three sub-adult groups, one from each of three separate economic and cultural phases, hunter-gatherer, transitional and agricultural, showed frequencies of 13.6 per cent, 31.2 per cent

Table 5–3 *Frequencies of cribra orbitalia for various populations around the world.*

Location†	n	SA%	AM%	AF%	CA%	SAU%	Source
Europeans	612	–	–	–	–	19.0	1
Germans	470	–	–	–	–	17.0	1
Germans	–	–	–	–	–	3.5	2
Southern Zealand (Denmark)	200	–	–	–	–	47.0	3
Northern Zealand (Denmark)	104	–	–	–	–	20.0	3
Austria	100	–	18.9	27.7	23.0	–	4
England	552	36.4	24.4	27.4	26.0	–	5
Scotland	743	52.0	—		6.6	–	6
Old Egyptians	434	–	–			8.0	2
Old Egypt	182	–	–	–	–	7.0	7
Sudanese Nubia	285	23.3	–	–	19.9	–	8
Modern Egypt	–	–	–	–	–	11.0	7
Socotrans (Arab descent)	42	–	–	–	–	48.0	9
East Sudan Negroes	–	–	–	–	–	35.0	9
Finno-Turks	–	–	–	–	–	4.0	10
Southeast Mongols	–	–	–	–	–	9.0	10
Mongols	70	–	–	–	–	37.0	10
Chinese	–	–	–	–	–	10.0	10
Japanese	121	–	–	–	–	15.0	11
Japanese	411	52.5	26.6	17.9	22.4	–	12
Japanese	695	26.0*	–	–	10.0*	–	9
Ainu	–	–	–	–	–	16.8	9
Malayans	–	–	–	–	–	22.5	9
Malayan Peninsula	51	–	21.6	28.6	23.5	–	4
Israel	35	93.3	12.5	75.0	50.0	–	4
Ein Gedi (Israel)	94	66.6	13.0	18.2	13.5	–	4
Polynesians	–	–	–	–	–	6.0	10
Micronesians	–	–	–	–	–	7.0	10
Papuans-Australians	–	–	–	–	–	30.0	10
Hottentots	–	–	–	–	–	4.0	10
Bantu	–	–	–	–	–	10.0	10
African Negros	–	–	–	–	–	21.0	2
Peruvians	–	–	–	–	–	9.0	9
Alaska (Eskimo)	90	54.6	11.0	17.3	15.2	–	13
North American Indians	120	62.8	10.9	22.8	14.3	–	13
British Columbian Indians	454	26.6	4.8	13.3	11.3	–	4
Late Woodland	44	13.6	–	–	–	–	14
Early Mississippian	93	31.2	–	–	–	–	14
Middle Mississippian	101	51.5	–	–	–	–	14
Eiden, Lorain, Ohio	31	51.6	–	–	–	–	14
Central Columbian Indians	60	42.9	12.9	27.3	18.9	–	4
South Columbian Indians	105	14.3	9.1	11.6	10.2	–	4
Southwest Indians (USA)	539	43.5	31.6	25.7	29.0	–	15

Key:
† Location names as used in original source
n – Total number of crania used in survey irrespective of age and sex
SA – Sub-adults

AM – Adult males
AF – Adult females
CA – Combined adult frequency irrespective of sex
SAU – Individuals of unknown age and sex
* – Average frequency

Sources:
1–Ahrens (1904, 2–Welcker (1888), 3–Møller-Christensen (1961),
4–Webb after Cybulski (1977), 5–Stuart-Macadam (1985), 6–Møller-Christensen & Sandison (1963),
7–Oetteking (1909), 8–Carson et al. (1974), 9–Koganie (1912), 10–Henschen (1961),
11–Adachi (1904), 12–Webb after Akabori (1933), 13–Webb after Nathan & Haas (1966),
14–Lallo et al. (1977), 15–El-Najjar et al. (1976)

and 51.5 per cent, respectively (Table 5–3) (Goodman *et al.* 1983). These findings not only support the idea that increasing sedentism brings with it a concomitant increase in the incidence of anaemia among children, but that it begins in earnest around the time of weaning. Among Aboriginal children living traditionally, weaning marks a delicate stage in the development of the child and this is when anaemia is most likely to become a problem. A number of other conditions may also arise at this time which, separately and synergistically, contribute to a general weakening of the child's constitution. Weaning nearly always means an initial reduction in nutritional intake, the loss of the natural immunity conferred by breast feeding, greater vulnerability to gastric infections, such as 'weanling' diarrhoea, the loss of adequate, hygienic, regular or frequent feeding, and nutritional stress from the introduction of unsuitable weaning foods (Britton 1963; Scrimshaw 1964; Scrimshaw *et al.* 1968; Stini 1971; Smith 1976; Hamilton 1981). All of this can result in poor health, undernourishment and iron-deficiency anaemia (Cook 1970). Aboriginal children living in all areas of Australia may have been subject to these stresses at some time and to varying degrees, which altered according to weaning age, the type of weaning food and the presence of other exacerbating factors such as infection. All these must be considered in any discussion which compares Aboriginal groups with different environmental or demographic backgrounds or both (Berndt and Berndt 1981; Hamilton 1981).

Consideration must be given also to parasite infestation, a particular hazard for all societies living physically close to the natural environment. Sub-adult parasitism can lower survival chances and depress natural growth rates (Anderson and May 1979). With the introduction of adult food there is an increased emphasis for the child to fend more for itself and explore its surroundings, all of which lead to a greater likelihood of parasite infestation, particularly in a traditional society. Moreover, what constitutes a substantial parasite load for a toddler may hardly be bothersome for older children or adults. So the degree of infestation and the individual's age are important when considering how infestation affects sub-adults.

Parasitism can counteract the benefits of an adequate diet because worm activity in the gastrointestinal tract prevents or severely reduces the ability of the intestinal mucosa to absorb nutrients. The resultant malabsorption causes nutritional inadequacy, diarrhoea and loss of body fluids which in turn removes electrolytes, salts and minerals. These effects often result in iron deficiency anaemia and have other, more serious, consequences for the child, typically affecting growth and later development as well as lowering its survival potential. The Murray valley and eastern coastal areas provide a natural environment for the support of various species of intestinal parasites, such as *Trichuris trichuris, Ascaris lumbricoides, Strongyloides stercoralis* and *Enterobius vermicularis* (Sweet 1924; Johnston *et al.* 1937). There is little doubt that these species were common in Australia long before the Australian Hookworm Campaign was undertaken between 1919 and 1923 (Sweet 1924). What is not clear, however, is whether they were here before 1788, although the world-wide distribution of these para-sites suggests that they might well have been. If they were, heavy loads of the first three types, particularly in children, would have produced symptoms which included diarrhoea, nutritional malabsorption, general weakness and anaemia.

With age comes a general strengthening of the sub-adult constitu-tion. In a hunter-gatherer society this includes increasing participation in the community's food quest, the lifting of any food taboos and full acceptance into the adult group, particularly in the case of young men. In these circumstances a reduction in anaemia among the oldest age group might be expected. On the other hand, with the onset of men-struation and early childbearing among females, together with the con-tinuation of food taboos imposed from an early age and the further imposition of others at different stages in the young woman's life, any extant anaemia persisting from childhood would be compounded (Eyre 1845 II:283; Berndt and Berndt 1981:155). Therefore, allow-ance must be made for the female component among the sub-adult 12–20 age group, as it is for the combined adult frequencies discussed below. With these considerations in mind, it is suggested that the majority of sub-adults having the worst form of cribra (trabecular) are likely to be females.

Although the sample size of sub-adults from the tropics is small (n=16), the 50 per cent frequency of anaemia in these children may reflect, in a general way, the susceptibility of toddlers in this region to anaemia, as we have already witnessed in other parts of Australia. Moreover, hookworm may have been a principal cause in this area. This helminth is particularly prevalent among people living in the tropics and one of the main causes of anaemia. Up to 40 per cent of young children living in these regions suffer in this way (Hennessy 1979). Both *Ankylostoma duodenale* and *Necator americanus* are found in Aboriginal communities in Australia's tropical north today, but we have little information about when these species were introduced or if they are endemic to this continent (Cilento 1942; Billington 1960; Jose *et al.* 1970; Moodie 1971; Walker 1975). There is every likeli-hood that if they were present in Australia before 1788 they would have caused the same sort of health problems as they do now. At the moment we have little prehistoric evidence for or against the presence of these particularly debilitating parasites, but future coprolite studies may enlighten us. Introductions of hookworm (*A. duodenale*) could have come through contact with people from Papua New Guinea or Macassan fishermen. The introduction of *N. americanus* is most likely to have taken place fairly recently, being brought into Australia by Chinese gold miners or Melanesian kanakas or both (Cilento 1942; Abbie 1960). With the many opportunities for the importation of hookworm prior to 1788, it may not be unrealistic to suggest that it probably contributed to the high rates of childhood anaemia seen in this survey in tropical regions.

The only obvious example of symmetrical osteoporosis that I have encountered in collections around Australia is one which occurs in a four-to-five-year-old child from the York Islands in Torres Strait, some

170 kilometres northeast of the Australian mainland (Plate 5–3). This individual also has a moderately severe category 2 cribra in the right orbit. Radiographic examination revealed no evidence of hyperplasticity of diploeic tissues, intratabular thickening or the hair-on-end morphology normally associated with diploeic expansion in the cranial walls. Nevertheless, gross morphological change in the form of a slight thickening can be seen at the centre of each lesion when viewed from above (Plate 5–4).

With the absence of a frontal lesion and intracranial thickening, I can only assume that this may be an example of severe chronic anaemia, perhaps from a heavy infestation with hookworm. It is unlikely that this symmetrical osteoporosis is associated with any of the balanced polymorphisms that initiate blood dyscrasias and which are endemic to many parts of the Papua New Guinea mainland which lies some 85 kilometres northwest of the York Island group. The nearest palaeopathological evidence for thalassaemia is situated on Motupore Island, off the New Guinea coast, and some 550 kilometres away from the York Islands (see Chapter 11). What is obvious is that the York Island child died. What we do not know is whether this was due to thalassaemia, but 4-5 years of age is when it usually claims its homozygous sufferers who do not obtain blood transfusions.

Adults

Adulthood cribra frequencies show a marked drop from those in sub-adults in all areas of Australia, presumably as a general reaction to the social, nutritional and physiological benefits of adulthood. With major growth processes completed, the more robust adult constitution is better able to cope with parasite infestation and other secondary pathological processes, as well as any nutritional imbalances. Another boost to the body's defences comes from the relaxation of any food taboos applied to sub-adults as well as from a more independent participation in food gathering and distribution processes. Nevertheless, it is interesting to note that adult frequencies reflect those of sub-adults from the same area, as though the general extent of the stress among a particular group applies to the old as well as the young. There is a world-wide trend for women to have a higher incidence of cribra than men and this is echoed in Aboriginal females (Tables 5–1 and 5–3). Childbearing, lactation, menstruation and the imposition of food taboos are probably the primary causes of this phenomenon.

Generally, coastal areas have significantly lower frequencies of cribra in men and women than the central Murray. With abundant, year-round food resources and a normally stable environment this is to be expected. In looking at various locations on the south coast (SC), a different picture emerges, however. Females from the Victorian coast (C) have rates of anaemia (34.2 per cent) approaching those of some places within the central Murray and over twice as much as their male counterparts (16.7 per cent). Similarly, the southern half of the east coast sample has a higher frequency for both men (22.1 per cent) and women (30.0 per cent) than it does as part of the larger area sample.

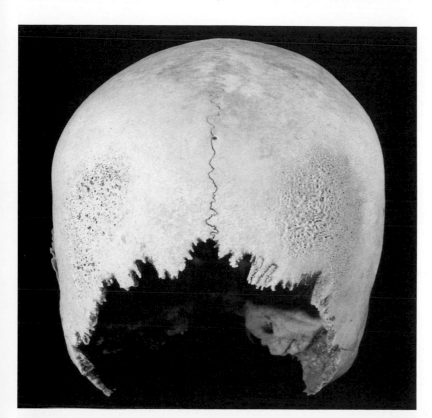

Plate 5–3
Symmetrical osteo-porosis on both parietals of a child's cranium from York Islands, Torres Strait.

Plate 5–4
The York Island skull in norma verticalis shows two raised areas of trabecula-tion associated with bi-parietal osteoporosis.

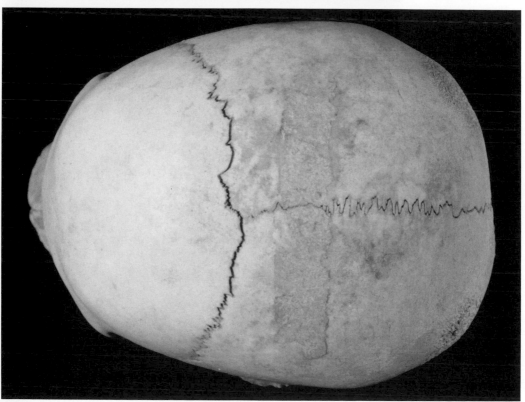

The relatively low rates of anaemia in men (10.9 per cent) and women (18.0 per cent) from the Northern Territory are very different from those in southeastern Australia and may indicate a capacity to overcome the stresses of childhood. These figures are similar to those of hunter-gatherers outside Australia and probably reflect a different lifestyle among the people of the north as opposed to those living in the southeast of the continent.

In the early 1960s, 57 Western Desert women living traditionally, all apparently without any previous association with Europeans, were medically examined and only 10.5 per cent were found to be sub-clinically anaemic (Elphinstone 1971). I am not sure whether to claim an actual reflection or just a coincidence for the figure of 9.8 per cent found in this survey, but the 10.5 per cent frequency is, I feel, significant in the light of this study. The reason given for the frequency of anaemia in desert women was that, after some observation, the medical researchers believed the women to be near the bottom of the food distribution chain. It is not the first time that European observers, usually males, have been misled by their lack of knowledge concerning women's food gathering activities, which are nearly always different from those of the men who are the ones normally observed (Meehan 1982). In the end, the low female frequency was largely attributed to infrequent or irregular menstruation. Although the latter does occur among nomadic women, menstruation would have been more regular among less nomadic or semi-sedentary people. This would have been so, for example, in the southeast of the continent where Aboriginal people have always been recognised as being less nomadic than those living in desert areas (Roth 1903:24; Roheim 1933:233; Abbie 1960:142). Physiological adaptation, such as infrequent ovulation, is of great advantage to those following a nomadic existence because it acts to reduce the chances of childbirth, creates greater spacing between births, thus helping to minimise population pressure and mouths to feed. It also directly and indirectly reduces the incidence of anaemia in females by relaxing metabolic, physiological and nutritional demands upon them.

Australian Aborigines experienced various degrees of mobility in their food quest and I discuss this in more detail in Chapter 12. They moved not only for economic reasons but because of a whole range of social, cultural and ceremonial factors also. The Murray Valley and east coast provided plentiful and varied amounts of food which included crustaceans, frogs, reptiles, fish, fowl, terrestrial fauna, vegetable foods and iron-rich shellfish (Bickford 1966; Lawrence 1967; Allen 1972; Thorne 1975). Most of these were subject to seasonal factors and environmental disturbances such as floods and drought (Bickford 1966). With such nutritional variety it is difficult to accept that so much anaemia existed in the southeast. Frequencies like those recorded here are usually found among people leading a sedentary life with aggregated populations, larger than are normally expected for hunter-gatherer societies (Lallo *et al.* 1977; Goodman *et al.* 1983). For example, the central Murray frequencies are similar to those found among Eskimos (Nathan and Haas 1966), Pueblo and Illinoian agriculturalists (El-Najjar 1976) and Mayan Indians (Saul 1972). These populations are known also to have been under considerable nutritional, pathological, social, demographic and environmental pressures. Thus, high levels of anaemia are normally attributed to increasing sedentism and, in this way, are a good indicator of population increase and aggregation as well as other more general socio-demographic changes (Lallo *et al.* 1977; Trinkaus 1977; Mensforth *et al.* 1978; Huss-Ashmore *et al.* 1982). Some of the high frequencies of cribra among some North American maize growers, however, are partly explained by the fact that this grain prevents proper metabolism of dietary iron (El-Najjar 1976). Nevertheless, as various groups changed their economic base from hunting and gathering to agriculture, there was an accompanying downturn in health standards due to the general reduction in community hygiene, a constant companion of those who faced the vast economic and demographic changes associated with settlement and village life. The root cause of this increase was inadequate sanitary arrangements which encouraged high levels of parasitism, a rise in infectious disease and, as frequently happens with population increase and the introduction of new forms of economic subsistence, reduced calorific intake and a change from a high protein to a high carbohydrate diet. The synergistic effect of all these factors produces widespread anaemia and the skeletal indicator cribra orbitalia which has become so useful in pin-pointing when these sorts of socio-economic changes took place.

Cribra frequencies similar to those recorded for the central Murray and, to some extent, coastal southeastern Australia, are rarely, if ever, found among hunter-gatherer groups that are not facing obvious hardship. It seems that at least some of the factors mentioned above are responsible for the high rates of cribra in the people of these areas. Overall, coastal adult frequencies are similar to those of the central Murray, but coastal children have substantially less. The southeastern coastal region comprises a second region in Australia where anaemic stress is great but it is not as high as that of the central Murray. There are other pathological indications that these stresses among coastal people may have a somewhat different origin than those found among Murray people. I draw together my arguments concerning the reasons for these differences at the end of this chapter.

The similarity between frequencies of cribra in desert men and women show that conditions causing anaemia operate equally for both sexes. In other regions this seems not to be the case. Besides low rates of anaemia, Elphinstone (1971) found also that there was little sign of parasite infestation in desert women. This reflects the ecology of these people who move their camps regularly, live in widely separated, small family groups in a relatively sterile environment and often bury their excreta to prevent its use by enemies for magic purposes (Dunn 1968; Abbie 1969; Berndt and Berndt 1981). Some parasitism must have been derived from consuming undercooked game and from close association with the dingo, though this was, no doubt, common to many Aboriginal communities (Mackerras 1958). The findings for the desert seem to underpin that we already suspected with regard to a rather pathogen-free, 'safe' ecology which revolves around nomadism. Early ethnohistorians believed that hardship and nutritional deficiency among those inhabiting arid areas caused their diminutive stature and slight build which was seen, for example, among Western Desert groups (Helms 1896). It is more likely, however, that in an area notorious for inflicting nutritional and physical hardship on people, mineral deficiencies may be the norm and humans have adapted to this during the 22,000 years or more that they have been living there (Smith 1989).

Recovery from anaemia

I have described elsewhere a category of cribra which I have suggested is a 'recovery' scar (Plate 5–2) (Webb 1989). I do not wish to go over arguments presented elsewhere, but it is helpful to mention briefly how it fits into the general picture outlined above.

With the exception of the desert sample, the frequency of the scar increases with age among adults Australia-wide and is seen most frequently in old adults. This pattern generally runs contrary to that of the active lesion and by doing so gives added support to the idea that the overall incidence of anaemia is reduced with age. When men and women are compared, old adult males have a greater potential for recovery than old females. Interestingly enough the one exception to this is among women who live in arid areas. Females from all but two areas show an appreciable recovery, whether it occurs in early adulthood, as in the tropics, later in life, as on the eastern seaboard or is steady throughout life (Rufus River and the south coast of Victoria). Women never show the consistency of continued recovery shown by males. Notable examples are those living in the central Murray, where there is little difference between young and old adult frequencies, and those in the arid regions.

It would seem logical to suggest that the potential for recovery would be highest in areas where frequencies of anaemia are at their lowest and the results presented here seem to support this as a general rule. In the central Murray, however, the situation is somewhat confused. Here, active cribra occurs in the highest frequencies found anywhere on the continent. Females follow the rule by displaying little evidence of recovery while males, particularly old men, experience a very substantial recovery. This evidence seems to suggest that cribra stress in females from the central Murray is continuous and they experience little relief, while the high recovery frequency in old men points to a real male/female differential which may possibly indicate cultural practices which favour males in terms of nutrition.

There is no uniform pattern to the prevalence of cribra among pre-contact Aboriginal people. While there are frequency differences between those living in various parts of the world who share the same general mode of existence, we must look closely at each group for answers explaining why these differences occur and not seek simple explanations merely to form general aetiological rules. The degree of stress revealed in the central Murray communities, for example, has no suitable explanation in terms of an ordinary hunter-gatherer lifestyle. They lived in one of the most bountiful environments in Australia, with abundant food choice, and there is no evidence for minerally deficient soils. Socio-demographic factors, therefore, would appear to be the only explanation for the high frequencies of anaemia found among these people and this will be discussed further at the end of the chapter.

Dental enamel hypoplasia

Introduction

It has been recognised for over 40 years that dental enamel hypoplasia (DEH) is caused by some form of nonspecific pathological stress (Sarnat and Schour 1941). (The abbreviation DEH follows that of Ogilvie *et al.* 1989.) DEH appears as a result of metabolic upset to normal developmental cell (ameloblast) function during enamel formation. It appears as a defect in the tooth enamel caused by a reduced thickness in this layer and manifests as single or multiple grooves, lines or pits (Sarnat and Schour 1941; Acheson 1960; Park 1964) (Plates 5–5a, b and c). Because these defects correspond to a particular time of enamel deposition in both deciduous and permanent dentitions, they provide a longitudinal record of stress events in the subadult which can be used to pin-point the age of the individual at the time they occurred. Several lines or grooves on one particular tooth indicate that a number of stressful events have taken place.

DEH has provided the palaeopathologist with another way of investigating ancient human stress and is now widely accepted as a standard tool in the interpretative arsenal of those wishing to understand more about the palaeobiology of past populations (Sarnat and Schour 1941; Giro 1947; Pindborg 1970; El-Najjar *et al.* 1978; Cook and Buikstra 1979; Goodman *et al.* 1980, 1984; Molnar and Molnar 1985; Ogilvie *et al.* 1989; Skinner and Hung 1989; Duray 1990; Lanphear 1990). Arguments continue over the exact aetiology of DEH, however, with some emphasising that simple interpretations applied to ancient groups avoid the complexity surrounding its appearance in human populations, different individuals and even individual teeth (Neiburger 1990). Poor nutrition, ingestion of toxic substances, surgery, acute infection, vitamin deficiency, trauma and genetic inheritance are all cited as possible causes (Clement 1963; Scott and Symonds 1977; Weinmann *et al.* 1945; Darling 1956; Rushton 1964; Neiburger 1990). During the first half of this century another range of nutritional and pathological causes was cited as responsible including syphilis, rickets, tetany, measles, whooping cough, pneumonia, gastrointestinal infection, highly fluoridated drinking water and vitamin and mineral deficiencies, to mention only a few (Giro 1947). Sarnat and Schour (1941), among others, found little correlation between hypoplastic events and exanthemous diseases and in 50 per cent of cases the cause of DEH remained unknown. As well as being artificially produced in experimental animals (Molnar and Ward 1975), DEH has been identified in wild and captive primate populations (Schuman and Sognnaes 1956; Molnar and Ward 1975), australopithecines (Robinson 1956; Tobias 1967; White 1978), *Homo erectus* (Brothwell 1963), Neanderthals (Sognnaes 1956; Ogilvie *et al.* 1989) as well as various other prehistoric populations from around the world (Sognnaes 1956; Brothwell 1963; Møller-Christensen cited in Alexandersen 1967b; Wells 1967; Molnar and Ward 1975; Schulz and McHenry 1975; McHenry and Schultz 1976; Rose 1977; Cook and Buikstra 1979; Sutton 1979; Clarke 1980; Goodman *et al.* 1980, 1983, 1984; Green 1982; Molnar and Molnar 1985; Duray 1990).

Study of recent populations has shown that there is a definite link between hypoplastic defects and socio-economic circumstances and that they are more prevalent in low-income groups who face economic and nutritional hardship (Giro 1947; Falin 1961; Sweeney *et al.* 1969; Cohen and Diner 1970; Jelliffe and Jelliffe 1971; Sweeney *et al.* 1971; Enwonwu 1973; Infante 1974; Infante and Gillespie 1974, 1977; El-Najjar *et al.* 1978; Skinner and Hung 1989). When traditional hunter-gatherer people are studied, and taking into account that DEH occurs only in the sub-adult during tooth formation, a number of causes can be disregarded. In a prehistoric context greater frequencies of dental hypoplasia have been seen among populations undergoing the sort of socio-economic and demographic changes which produce nutritional and pathological stresses (Cook and Buikstra 1979; Clarke 1980; Goodman *et al.* 1980, 1983). Most of those working in the field of palaeopathology at present favour some form of nutritional or pathological stress, or both, as a cause of DEH among archaeological populations and this is the aetiology favoured in this survey.

Methodology

Only two teeth were used for this survey: the permanent maxillary canine and third molar. The reason for this was dictated by the time of their respective enamel formation: between 4 months and 6–7 years for the canine and between 7–9 and 12–16 years for the third molar (Barrett 1957; Moorees *et al.* 1963; Scott and Symonds 1977). Individual variation in these times is not important. What is important is that two distinct sub-adult age groups can be monitored using this method. DEH was classified following Sarnat and Schour (1941: 1997), but the 'single' (acute), 'wide' (chronic) and 'multiple' definitions used also by these researchers have been ignored. Lines, grooves and pits were recorded as a single manifestation of DEH (Plates 5–5a, b and c). Dental attrition in Aboriginal populations is often extensive enough to reduce crown height to gum level, reducing sample sizes.

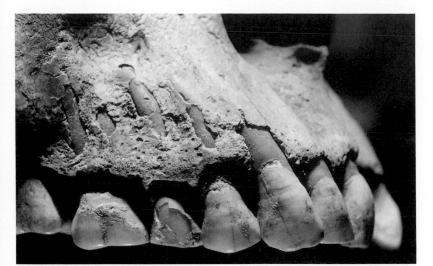

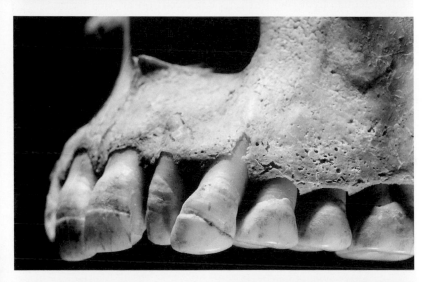

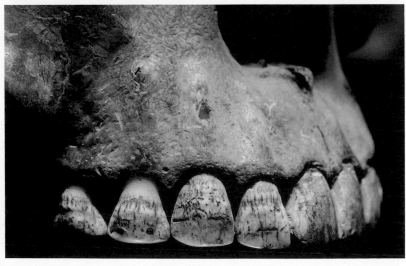

**Plates 5–5a, b
and c**
*Three forms of DEH
(dental enamel
hypoplasia) mor-
phology: lines (a),
grooves (b) and pits
(c).*

Results

Canine

All over the continent the frequency of third molar DEH is much smaller than for the canine and this is statistically significant (p=<0.005) (Table 5–4a). Population frequencies (males plus females) range from 18.9 per cent in Western Australia to 59.4 per cent along the Queensland coast. The latter has the highest individual male (61.4 per cent) and female (55.0 per cent) frequencies, while the lowest are found in Western Australian males (23.7 per cent), and females living at Rufus River (15.3 per cent). On an area basis, the east coast has the highest population (45.6 per cent) and male (50.5 per cent) frequencies but this includes the Queensland coastal people. Rufus River has the lowest for both these with 20.7 per cent and 24.5 per cent, respectively (Table 5–4b). The central Murray has the highest female frequency with 42.1 per cent on an area basis.

Table 5–4a *Canine and third molar DEH frequencies for all parts of the continent combined.*

	MALE			FEMALE			TOTAL	
	n	*n̄*	%	*n*	*n̄*	%	*n̄*	%
Canine	626	253	40.4	381	116	30.5	369	36.6
Third Molar	649	90	13.9	404	53	13.1	143	13.6

Table 5–4b *Canine and third molar DEH frequencies for various areas of Australia.*

		CANINE			THIRD MOLAR		
		n	*n̄*	%	*n*	*n̄*	%
CM	M	182	80	44.0	189	48	25.4
	F	107	45	42.1	111	27	24.3
	T	289	125	43.3	300	75	25.0
R	M	102	25	24.5	100	9	9.0
	F	72	11	15.3	70	11	15.7
	T	174	36	20.7	170	20	11.8
SC	M	88	35	39.8	101	6	5.9
	F	70	25	35.7	80	4	5.0
	T	158	60	38.0	181	10	5.5
DES	M	80	27	33.8	81	5	6.2
	F	31	5	16.1	32	1	3.1
	T	111	32	28.8	113	6	5.3
TRO	M	73	35	47.9	75	8	10.7
	F	44	9	20.5	46	1	3.1
	T	117	44	37.6	121	9	7.4
CTL	M	101	51	50.5	103	14	13.6
	F	57	21	36.8	65	9	13.8
	T	158	72	45.6	168	23	13.7

Key:
M–Male, F–Female, T–Population Total (males plus females)

Area Codes:
CM–Central Murray, R–Rufus River, SC–South Coast, DES–Desert, TRO–Tropics, CTL–East Coast

There is a large variation in the frequency of canine DEH in different parts of the continent. In some locations male and female frequencies are similar (for example, Euston in the central Murray); in others they are totally different, for example, central Australia where males have 37.3 per cent and females 16.7 per cent. Men have more hypoplasia than women but several marked reversals of this trend, at Baratta in the central Murray and along coastal Victoria, for example, have been observed. It should be noted, however, that female sample size in these groups is below the normal minimum of 25. With few exceptions, a location with a high male frequency will have also an accompanying high female frequency. The Broadbeach group from southeast Queensland has the highest population frequency of DEH anywhere in Australia, but the male and female sample sizes of 17 and four, respectively, are too small to compare properly with those from elsewhere.

Third molar

Rufus River is the only place where a molar frequency (15.7 per cent) is higher than the canine (15.3 per cent), and it occurs in females (Table 5–4b). Third molar hypoplasia was not observed among Northern Territory people, as part of the tropics sample, and females from Western Australia, while the lowest registered frequencies for a particular location were 2.1 per cent and 2.5 per cent for Swanport males and females, respectively (Map 2–1, 12). The greatest frequency difference between the canine and third molar is 47.9 per cent and 10.7 per cent, respectively, in males from the tropics. It is significant that the central Murray displays the highest overall frequency of molar DEH for both males and females where frequency differences (from 33.3 per cent to 31.3 per cent) in locations like Kerang are the smallest recorded anywhere.

Discussion

The general pattern of DEH among sub-adult Aboriginal people is as follows. With few exceptions, stress in the infant-toddler group is generally of a much higher order across the continent than it is in older children. The canine pattern shows that infant males almost always suffer greater stress than females of the group and this is particularly evident among sub-adults in tropical regions of Australia. These results reflect also the pattern observed in other studies, whereby male toddlers seem to have a greater susceptibility to stressful events in their formative years. Male and female frequencies reflect, proportionally, the degree of stress occurring at that location and/or area. A substantial reduction in stress takes place as Aboriginal children grow into their teenage years and this is the general pattern Australia-wide. It is variable, however. Evidence for the smallest amount of stress reduction comes from the central Murray and east coast. In these areas there is an absolute and relative maintenance of stress or stresses that do not decline with age in the same way that they do in other parts of the continent.

Canine

Dental hypoplasia has been studied in contemporary Aboriginal people (Cran 1955; Moody 1960; Schamschula *et al.* 1980). But these results are of little value for providing an aetiology for the condition in pre-contact people or for comparisons with those presented here because of radically changed social and demographic circumstances. The only study of dental hypoplasia in precontact Aboriginal remains is that of Green (1982) and I discuss these at length elsewhere (Webb 1989). The major contribution of this study was that it showed that among Murray River people DEH on the canine peaked at around four years in both males and females. It is interesting to compare this peak with those obtained from studies of North American Indian skeletal populations (Fig. 5–1) (Schulze and McHenry 1975; Rose 1977; Rose *et al.* 1978; Clarke 1980; Huss-Ashmore *et al.* 1982; Goodman and Armelagos cited in Huss-Ashmore *et al.* 1982; Goodman *et al.* 1984). Both the amplitude of the curve and the age at which the frequency peaks is different for each population, so that among Californian Indians the highest frequency (39.5 per cent) appears between four and five years (Schulze and McHenry 1975), while a 53.8 per cent peak among Illinoian Dickson Mound children occurs between a tighter, narrower age group (3–3.5 years) (Rose 1977). An Anasazi-Dickson Mound sample shows about 50 per cent affected at three years (Clarke 1980), while among Aboriginal children living in the central Murray the peak formation time occurs around 3.75–4.0 years. All these peaks are thought to coincide with the most favoured weaning age and the periodicity with the age spread of children undergoing this process. Both these are culturally determined.

Weaning best explains both the age at which the greatest frequency occurs and the rapid rise and decline of values on either side. Moreover, the timing broadly corresponds to the weaning age in tribal societies (Saul 1972; Clarke 1980). The weaning 'shock', caused by the negative effect of the rather sudden and nutritionally inadequate dietary change, together with any resulting illness, is the most plausible aetiology for the widespread occurrence of canine DEH among Aboriginal children. Although the maximum frequencies in Fig. 5–1 are not large, their amplitude depends upon the age spread of the affected group. Two-thirds of the dental hypoplasia in a Chicago group (Sarnat and Schour 1942) appeared during the first 12 months of life, then tapered to almost nothing in the next 20 months. This peak is large because weaning in western society at that time occurred mostly towards the end of the first 12 months of the infant's life. Among Aboriginal and Indian people it took place later and over a greater time period to take into account unsuitable weaning foods and also possibly to maximise the effects of breast feeding for child spacing. Hence, the wider spread of incidence and lower peak frequency compared to modern human populations.

Rufus River, Western Australia and central Australia seem to have the lowest incidences of canine DEH. The highly significant difference (p=<0.001) between these groups who inhabit different parts of arid

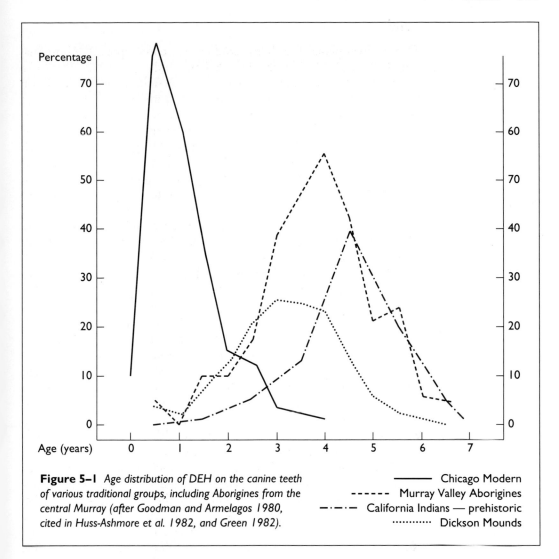

Figure 5–1 *Age distribution of DEH on the canine teeth of various traditional groups, including Aborigines from the central Murray (after Goodman and Armelagos 1980, cited in Huss-Ashmore et al. 1982, and Green 1982).*

——— Chicago Modern
- - - - - Murray Valley Aborigines
—·—·— California Indians — prehistoric
············ Dickson Mounds

Australia, and those living in the more fertile southeastern and coastal regions, could be a reflection of the similarity of child-rearing practices among people living in desert areas. While this is open to speculation, a limitation on and greater spacing between births, for example, would give a mother more time to wean and care for a toddler, thus reducing nutritional pressure on the infant from competing peers. But weaning may be only one contributor to these high frequencies of DEH. The continued formation of DEH on the third molar requires another explanation.

Third molar

The reason why DEH frequencies are lower for the third molar than the canine is that weaning no longer contributes to the formation of this lesion. This could imply, of course, that weaning is not the major cause of high rates in the younger age group because the stress persists in the older age group. There is little doubt, however, that the curves produced by Green and others demonstrate a link between weaning and dental hypoplasia and the frequency pattern presented above underpins this interpretation. In other words, while the third molar pattern shows a definite reduction in the amount of stress on older children it has a different aetiology also. While less DEH is recorded in this group, in some locations substantial frequencies of dental hypoplasia still occur. Generally, the older child is physically more able to cope with other forms of stress and this probably accounts for the observed drop in the frequencies in this age group, but the lower frequencies themselves are an indication of the *real* stress that the young continue to face. Such stress must come from how people lived, their nutrition and their general health which, in turn, are all a function of their demography and socio-economic status.

Variable levels of other stresses continue to influence the metabolism of the growing youngster. Naturally, the bigger the sub-adult the more able he or she is to withstand these, although growth spurts in this age group increase the individual's vulnerability to stress at those times. So the concept of *continuing* or *persistent* stress is, more accurately, one of the imposition of new stresses, supplanting or in addition to others which occur throughout the life of the child. If frequency reduction is due to physical growth alone, it should be equal in all parts of Australia. Clearly, this is not the case. There is a stark intergroup differential but, once again, the central Murray has significantly more of this kind of stress than any other area. In the face of this the desert and tropics show the least stress and the east coast and Rufus River trail the central Murray.

Before continuing with a more general discussion concerning the aetiology of DEH among Australian Aborigines, I want to briefly discuss the phenomenon of hypoplastic pitting. It has been accepted that lines, grooves and pits are all manifestations of the same DEH complex (Goodman *et al.* 1984). Although pits occur in horizontal rows in a similar manner to lines and grooves, they suggest a more severe process of ameloblastic disturbance than the other two because they are etched more deeply into the tooth enamel, often exposing dentine (Plates 5a–5c). Pitting frequencies among Aboriginal people are not great, with many locations having little or none. The bulk of canine DEH consists of lines and grooves with pits contributing minimally to the overall frequency. Third molar DEH presents a different story, however. In this tooth, pitting accounts for proportionally more hypoplasias than either lines or grooves. This is particularly evident among central Murray people, where between 80–85 per cent of hypoplastic scarring on the third molars of males (23 per cent) and females (29 per cent) from Kerang is in the form of pits. The next highest frequencies outside the central Murray are found along coastal New South Wales where frequencies of 9.4 and 11.1 per cent exist for males and females, respectively.

It is interesting that pitting occurs in locations with the highest frequencies of lines and grooves as well as anaemia. It is suggested, however, that this association does not stem from the likelihood that populations with more hypoplasia will, by chance, have more pits. The evidence points to increased frequencies of pits between the two age groups while there is an effective reduction in other forms of DEH. If there was a genetic predisposition for pit formation among certain individuals, rather than lines or grooves, it might be expected that: one, there would be an even reduction in the incidence of pits from the younger age group to the older because the latter has less hypoplasia; two, they might favour one sex over another; and three, individuals with an inherited tooth defect would, particularly in a society bearing considerable dental attrition and stress, have been selected out or reduced to a minimum over hundreds of generations. Another possible explanation for this pattern is that molar teeth could be more susceptible to this form of hypoplasia. If this were the case, however, surely a more even distribution of pitting in all locations might be expected?

I propose, therefore, that hypoplastic pits are a result of ongoing stressors which, because of extended chronicity, act upon the formation of tooth enamel in a more dramatic manner than those which produce lines and grooves. Such chronic, unrelieved stress is, once again, expressed more obviously in Murray River people than in those living elsewhere.

An aetiology for stress among Aborigines

In the light of the results discussed so far in this chapter, I want to review similar sorts of evidence from other parts of the world. I feel this is required particularly because of the high frequencies of anaemia (cribra) and non-specific stress (DEH) emanating from the central Murray region.

There is great variation in the degree and frequency of both anaemia and DEH among Australian Aborigines. There are particularly high, if not higher, incidences of DEH which are similar to those of North American Indians. As I mentioned before, the socio-economic circumstances of a given community play an important role in the incidence of DEH in that community (El-Najjar *et al.* 1978). It has been known for some time that the frequency of DEH and Wilson bands, another dental indicator of metabolic insult, increases in those societies undergoing socio-economic change. For example, among North American Indian populations both the number of hypoplastic events per individual and the total incidence of dental hypoplasia in the population rose when hunter-gatherers took up agriculture (Rose *et al.* 1978; Goodman *et al.* 1980, 1983, 1984). Rises from 45 per cent to 60 per cent and again to 80 per cent have been recorded for Indians moving from a traditional hunter-gathering lifestyle (Late Woodland) through a more settled transitional phase (Mississippian Acculturated) to the fully sedentary farming stage (Middle Mississippian), respectively. It is interesting that the male–female frequencies for the latter horizon are 81 per cent and 76 per cent respectively, similar to Green's results for the Murray people, although I in no way infer that Murray Valley

Aborigines were secret maize farmers – there was no maize to cultivate. Studies of Wilson bands have produced similar results (Rose *et al.* 1978). Cultural changes among those occupying the Ohio Valley between 4000BP and 1600AD seem to have also identified increases in dental hypoplasia with increasing sedentism (Sciulli 1977). Greater nutritional stress in the later agricultural people (post-Hopewell) has been cited as the most likely cause of the increase. Sciulli (1978:193) says that: 'severe linear enamel hypoplasia ... is found in every Amerindian group and is present at a significantly higher frequency in focal agricultural groups'. The reasons for this are understood and stated clearly by Cook and Buikstra:

> increased population pressure on food resources,
> increased reliance on carbohydrates for weaning diets,
> and environmental deterioration. It seems plausible to
> suggest that all of these factors were at work, and that
> enamel defects have provided us with an indirect
> measure of the pressures associated with increased
> reliance on agriculture. (1979:658)

Elsewhere, a significant relationship ($p = <0.05$) exists between dental hypoplasia and cribra orbitalia (Cook and Buikstra 1979). In this study, however, the only significant association between these two involved the canine frequency of east coast women ($p = <0.005$) and the third molar in desert men ($p = <0.001$). Because only two of the 28 possible groupings tested showed any association, it is suggested that these results are coincidental. The largest frequency of cribra (anaemia) and the most obvious persistence of DEH that occurs among people living in the central Murray is not considered coincidental, however.

Harris lines

> ... by far the greatest technical advance was made when
> radiology began to be used in the examination of
> anthropological and palaeontological materials.
> (Sigerist 1955:41)

Introduction

Harris lines were first observed in sectioned dry bone before the discovery of X-rays (Wegner 1874). Forty years later it was discovered that they were the result of some sort of metabolic insult or pathological stress (MacConaill 1969). It took another 50 years before experimental work showed this association conclusively (Asada 1924; Harris 1926, 1931, 1933). Harris (or Harris') lines are transverse networks of trabecular bone that either completely or partially span the medullary cavity of tubular bones or trace the outline of irregular or flat bones. They range from 1 mm to 1 cm in thickness and are found most commonly in the distal tibia and, decreasingly, in the proximal tibia, distal femur, distal radius and metacarpals (Steinbock 1976).

The mechanism of their formation is thoroughly understood but doubt still surrounds their exact aetiology (Park and Richter 1953; Park 1954, 1964). They begin with a reduction in the thickness of the epiphyseal cartilage plate beneath which osteoblasts form a thin bone layer (primary stratum). With stress relief, osteoblastic activity lays down bone on the inferior surface of the primary stratum, thickening it and producing the thin line of bone visible in radiographic examination (Steinbock 1976). From a palaeoepidemiological standpoint Harris lines are not only indicators of a stress event but show also recovery from that event. Broadly speaking, they appear after bouts of mild or severe illness, whether chronic or acute (Follis and Park 1952; Acheson 1959; MacConaill 1969). Other known causes include malnutrition, starvation in particular, and systemic pathology of one kind or another (Wells 1961; Steinbock 1976). Experimentally induced protein calorie malnutrition has produced Harris lines in pigs (Stewart and Platt 1958; Platt and Stewart 1962), while 84 per cent and 74 per cent of boys and girls suffering kwashiorkor had lines respectively, compared to 22 per cent and 10 per cent respectively in non-sufferers (Jones and Dean 1959). Ingestion of heavy metals (Caffey 1931; Park *et al.* 1933), testosterone treatment and repeated blood transfusions (Garn *et al.* 1968), surgery, chicken pox, smallpox immunisation and whooping cough also produce lines of arrested growth (Gindhart 1969).

The majority of Harris lines seem to form in the first five years of life (Dreizen *et al.* 1964). Peaks occur at about two and three years coinciding, it is thought, with the prevalence of childhood diseases (Garn *et al.* 1968; Gindhart 1969). Boys produce more lines than girls but have greater rates of resorption, where bone undergoes greater restructuring due to increased physical activity, muscular function on the bone and overall body size. So the adult pattern biases females, making them look more susceptible to stress (Garn and Schwager 1967; Garn *et al.* 1968). Some redress in this differential pattern takes place the longer females live because resorption removes many lines as the individual ages. Garn and Schwager (1967) have shown that line frequencies drop from 14 per cent in young males to 8 per cent in old males, and from 30 per cent in young females to 14 per cent in old females. Similarly, others have shown that while 53 per cent of young adults have such lines, only 28 per cent of old adults have them (Garn *et al.* 1968). This is mainly due to age-associated bone remodelling through endosteal resorption processes which reach their maximum in the fifth decade.

Because Harris lines form only while the bone is growing, they have become accepted as natural markers, showing not only periods of pathological or nutritional stress in the sub-adult but the age at which they took place. In this way they provide the palaeopathologist with a longitudinal record of an individual's health during childhood and help refine the general picture of morbidity in a skeletal population. Wells (1961, 1963, 1967) seems to have been the first to realise the value of these lines for assessing, comparing and contrasting stress in different archaeological populations. Since his work, Harris lines have been recorded in human skeletal material from many parts of the world (Gill 1968; McHenry 1968; Woodall 1968; Garn and Baby 1969; Allison *et al.* 1974; Sutton 1979; Houghton 1980; Kuhl 1980; Clark 1981; Hummert and Van Gerven 1985). The negative correlation between Harris lines and other pathological indicators noted by some workers has, however, somewhat dampened enthusiasm for their use in concert with other indicators such as cribra orbitalia and dental hypoplasia (Schultz and McHenry 1975; Clarke 1982; Goodman *et al.* 1983; Maat 1984). This has led to a healthy scepticism among some researchers about their use in palaeopathology and the kinds of interpretation that can be made from them. Increasingly, there is a belief that they may be an osteological reaction to stress similar to cribra orbitalia and dental hypoplasia but that they appear for entirely different reasons (Maat 1984). The main drawbacks in using them seem to lie in the differential adult resorption rates and the fact that they appear in people who have apparently not undergone any form of stress or trauma whatsoever. In the light of these points, an exact assessment of what they mean is difficult. Obviously, this limits their value, but it is worth adding that some other stress indicators we use do not have an exact aetiology either. But it is not imperative to have one. The weight of evidence points to their representing an episode of stress, which is the main aim of using Harris lines in this study. Further, as obvious as it might seem, it needs to be emphasised that although a number of causes for Harris lines seem likely, in the context of traditional Aboriginal society many of these, such as surgery, European infectious diseases as well as other causes associated with post-industrial society, including pollution and the ingestion of heavy metals, can confidently be ruled out.

The only Australian study that mentions Harris lines is that of Gill (1968:215) who investigated three recent Aboriginal skeletons and one mid-Holocene example. Hackett (1936a:50) also noted lines which had formed in bones he inspected during his work on 'boomerang' tibia (see Chapter 6). Certainly no systematic study of these lines among Aboriginal skeletal remains has been carried out until now.

Methodology

Before going on with a discussion of the results, it is worth recalling how the data was gathered. One thousand and two tibiae were radiographed, mainly at the Department of Prehistory, Australian National University. Some difficulty was experienced with certain specimens. These included those that had different cortical densities, some pathological specimens, very large or rugose individuals and those that were fossilised or filled with calcium carbonate or both. Right tibiae were used unless damaged and all were X-rayed in an antero-posterior aspect unless for some reason, such as thick cortices, another posture proved better.

The distal end of the tibia was divided into three developmental sectors, roughly following the method used by Hunt and Hatch (1981). These sectors correspond to age groups of less than 5 years, 5–10 years and greater than 11 years; in this study I refer to these as H1, H2 and H3, respectively. With different growth rates for males and females and, possibly, between different groups around the continent, not to mention variations in activity and nutrition levels, these sectors are used as a general guide only. I have adopted the Index of Morbidity (IM) developed by Wells (1967) as the most convenient way to express the frequency of Harris lines and compare different populations. It was adopted also because of its compatibility with other studies around the world.

Results

Aboriginal people living on the south coast have over three lines per individual, nearly twice that of the next highest group, the central Murray, and only 20 per cent of people in both these areas have no lines at all (Table 5–5). While central Murray people have the second highest IM (1.64), they are followed closely by desert dwellers (1.56), 30 per cent of whom have no trace of growth arrest lines. On the east coast there is a very low IM (0.80) and it is equally significant that lines appear in only 40 per cent of people. The small tropical sample disqualified it from this survey.

Swanport (3.54), on the lower Murray and Goolwa (2.88) on the southeastern coast of South Australia have the highest IMs in Australia (Map 2–1, 12 and 13). In the Swanport and Adelaide groups males have more lines than females and they have multiple lines, with some displaying more than four. The male propensity for line formation is further supported by the fact that they have more lines than females in the first two age groups (H1, H2) (Table 5–6).

Table 5–5 *Frequency of Harris lines for each area.*

	%F	IM
CM	21.5	1.64
R	54.4	1.31
SC	19.9	3.18
DES	28.9	1.56
CTL	57.7	0.80

Key:
%F – Percentage of line-free bones
IM – Index of Morbidity

Area Codes:
CM–Central Murray, R–Rufus River, SC–South Coast, DES–Desert,
CTL–East Coast

Table 5–6 *The number of Harris lines and morbidity indices among three sub-adult age groups (H1, H2 and H3).*

	H1	nL	H2	nL	H3	nL
CM	0.66	190	0.65	188	0.34	97
R	0.41	37	0.59	53	0.31	28
SC	0.86	155	1.85	335	0.47	85
DES	0.72	31	0.44	19	0.40	17
CTL	0.49	79	0.23	37	0.09	15

Key:
H1 – Lines forming between 0-5 years
H2 – Lines forming between 6-11 years, inclusive
H3 – Lines forming between 12-18 years, inclusive
nL – Number of lines in the age grade

Area Codes:
CM – Central Murray, R – Rufus River, SC – South Coast, DES – Desert,
TRO – Tropics, CTL – East Coast

The Harris line pattern in the central Murray is very different from that of the Swanport–Adelaide area. Males and females from there have similar IMs but in certain locations, such as Baratta and Swan Hill, they have lines in all age categories. One individual from Swanport has 20 lines and over one-third of the population (34.4 per cent) from there has more than four (Plate 5–6), but in the central Murray the frequency is far lower, with only 8.5 per cent at Baratta and 13.3 per cent at Swan Hill with more than four. Rufus River is similar to these central Murray locations with 8.8 per cent.

Discussion

If we look at stress episodes, three distinct population groupings emerge. In decreasing frequency these are: the south coast, the desert with the central Murray and Rufus River, and the east coast. If the number of individuals affected is considered, group clustering changes to central Murray with south coast, the desert and the east coast, and Rufus River. South coast people not only have the greatest number of lines but the highest percentage of individuals with them, while those living along the east coast have the least in both these categories. So what do these results mean?

Any Harris line survey essentially looks at childhood stress and because lines are resorbed throughout life, frequencies represent only minimum numbers of stress episodes. In places where large numbers of lines are found, like the south coast, resorption seems to have been minimal. The distribution of lines between males and females seems to be opposite to that found in other studies (Garn *et al.* 1968). Rather than fewer Harris lines in males, which seems to be the general pattern elsewhere, on the south coast they have more, as do those living in the central Murray. In the light of what is known about line resorption, the following are possible reasons for this distribution:

1) Aboriginal people have different resorption processes from other people around the world;
2) females are not subject to the stresses that cause lines in males;
3) males have more stress episodes than females;
4) both males and females undergo similar degrees of stress but there is greater resorption among females;
5) males are less active than females, thus, line resorption is less and lines are retained;
6) women are living longer than men, thereby increasing the chances of line resorption, or
7) males and females undergo similar amounts of stress but males have a better chance of recovery and, thus, line formation.

In the absence of direct evidence to support notion one, it must be rejected. As regards the second and third, it is clear that Aboriginal females are subject to more stress than males, as we have seen in the cribra and DEH studies. However, the stresses that cause these conditions may not be the same as those that form Harris lines. We may, then, be dealing with a stress to which males are more vulnerable than females, which is similar to reason two. Reasons four, five and six are essentially linked in that the loss of lines in females might be due to greater activity levels than males or because they live longer, or both. The latter is clearly not the case, as we shall see in later chapters. This leaves us with reason seven. We must not forget that Harris lines not only indicate a stressful episode but they also indicate recovery from that episode. One possible reason for the difference in line frequency between men and women might be that the former often enjoyed better nutritional circumstances in traditional Aboriginal society and, therefore, had more opportunity to recover, thus producing growth arrest lines.

South coast

It seems that individuals with many lines have them spaced equally, in a 'step ladder' pattern (Plate 5–6). The periodicity between each line closely follows the spacing one might expect for annual tibial growth increments (see also McHenry 1968). When seen in hunter-gatherers a pattern like this is best explained by regular stress episodes. For example, annual or biannual nutritional shortages rather than regular bouts of acute illness or regular surgery. Males in the Swanport and Adelaide samples display this pattern more clearly than females, which might suggest that they have a greater potential for recovery from these events and the results of the DEH study above could be used to support this conclusion. It could be suggested that age plays a major part in male/female differentials and that if lines are lost with age, then perhaps men were dying earlier than women. Using the basic ageing technique explained in Chapter 2, it is clear that males in all areas generally live longer than females, the majority of whom succumb before their early forties (Fig. 5–2). In this case, they are less likely to have experienced the resorption processes of old age than their male counterparts.

Plate 5–6

An individual from Swanport with eighteen Harris lines in a typical 'step ladder' pattern that probably indicates a regular, perhaps seasonal, stress.

It is reasonable to conclude, therefore, that the pattern of Harris lines in south coast people reflects annual or biannual periods of nutritional shortage. The evidence also suggests that males are not more susceptible to stress but rather are more capable of recovery, which could reflect a cultural bias towards male children in this region. It should be noted also that, unlike the central Murray, neither sex from this area shows undue morbidity as reflected by other pathological markers or early mortality. The prevalence of both sexes to line formation during their second trimester of growth may indicate a particular susceptibility at this time. Breast-feeding would play some part in the amelioration of nutritional stress experienced by the H1 group,

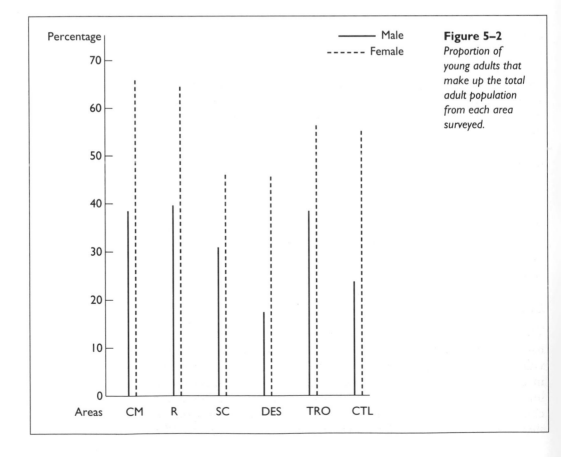

Figure 5–2

Proportion of young adults that make up the total adult population from each area surveyed.

but with the complete cessation of this source of nutrition the H2 group is fully exposed to the vagaries of a seasonally structured adult diet in a hunter-gatherer community.

Central Murray

The stress acting on south coast people is different from that experienced in other areas. The percentage of affected central Murray people, for example, is similar to the south coast, but the difference between male and female frequencies is not so pronounced. This gives the impression that both sexes are affected almost equally and, unlike the south coast, they have equal chances for recovery. What does the lower IM of the central Murray tell us then? It could be argued that it is real and reflects a less stressful environment. Clearly, however, this would be difficult to sustain in view of results obtained from other stress markers and presented earlier. Another interpretation is that recovery is not as readily achieved as it is on the south coast and that the lower IM of the central Murray further reflects the constant stress that we have already seen in the high frequencies of other stress indicators in the area. So, although the chances of recovery are almost equal for both men and women, they are depressed for everyone.

But how many lines have disappeared from the central Murray population through the processes of resorption? If we look at Fig. 5–2 we see that resorption is less likely to occur among this group than among south coast people, especially for females, because they experience a shorter life span than their male counterparts. At Swan Hill, 80 per cent of female crania represent young adults. With men living longer we should expect women to have more lines, therefore, the almost equal distribution of Harris lines between the two sexes suggests that men do undergo some resorption with age and this brings their observed frequency closer to that of women. In fact, they may have had more stress episodes than females, suggesting many stress episodes but a greater chance of full recovery than females. In other words, females had more constant stress than males with fewer chances of recovery. Whatever the reasons for the central Murray line patterns, they seem different from those of the south coast. Further, if the IM is a true reflection of specific stress events in this area, then they do not correlate with the other stress markers discussed previously. On the other hand, if recovery from stress is non-existent, impeded or slow, Harris line indices can only be used as a negative stress correlate in the central Murray.

East coast

The east coast provides us with a third distinctive pattern. This area has the lowest indices; the least number of people affected; no individual with more than four lines and most stress events taking place in the youngest age group. Moreover, less than half the sample has lines, the 'step ladder' pattern is missing and few lines form after children reach six years. Studies carried out on modern populations show a pattern similar to this (Dreizen *et al.* 1964; Garn *et al.* 1968).

If for the moment we accept the H1 figures as 'normal' or 'expected' for everyday living, the IM for the east coast drops from 1.00 to an almost insignificant 0.36. I have already described why the youngest age group is more vulnerable to stress events but on the east coast this group is not as affected as it is on the south coast and in the central Murray. It could be argued, as I did for the latter, that the absence of lines in eastern coastal groups is no proof that stressful periods did not occur and that no recovery phase took place. I suggest, however, that there is a *real* absence of the kind of stress which causes growth arrest lines, perhaps because there is a secure source of all-year-round nutrition on this coast. In other words, the cycle of feast and famine, suggested as being responsible for the south coast pattern, was not experienced to the same degree on the east coast. Adult morbidity is not as high on the east coast as it is in the central Murray, but it is close to the south coast pattern, although female morbidity is higher. If minimal resorption takes place in young adults then there is a real absence of lines, at least among females. Once again, I point to the results from other stress indicators and suggest that the Harris line pattern on the east coast does not correlate well with these.

Rufus River

The Harris line pattern among Rufus River people presents a mix of characters already noted for the other areas. Less than half the population is affected (45.6 per cent), which is similar to the east coast but quite unlike other parts of the Murray. The overall IM is the second lowest of any area, while peak line formation occurs in the H2 group, as it does for other parts of the Murray and the south coast. So, like most other areas, Rufus River presents its own line pattern. Most importantly, this pattern is not like those found in other parts of the Murray River. There is multiple line formation with up to 11 in some individuals, strongly indicating seasonal nutritional stress, in a similar way to that displayed among the south coast people. Perhaps stress relief came less often to the Rufus River than it did on the south coast.

A possible meaning for Harris lines in Aboriginal Australians

Because of their equivocal aetiology, interpretations of what Harris line patterns might mean often depend more upon the results of surveys of other stress markers. The use of Harris lines as 'stand-alone' stress indicators, therefore, is limited and relies on the amount of other relevant pathological and palaeobiological data for their interpretation (Goodman *et al.* 1983; Hummert and van Gerven 1985). It is for this reason that it is difficult to give an accurate idea of what they indicate in various Australian populations. On top of this is the shortage of data from elsewhere with which to compare these results. An IM of 3.18 for the south coast cannot, for example, be readily compared to the 3.4 obtained by Wells (1961, 1967) for an early Saxon population.

Clearly, the respective aetiologies in these groups are very different. At first glance Wells' study leads to the conclusion that a high IM can be associated with rising social complexity and the formation of large towns and villages (Wells 1967:392). A study of two communities in Peru has also shown that a sample of sedentary coastal agriculturalists had the highest IM (2.63), while people living at higher altitudes were not so susceptible (Allison *et al.* 1974). These findings seem to contradict other data indicating that 70 per cent of individuals from a nomadic Mexican group had lines, while only half the members of a contemporary sedentary group (1200AD) were affected (Allison *et al.* 1974). Before going on it is worth asking whether an IM of between 2 and 4 is high or low.

McHenry's (1968) study of Californian Indians clearly shows an inverse relationship between line formation and increasing infectious disease, morbidity, sedentism and general social and economic intensification. The IM among these Indian groups changed from 11.32 to 7.68, then to 5.03 as they settled down. One could be tempted to suggest these results are the reverse of Wells' findings. McHenry has suggested that feast and famine was the best explanation for the cause of the multiple line pattern observed among the least sedentary hunter-gatherers in his study. The reason for the observed drop in line frequency could be either more regular food supplies, perhaps from increased yields as people began to use cultivation, or an increase in infectious disease which prevented sufficient recovery from bouts of famine. Similar findings have been published from a study of the Dickson Mounds population (Goodman *et al.* 1983). The IM among these people dropped also, from 1.3, to 1.19 to 1.06, across three increasingly sedentary cultural phases.

Clearly, these results do not support the view that growth arrest lines correlate with increasing community stress. But we know that human health deteriorated with developing sedentism and population aggregation and growth, so reduced line frequencies among societies known to be undergoing such stresses is not what might normally be expected. We must, however, take into consideration the frequencies of other stress indicators and remember that Harris lines form essentially when there is adequate stress relief. With high frequencies of cribra orbitalia, infectious disease and DEH but a low IM, for example, there are sufficient grounds to believe that pathological, metabolic or nutritional stress, or all these, is more constant or chronic in that particular population. In contrast, a pattern of high IM and low frequencies of other stress markers is likely to mean a fairly stress-free society experiencing a regular, perhaps annual, nutritional shortage, typical of that experienced by many hunter-gatherers. Interpretation, then, depends upon the type of society being studied. Many or few lines in a given population can mean the same thing: that the population is stressed, but in different ways. Harris lines can, then, be used as both positive and negative stress indicators; there are examples of both these in this survey.

People with multiple lines show that, first, they have regular periods of stress, probably resulting from seasonal shortages of food, and, second, that they adequately recover from these. The variability of line frequency between different Aboriginal groups is surprising, particularly when we compare people living along adjacent coastlines or different parts of the same river. There is wide variation both in the number of lines per individual and the number of individuals with them. In my opinion there is little doubt that seasonal food shortages were much more common for people living on the south coast than they were for those occupying the warmer and more protected coastlines of New South Wales and Queensland. In other words, the south coast had a typical feast and famine diet and the east coast did not. Surprisingly, the picture from the desert does not reflect that type of pattern which is often associated with those living in this area. Multiple lines are not particularly common and the IM is similar to that of the central Murray. Taking into consideration the low frequencies of other stress markers among those living in arid areas, it can only be assumed that millennia of cultural and physiological adaptation to the harsh conditions of desert life have provided these people with constitutions that can cope with the vagaries of that particular environment.

The Murray River presents a consistently changing picture as we move up from the Swanport area of the lower Murray, past Rufus River and into its central portions. Near the mouth, around Swanport, there is the seasonal pattern of nutritional stress and minimal frequencies of other stress indicators. This is a pattern not unlike that of the nearby south coast. Several hundred kilometres upstream at Rufus River, the IM is lower than Swanport's but other forms of stress are prevalent. It is, in fact, a suitable intermediary between the lower and central portions of the Murray River and in terms of Harris lines looks more like the desert with which it shares many environmental similarities. The central Murray presents a completely different picture of stress from the lower and, for once, it does not show the large amounts of stress, in terms of lines, that we might expect. High frequencies of other stress markers strongly indicate, however, that stress among these people is more chronic or permanent or both, rather than the transitional type found on the lower Murray.

The evidence points to an acute rather than chronic stress, probably stemming from inadequate food supplies at certain times of the year, as the most likely reason for Harris line production among Aboriginal people. Even if disease is an occasional causative agent, it can, together with trauma, be discounted as a major influence on line production. This makes any association between Harris lines and other stress indicators, such as cribra orbitalia and DEH, remote. This may go some way to explain the different patterns of these lines compared to other stress markers not only in this study but in studies undertaken elsewhere. With this in mind, it seems essential that other forms of skeletal stress marker should always be used together with Harris lines.

Chapter 6

Infectious disease

Non-specific infection
Treponemal infection
Tibial bowing

General introduction

In one sense this chapter is a continuation of the previous one. There I described indirect indicators of stress but I also alluded to a contributor to them: infectious disease. This chapter describes the evidence for infection as it appears on the skeletal remains of Australian Aborigines. To do this I have divided bone infection into two types: non-specific and treponemal. My definition of non-specific infection uses three different pathological conditions: periostitis, osteitis and osteomyelitis. The treponemal section discusses the evidence for this condition as it appears on the cranium only and uses well known morphological criteria to describe lesions of this type. At the end of the chapter I discuss tibial bowing. I have included it because it has often been observed among Aboriginal people living in northern and arid areas of the continent who, at the same time, are suffering from a form of treponematosis endemic to those parts of Australia. The apparent association between treponemal disease and bowing, suggested by some, makes its inclusion here important (Hackett 1936a,b; Jaffe 1975; Steinbock 1976).

Non-specific infection

Introduction

Infection of the bone has probably occurred ever since it was possible for bacteria and bone to come together. Evidence for it goes back a long way, all the way, in fact, to its appearance in Permian dinosaur remains (Moodie 1923). Bone infection among humans is, and probably always has been, universal. It has been recorded in many ancient peoples living all over the world and no doubt dates back to the first time a hominid gouged a piece out of its hand with a sharp rock (Goldstein 1957; Brothwell 1963; Saul 1972; Shermis 1975; Clabeaux 1976; Goldstein *et al.* 1976; Walker 1978; Blakely 1980; Larsen 1981, 1982; Trinkaus and Zimmerman 1982; Trinkaus 1984).

On this level there is nothing outstanding about the appearance of the condition in human skeletal populations. Nevertheless, in recent years non-specific infection has provided clues as to the general health, demography and, to a certain extent, even the social construction of human societies. The amount of infection that exists in a community often means more to the palaeopathologist than the mere presence of infective organisms. Its frequency, type and distribution depends on a number of factors including the way people live, their behaviour, population size, their nutritional status and so on. In this way the study of prehistoric infection provides further evidence about people and their wider social circumstances. For example, the build-up of such disease correlates with an enhanced environment for pathogenic organisms which emerges when human populations grow, people become more sedentary and community refuse is not adequately disposed of. It is in this context that the incidence of non-specific infection among recent Aboriginal groups from various parts of the continent is of interest here.

A brief aetiology of non-specific infection

Some of the pathogens which produce bone infection include *Staphylococcus aureus*, which accounts for up to 90 per cent of cases, and the streptococcus group comprising organisms such as *Escherichia coli*, *Salmonella typhi* and *Neisseria gonorrhoea* (Aegerter and Kirkpatrick 1975; Steinbock 1976). They are introduced into the bone either through trauma, such as a compound fracture, or through soft tissue wounds or abrasions. Osteomyelitis can begin as an infection of the periosteum (periostitis) and if left untreated can eventually cause swelling of the bone cortices beneath (osteitis). Occasionally, chronic or long-term infection results in the penetration of the bone cortex and the infectious pathogen then enters the medulla. A more common cause of medullary infection takes place through the introduction of bacteria via the bone's own arterial system. Once there, a site of infection (gumma) forms which, over a number of years, gives rise to a suppurative condition at the site of infection (osteomyelitis). Necrotic destruction of the cortex follows, producing holes (cloacae) through which the exudate or pus drains. These are usually accompanied by surrounding patches of new, woven bone and other small, rarefied foci of cortical destruction. The presence of cloacae in the dry bone is, therefore, a distinctive diagnostic feature of osteomyelitic infection.

Defining non-specific infection in bone

Periostitis and osteitis can be regarded as primary and secondary stages in the onset of osteomyelitis, respectively (Steinbock 1976). So, while it is possible to differentiate between them in dry bone, each may only mean that the individual died before the infection reached the next stage. The terms periostitis and osteitis, therefore, are, in one sense, not medically accurate because they may indicate only one stage or phase in an increasingly severe pathological continuum. On the other hand, the palaeopathologist cannot assume that the periostitis on an ancient tibia, if left untreated, would have automatically progressed to osteomyelitis. Ultimately, periostitis and perhaps osteitis indicate only the presence of an infectious condition *per se*. As all palaeopathologists will agree, lesion 'categorisation' is a constant dilemma in the diagnosis and interpretation of disease using skeletal tissues only. While it may be wiser, therefore, to record individual categories and let others form their own opinions about individual meanings, for this survey I have combined periostitis, osteitis and osteomyelitis as one lesion termed 'non-specific infection' or 'infection'.

Having done this, I am aware that osteomyelitis may not be so 'non-specific'. It can result, for example, from treponemal infection, which is quite specific. I have chosen to ignore this particular aetiology for osteomyelitis in Australian post-cranial remains because of our inability to accurately separate treponemally derived infection in these remains from non-specific forms. Tertiary stage treponemal disease normally produces distinctive cranial lesions beside osteomyelitic infections in the post-cranial skeleton. Crania are almost always separated from post-cranial remains in Australian collections, however, and it is because of this that the frequency of treponemal disease used in this survey is determined on cranial evidence only (see below).

Frequencies of non-specific infection in Australian Aboriginal populations

Because there are so few sub-adult post-cranial remains, for this survey they have been included with adult remains. Frequencies of non-specific bone infection were assessed separately for each of the six major long bones (humerus, ulna, radius, femur, tibia and fibula) and by left and right sides (Table 6–1).

Infection in coastal areas is minimal, the highest frequency is 6.1 per cent in right tibiae from the east coast. If, however, the biased sample from Broadbeach is ignored and the separate tibial samples from the New South Wales and Queensland coasts are viewed individually, their respective frequencies rise to 8.6 per cent and 10.3 per cent. Only one individual from the Broadbeach sample showed any sign of infection and there were none at all in the small sample from the southwest coast of Western Australia. The south coast frequency

(3.3 per cent) is low and contrasts somewhat with east coast people. The highest frequency occurs among the desert group, in which 16.7 per cent of femora display some sort of infection. While this sample is small (n=24), the high rate of infection may reflect the presence of treponematosis which is endemic to the region. The second highest frequency comes from the central Murray where it occurs most often in right ulnae (12.8 per cent) and humeri (9.5 per cent).

Table 6–1 *Non-specific infection frequencies for the post-cranial skeleton.*

UPPER LIMB

LOWER LIMB

HUMERUS

FEMUR

	Left			Right				Left			Right		
	n	ñ	%	n	ñ	%		n	ñ	%	n	ñ	%
CM	176	15	8.5	189	18	9.5	CM	216	11	5.1	202	8	4.0
R	128	4	3.1	134	4	3.0	R	94	4	4.3	88	2	2.3
SC	152	1	0.7	147	2	1.4	SC	144	2	1.4	140	4	2.9
DES	28	2	7.1	27	–	–	DES	22	–	–	24	4	16.7
TRO*	10	1	10.0	8	1	12.5	TRO*	8	–	–	9	–	–
CTL	99	1	1.0	106	2	1.9	CTL	100	5	5.0	111	2	1.8

ULNA

TIBIA

	Left			Right				Left			Right		
	n	ñ	%	n	ñ	%		n	ñ	%	n	ñ	%
CM	127	8	6.3	130	8	6.2	CM	261	17	6.5	254	20	7.9
R	78	2	2.6	84	5	6.0	R	98	6	6.1	101	8	7.9
SC	108	1	0.9	117	2	1.7	SC	138	4	2.9	145	4	2.8
DES	24	1	4.2	26	1	3.8	DES	28	2	7.1	36	4	11.1
TRO*	6	–	–	8	1	12.5	TRO*	9	–	–	11	2	18.2
CTL	93	–	–	100	1	1.0	CTL	90	5	5.6	114	7	6.1

RADIUS

FIBULA

	Left			Right				Left			Right		
	n	ñ	%	n	ñ	%		n	ñ	%	n	ñ	%
CM	128	7	5.5	131	7	5.3	CM	151	8	5.3	143	8	5.6
R	110	3	2.7	113	5	4.4	R	87	2	2.3	87	6	6.9
SC	120	2	1.7	92	3	3.3	SC	41	–	–	36	1	2.8
DES	25	2	8.0	24	–	–	DES	22	1	4.5	19	1	5.3
TRO*	7	1	14.3	6	–	–	TRO*	8	1	12.5	7	1	14.3
CTL	93	1	1.1	93	–	–	CTL	75	–	–	72	1	1.4

Key:
*– TRO (Tropics) not analysed because of small sample size

Area Codes:
CM–Central Murray, R–Rufus River, SC–South Coast, DES–Desert, TRO–Tropics, CTL–East Coast

Discussion

Overall, infection among Aboriginal populations occurs most often in the right arm and leg. Handedness may play a part in determining the upper limb pattern but the reason for the lower limb involvement is more obscure. The frequency of non-specific infection reflects some-what the pattern we saw for stress indicators in the previous chapter. If the stress marker data are ignored for the moment, it could be argued that the differences in the frequency of non-specific infection between the Murray and the coast are more apparent than real. However, the stress picture makes these non-specific infection results interesting. Bone infection is intimately related to lifestyle: a high incidence can be caused, for example, by population increase and crowding which promotes the expansion of pathogenic organisms. This palaeoepidemiological link between human ecology and infection is only one of a number of associations between society and pathology:

> The relationship is often intimate: osteoarthritis and the
> economy; infectious diseases and population; oral sepsis
> and diet; parasites and available animal vectors;
> nutritional diseases and the level of technology are all
> examples of the dependency between man and his
> environment. (Shermis 1975:55)

The relationship between the total social composition of a society and its infectious environment has been amply demonstrated using palaeo-pathological data gathered in a number of North American studies (McHenry 1968; Blakely 1971, 1980; Shermis 1975; Lallo and Rose 1979; Larsen 1981, 1982). Increases in rates of infection have, however, been variable and the following examples are worth review-ing from the epidemiological stand-point. At the Dickson Mounds Lallo and Rose (1979) discovered a significant rise in the incidence and severity of non-specific bone lesions between the Mississippian Acculturated and Late Woodland group (30.8 per cent), whose hunter-gathering activities were supplemented with some agriculture, and the subsequent Middle Mississippian phase (67.4 per cent), which had an economy based on maize agriculture. Larsen (1982) found that periosteal infection among Indians living along the Georgia coast increased in all bones between the pre-agricultural and agricultural phases. This increase was highly significant in tibial infection, which rose from 4.5 per cent to 15.0 per cent. Larsen attributes this rise to '... crowded conditions associated with permanent occupation of large, densely populated sedentary villages' (1982:252). It is interesting to note the differences in frequencies between the Dickson maize growers and corn farmers along the Georgia coast. Shermis has high-lighted these differences among other prehistoric Indian groups:

> Certain aboriginal American groups display low
> incidences of [infectious] disease, such as the Archaic
> Indian Knoll population of Kentucky or the Pecos
> Pueblo population of New Mexico (Hooton 1930). In
> other groups, late or proto-historic or historic
> populations such as the Fort Ancient population of Ohio
> and Kentucky or the Arikara of the Dakotas, the disease
> reached virtual epidemic or pandemic proportions.
> (1975:43)

While some groups have higher frequencies of infectious disease than others, Blakely has determined that an average figure for prehistoric Americans lies somewhere ' … between ten and fifteen percent' (1980: 31).

In Australia, not only is there a significant difference in the frequency of infectious disease between Murray River and coastal groups, lesions are distributed differently between the two also. In the former there is a more even involvement of all bones from upper and lower limbs, while on the coast upper limb infections are negligible. This pattern suggests that either injuries, from which infection arose, were more common in the Murray for all limbs, or infection without injury was high. In Chapter 8 I show that Murray people suffer less post-cranial trauma than those inhabiting other parts of the continent, which would reduce the potency of the trauma argument as a cause. If the Murray has an 'infectious environment', stemming from population clustering, there would be a greater likelihood that infections would be more evenly spread throughout the body from the cuts and abrasions of everyday living. The upper limb predominance could be related to the pattern of mechanical stress which is reflected in the high incidence of bilateral upper limb osteoarthritis in this area (see Chapter 7). This in itself is not a pattern normally associated with hunter-gatherers, where handedness is usually quite strongly visible.

Tibial infection is predominant at Rufus River and on the east coast while it is a close second in all others. This is a pattern noted elsewhere in both hunter-gatherer and sedentary groups (Clabeaux 1976; Larsen 1982). Continuous blows to and bruising of the lower legs, encountered as a natural part of living, might be one explanation for this, but it must be noted also that of all the long bones the tibia is the most commonly affected in syphilitic or treponemal disease (Adams 1976).

There is less bone infection at Rufus River than among people living further east in the central Murray, but there is more than among the Swanport population near the mouth of the river. In other words infection frequencies are reduced as one moves down the Murray River towards the coast. The eastern coastal group has more infection than people living on the south coast and this overall pattern of infection, it may be remembered, matches the results obtained for stress indicators, although the reverse is true for Harris lines.

Osteomyelitis

During his survey of Aboriginal remains, Sandison (1980) noted the complete absence of haematogenous pyogenic osteomyelitis. There is, however, some very convincing evidence for chronic pyogenic osteomyelitis among Aboriginal groups in the Murray Valley. Two particularly notable examples of this severe form of bone infection, both in adult individuals, are worth describing briefly. The first of these is a chronic infection in the distal end of a left femur. The focal site lies just above the knee and displays a large cloaca that drains onto the anterior surface of the bone (Plate 6–1). The hole is slightly oval and measures almost 25 mm across. The fine cancellous appearance of the bone surrounding the entrance testifies to the active condition of the infection at the time of the individual's death. Superior and medial to the cloaca is a fairly large area of raised, irregular new bone which has formed a 'skin-like' scrolled sheath but there is no sign of a sequestrum beneath. The whole distal half of the diaphysis is thickened due to sub-periosteal bone apposition, giving the femur a rather swollen appearance. This femur is only one of several examples that have a single but smaller cloaca positioned above the knee. A lesion like this one develops through the introduction of an infectious organism, like *Streptococcus* into the bone through the nutrient artery. This may have occurred from a thigh wound which penetrated the bone or from an adjacent soft tissue lesion. Such a prominent and deep-seated lesion suggests a long-standing, low-grade suppurative infection. The condition probably began as a haematogenous osteomyelitis, progressing into a chronic condition of long-standing.

The second example of chronic pyogenic osteomyelitis occurs in a left tibia and is more extensive than the first. Its most notable feature is the widespread formation of new bone that covers most of the distal half of the diaphysis and the distal articular surface (Plate 6–2). The bone displays the shiny, irregular, and 'melted' appearance typical of pyogenic osteomyelitis. This is accompanied by a plethora of spiky projections of various lengths which have formed along the line of attachment of the interosseous membrane (Plate 6–3). A similar case history is envisaged for this individual as that described for the previous case.

Plate 6–1
Chronic, non-specific osteomyelitis in a distal femur from the central Murray. The irregular woven bone above the large cloaca is reminiscent of pyogenic osteomyelitis but there is no evidence of a sequestrum.

Plate 6–2 (left)
The infection in this distal tibia from the central Murray has many features of chronic pyogenic osteomyelitis, for example, the 'melted candle wax' appearance of new irregular woven bone. There is no evidence of a sequestrum, however. The infection has spread across much of the bone surface and probably extended distally to the talus, resulting in a possible ankylosis of the ankle joint.

Plate 6–3 (right)
This section of the diaphysis of the bone featured in Plate 6–2 shows a series of bony spikes on the lateral surface. They probably originate from ossification of the interosseous membrane between the tibia and the fibula as a result of the primary infection.

A third example of chronic osteomyelitis, and the most extraordinary pathology of its type that has come to my notice, is that in a left femur from the central Murray. It is positioned just above the condyles and has removed all the cancellous and most of the cortical bone in that region. As a result only a tripod of compact bone spindles is left joining the condyles to the rest of the shaft (Plate 6–4). The infection has remained comparatively localised, with no new bone formation or other features normally associated with pyogenic osteomyelitis. Even though healing is evident throughout much of this extensive lesion, several foci on the 'legs' of the tripod and a large cloaca on the posterior side of the bone, above the main cavity, testify to the presence of infection at the time of the individual's death.

Other forms of chronic bone infection can also be found in Australian collections. Many of these show different stages in the osteomyelitic process and are particularly notable among long bones from the central Murray region. The majority of cases display a multifocal,

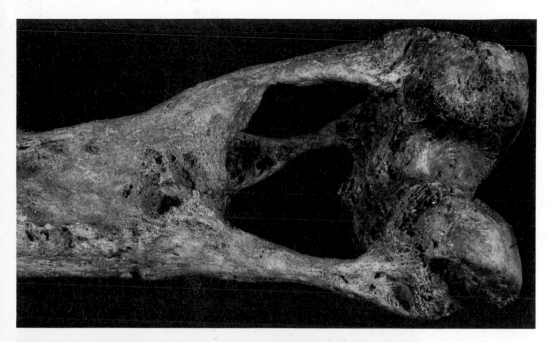

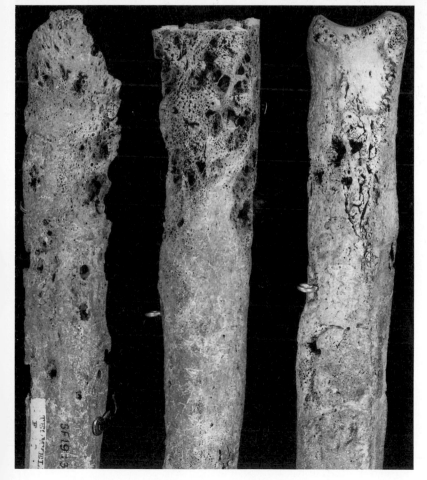

Plate 6–4
The extraordinary lesion just above the knee of this individual from the central Murray is testimony to a chronic infection of long standing. The tripod of bone joining the condyles to the rest of the femur must have been very hard to have continued to withstand the weight of the individual. Once broken there would be little chance of its mending and amputation may have been the only treatment.

Plate 6–5
Three distal ends of osteomyelitic tibiae from the central Murray each showing multiple cloacae.

Plate 6–6a (left)
This picture presents a wider view of the left and middle tibiae featured in Plate 6–5. Osteomyelitis affects almost all parts of the diaphyses with widespread cloacae which cluster at either end of the bone, with some coalescing to form larger openings. It is difficult to know whether these lesions are a product of treponemal infection or have a non-specific origin. The former is favoured.

Plate 6–6b
(right) *While the external effects of infection are different for these bones, internally they have a similar morphology. Both clearly show that infection stems from multiple foci which reside in many parts of the diaphysis. Areas of thickened cortex due to subperiosteal new bone formation are prominent and these have filled the medullary cavity, almost blocking it in some places. There must have been an enormous amount of suppuration as well as odour associated with a long-standing infection of this type.*

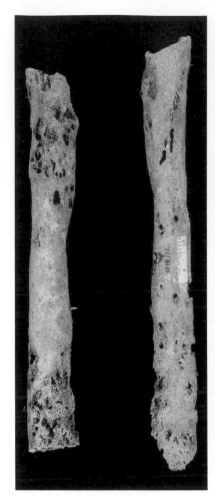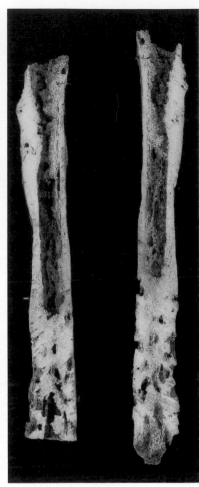

gummatous infection of the medulla which is reflected in a honeycomb of necrotic cavities and cloaca peppering the external surface, sometimes along the whole length of the diaphysis (Plate 6–5). Often there is a generalised involvement of many parts of the bone including a thickening of the cortex due to subperiosteal bone apposition which often invades the medulla (Plates 6–6a and b). This type of chronic infection suggests years of suffering and in some cases may have its origins in childhood. It is for this reason that others have associated these extreme examples of post-cranial infection with treponemal disease (Hackett 1976; Steinbock 1976). Unfortunately, cranial and post-cranial bones of these individuals were separated when they were collected, over fifty years ago. For this reason, the severe gummatous osteomyelitis that appears in post-cranial remains cannot be firmly linked to the more diagnostic cranial scarring that occurs in tertiary treponematosis. It is likely that an endemic form of treponematosis did, in fact, exist in parts of the Murray Valley in pre-contact times and was responsible for some of the gummatous osteomyelitis that can be seen in long bones from this area today.

Treponemal infection

Introduction

The greatest pitfall in studying and diagnosing non-specific infection in post-cranial remains is in assessing what proportion is due to treponemal disease. There is no doubt that an endemic form of treponemal disease (treponarid), as well as yaws, existed among Australia's Aboriginal population in some areas of central and northern Australia prior to the arrival of Europeans. Aboriginal stories and beliefs concerning the origin and magical potential of this infection testify to their familiarity with it and accounts by early explorers graphically describe the infection. It is entirely possible, therefore, that some of the infection which I have designated 'non-specific' could, quite easily, have a treponemal origin. We have another problem, however. No one is sure how widespread this disease was or how long it has been in Australia. It is for this reason that I want to take this opportunity to document some of the evidence for this chronically disfiguring and debilitating disease in order to put the palaeopathological evidence in a more secure epidemiological framework and, hopefully, to improve our understanding of the age and distribution of treponematoses on this continent.

There is an extensive literature covering the palaeoepidemiology, differential diagnosis and historic spread of treponematoses (yaws, endemic treponarid and syphilis) throughout the world. (For some of the major contributions and reviews see Butler 1928; Williams 1932; Hudson 1958a, b, 1961, 1963, 1965; Dennie 1962; Hackett 1963, 1968; Goff 1967; Crosby 1969; Brothwell 1970; Steinbock 1976, and Baker and Armelagos 1988). Most of these discussions cover the arguments for and against the presence of syphilis in the pre-Columbian New World and its origins in Europe. I do not want to review this literature here because it is too easy to become side-tracked and entangled in a controversial and inconclusive web of information concerning this subject and what is, in my view, the impossible task of differentiating between bone lesions caused by one or other of the treponematoses. Moreover, in Australia's case and for this work the bulk of these arguments are irrelevant. Nonetheless, having said this, the place of the Australian evidence for understanding how treponemal disease has affected humanity across the globe is very important. Certain aspects of the main arguments need to be reviewed because they have some bearing on the Australian evidence I present later.

In recent years some very convincing evidence for the existence of pre-Columbian treponematosis has been found in North America. This has come from pre-Columbian human remains found in a number of sites stretching the length of the Americas, with the oldest discovered at the Indian Knoll site, Kentucky, and dated to about 5000BP (Brothwell 1970; Steinbock 1976; El-Najjar 1979; Baker and Armelagos 1988). While there is still some disagreement among researchers concerning certain interpretative details of the evidence, there is now a general acceptance that this disease existed among the North American Indians long before the trees used to build Christopher Columbus' *Santa Maria* began to sprout.

> The abundance of New World human skeletal material exhibiting lesions suggestive of treponemal infection, particularly when encountered in large skeletal populations, and the discovery of treponemal antigens in the remains of a Pleistocene bear ... clearly demonstrate the presence of the disease prior to 1492. (Baker and Armelagos 1988:720)

Our evidence for a long history of the treponemal spirochaete among humans is stronger than ever, although when it first appeared in other parts of the world still remains a mystery. Another intriguing question is: how did this disease spread to other continents and when? Perhaps yaws and the non-venereal syphiloids, such as bejel of the Middle East and the treponarid of Australia, developed independently! It might be that there is little mystery to all of this. Like *Streptoccocus* and millions of similar organisms, treponemes probably developed as just another evolutionary product of this planet, perhaps spreading sub-clinically across the globe via certain animal carriers. Later, varieties with slightly different clinical appearances may have arisen in centres of human population growth where intensification of the pathological environment provided suitable conditions for highly infectious forms to be successful and thrive in a new host: humans.

Non-venereal or endemic treponematoses have been given a variety of colloquial names, suggesting that some people have had a long-term familiarity with them. In Scotland it was known as the 'sibbens' (Morton 1967), the 'radesyge' in Norway, 'saltfluss' in Sweden, 'spirocolon' in Greece and Russia (Steinbock 1976) and the 'frenga' in Bosnia (Grin 1953). 'Pinta', of course, is another form, but this is confined to the Americas and does not manifest itself skeletally. 'Bejel' of the Middle East is another form of 'treponarid' which is the most familiar term used for this disease in Australia (Hackett 1963). It is, as its compound blend name implies, a treponemal infection found in arid desert regions, but among the Aranda people of central Australia it is called *erkincha* (Hackett 1936a, the spelling used here conforms to Spencer and Gillen 1969:443).

For this study I include yaws in the Australian endemic forms simply because it *is* endemic to the tropics, and was present in Papua New Guinea, as well as other neighbouring regions of Oceania in pre-colonial times (see Chapter 11 also). All these equatorial and sub-equatorial regions provide a suitable environment in which the yaws spirochaete (*Treponema pertenue*) can live and be transmitted (Cilento 1942; Hackett 1947; Manson-Bahr 1961). The important palaeo-epidemiological question is how long has treponemal disease been in the region? We may never know the answer to this, but if it was around in the early Holocene then there is no reason why it would not have entered Australia from Papua New Guinea when these two large land masses were joined by lingering low sea levels. Others have already suggested that 'Yaws was probably universal [in Papua New Guinea] in the pre-contact period' (Maddocks 1973:70). Early serological testing programs carried out in the 1960s among various New Guinea communities having little or no contact with outside influence have clearly shown yaws to be endemic and widespread in both Highland and lowland coastal communities (Garner and Hornabrook 1968, 1970, 1973; Garner, Hornabrook and Backhouse 1972). Earlier observations also noted the bodily ravages of the disease among Papua New Guinean people as well as gangosa, a destructive, ulcerous rhino-pharyngitis (*Rhinatrophia mutilans*) now generally accepted as a sequel to yaws (Breinl 1915; Haddon 1935; Cilento 1942; Manson-Bahr 1960).

Ninth-century crania from the Marianas Islands clearly show Hackett's 'discrete' lesion of treponematosis (Stewart and Spoehr 1952; Hackett 1976:372 and Fig. 4a). We know also that caries sicca, a long accepted diagnostic lesion of tertiary treponematosis, was present in Sarawak in the 16th century (Brothwell 1976). The palaeopathological evidence from New Guinea is confined to the island of Motupore, just off the south coast, and Nebira on the mainland. Calvarial caries sicca has been clearly identified in pre-contact, archaeologically-derived skeletal remains from both these areas, but these will be described further in Chapter 11. In the Pacific, Pietrusewsky (1969) has identified treponematosis in prehistoric Tonga and Bowers (1966) has raised the possibility of yaws causing some of the infections he noted among 864 traditional burials from the other side of the Pacific at Mokapu, Hawaii. There is no evidence for treponematosis in prehistoric New Zealand which tends to suggest that the trans-Pacific migrations to that country, which took place over 1000 years ago, came from areas unfamiliar with this disease (Houghton 1980). It seems reasonable to accept, therefore, that yaws was distributed widely throughout the region to the north of Australia, was very common in some areas and its origins in Melanesia go back as much as 1000 years. If one tentatively puts together these very small pieces of information from Micronesia, Polynesia and Melanesia, the direction of origin for treponematosis seems to point to the north.

Cecil Hackett and the Australian treponematoses

No discussion of treponematosis in Australia or this part of the world can ignore the work of Cecil Hackett. He devoted many years of his life to improving our understanding of the aetiology and epidemiology of the disease, including tibial bowing, as well as developing meticulous criteria for identifying skeletal lesions caused by the various forms (Hackett 1936a,b,c, 1968, 1974, 1975, 1978). These criteria have not been accepted by all workers but there is no doubt palaeopathology has benefited enormously from his research and for this owes him a lot. His first research in Australia during the 1920s and 30s was prompted because endemic forms of treponematosis were known to be present among groups of Aboriginal people living in central and northern parts of the continent. While working here, he also examined crania in various collections around the country. For example, in 1967–68 he examined over 9000 Aboriginal bones many of which, in his view, showed typical treponemal lesions that left heavy scarring on the vault and occasionally a gangosa-like destruction of the face (Hackett 1975). Among living populations, however, diagnosis of treponematoses is not normally undertaken by observing bone lesion morphology. It follows one or other of a series of serological examinations such as the Wasserman, Kahn, Kline, Hinton and VDRL tests (Robbins and Cotran 1979:406). Obviously, cutaneous lesions provide an immediate assessment of the stage which the disease has reached. Bone lesions are encountered only during the tertiary stages of the disease, which today, in most industrialised countries, rarely occurs. Lastly, and by no means least, the living patient can provide a history and possible origin of the condition. Needless to say, none of these are available to the palaeopathologist. In this case the benefits of Hackett's diagnostic criteria for identifying cranial lesions are obvious. Even so, bone infection tells us only that the disease reached a tertiary stage. There is some concern over the accuracy of these lesion criteria and doubt whether in fact a particular lesion has been caused by yaws, *erkincha* or venereal syphilis. Hackett's criteria are the best we have; they are used here for that reason and because they were developed mainly from observations made on Australian crania and as evidence of my respect for the extensive research he put into this work over many years.

For this survey I recorded all cranial lesions conforming to Hackett's (1976) 'contiguous' and 'discrete' scarring forms. In the contiguous series these included: nodular cavitation (Plate 6–7), serpiginous cavitation (Plate 6–8) and caries sicca together with stellate cracking within healed scars (Plate 6–9). In the discrete series only circumvallate cavitation (Plate 6–10) and radial scars were recorded (Plate 6–11). Naso-maxillary and/or palatal destruction and sub-glabellar nasal bridge collapse ('saddle nose') were observed also (Plates 6–12, 6–13 and 6–14). It is worth noting that these lesions are not always mutually exclusive and, in some cases, both serpiginous and discrete lesions were observed on the same cranium.

Plate 6–7
Nodular cavitation, typical of treponemal infection, in an individual from Rufus River.

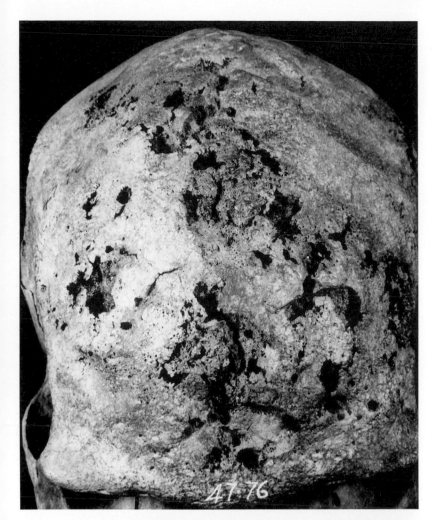

Plate 6–8
A good example of widespread serpiginous cavitation across the frontal bone of a man from the central Murray region. The scarring that lies across the sagittal suture indicates a chronic treponemal infection and one that has undergone healing. A treponematosis of this nature must have been similar to or part of the endemic form (erkincha) of central Australia.

Plate 6–9
Extensive caries sicca and healed scars surround a large hole in the left parietal of a woman from northern New South Wales.

Plate 6–10
This large scar on a cranium from the central Murray is typical of circum-vallate cavitation. It is almost identical to a lesion found on a ninth-century cranium from Tinian Island in Micronesia and described by Hackett (1976) as indicating an endemic treponemal infection.

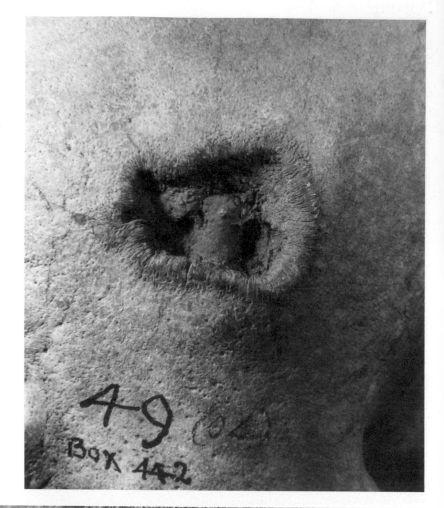

Plate 6–11
Radial scars with stellate cracking formed during healing of a large treponemal lesion in a person from the central Murray.

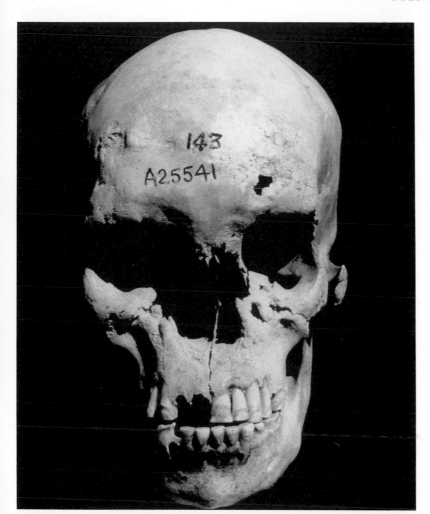

Plate 6–12
Widespread facial destruction in an individual from the Northern Territory. The infection has focussed particularly on the nasal opening and periorbital structures, typical in tertiary yaws sufferers.

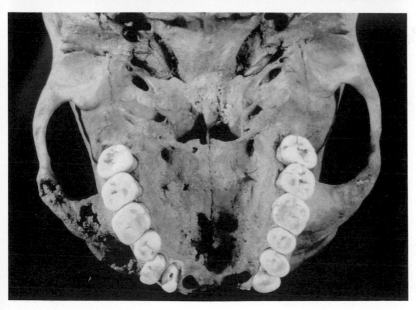

Plate 6–13
Treponemal infection has caused widespread damage to facial structures in this individual, partially destroying the palate, sphenoid and inferior surface of the left zygomatic arch.

Plates 6 – 14a, b

This central Murray individual had active lesions on the forehead, cheek and sub-nasal region at the time of death. One of the most notable areas of destruction is on the bony bridging of the nose, causing the typical collapsed appearance of these structures ('saddle nose') seen in long-standing cases of erkincha and yaws. Both the extent of the bony destruction and healed scars on the frontal bone suggest that this woman had the condition some considerable time. The healing indicates a biological familiarity with the disease and while the condition is not pleasant it rarely causes death.

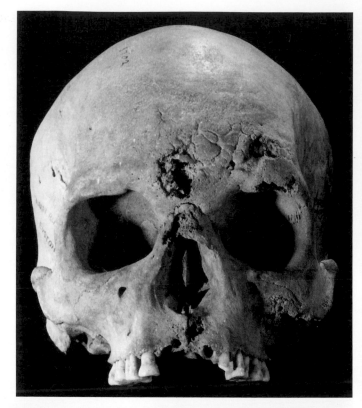

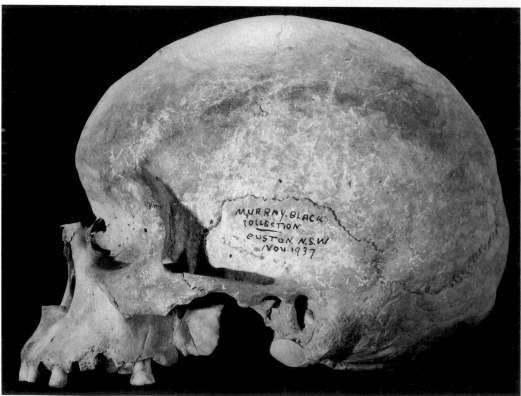

Treponemal infection in Australian Aboriginal populations

The central Murray has the most treponemal infection with the highest frequencies occurring at certain locations within it. These are: 16.1 per cent for males from Swan Hill and 14.3 per cent in females from Baratta; another frequency of 17.7 per cent in females from the Kerang location further east was obtained but the sample consisted of only 17 crania. Elsewhere, there is great variability of infection from one place to another among men and women. Females seem to suffer more from this disease than males, albeit the reverse is true on the east coast (Table 6–2). Frequencies are generally not very high anywhere, although the central Murray is the most prominent, with Rufus River to the west and then the tropics and desert areas (Table 6–3). It is interesting to note that with the exception of Tasmania and coastal Queensland, this type of infection is observed among skeletal remains from most parts of Australia and prominent among these are the arid and tropical regions.

Table 6–2   *Treponemal infection on crania.*

	MALES			FEMALES		
	n	*n̄*	%	*n*	*n̄*	%
CM	247	18	7.3	151	14	9.3
R	122	6	4.9	83	7	8.4
SC	138	3	2.2	123	4	3.3
DES	132	6	4.5	51	3	5.9
TRO	92	3	3.3	62	3	4.8
CTL	133	3	2.3	86	1	1.2

Area Codes:
CM–Central Murray, R–Rufus River, SC–South Coast, DES–Desert,
TRO–Tropics, CTL–East Coast

Table 6–3   *Comparison of non-specific and treponemal disease frequencies.*

	Non-specific Infection	Treponemal Infection
	%	%
CM	9.5	8.0
R	8.0	6.3
SC	3.3	2.7
DES	16.7	4.9
TRO	–	5.2
CTL	6.1	1.8

Area Codes:
CM–Central Murray, R–Rufus River, SC–South Coast, DES–Desert,
TRO–Tropics, CTL–East Coast

Discussion

Before moving on to the general discussion I want to try and clear up one point raised at the end of the last section. In 1974 Cecil

Hackett described an undated, but fairly recent, Tasmanian Aboriginal cranium held in the Anatomy Department of Edinburgh University, which he described as having lesions consistent with treponemal disease (Hackett 1974). A photograph of this cranium appears in an article by Møller-Christensen and Inkster (1965) and shows the lesions quite clearly. Although I have not personally inspected this cranium, the lesions, as they appear in the article, do seem to correspond to those originating from treponemal disease. Hackett concluded that the origin of these treponemal changes were possibly due to 'a childhood, and hence indigenous, treponemal infection which accompanied the original inhabitants on their migration into Tasmania from Australia about 10,000 years ago' (1974:442). With the benefit of hindsight and recent research, however, certain aspects of this conclusion can be reassessed. There is no evidence for treponemal disease in Australia crania from as far back as 10,000 years or the time at which Tasmania became separated from the mainland, about 6500 years ago. It is worth bearing in mind also that there was no real possibility of this disease being introduced from the mainland during that island's long isolation prior to European colonisation. Moreover, all the Tasmanian crania that I have inspected are completely free from treponemal lesions. The infection on this cranium is treponemal but it points more persuasively to European syphilis rather than an endemic form. This seems the most likely origin for the lesions when one considers the often inhumane treatment that befell many Tasmanian Aboriginal women at the hands of the sealers and whalers who frequented the southern coasts of Tasmania, even before the first official colony was formed in 1810.

Non-specific infection or not?

It is certain that some of the non-specific infection reported earlier in this chapter has treponemal origins, but just how much is difficult to say. All we can do is compare the frequency of cranial treponemal disease with that of the non-specific infection in post-cranial material (Table 6–3). In all areas of Australia the frequency of treponemal infection is lower than that of the non-specific type. I doubt whether by subtracting treponemal infection from the non-specific variety we can arrive at the *real* incidence of non-specific disease. It is better merely to provide both frequencies without explanation of either than speculate in such a way. In most cases, crania and post-crania cannot be matched, so it is not possible to link their respective lesions; Plate 6–15 shows a rare exception to this. These scapulae from the central Murray are associated with a cranium having typical treponemal lesions. Steinbock (1976:113) has indicated that while 42 per cent of tertiary syphilis sufferers have cranial lesions, only 26 per cent of them have osseous lesions of the post-cranial skeleton. Using these data, cranial lesions outweigh post-cranial lesions by almost 2:1, which would, in theory, suggest that even less of the non-specific infection

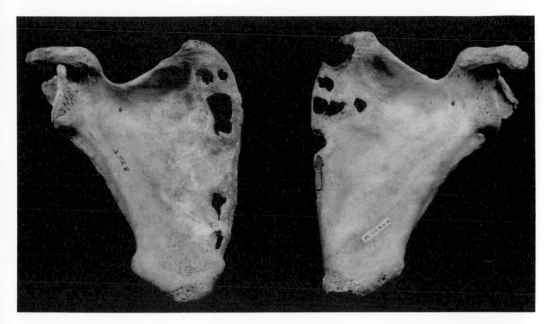

Plate 6–15
The bilateral lesions on this pair of scapulae from the central Murray are typically treponemal in origin. Scarring was also prominent on the associated cranium.

tabulated here has its origins in treponemal disease. It is impossible, therefore, to know how much post-cranial non-specific infection may have originated among the treponematoses although there might be much less than we think.

Syphilis or treponarid?

Is the treponemal disease in Australian Aboriginal skeletal material of an endemic or introduced variety? It took Cecil Hackett 40 years to assemble enough data to establish criteria for identifying syphilis in dry bone. In 1975, one year before the publication of his large monograph, he published a shorter paper in which he presented a differential diagnosis of European venereal syphilis and *erkincha*/yaws. It is important to include here a large section of what he had to say about this.

> For simple and immediate diagnostic criteria of syphilis the caries sicca sequence of calvarial changes, and nodes/expansions with superficial cavitation in long bones are recommended with confidence. Because the late [tertiary] bone lesions of acquired syphilis cannot be distinguished from those of yaws and treponarid [endemic treponematosis or erkincha], diagnostic criteria of syphilis are really evidence of treponematoses. Which of these three related infections is the cause of the bone changes can only be indicated by the provenance of the specimen (humid or arid), its accurate dating, and the way of life (urban or rural) that the population concerned might have lived. (1975:238)

He goes on:

> In European bones most calvarial sequestra are labelled syphilis but in a few diagnoses this is accompanied by (pyogenic) osteomyelitis. ... The absence of sequestra in Australian calvariae casts doubt on the purely syphilitic origin of these changes labelled syphilis in European calvariae. In Australian long bones sequestra are also absent. Most of the changes in aboriginal [*sic*] bones in Australian national collections are of the caries sicca sequence. A similar occurrence of yaws bone changes and absence of osteomyelitis were found in the 1950s in Western New Guinea by the first medical service doctors. In the Pacific area, skulls from a number of islands have caries sicca changes, e.g. New Hebrides, Solomon Islands, Samoa, and New Guinea, where clinical yaws was present until the recent penicillin mass treatment campaigns. (1975:238)

These statements raise several questions. Firstly, even though caries sicca can be indicative of syphilis, unless it is accompanied by pyogenic osteomyelitis, it does not necessarily indicate syphilis, merely the presence of a treponematosis of some kind. Secondly, when the distinctive caries sicca lesion does occur, it should be related to the individual's natural and pathological environment and not assigned immediately to a syphilitic origin. Thirdly, cranial lesions alone are not reliable indicators of the type of treponemal infection which caused them. Finally, neither European pyogenic osteomyelitis nor the 'nodes/expansion' changes have been found in Aboriginal remains, either in this study or others (Sandison 1980). By using Hackett's criteria, therefore, there seems to be an absence of overt signs of syphilis among Aboriginal skeletal collections.

While based on long-term clinical and comparative investigation, Hackett's work cannot be used for accurate differential diagnoses of the various forms of treponematoses. What it does do is illustrate the problems of diagnosing *any* specific treponemal disease in dry bone. Even if we cannot properly identify a particular type of treponemal infection, we do know one when we see it. At this point it is appropriate to ask: was it possible for syphilis to be present among Aboriginal populations before the arrival of the first European colonists in 1788? If not, then any pre-contact evidence for treponemal disease must indicate an endemic form.

Although it seems unlikely that syphilis was here before colonisation, there may have been a slim chance of sporadic introductions into parts of northern Australia. Transmission may have been facilitated by contact with Asian and Indonesian fisher-traders, if they, in turn, had the disease, or by an occasional brush with one of the rare European visitations which began at least 150 years before Captain Cook landed here in 1770. We have to consider, however, that syphilis is not usually present in a population in which yaws is endemic, such as Indonesia (Hackett pers. comm.). In that case, it seems highly unlikely that it would have entered Australia through contact with northern neighbours. The Macassans, who fished Australia's warm northern waters for sea cucumber (*bêche-de-mer*) for several hundred years before Cook's arrival and were well known to the Aboriginal people of the north, are, therefore, not likely to have carried this disease. Nevertheless, even in the unlikely event that it was brought here from time to time, the natural cross-immunity between syphilis and the endemic yaws that was already here, would have prevented its spread. But yaws must have been introduced at some time in the past and the Macassans may have been the origin of that introduction. If it is unlikely that venereal syphilis existed in Australia before first white settlement, therefore, any disease causing similar bone lesions is more likely to have been tropical yaws. Away from the coast, in central parts of the continent, such lesions were caused by *erkincha*, an arid region version of yaws. An assumed absence of yaws in the south of the continent automatically puts any treponemal lesions found among people there in the syphilis category and, by definition, post-contact in origin. Hence the circular argument used by those who believe all these lesions have their origins in European syphilis even though crania from the Murray River, for example, were found in large, traditional burial grounds. Therefore, the firmest evidence for endemic treponematosis would come from skeletal remains displaying diagnostic lesions and dated to before 1788. No material with these scars has yet been individually dated.

In reviewing some of the earliest observations of treponemal disease in Australia, Hackett (1936c) was persuaded that most accounts were probably wrong in their diagnoses that European syphilis was prevalent among Aborigines. He believed a large number of the symptoms described were more reminiscent of yaws which, as many accounts were recorded in southern areas of Australia, must have been related to the *erkincha* or endemic treponematosis of central Australia rather than tropical yaws. Hackett pointed out also that reports of 'leprosy' and 'cancer', believed by early settlers and explorers to be the causes of terrible facial destruction among Aborigines, were almost certainly cases of the gangosa-like lesions that often accompany the tertiary stage of yaws and *erkincha*. He cites Mackillop's observations along the Daly River in the Northern Territory as an example: 'Cases of cancer are frequent … and there are cases also of something very like leprosy …' (1893:258–9). It should be noted, however, that bone cancer affects between one and three people per 100,000, and I have encountered comparatively few cases of cancerous lesions in Aboriginal remains (see Chapter 9). It seems, therefore, extremely unlikely that Mackillop saw 'frequent' cases of cancer; it is more likely they were tertiary stage treponemal lesions or gangosa. Similarly, Cadell reported women 'without noses' near the Blyth River, also in the Northern Territory, which was probably destructive gangosa, resulting from yaws, rather than the syphilis he attributed it to or the leprosy which a medical acquaintance of Cadell's thought it could have been (1868:21). The woman in Plate 6–16 photographed at Hermannsburg Mission early this century probably typifies the kind of condition Cadell observed. According to reports from medical officers residing in the area, yaws

Plate 6–16
This Aboriginal woman has suffered general facial destruction particularly around the perinasal region. There is total collapse of the nasal bridging and altered features in the sub-nasal area together with scarring of the forehead. Such destruction has a long history; the treponemal condition in this woman must have begun in her early years and at a time when she lived among traditional people in the Western Desert region.

was widespread among Northern Territory Aborigines at the end of the nineteenth century (Breinl 1912; Holmes 1913; Breinl and Holmes 1915). The ethnohistoric photographs of Baldwin Spencer (Vanderwal 1982) and Herbert Basedow (1932) provide further graphic evidence of this (see below).

Other support for the endemicity of treponemal disease in north and central Australia, comes from an Aboriginal story relating the tradition of *erkincha*. This Dreamtime story of the central Australian Aranda people was related to the ethnographers Baldwin Spencer and Francis Gillen and is tied to a myth associated with the transmission of a disfiguring disease (1899:443). Part of the myth is concerned with native cat or Achilpa men who were the creators of landmarks and Dreaming tracks across Aranda country. It was these mythical supermen who first had the disease and who died when the land was flooded by other Dreamtime spirit people representing another totem. A stone arose where the Achilpa men died and since then it has become known as *Aperta atnumbira*, meaning a stone which causes a diseased growth to issue from the anus, a common symptom among *erkincha* sufferers. In a footnote Spencer and Gillen described the disease:

> The disease is one which is common amongst young people, only attacking each individual once. It affects only the glands of the part of the body in the

neighbourhood of the sore. At first sight it has much the appearance of being syphilitic in nature, but Dr Eylmann, who has studied it, is of the opinion that it is distinct from syphilis. It usually appears in the anal region, under the arms or legs, or close to the mouth. (1969:444)

Spencer and Gillen noted that the Aranda employ a restriction on the eating of native cat (*Dasyurus geoffroyi*) not just by the members of the Achilpa totem but on almost everyone. Only small amounts are allowed to be eaten by the old people because: 'it is supposed that any one, save an old man or woman, eating Achilpa would be afflicted with a special disease called *Erkincha*' (1899:168). The way this myth is related is interesting. Implicit is the association of age with the onset of the disease: it is only contracted by the young. After reaching adulthood the danger is past and it becomes very difficult or impossible to contract. Those that develop the symptoms are believed to have broken the food taboo, thus there is a reason for the existence of the infection. This account strongly suggests that the Aranda know the aetiology of the disease through an intimate familiarity with it that existed long before any non-Aboriginal people entered the region. Further support for this conclusion comes from the Dr Eylmann (1908) mentioned by Spencer and Gillen and who confirms that Aborigines said they could only contract *erkincha* once, and that was during childhood. Endemic treponematosis is contracted only by children and young adults. *Erkincha* may also have been the disease the explorer Stuart encountered at Attack Creek (Northern Territory) in 1862, when he saw one of two elderly men who was 'very much diseased and lame' (1865:440). Basedow (1932) published several photographs of Aboriginal people suffering severe facial lesions (gangosa). These lesions are normally accompanied by shiny scar tissue indicative of a long-standing, localised infection with treponematosis which has destroyed underlying structures of the facial skeleton. A notable example is seen in an old woman from the Cooper Creek area in whom it has also caused blindness (Plate 6–17). Plate 6–18 shows how treponemal infection could severely affect the young. Here, we see a 15-year-old boy from the Kimberley region of northwestern Australia with extensive, active and very destructive facial lesions around the nose and mouth.

Apart from the tradition of *erkincha* reported by Spencer and Gillen (1899) and Eylmann (1908, cited in Hackett 1936a:738), a number of reports from medically-qualified people have confirmed the existence of gangosa over large areas of the continent (Gray and Cleland 1933; Hackett 1936a; Black and Cleland 1938). Cilento (cited in Cleland 1928:143) states that syphilis was rare around Townsville, northern Queensland, and the treponemal disease of Aborigines there was due to yaws. Labour from island Melanesia and Polynesia was brought to the Townsville area to work in the sugar cane fields during the latter half of the nineteenth century. So it is difficult to know whether tropical yaws may not have been introduced into the region at that time. The common socio-economic status of both the islanders

Plate 6–17

This picture of a 50-year-old woman from Coopers Creek in northwest South Australia was taken by Herbert Basedow in 1919. It shows another example of gross facial destruction (gangosa) due to treponemal infection which has also caused blindness in the left eye. The primary focus of the infection is around the nose and mouth, causing severe disfigurement of the facial features. (The Basedow Collection, courtesy of the National Museum of Australia)

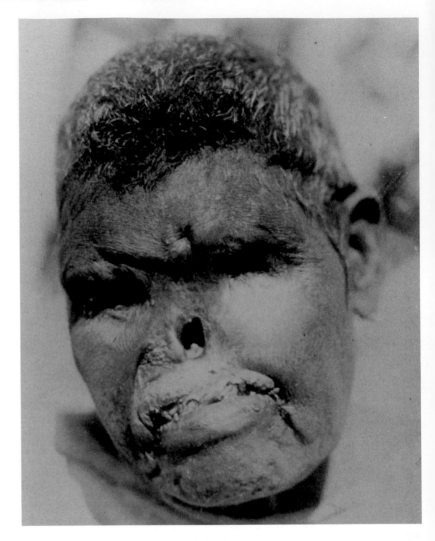

and the Aboriginal population in this area automatically drew them together on many levels and subsequently any tropical yaws could have been introduced into the latter community with comparative ease.

I have already cautioned that ethnohistoric observations of Aboriginal disease must always be carefully assessed, but the presence of an Aboriginal myth to explain *erkincha* is compelling evidence for its pre-European origins, not to mention the many traditional bush medicines used for curing endemic yaws in the Northern Territory (Foelsche 1882; Webb 1933). The syphilitic-like disease described at the time of first contact, which caused facial disfigurement, was probably a tertiary stage treponemal disease. Its symptoms are strongly indicative of a chronic infection and its wide distribution among Aboriginal people living in widely separated regions stretching from northwestern New South Wales and northern South Australia across to the northwest and north Australian coasts, is further convincing evidence for its pre-European origins. I find it difficult to believe that syphilis would have spread so far, so quickly and so thoroughly, particularly

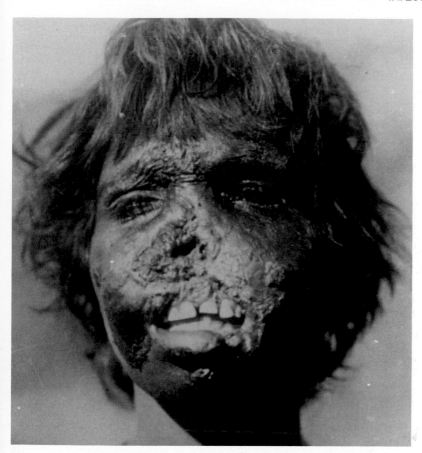

Plate 6-18
Herbert Basedow recorded this case of gangosa in a 15-year-old boy from Port George IV in northwest Australia. The picture was taken in 1916 and shows the typical oro-nasal destruction seen in the preceding two plates. This graphically illustrates the active state of the disease, which has destroyed much of the facial region and forehead, caused damage around the right orbit and has extended to the eye itself, causing blindness. (The Basedow Collection, courtesy of the National Museum of Australia)

through relatively sparse, very remote and isolated populations, from a 1788 introduction at a very distant Sydney Cove. Even recent medical examination of Aboriginal people still living a traditional lifestyle in remote parts of the western desert region of Western Australia and the Northern Territory continues to testify to the continuing endemicity of yaws in these areas (Garner *et al.* 1972).

It is likely, therefore, that the infectious disease in post-cranial bone from the desert sample used in this survey is an indication of the presence of endemic treponemal disease. Note also that most of the desert crania examined were collected in the late nineteenth century and if we take into account the death of the individual, which must have occurred at least twenty or thirty years previously, and the long standing and tertiary nature of the condition, the treponematosis was almost certainly contracted before Europeans entered this region or lived anywhere near it. This notwithstanding, it is extremely unlikely, in my view, that these crania are even as recent as that. With the minimal likelihood of staphylococcal infection in the hot, dry desert environment, there is little to explain the frequency of chronic infection that appears in remains from this area (Table 6-3). I can only draw the conclusion that from a careful assessment of the historic accounts and the palaeopathological evidence there seems to have been a widespread existence of an endemic form of treponemal disease among traditional Aboriginal groups living in central and northern parts of Australia before non-Aboriginal settlement. These two sources of evidence point also to an extension of this disease into southern parts of the continent, so let us now turn to these areas.

I have left southern and southeastern Australia out of the discussion so far because of the complexity of trying to understand the origin, prevalence and distribution of endemic treponematoses in this region. The main reason for the complexity is the equivocal and often conflicting nature of early observations as well as the general lack of understanding about the speed at which syphilis spread through Aboriginal groups living close to the first European settlements. Some accounts suggest that treponemal disease was endemic, while others were convinced that this was the introduced European syphilis. For example, Aborigines around Melbourne could not remember having the syphilis-like disease before Europeans arrived (Eyre 1845). Further east, Eyre says that within three years, from 1841 to 1844, Aborigines living around Murundi on the lower Murray had become badly infected with it by their association with the townspeople. But Moorehouse (1840, cited in Basedow 1932:11), Protector of Aborigines in South Australia during the earliest days of the colony, relates that the Adelaide Aborigines knew of treponemal disease before Europeans arrived and believed that it came originally from the east (from the Murray River?). On the other hand, whalers and sealers visited the South Australian coast for many years before a permanent settlement was founded. Westgarth writing a little later, however, epitomises the problem that I have already outlined:

> But by far the most terrible of these accompaniments of colonization has been the spread of syphilitic disease. It has indeed been doubted that the introduction of this malady is due to Europeans, as it has been found to exist among tribes which had never previously communicated with the colonists, and who, when questioned upon the subject, could afford no satisfactory information as to how or when it appeared amongst them. But it is thought to be of a milder character and of less frequent occurrence among those tribes that have not mixed with Europeans. (1848:81–2)

His words ring as true today as then, describing the two main questions that still face us: yes, syphilis was a problem among Aboriginal people but there was evidence to suggest that an endemic form existed also. I want to pursue some of the ethnohistoric evidence further in order to understand the results that have been presented here.

In his well known description of Aborigines inhabiting the Murray, Lachlan and lower Darling rivers, Beveridge says:

> ... in general, it is supposed that the venereal disease amongst the aborigines [sic] is entirely due to the Europeans, but a greater error than this never had promulgation, for long before the advent of the white man it was one of the vilest scourges this ... people had to bear. The probabilities are that the trepang hunting

> Malays and Chinese first introduced it on the northern
> coast, centuries ago, whence it spread from one tribe to
> another, until at last the foul disease became a national
> calamity. (1883:22)

I have already suggested that treponemal disease of some kind may have been introduced into northern Australia some time in the past. The continental spread of syphilis would certainly have been possible through the widespread system of Aboriginal trade routes that crossed the entire continent, but over hundreds of years yaws/*erkincha* could have been communicated in this way also. Traditional trading routes provided lines of communication between widely separated groups of people who were normally separated by hundreds of kilometres. Sometimes gatherings numbering in the hundreds would congregate at trading centres after weeks of journeying. Once there they would participate in ceremonies that reinforced alliances and ties with other groups and barter and exchange various sorts of material culture, the narcotic native tobacco or *pituri* (*Duboisia hopwoodii*), and swap songs and stories. In fact, even in remote areas, such as far western Queensland, groups of over 500 people regularly came together from as far afield as the Gulf of Carpentaria and the Flinders Ranges of South Australia (Watson 1983). With regular connections between the far north and deep south of the continent, disease entering the network from north or south could easily travel to the centre and opposite ends of the country and, indeed, some have argued that this is how smallpox crossed the continent: from south to the north and vice versa (Butlin 1983; Campbell 1983).

While Beveridge's comment above seems straightforward enough, at the same time it is easy to see why the early settlers might not have wanted to accept the responsibility for the introduction of syphilis and would want to shift the blame to Macassan fishermen or explain it as an indigenous disease. Nevertheless, it is interesting that the disease was reported to be of an allegedly milder character than syphilis and that Aborigines could not remember when it was first introduced. At this point is is worth recalling what we have already learned from the central and northern parts of the country in this regard. One of the earliest comments comes from Collins, writing at the time of the First Fleet:

> It was by no means ascertained whether the lues venerea
> [venereal syphilis] had been among [the Aborigines]
> before they knew us, or whether our people had to
> answer for having introduced that devouring plague.
> Thus far is certain, however, that [the Aborigines] gave
> it a name, Goo-bah-rong; a circumstance that seems
> rather to imply a pre-knowledge of its dreadful effects.
> (1798:496)

This is not necessarily true. Interestingly, Collins also tells us that the Aborigines around Sydney gave smallpox a name (*Gal-gal-la*) indicating that an Aboriginal name for a disease does not necessarily prove its endemicity. Nearly 30 years later Cunningham made an interesting observation:

> I have often observed the men, too, labouring under the
> eruptions of the skin resembling syphilis, and open
> tumours also in their groins apparently of the same
> nature; but time with them cures all disorders. (1827:45)

Some of the confusion surrounding early observations of treponemal disease could be avoided if we concentrate on the presence of destructive lesions. These constitute inordinately stronger evidence of tertiary infection than interpretations based on 'ulcerations', 'pustules' and other skin lesions in groins, necks and under arms. Also, it is clear that because obvious signs of this disease were not reported by the majority of early explorers, this does not mean that it was not present in a sub-clinical sense.

All cutaneous lesions and swellings prominent enough to be described are of little value for differentiating between endemic and introduced treponemal infection as these can occur in both conditions (Manson-Bahr 1961; Robbins and Cotran 1979). Symptoms such as *granuloma pudenda*, swellings in the groin and under the arms, gangosa or facial destruction, rashes and curved (boomerang) tibia seem to occur in, or be associated with, most of the treponematoses (see below). However, the first of these, *granuloma pudenda (granuloma inguinale)*, which is often associated with treponemal disease among Aboriginal people (Basedow 1932), has recently been reappraised:

> Because it is so often associated with other venereal
> infections and because the usual site of involvement is
> the genital region, it has been called a venereal disease.
> However, this designation might well be inappropriate
> since the evidence that the disease is spread by sexual
> contact is somewhat equivocal. Concurrent infections in
> husband and wife are uncommon. (Robbins and Cotran
> 1979:420)

There are a number of comments to be made about these remarks. The first is that observers often do not seem to be sure of what they are seeing, or at least the earlier ones do not, otherwise they would have made a positive identification of at least venereal syphilis. Or, perhaps Aborigines were suffering two diseases: syphilis and an endemic form of treponematosis. This is difficult to believe because of the cross-immunity believed to exist between the two (Cannefax *et al.* 1967; Abbie 1969; Garner *et al.* 1972; Jacobs 1978). Such a situation would be very confusing because of the various symptoms involved. Is the cure of which Cunningham speaks, however, indicative of endemic treponematosis, rather than the more fatal syphilitic type? It could be argued that Aboriginal recovery, in the majority of cases, implied a familiarity with it. Further, if the disease was milder than the imported syphilis, this too might suggest a long-standing familiarity. We must not forget also the fact that some Aborigines believed they had the disease before the arrival of colonists; but if this is true where does this leave the cross-immunity arguments? Perhaps syphilis did not cause the health problems among the Aboriginal com-

munity that we are often led to believe. Observations of lesions may
have largely been of the endemic variety and cross-immunity among
these sufferers afforded them protection from syphilis. The last point
to make is that any recently introduced infection, particularly one that
severely maimed, would surely have been fresh in the minds of older
Aborigines and not forgotten as implied in some accounts. Perhaps
the long-held belief that syphilis had devastating effects on the Aboriginal population at large, should be reconsidered. It may be that in
some areas the presence of endemic treponematosis pricked the con-
science of European observers and falsely led them to believe that all
syphilis-like lesions were indeed syphilis and did not stem from an
endemic infection. This line of argument cannot be taken further
because it raises many imponderables to which there are no suitable
answers at this time. One thing is certain, however, the ethnohistorical
evidence alone is not good enough to present a clear picture of the
problem. I offer this interpretation of the evidence as just that—an
interpretation; but it cannot be said that syphilis was not a problem
among the Aboriginal community in some parts of the continent.

What about the geographical distribution of endemic treponematosis? I implied above that perhaps not all areas had this form of
infection. In this regard, it is worth noting one more account and one
of the earliest and most famous of its type concerning a treponemal-
like disease among, what were then, remote living Aborigines. It is
that of Sturt, written during his exploration of the Murray River
between Euston and Rufus River in January 1830: 'The most loath-
some diseases prevailed among [the Aborigines]. Several were disabled
by leprosy, or some similar disorder, and two or three had entirely
lost their sight (1833:94). (I refer the reader again to Plates 6–16, 17
and 18.) As he went a little further west, his remarks are more
extensive:

> The most loathsome diseases prevailed throughout the
> tribes, nor were the youngest infants exempt from them.
> Indeed, so young were some, whose condition was truly
> disgusting, that I cannot but suppose they must have
> been born in a state of disease; but I am uncertain
> whether it is fatal or not in its results, though, most
> probably it hurries many to a premature grave. How these
> diseases originated it is impossible to say. Certainly not
> from the colony, since the midland tribes alone were
> infected. Syphilis raged among them with the most fearful
> violence; many had lost their noses, and all the glandular
> parts were considerably affected. (1833:124–125)

A couple of points need to be made. First, Sturt sees a disease which
certainly resembles tertiary treponematosis among people separated
from the colony by uninfected groups. This seems to me firm evidence
that it was not spreading from settlements in the east or upriver from
seafarers at Encounter Bay on the South Australian coast. Second, even
if the occasional convict escapee, infected with syphilis, fled into the
interior and survived, it seems highly unlikely that a lone individual
would have caused such widespread infection among so many

Aboriginal people. Then the disease would have had to reach a tertiary stage before it caused such prominent facial destruction. Third, there is no evidence for the existence of leprosy among Aboriginal people living in southern or any other part of Australia at that time. Sturt's observation that ' ... the midland tribes alone were infected' is interesting because endemic treponematosis among Amazonian Indians has been shown also to be confined to a group of tribes, while those living around them often remain unaffected (Black 1975). Similar results have emerged in Papua New Guinea, where great variability in seroreactivity has been observed between different villages and language groups (Garner and Hornabrook 1973).

So, early observations and descriptions of disease among Aborigines cannot be considered firm evidence for the presence of venereal syphilis and other forms of treponemal disease. This, of course, must be tempered by considering the area in which the observations were made, such as the Northern Territory, where encounters with yaws were more likely, and the time at which observations were made. The evidence from this survey points to an indigenous form of treponemal disease being present among people in north and northwestern Australia, arid areas of central Australia, South Australia, the channel country of western Queensland, parts of the Murray and Darling Rivers and maybe even further east. There is little doubt that endemic treponemal infection in Australia had a much wider distribution than we have previously thought and the palaeopathological evidence has certainly provided us with a better understanding of this distribution than we had before.

Tibial bowing

Anterior bowing of the leg occurred in a number of prehistoric groups (Stewart and Spoehr 1952; St Hoyme 1969; Goldstein *et al.* 1976) as well as modern populations from all over the world (Bahr 1914; Chesterman 1927; Wilson and Mathis 1930; Hackett 1936a, 1951; Zivanovic 1982). One of the first reports concerned with sabre-like or bowed tibia is that of Topinard (1894:299–300): 'The first time it was observed was in the tibias of the family buried at Cro-Magnon'. He tells us that 14 per cent of 200 tibiae from Parisian cemeteries, dated from the fourth to the tenth centuries, were bowed and comments on 'the character which the tibia sometimes presents, and which bears the name platycnemia, or sabre-like' (1894:299). It is not clear whether platycnemia, or the lateral flattening of the tibia, appeared to Topinard sabre-like or whether there was a real diaphyseal bowing of the tibia. Platycnemia often accompanies bowing but in the present study only a distinct curvature of the tibia has been accepted as diagnostic. Wood (1920) has pointed out that more than 34 per cent of Aboriginal tibiae show platycnemia to some degree and he regards it as an anatomical variation rather than a pathology. Moreover, he does not mention bowing as an accompanying feature of platycnemia.

It is true that many tibiae have a platycnemic morphology but these are not necessarily bowed. Stirling (1894) referred to Topinard's findings when writing about the tibial curvature he observed in central Australia. Spencer and Gillen (1899) also noted it among the Aranda of the same region. Gillen thought that the bow resulted from the legs of the child hanging over the edge of a food container (coolamon) in which it lay. As the child grew and the leg became longer so its increasing length and the weight of the foot pulled the leg downward. Being 'soft', it, allegedly, would gradually bow, taking on the shape of a boomerang (Basedow 1932:21-22). On the upper Darling River of New South Wales, Newland (1926) knew an Aboriginal man who had antero-posterior bowing of the shins, while Spencer says that: 'an anterior curvature of the shin bone … gives rise to what the white settlers have described by the apt term "boomerang leg" ' (1928:194). Other references to this type of deformity have come from a number of clinically trained individuals who saw it in central Australia (Basedow 1932; Hackett 1936a; Black and Cleland 1938), northern Australia (Breinl and Holmes 1915; Breinl and Priestly 1915; Binns 1945) and Torres Strait (Elkington 1912). In the latter two areas, it occurred in association with yaws.

Bowing of the shins is known to be caused by yaws and other treponemal infections. For example, in late congenital syphilis it is caused mainly by longitudinal growth, which is stimulated by irritation of the epiphysis. Because the fibula largely remains unaffected by this process the diseased tibia bows antero-posteriorly between the two fixed points represented by the ends of the fibula (Murray and Jacobson 1972; Jaffe 1975:921). Subperiosteal and endosteal deposition of new bone (hyperplastic osteoperiostitis) of late congenital and acquired syphilis are other processes which cause tibial bowing (Steinbock 1976). Both these processes tend to thicken the tibial cortex, usually in the middle third of the diaphysis, blunting the anterior margin and giving the bone its bent look (King and Catterall 1959:118; Jaffe 1975:937). This 'pseudobowing' morphology, together with some other naturally occurring features which confer a bowed appearance on the tibia, such as a retroverted head, can trap the unwary into a completely erroneous identification of the condition.

The first thing to be noticed about the results of this survey is that tibial bowing is not a common condition (Table 6–4). The highest frequency is found in the tropics, but the small sample size from there makes the results unreliable. It is surprising that the east coast has the next highest frequency because of the minimal amount of infection already noted in this area. It also contrasts strongly with results from the south coast. Another surprising result is that from the central Murray, which has a marginally higher frequency than that found among desert dwellers. Another sample of 1052 tibia without precise location, but known to come from somewhere along the Murray River, revealed a frequency of 3.7 per cent. The bowing frequencies do not follow the trends already noted for either treponemal or non-specific infection. Only four of the 26 bowed tibia (15.6 per cent) from this unprovenanced sample have infectious lesions resembling

Plate 6–19a
The tibia at top appears to be bowed but, in fact, has a general osteitis causing sub-periosteal thickening of the cortices down the entire anterior border and part of the posterior border of the shaft. Irregular thickening of the diaphysis accompanies a large infectious lesion below the head of tibia on the bottom specimen. This may be an example of non-suppurative or sclerosing osteomyelitis which, because of the change in the shape of the diaphysis brought about by the infection, causes a bowing that is more apparent than real.

Table 6–4   *Tibial bowing.*

	n	n̄	%
CM	523	11	2.1
R	199	3	1.5
SC	283	2	0.7
DES	64	1	1.6
TRO	21	1	4.8
CTL	207	8	3.9

Area Codes:
CM–Central Murray, R–Rufus River, SC–South Coast, DES–Desert, TRO–Tropics, CTL–East Coast

either periostitis or osteitis. No osteomyelitis was found on any bowed tibia but its presence on other non-bowed specimens gave the appearance of 'pseudobowing' which comes from the general alteration of surface features of the bone shaft due to cortical swelling in the middle and anterior parts of the bone. The swollen appearance gives the effect of a bent shaft, rather than the presence of an actual diaphyseal curvature (Plate 6–19a). The remaining 22 tibiae in this sample are bowed in the classical fashion (Plate 6–19b).

These results support those of others who have noted bowing to the exclusion of overt signs of disease, particularly treponemal infection. It is possible, however, that in these individuals it is caused by some sort of sub-clinical treponemal infection in its primary or secondary stage. Serological surveying (TPI) of 1542 Aborigines living in

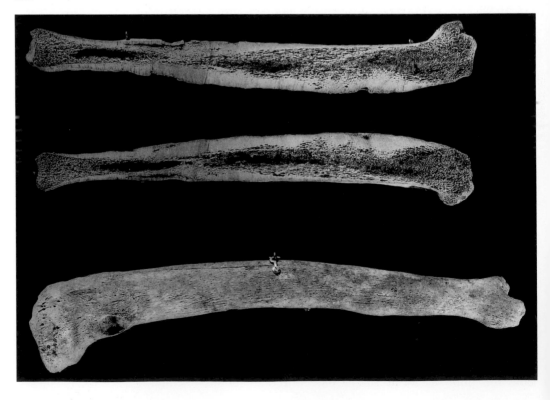

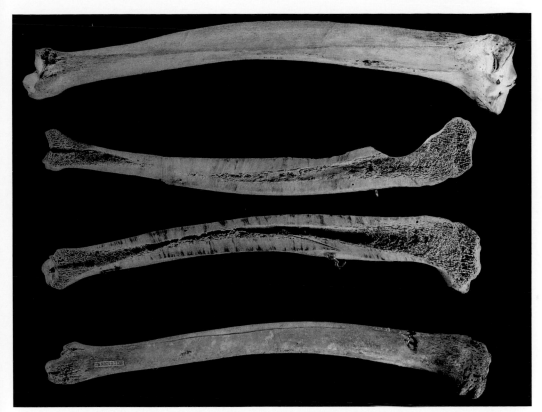

the Northern Territory revealed that 23 per cent tested positive for treponemal infection and in the vast majority of cases they were suffering endemic *erkincha* and yaws (Garner *et al.* 1972). Of these only 'a few cases of marked anterior bowing of the tibia were seen ... but ... there were many cases of slight bowing of the tibia ... (Garner *et al.* 1972:287). The bones of these individuals could not be examined in the same way as those in this study and the link between bowing and TPI positives was not explained. Hackett's data from the Northern Territory show that 49 per cent of 322 Aborigines who had boomerang leg also had associated scarring from tertiary treponematosis and only 9 per cent had boomerang leg alone (see Hackett's Table VIII, 1936a:22). Hackett's data is extremely interesting in the light of results obtained here. There is a very obvious discrepancy between the two, but tibial samples from areas where endemic *erkincha* and yaws are found are small. On the other hand, this condition may be more obvious in the living when different diagnostic criteria are used. If not, then the only conclusion that can be reached at this time is that there has been an enormous increase in the incidence of bowing among Aboriginal people between pre-contact and modern times. Before accepting this conclusion, however, let us investigate further.

Earlier research proposed a definite association between bowing and treponematosis. In a palaeopathological sense, however, bones that are bowed but which have no sign of infection cannot be categorised one

Plate 6–19b
None of these tibiae show any sign of infection. The cause of their bowed shape is unknown but examination of the internal structures reveals strong cortical bone formation (centre) which tends to eliminate any metabolic or nutritional deficiency as reason for their misshapen appearance. The reinforcement of compact bone, particularly in the mid-shaft region, could be a natural response to the bending of the diaphysis and the possible weakening that follows.

way or another. Alternatively, this deformity may have nutritional or metabolic causes, either stemming from or indirectly related to treponemal disease. One non-treponemal origin for such bowing is hyperfluorosis (Zivanovic 1982). It is worth noting, however, that the bones of people suffering from this condition quickly disappear during interment because of their very fragile nature. All the bones in this survey were very sturdy and in many cases thickened cortices suggest good nutrition and a normal metabolism (Plates 6–19a, b). One avenue of analysis might be to see whether those individuals having treponemal cranial lesions also have bowed tibiae, but this is not possible in the vast majority of cases for reasons discussed previously. Where possible, however, this has been carried out, particularly on eastern and southern remains where more whole skeletons are represented. Not one single example of associated bowing with accompanying cranial lesions has been observed, however.

Obviously the aetiology of bowed tibiae demands further investigation. Spencer raised the question of whether bowing (and camptocnemia) was pathological or not:

> To what extent either, or both, of these conditions are pathological is difficult to say. They do not seem to be associated with any indication of debility in the man or woman in whom they are present. (1928:194)

Similarly, those describing Bedouin remains in Israel have said: 'Whether the pronounced bowing in the long bones can be considered pathological, is not certain' (Goldstein *et al.* 1976:628). The same can be said for Australia. There is, then, little evidence for tibial bowing being associated with other forms of disease, particularly treponemal infection. Nevertheless, there is little doubt that it represents some form of pathological alteration to normal bone morphology. It is widely distributed and it certainly is not confined to northern and central parts of the continent alone. The frequencies in which it is found suggest that pronounced bowing affected few people. From the palaeopathological evidence it seems that it was most prevalent in the central Murray and along the east coast, not in central Australia where the main focus of attention on it has been placed. While these results extend the known range of this deformation, the prevalence of the condition along the Murray River may be more apparent than real in that the sample sizes from there are much better than those from areas where we know the condition to be endemic, such as central Australia.

Chapter 7

Osteoarthritis

General introduction

Osteoarthritic disease probably began as soon as skeletal tissues first evolved. At present our earliest evidence for this disease is found among the dinosaurs. Prominent examples include the aquatic Mesozoic reptile, *Platycarpus* and the giant *Diplodocus longus*, both of which lived around 100 million years ago and a case of ankylosing spondylitis has been reported in a 140-million-year-old armoured reptile from Britain, *Polycanthus foxi* (Moodie 1923: Karsh and MacCarthy 1960; Zorab 1961; Hollander 1962; Steinbock 1976). Similar bony changes appear in Miocene crocodilians and Pleistocene cave bears, sabre tooth tigers, mammoths, cattle (*Bos primagenius*), hyenas as well as large flightless birds like the Moa and Aepyornis (Wells 1964, 1973).

Osteoarthritis in humans also goes back a long way. Neanderthals were variably but sometimes severely affected by degenerative joint disease (Trinkaus 1983, 1985). It is now well known that it was arthritic changes to their skeletons that precipitated the initial misinterpretation of their posture and carriage and provided the unflattering image which has become synonymous with all that is brutish and primitive from our ancient past (Boule 1911-13, 1923; Smith 1924 cited in Straus and Cave 1957; Trinkaus 1985). Neanderthal remains from La Chapelle-aux-Saints, La Quina and La Ferrassie have arthritic damage to the temporomandibular joint, spine and hip, while at Shanidar it is confined generally to the major joints (Trinkaus 1983). Many of these changes can be directly attributable to activity levels associated with a lifetime of strenuous movement.

Skeletal studies of more recent populations show many forms of arthritic disease in varying frequencies and levels of severity. Some peoples studied include: Egyptians (Ruffer and Rietti 1912; Smith and

Dawson 1924; Wells 1964; Bourke 1971), Byzantines (Angel 1979), Europeans (Wells 1965; Gladykowska-Rzeczycka and Urbanowicz 1970; Edynak 1976), Peruvians (Hooton 1930) and North American Indians (Blumberg 1961; Chapman 1962, 1968; Angel 1966; Ortner 1968; Hudson *et al.* 1975; Jurmain 1977a, b; 1990; Hartney 1978; Kelley 1979; Martin *et al.* 1979; Pickering 1979; Larsen 1982; Bridges 1989). It is, however, the study of arthritis among hunter-gatherer people that has enabled us to assess the skeletal impact of work-related biomechanical stresses associated with a lifestyle that humans have followed for 99 per cent of their existence.

Arthritis (as I will refer to it) appears in many forms including pyogenic arthritis (Steinbock 1976), ankylosing spondylitis (Aufdermaur 1957; Zorab 1961; Hudson *et al.* 1975; Hochberg *et al.* 1978; Beute 1979), vertebral osteophytosis (Stewart 1966; Pietrusewsky 1969; Clark and Delmond 1979), rheumatoid arthritis (Blumberg *et al.* 1961; Short 1974; Klepinger 1979; Leisen and Duncan 1979; Riddle 1979), osteoarthritis (Duncan 1979) and arthritis of the temporomandibular joint (Pales 1930; Blackwood 1963; Alexandersen 1967; Seward 1976; Alpagut 1979). (For general overviews of the palaeopathology of arthritis and its aetiology see Karsh and McCarthy 1960; Bourke 1967; Steinbock 1976; Jurmain 1977a, b; Beute 1979; Cassidy 1979; Cockburn *et al.* 1979; Reyman 1979 and Ortner and Putschar 1981).

We know very little about the effects of biomechanical stress on the joints of traditionally-living Aboriginal people. This chapter makes a start by offering some general observations on the variety and frequency of arthritis from different parts of the continent and from these I make some interpretations concerning behaviour and socioeconomic status in different regions. The two major parts of the study include an analysis of arthritic degeneration (osteoarthritis) of the knee and elbow joints and the prevalence and severity of arthritic wear in the temporomandibular joint. Some individual examples of other related conditions, such as ankylosing spondylitis and vertebral osteophytosis, will be made at the end of the section dealing with the postcranial skeleton.

Osteoarthritis of the knee and elbow

I have referred before to the importance of describing methods, so I want to include a brief description of the three bony changes used here to record arthritis. These are: marginal osteophytosis, eburnation and erosion or pitting of articular surfaces. Generally, the degenerative sequence begins when the articular cartilage cushioning joint surfaces begins to deteriorate. This occurs principally when the subchondral bone contour becomes remodelled and changes shape. The consequent alteration then predisposes the joint to damage through injury or repetitive stressing. Erosion of the articular cartilage continues until

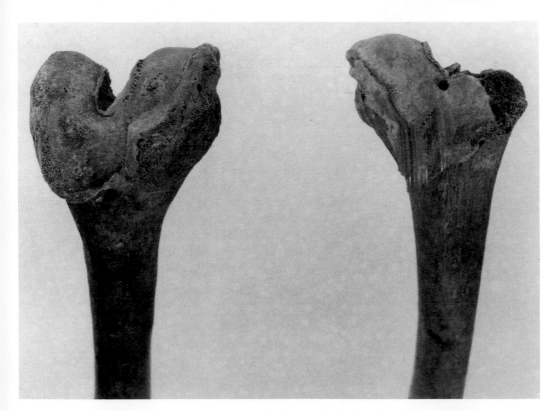

patches of tissue are lost, exposing small areas of unprotected bone. Bone-on-bone contact begins an irreversible destructive process through the rubbing together of the bare surfaces which tends to remove remaining sections of articular cartilage. The opposing bone surfaces which are exposed beneath become polished and the resulting eburnation appears as shiny patches composed of hard, dense but very thin compact bone (Plate 7–1). With continued joint use the polished surface eventually wears through, becoming pitted and grooved. Sub-cortical cystic defects, probably brought on by the degenerative process, also undermine this thin layer which contributes towards an inevitable and painful complete break-up of joint surfaces (Steinbock 1976).

A commonly associated feature of arthritis is osteophytosis. These exostotic bony outgrowths are usually located at the joint periphery (Plate 7–1). They can grow in three sorts of tissue, primarily the insertions of ligaments; in fibrocartilage, or even the periosteum (Rogers *et al.* 1987). They normally appear along the outline of the joint capsule insertion and margins of the articular cartilage but they can also form in areas away from the joint margin. Opinions differ as to whether osteophytes indicate the presence of arthritis (for opposing views see Bourke 1967 and Jaffe 1975). Nevertheless, most researchers seem to accept them as indicative of some sort of primary arthritic change and use them when diagnosing degenerative joint disease in both modern clinical as well as skeletal populations (Copeman 1955; Chapman 1968; Jaffe 1975; Adams 1976; Steinbock 1976; Jurmain

Plate 7– I
The left bone has been severely eroded on the anterior portion of the medial femoral condyle. Repetitive wear in this area has caused deep scoring of the surface together with eburnation and wide osteophytic flanging on both condyles. The hole in the intercondylar area is a post-mortem arti-fact. Well-formed flanging can also be seen tracing the joint capsule of the bone on the right.

1977a,b; Angel 1979; Clark and Delmond 1979; Cassidy 1979; Pickering 1979; Martin *et al.* 1979; Ortner and Putschar 1981). Jaffe's view, for example, is that osteophytes 'appear so commonly in primary osteoarthritis that they constitute a characteristic feature of its pathology' (1975:751). Osteophytes can be very prominent and in this survey were seen to project from the main body of the bone by as much as 8 mm on the distal humerus, 10 mm on the proximal tibia and 12 mm on the distal femur (Plate 7–2).

Some caution has been expressed concerning the interpretation of arthritis using single elements or joints only from skeletal populations (Rogers *et al.* 1987). While there is little disagreement in principle with these sentiments, the palaeopathologist working on hunter-gatherer populations is often faced with choices dictated by the material at hand. In many cases the available samples are not complete, fragmentary and often the researcher is at the mercy of history in terms of the way the individual(s) was collected and subsequently stored and cared for. The choice is, then, either to make use of what is available or ignore it completely. In many cases today, to ignore it is to lose it because of the disappearance of many collections of human remains. In the case of Aboriginal remains, almost all the major elements of the samples used here were separated from one another over fifty years ago and other elements, believed to be of little importance at the time, were discarded. While the whole skeleton is needed for the best interpretation to be made, we can learn little if those elements that are remaining are not surveyed.

Plate 7–2
Massive osteophytic lipping along the margin of the joint capsule attachment in this example reaches a maximum width of 12 mm.

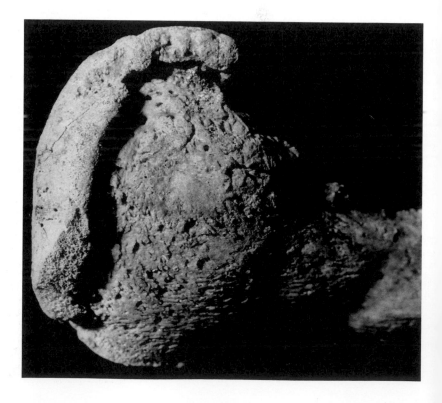

Results

The basic pattern of arthritis among Aboriginal groups shows that it affected males more than females, elbows more than knees and Murray people more than anyone else (Table 7–1). The most affected parts are the left knee and right elbow, the latter not surprising given the predominance of right handedness. The only exception to these general patterns is found on the east coast. Women there seem to have more arthritis in both elbows and knees than their male counterparts. By sub-dividing this coast into New South Wales and Queensland sections, however, knee arthritis among females from the latter group averages around 15 per cent whereas none was recorded in females from New South Wales. This frequency is higher than for males or females from anywhere else on the continent, except for the 18 per cent recorded in males from Kerang in the central Murray. Chronic forms of arthritis, involving eburnation or erosion of the articular surface, or both, are prominent in both knees and the right elbow of the Queensland coastal women. So, taken as a group, they not only have the highest frequency of arthritis, these women also have the most severe form of the condition. The only other area where females have arthritis of the knee is in the Murray, but it is not of the order of frequency seen in Queensland. In a sort of reverse situation, Murray Valley females have much higher frequencies of chronic degeneration of the elbow joint than their Queensland sisters.

Table 7–1   *Frequencies of arthritis in the major joints.*

		CM			R			SC			DES			CTL		
Elbow																
		n	n̄	%	n	n̄	%	n	n̄	%	n	n̄	%	n	n̄	%
Male	L	182	21	11.5	140	7	5.0	75	1	1.3	41	3	7.3	153	2	1.3
	R	216	44	20.4	149	15	10.1	86	7	8.1	36	5	13.9	167	7	4.2
Female	L	110	9	8.2	70	2	2.9	27	–	–	12	–	–	70	–	–
	R	106	8	7.6	76	–	–	54	–	–	17	–	–	70	3	4.3
Knee																
Male	L	194	15	7.7	99	3	3.0	87	7	8.1	29	3	10.3	94	4	4.3
	R	173	12	6.9	108	10	9.3	96	4	4.2	31	2	6.5	122	5	4.1
Female	L	100	1	1.0	55	2	3.6	70	–	–	7	–	–	48	4	8.3
	R	116	3	2.6	49	–	–	67	–	–	9	–	–	46	4	8.7
Knee and elbow combined																
Male	L	376	36	9.6	239	10	4.2	162	8	4.9	70	6	8.6	247	6	2.4
	R	389	56	14.4	357	25	7.0	182	11	6.0	67	7	10.5	289	12	4.2
Female	L	210	10	4.8	125	4	3.2	97	–	–	19	–	–	118	4	3.4
	R	222	11	4.5	125	–	–	121	–	–	26	–	–	116	7	6.0

Key:
L–Left, R–Right

Area Codes:
CM–Central Murray, R–Rufus River, SC–South Coast, DES–Desert, CTL–East Coast

With the exception of east coast people, arthritis of the knee is much more prominent in men than women but, interestingly, it is not common in the central Murray (Table 7–1). Another point to observe is that when it does occur, arthritis is much more bilaterally distributed in the men here than it is elsewhere, such as Rufus River and the desert. Desert men have the highest overall frequency of knee arthritis and while both elbows are affected, it is the right that is affected most. The pattern of degeneration in the knee displays a greater proportion of arthritic damage on the femoral condyles than on the opposing surface of the proximal tibia. I have no explanation for this (Table 7–2).

Extensive degeneration of both elbow joints, with a significant bias towards the right arm, is much more common among central Murray men than anyone else (Table 7–1). The highest frequency of arthritis from a specific location within the central Murray is 24 per cent in the right elbow of men living in the middle of the area at Swan Hill

Table 7–2 *Post-cranial osteophytosis, by area.*

		MALES						FEMALES					
		Left			Right			Left			Right		
		n	*n̄*	*%*	*n*	*n̄*	*%*	*n*	*n̄*	*%*	*n*	*n̄*	*%*
CM	a	99	7	7.1	111	21	18.9	54	5	9.3	55	3	5.5
	b	57	9	15.8	60	8	13.3	36	4	11.1	28	2	7.1
	c	49	3	6.1	56	3	5.4	40	3	7.5	36	4	11.1
	d	124	13	10.5	98	13	13.3	58	1	1.7	66	2	3.0
	e	78	1	1.3	77	6	7.8	50	–	–	49	–	–
R	a	34	1	2.9	35	3	8.6	21	–	–	23	–	–
	b	43	1	2.3	46	4	8.7	22	1	4.5	23	–	–
	c	64	2	3.1	62	4	6.5	30	1	3.3	32	–	–
	d	52	3	5.8	54	2	3.7	33	2	6.1	29	–	–
	e	52	–	–	52	2	3.8	26	–	–	25	–	–
SC	a	32	–	–	36	1	2.8	31	–	–	23	–	–
	b	21	–	–	28	6	21.4	21	–	–	19	–	–
	c	25	1	4.0	25	–	–	21	–	–	20	–	–
	d	34	2	5.9	33	1	3.0	35	–	–	32	–	–
	e	55	5	9.1	64	3	4.7	41	–	–	41	–	–
DES	a	23	3	13.0	21	2	9.5	4	–	–	6	–	–
	b	19	1	5.3	19	2	10.5	5	–	–	5	–	–
	c	21	–	–	15	3	20.0	4	–	–	6	–	–
	d	18	2	11.1	19	1	5.3	4	–	–	5	–	–
	e	24	1	4.2	28	1	3.6	4	–	–	6	–	–
CTL	a	56	2	3.6	64	2	3.1	27	–	–	26	1	3.8
	b	53	–	–	60	1	1.7	26	–	–	24	1	4.2
	c	59	–	–	56	1	1.8	20	–	–	21	1	4.8
	d	56	2	3.6	65	2	3.1	25	2	8.0	28	2	7.1
	e	49	2	4.1	66	3	4.5	24	2	8.3	26	2	7.7

Bone Code:
a–Distal humerus, b–Proximal ulna, c–Proximal radius, d–Distal femur, e–Proximal tibia

Area Codes:
CM–Central Murray, R–Rufus River, SC–South Coast, DES–Desert, CTL–East Coast

(Map 2–3). There is proportionally less arthritis in the knee than in the other major joints, particularly among women. The pattern of bilateral stress in the elbows of central Murray females emphasises the work imposed on both joints and suggests a greater use of the upper limb by these women than occurs in other areas. The slight left arm bias in these females is probably an artefact of the sample.

The small post-cranial samples available for the tropics made the inclusion of this area meaningless. In the 42 left and right, male, female and unsexed bones of all types from there, only three (7.1 per cent) showed any sign of arthritis. The female desert sample is very small also.

Other forms of arthritis

Only five (0.1 per cent) of 4777 assorted, but locally unprovenanced, post-cranial bones from the Murray and two (0.1 per cent) of 2770 from all other areas combined showed obvious signs of traumatic arthritis. These consisted of two male, one female and two of unknown sex in the Murray River group and two females from the combined sample. All cases of infectious arthritis come from the Murray. These include eight male, three female and another eight unsexed individuals (0.4 per cent). In several cases this infection has resulted in a complete ankylosing of various joints. Specific sites of fusion include the elbow, knee, ankle and toes (Plates 7–3 to 7–6).

Frequencies of vertebral arthritis have not been recorded for several reasons. The first is that in almost all collections the vertebral column has been separated from the rest of the skeleton and then disassembled

Plate 7–3
Infectious arthritis has brought about a complete ankylosis of the knee joint in this individual.

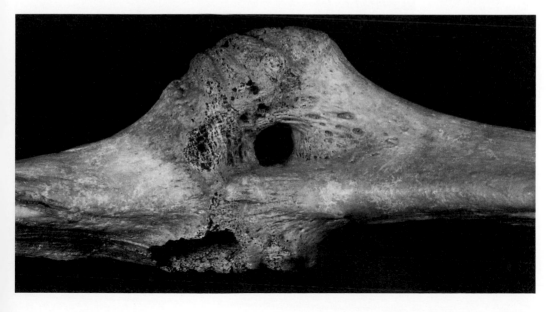

Plate 7–4
The ankylosed knee joint in this individual was probably the result of a wound that became infected. The damage around the knee area has occurred during interment.

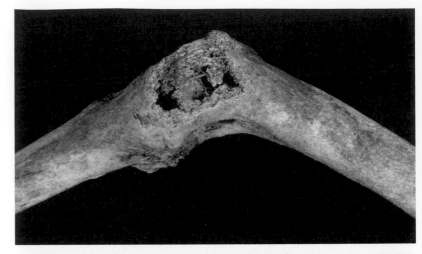

Plate 7–5
In this example of infectious arthritis there is multiple ankylosing of the bones of the foot and ankle, including the metatarsals, as though adjacent articular facets have melted into one another.

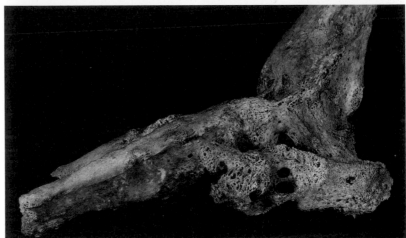

Plate 7–6
The ankylosis in this left foot involves both the intertarsal and tarso-metatarsal joints.

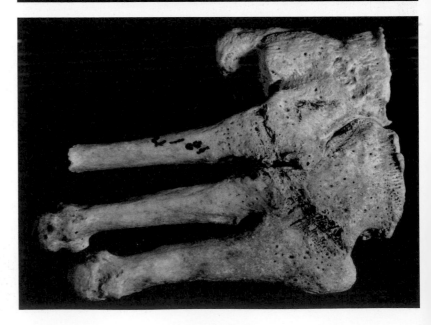

into its component parts which precludes any ageing or sexing. Secondly, there is no precise origin given for most of the vertebrae except to say that the majority come from somewhere along the Murray River. Thirdly, because of these factors and scope of my survey there has been little time to carry out a thorough investigation of this condition.

Severe forms of vertebral arthritis have, nevertheless, been observed among Aboriginal populations. Vertebral osteophytosis is the first of these conditions I want to mention. Osteophyte formation is very prominent in some cases. These have produced the 'parrot beak' projections around the superior and inferior margins of the vertebral body, often fusing the anterior sections of adjacent vertebrae in the classic form of vertebral osteophytosis (Plate 7–7). Although these changes could indicate an early stage of diffuse idiopathic skeletal hyperostosis (DISH), the fact that they appear on the lumbar vertebrae suggest that vertebral osteophytosis is a better diagnosis for them.

Ankylosing spondylitis is the second and much rarer of the vertebral arthroses observed. The condition has now been linked to an autoimmune disease which has a modern Caucasian frequency of 0.4 per cent (Manchester 1983). This chronic and progressive pathology may fuse several vertebrae or, in some cases, the whole vertebral column ('bamboo' spine) and nearly always affects the sacroiliac joint of the individual in the same way (Robbins and Cotran 1979). Ankylosing

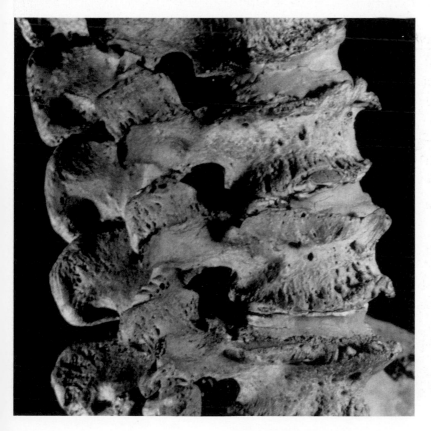

Plate 7–7
Vertebral osteophytosis with large anterior osteophytes on the vertebral bodies and fused apophyseal joints, both common features of the condition.

spondylitis is not degenerative but is most distinct because of the very smooth, 'melted candle wax', appearance of the vertebral column, which is caused by ossification of the apophyseal and costovertebral joints as well as the spinal ligaments (Plates 7–8 and 7–9). In the examples shown here the process has enclosed the spaces normally reserved for the intervertebral disc with a bony cover which is punctured in several places by foramina that continued to allow the passage of vessels. The new bone extends posteriorly as far as the pedicle and articular process to secure complete immobility of the spine in this region. Ankylosing spondylitis is also known as rheumatoid spondylitis or Marie-Strumpell disease, but although it is not associated with other forms of rheumatoid arthritis it is just as painful. Rheumatoid arthritis is more common in females whereas ankylosing spondylitis is predominantly a male disease by a large ratio of between 7 or 9 to 1 (Steinbock 1976). Unlike other forms of arthritis, it also occurs in younger men (between 20 and 40 years of age). Although its aetiology is largely unknown a firm association with the genetically controlled Human Leukocyte Antigen (HLA) system has been established. It has a particular link to the HLA-B27 antigen which occurs in 90 per cent of all those who suffer the disease and the highest linkage with disease for the HLA antigen system (Bodmer and Cavalli-Sforza 1976; Robbins and Cotran 1979; Stansfield 1981; Hoffbrand and Pettit 1984). The presence of ankylosing spondylitis in a particular cemetery population provides vital evidence, therefore, for genetic relationships

Plate 7–8
Ankylosing spondylitis in two lumbar vertebrae. These bones have been completely welded together by the ossification of the diarthrodial joint. While having the typical 'squared off' appearance of the vertebral body, fusion has taken place only on the right side.

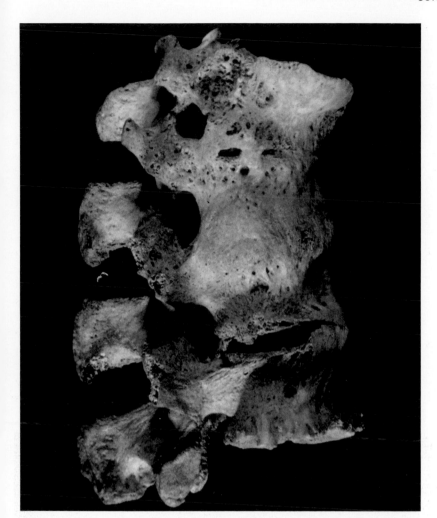

Plate 7–9
*Ankylosing spondylitis
in this fused section
of vertebral column
has joined the two
upper lumbar verte-
brae to a third
above and which is
now missing. The
general appearance
is mixed, however,
with the upper
section showing the
typical 'bamboo
spine' of ankylosing
spondylitis, while the
lower two vertebrae
have a less complete
fusion. They show
the anterior 'parrot
beak' join of
encroaching osteo-
phytes from the
anterior border of
the vertebral body,
typical in vertebral
osteophytosis.*

between populations. The original genetic disposition of the Australian Aboriginal population, particularly in terms of the HLA-B27
complex, is largely unknown, with the most reliable information
coming only from a few communities across the north of the continent (Kirk 1981). It is interesting, therefore, to find these examples
of ankylosing spondylitis because they add something to our extremely
limited knowledge of the genetic disposition of Aboriginal people that
lived in the southeast of the continent.

Bony ankylosing is evident also in the chest region. In one example
the first ribs have fused with the manubrium and lower ribs with the
sternum (Plate 7–10). There are examples also of costovertebral fusion
of ribs with thoracic vertebrae at the costovertebral articulation (Plate
7–11). Both examples shown here are from the central Murray area
but nothing further is known about them. It may be possible that
they are linked in some way with the wider ankylosing spondylitis
syndrome mentioned above.

Plate 7–10
The ankylosing spondylitis in this individual has involved the sterno-costal and sterno-clavicular joints.

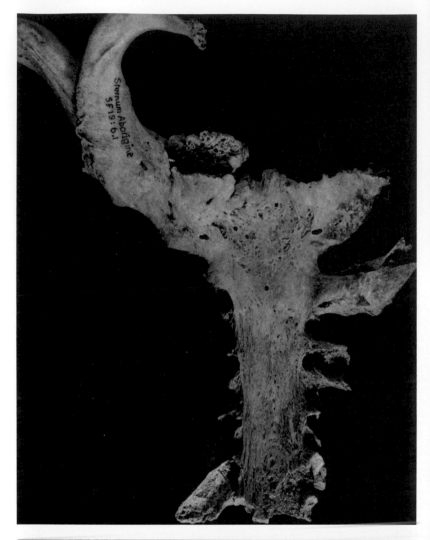

Plate 7–11
This individual presents an example of thoracic ankylosis at the costo-vertebral joint.

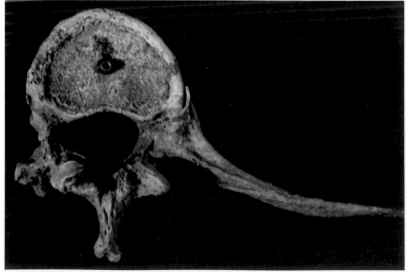

Discussion

In modern populations arthritic changes in the weight-bearing joints appear in about 4 per cent of people as early as the second decade of life and by 40 years of age 90 per cent of us will have them to some extent (Sokoloff 1974). An American survey revealed that nearly all cases under 45 years were mild, but by 75–79 years 23 per cent of sufferers have moderate to severe changes. In England 85 per cent of individuals between 55 and 64 years were found to have arthritis in at least one joint (Moskowitz 1974). Men under 45 years seemed to be affected more than women; a situation reversed after reaching 55 years when male–female frequencies become more equal. Equal numbers of black and white people have arthritis, although the knee joint of black people is affected more often. Contemporary North American Indians have a higher prevalence than either white or black people. Rather than a racial susceptibility towards the disease, however, these results are believed to reflect the generally lower socio-economic status of Indians and black Americans in that they undertake proportionally more manual occupations than whites.

Although ageing and mechanical stress play important roles in the onset of arthritic disease, environmental factors are thought to contribute also. Studies in northern Europe and America have suggested that the frequency is inversely related to latitude. Evidence for this has emerged from studies in Finland and Holland, which show that Finns have far less arthritis than Dutch people (Moskowitz 1974). A study of Jamaicans and Britons revealed, on the other hand, an equal incidence. Contrary to popular belief, there is no proof that cold, wet environments predispose individuals to arthritic disease; rather these climates stimulate muscular pain mechanisms which tend to simulate 'rheumatic' pain. Moskowitz (1974) tells us also that obesity may be an important cause of joint degeneration, particularly in the knee, since 61 per cent of overweight people suffer from arthritic degeneration, compared with 26 per cent of non-obese individuals. Whatever the complicating effects of other factors, overall it is probably the amount of wear and tear on a joint that determines its mild or severe degeneration at an early or late age.

A number of studies have established clear links between occupation and arthritis (Tempelaar and van Breeman 1932; Lawrence 1955; Kellgren and Lawrence 1958; Brodelius 1961; Anderson *et al.* 1962; Solonen 1966; Kouba 1967). The functional stress hypothesis has been used widely to make predictive statements concerning human behaviour patterns in past societies, especially hunter-gatherer and early farming communities. This logical approach has been recently questioned, however, in terms of its value, particularly if it cannot be supported by ethnohistorical or ethnographic data (Jurmain 1990). In other words, one should not expect to be able to say too much about specific activities from the pattern and frequency of arthritis but rather aim to present a wider and more generalised interpretation concerning work or activity-related stresses. We have to be careful here with how we use and apply such interpretation because it is easy for it to become an alibi for ethnohistoric observation rather than contributing to a new synthesis in its own right.

The age and sex of the population play an important part in any final analysis, but unfortunately, there is no absolutely reliable method for ageing Aboriginal skeletal remains other than employing the categories of 'young' and 'old' adult used here. Ageing by dental attrition is not accurate because differences between known individuals of like-sex and age precludes development of a standard method (Richards and Millar 1991). The fact that most post-cranial remains used in this survey have been separated from associated crania compounds this problem and renders them impossible to age using non-destructive methods.

In any palaeopathological analysis certain variables must be assumed to be constant. Here, for example, I can only assume that age predisposes Aboriginal people to arthritic degeneration, as it does others, and that this degeneration is made worse by human levels of physical activity. Obviously, these will vary between males and females and between groups living in different and even similar environments. Therefore, it is expected that the range of arthritic variation in a given population or across a continent like Australia will be a general reflection of variation in work related stress which, in turn, can be directly associated with demographic, behavioural, socio-economic and environmental factors.

The generally small frequencies of knee arthritis among Aboriginal people are surprising. One might expect them to be much higher among people leading a hunter-gatherer existence. It is hard to believe that female work loads, for example, varied so much that they would produce big differences in the frequencies of arthritis. Activities such as gathering of vegetable foods and shellfish and some minor hunting, were probably similar for almost all groups of Aboriginal women, wherever they lived. Shellfish gathering, particularly pipis (*Plebidonax deltoides*), may have been one activity that was more prevalent along the Queensland and northern New South Wales coast than elsewhere. Gathering of these shellfish was done using the toes to dig into the soft, sticky mud and sand along the littoral. This would produce strong, twisting, mechanical stresses on the knee and ankle joints as the toes bored down into the sand to feel for and expose the burrowing pipis. This form of shellfish gathering could have been more widely adopted in Queensland than on the south coast, thus accounting for the differences in the frequency of knee joint degeneration between these two areas. Age, of course, may play some part in these results but I am sceptical that there are large differences between female age structures in these two areas as there seems to have been between coastal and central Murray women, for example. On the other hand, Swanport women from further down the Murray seem to live longer than women in either the coastal or Murray groups and they do not show any incidence of arthritis of the knee. This suggests that the Queensland frequencies probably do reflect mechanical stresses and, thus, the type of work stress that was placed on the legs.

It might be expected that Aboriginal males would have more arthritis of the major weight-bearing joints than females, particularly in the knees. There are two reasons for this. One, their activity levels are believed to be higher and more vigorous and, two, in all areas of Australia men seem to attain the status of 'old adult' in greater frequencies than women. Arthritic changes in the knee rarely reach 10 per cent for any population examined and, generally speaking, there is greater involvement of the left than right knee. I suggest that these results can be accepted as a normal percentage of knee joint arthritis for males in any population, tribal or urban. Generally, therefore, the results obtained in this study for the lower limb are not unusual and, indeed, from studies on hunter-gatherer groups elsewhere they are somewhat as expected.

In modern populations, arthritis 'almost never involves the first metacarpophalangeal joints, wrists, elbows, or shoulders, except after trauma' (Moskowitz 1974:1043). Adams confirms this view: 'Osteoarthritis seldom occurs in an elbow that was previously normal' (1976: 249). Can we take it then that any incidence of degeneration in this joint is a reflection of unusual and/or excessive use and repetitive movement? Palaeopathological interpretations have generally supported this view, but they have also had to rely on explanations derived from known activities of individual groups or those being studied. Jurmain (1977b) has shown that arthritis in the elbow joint is not necessarily age related, has a slightly earlier onset than it has in other joints and occurs more often in the right arm of men than women, although some variation in this pattern occurs with different lifestyles. Inuit, for example, traditionally experience a great deal of functional stress; as a result they have higher frequencies of arthritis in the elbow joint than other groups, and young men experience severe degeneration of the elbow joint in the right arm (Jurmain 1977b). A similar pattern appears in women, albeit to a lesser extent, reflecting their equal share of the arduous tasks associated with an Arctic lifestyle. Degenerative changes are not so obvious among Californian hunter-gatherers, however (Jurmain 1990). Changes in the frequency of arthritis over time in both the knee and elbow joint have been observed in people undergoing socio-economic change. In a sample of pre- and post-agricultural Indians from the Georgian coast, a reduction from 13.7 per cent to 6.1 per cent for men and 9.6 per cent to zero per cent for women has been recorded, which follows reduced activity levels corresponding to socio-economic change (Larsen 1982). Agriculture is probably no less strenuous than hunting and gathering, but the duration of strenuous tasks is often shorter. This factor, together with periods of minimal activity during growing seasons, tends to be reflected in the skeletal remains of people living in this way. Moreover, the degree of stress upon joints would not be the same as that experienced by a hunter. Larsen's data match those of Jurmain (1977a,b) which show that Pecos Pueblo Indian farmers had substantially less arthritis for all ages and both sexes than for Inuit.

The elbow is probably the best indicator of the amount of work stress in a population because the knee is subject to a lifetime's weight-bearing and repetition stress from standing, walking, climbing and so on. Thus, it will inevitably sustain a certain amount of wear and tear in everybody from everyday living. In this light the pattern for the central Murray is interesting. Here, both elbows are involved in a way not seen in other areas where the prevalence of right elbow involvement is common. This stark inter-regional variation suggests the upper limb being put to a different use. These results are particularly significant in the light of the commonly-held belief that Aboriginal activity patterns were pretty much homogeneous throughout the continent. I suggest, therefore, that the bilaterality and extent of elbow use observed in men and women living in the central Murray is probably the most significant result of this arthritis survey.

The frequency of radial head involvement among desert men is quite different from that seen in the central Murray. Repetitive arm rotation when using a spear thrower, for instance, could be one reason for the difference. Moreover, the obvious right hand bias among these men tends to support this interpretation, given the common use of this weapon in the area. I refer the reader to the biomechanical consequences of using this type of weapon discussed in Chapter 3. Male activity in the central Murray seems to be different from that in the desert. Take, for example, the substantial difference in wear patterns between the left and right distal humeri. In the central Murray, the pattern emphasises the use of the elbow as a hinge joint, with the associated articular surfaces of the ulna and humerus bearing the brunt of wear rather than the radial head. This is different from the emphasis on rotation seen among desert dwellers. Moreover, the bilateral involvement of the ulnae and radii from the central Murray suggests equal use of both arms which is particularly obvious in females. I can only conclude that people in the central Murray present a pattern of upper limb arthritis that is unique to them in that it clearly displays an equal use of both arms by both sexes that is not seen elsewhere in Australia.

Minimal frequencies of arthritic wear on the east and to some extent the south coast, tend to suggest that elbow stress is almost non-existent. One can only assume that people in those areas were not using the joint in the same way or to the same extent as Murray and desert groups. The frequency and distribution of arthritis that emerge from this survey clearly point to different work regimes in different areas. An explanation for this must lie in the various subsistence strategies or the amount of work involved in procuring food or both. Those living in the central Murray use the upper limb to a far greater extent than people living elsewhere. Even though we have seen that age has little to do with arthritis of the elbow joint in a modern population, some association is more likely to exist in those that work hard all their life. Age, however, is not the reason for higher frequencies in Murray people, although this argument might be used to explain the prevalence of arthritis of the elbow joint among desert men.

Osteoarthritis of the temporomandibular joint

Introduction

Like other forms of arthritis temporomandibular arthritis has been noted among various human groups. These include Neanderthal remains from Krapina, La Quina, La Ferrassie and La Chapelle-aux-Saints (Pales 1930; Alexandersen 1967b), in neolithic groups from Turkey (Alpagut 1979), North American Indian (Leigh 1925; Rabkin 1942; Goldstein 1957) and a variety of other fossil populations (see Alexandersen 1967). Nevertheless, population frequencies are not widely published in the literature. The following examples provide a few comparison: Black Americans 4.5 per cent, New Hebrides 5.6 per cent, New Caledonia 24 per cent, Loyalty Islands 26.4 per cent (Pales 1930:166–167), and 43 per cent and 33 per cent in male and female Aborigines, respectively (Richards and Brown 1981). Among contemporary European groups frequencies of 16 per cent for men and 33 per cent for women seem to be the norm (Oberg *et al.* 1971:380). The incidence is, therefore, very variable but standardised categories enabling direct comparisons are few. Other than these studies arthritic disease of the temporomandibular joint in skeletal populations has attracted minimal attention from palaeopathologists, particularly with regards to its frequency and aetiology (Ortner and Putschar 1981).

It is well known that Australian Aboriginal people have rather robust chewing mechanisms which include large jaws and teeth. This adaptive apparatus has, no doubt, partly developed in response to a traditional diet which includes large quantities of meat and vegetable fibre, often liberally sprinkled with sandy inclusions. The development (or retention) of a robust temporomandibular complex has been, therefore, a distinct advantage. It has served to absorb and withstand the severe stresses that are constantly put on it, not only from chewing but from those times when the mouth is used for gripping objects. A number of recent studies have been carried out focussing on dental morphology, kinesiology, functional use and dental attrition among Aboriginal people (Brown *et al.* 1990; Brown and Molnar 1990; Townsend *et al.* 1990; Yamada and Brown 1990; Danenberg *et al.* 1991; Richards and Miller 1991). In the light of this research and to avoid repetition, I have confined my observations of the temporomandibular apparatus, namely within the glenoid fossa. Assessment criteria basically follow those used by Richards and Brown (1981) with some minor changes. I have employed two wear categories. Category 1 is a localised erosion or wear of the fossa which lacks arthritic lipping (Plate 7–12a). Category 2 is major erosion or wear of the joint surface and includes erosion, eburnation, grooving and osteophytic lipping. Sometimes these changes cause substantial alteration of the joint area or obliteration of the fossa(e) with proliferative bone (Plate 7–12b). 'TMJ' is used in this section as a convenient abbreviation of 'temporomandibular joint'.

Plate 7–12a
This primary stage was used as the standard for Category 1 TMJ arthritis. Minor arthritic erosion and slight pitting has ensued on the articular tubercle of the glenoid fossa.

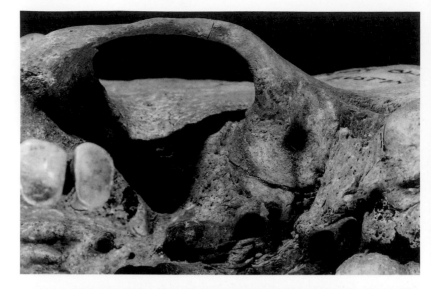

Plate 7–12b
The destructive changes shown here constitute the advanced Category 2 TMJ arthritis. The glenoid fossa and the articular tubercle have been so badly eroded that their original architecture has been destroyed. The only remaining portion of the articular surface is where eburnation has occurred; the rest consists of a fragmented surface surrounded by marginal osteophytosis.

Results

The highest frequencies of TMJ arthritis occur in the central Murray populations as well as groups from Adelaide and coastal Victoria. There is also a rather high frequency among the late Pleistocene Kow Swamp and Coobool remains from the Murray River where 48 per cent of males and 46.7 per cent of females are affected, but only the old adults have the more severe form of the condition. It is interesting to note that modern populations from this same area have comparable, if not higher frequencies, such as 80.0 per cent and 75.0 per cent for males and females from Kerang; 52.5 per cent and 57.1 per cent from

Baratta, respectively, and 72.2 per cent and 55.0 per cent from Swan Hill. Nowhere else on the continent do frequencies rise to these levels. The 52.5 per cent from Baratta is the minimum frequency from this area and all others outside the Murray Valley are below 50 per cent. Males usually have higher frequencies of TMJ arthritis than females but nowhere is this difference statistically significant (Table 7–3). Moreover, it is more evenly distributed between central Murray men and women than it is between males and females from other areas.

Table 7–3   *Temporomandibular (TMJ) arthritis in young and old adults.*

		YA	OA	T	S
CM	Male	48.4	67.8	60.3	24.2
	Female	51.0	74.5	59.1	15.4
R	Male	48.9	66.2	59.4	16.5
	Female	43.4	50.0	45.8	2.4
SC	Male	47.6	59.4	48.6	20.3
	Female	36.8	54.6	46.3	8.9
DES	Male	4.2	40.6	33.9	4.6
	Female	17.4	32.1	25.5	5.9
TRO	Male	13.9	42.9	31.5	3.3
	Female	18.5	32.4	26.2	9.8
CTL	Male	16.7	40.8	35.3	3.8
	Female	22.2	34.2	27.7	6.0

Key:
YA – Young adults
OA – Old adults
T   – Total frequency of temporomandibular arthritis
S   – Frequency of severe arthritic degeneration

Area Codes:
CM–Central Murray, R–Rufus River, SC–South Coast, DES–Desert, TRO–Tropics, CTL–East Coast

So far, I have talked about the overall frequency of TMJ arthritis but if these frequencies are divided into minor and severe degenerative wear patterns the largest incidence of the latter, by far, occurs among central Murray people. Of particular interest is the fact that the severe form is much more prevalent among young adults from this area, with 24.2 per cent of males and 15.4 per cent of females affected. Young men from Rufus River and the south coast feature prominently with 16.5 per cent and 20.3 per cent respectively, as do females from these areas. Frequencies rise with age, particularly in the Murray where among old adults they are inordinately greater than in the same group living in other areas. The central Murray and the south coast, therefore, stand out as areas having the most severe form of TMJ arthritis in both males and females, and places where it develops at an early age in both sexes. With this trend among young adults, it is to be expected that these populations will automatically show very large frequencies in older people. These results contrast strongly with those from other areas of Australia; for example, severe arthritis does not occur among young women from the tropics. The desert pattern is very interesting because frequencies are, overall, very close to those for the tropics. Severe degeneration, therefore, is much less common in the centre and north than it is in other parts of the continent but, interestingly, it affects both men and women to the same extent.

Discussion

Tooth attrition is common among many groups of hunter-gatherers (Leigh 1925, 1929; Rabkin 1941, 1943; Roydhouse and Simonsen 1975; Scott and DeWalt 1980), including Australian Aborigines (Campbell 1925, 1937, 1939; Campbell and Barrett 1953; Beyron 1964; Barrett 1969, 1977; Seward 1976; Brown and Molnar 1990; Richards and Miller 1991). Dental attrition was not studied in this survey but it has been linked as a contributory factor in the onset of TMJ arthritis in Aborigines (Seward 1976; Richards and Brown 1981). Tooth wear is primarily a product of the amount of chewing that an individual does. The type of diet and age are other important factors also together with dental attrition and tooth loss which in themselves depend on a number of factors. These include the amount of fibrous food consumed; how much grit, abrasives or other inclusions are in the food, the type of abrasive, how food is prepared, the environment in which people live, eating habits and whether the mouth and jaws are used in the manufacture of cultural items (Molnar 1972; Barrett 1977).

As we have seen in the previous section, age is intimately linked with the degeneration of synovial joints and the onset of arthritic disease (Jaffe 1975; Adams 1976). This is no less true for the TMJ than it is for other synovial joints, but, unlike these, TMJ arthritis is rare before the fifth decade of life in modern populations (Blackwood 1963). Besides natural ageing processes, tooth loss, dental attrition, facial trauma and 40–50 years of repetitive mechanical overloading of the joint complex are major contributors to the breakdown in the diarthrodial integrity of the masticatory apparatus. These factors are not mutually exclusive, however, but unfortunately the extent of their individual contributions to this process is not well understood. Excess in any of these factors can initiate joint breakdown and begin the processes of degeneration at an earlier age than might be expected otherwise. The result of this process is the ultimate destruction of facial structures causing jaw malfunction and loss of occlusal integrity all of which produces, first, a maladapted chewing mechanism and, second, a feedback mechanism that aggravates the situation. If we know something about how the jaws and teeth are used it helps us in the analysis of TMJ arthritis and can give a better understanding of why the degeneration appears in the form and frequency it does.

Osteoarthritis: a selective stress in Aboriginal cranial morphology

Why are Murray River people more prone to TMJ arthritis than those living elsewhere? The answer to this seems to lie in the amount of mechanical stress people in this area put on their jaws. It has already been established that old age is not necessarily a causative factor in the onset of TMJ arthritis in this group; therefore, it must be a product of use, the frequency of that use and TMJ morphology. The latter will, of course, change in relation to the amount of tooth attrition and the teeth involved (Richards 1984). Such alterations may, in turn, become maladaptive and tend to accelerate the degenerative process. In short, joint stress in Murray River people is greater than elsewhere and any tooth loss amidst such high stress rates will only exacerbate the susceptibility of the joint to break down further. These stresses must take place in other groups but they obviously do not occur to the same extent. Late Pleistocene evidence from the Murray suggests that these stresses may have been operating there for a very long time (perhaps >12–14,000 years) which begs the question: would not such stress on the orofacial complex maintain selection towards reinforcement of that complex over hundreds of generations, or both?

Pre-mortem tooth loss and TMJ arthritis

The highest frequencies of pre-mortem tooth loss with TMJ arthritis occur in the central Murray (Table 7–4). Males are affected somewhat less than females in whom 80 per cent of young adults and 100 per

Table 7–4   *Adults with missing teeth as a percentage of those with TMJ arthritis.*

	MALES		FEMALES	
	YA	OA	YA	OA
	%	%	%	%
CM	100.0	78.3	80.0	100.0
R	100.0	73.3	25.0	100.0
SC	50.0	51.6	60.0	63.6
DES	–	75.0	40.0	20.2
TRO	–	31.6	25.0	33.3
CTL	–	22.7	–	53.9

Key:
YA – Young adults
OA – Old adults

Area Codes:
CM–Central Murray, R–Rufus River, SC–South Coast, DES–Desert, TRO–Tropics, CTL–East Coast

cent of old adults have both conditions. Tooth loss in other parts of the continent is far greater for both young and old adults than it is in the central Murray-Rufus River area (Table 7–5 and Figs 7–1, 7 –2, 7–3 and 7–4). Men and women in the Murray have tooth loss frequencies of 14.2 per cent and 12.0 per cent, respectively, as opposed to an average of 28.7 per cent for males and 27.2 per cent for females for the rest of Australia which is highly significant for both sexes (p=<0.001). This pattern is obvious when we look closer at a comparison between a Murray River population from Swanport and

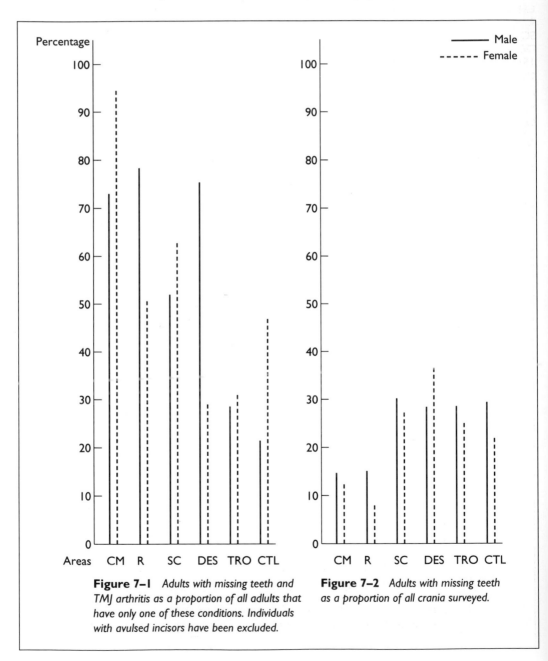

Figure 7–1 *Adults with missing teeth and TMJ arthritis as a proportion of all adlults that have only one of these conditions. Individuals with avulsed incisors have been excluded.*

Figure 7–2 *Adults with missing teeth as a proportion of all crania surveyed.*

coastal people (Fig. 7–5). Swanport people retain their teeth as other
Murray inhabitants do further upstream, while the combined Adelaide
and coastal Victorian groups experience a similar pattern of tooth loss

Table 7–5 *Adults with missing teeth as a percentage of those without TMJ arthritis.*

	MALES		FEMALES	
	YA	OA	YA	OA
	%	%	%	%
CM	10.8	16.2	5.4	24.0
R	2.0	21.2	7.7	10.0
SC	16.7	35.6	17.5	35.5
DES	–	33.9	22.7	52.9
TRO	6.9	41.3	14.8	34.6
CTL	10.5	33.3	5.7	37.1

Key:
YA – Young adults
OA – Old adults

Area Codes:
CM–Central Murray, R–Rufus River, SC–South Coast, DES–Desert,
TRO–Tropics, CTL–East Coast

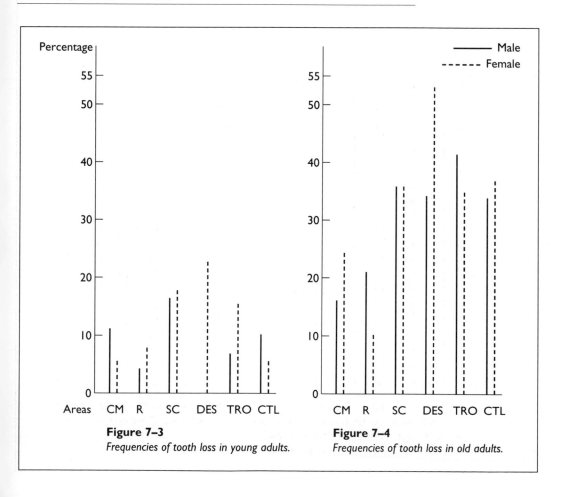

Figure 7–3
Frequencies of tooth loss in young adults.

Figure 7–4
Frequencies of tooth loss in old adults.

to that of other groups around Australia. Those that lose teeth are affected most by TMJ arthritis; this is particularly obvious among young adults from the central Murray. Young men from the desert and tropics and young adult men and women from the east coast are entirely unaffected by arthritis, however. While tooth loss occurs far more often in young women from the tropics than in central Murray women, only 25 per cent have arthritis as opposed to the 80 per cent among the latter (Table 7–4).

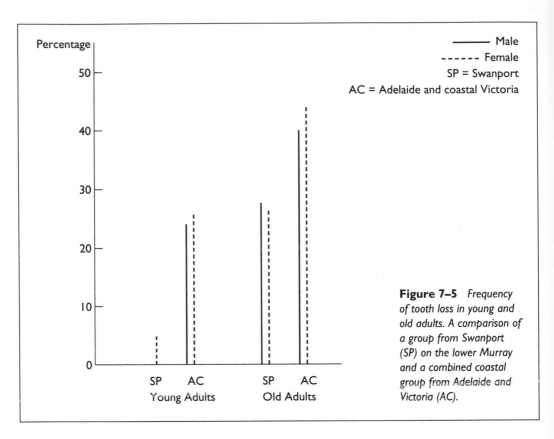

Figure 7–5 *Frequency of tooth loss in young and old adults. A comparison of a group from Swanport (SP) on the lower Murray and a combined coastal group from Adelaide and Victoria (AC).*

Pathology and culture: selective forces in human morphology

Selection towards rugged craniofacial features was the essence of Wright's (1976) argument to explain why such a robust morphology should appear among the Murray River Kow Swamp people (9–12,000BP) almost 20,000 years after gracile individuals inhabited Lake Mungo in western New South Wales (28–32,000BP approx.). Since his publication, however, the morphological picture of the earliest Australians has become a little easier to understand. In those 15 years fossil evidence for both gracile and robust morphological types, as well as intermediate forms, has been accumulated from the Willandra Lakes region to the northwest. Some, like WLH50, display features that are more robust than those found at Kow Swamp. Many individuals are a lot older than Kow Swamp and WLH50 may be older than 30,000 years (Caddie *et al.* 1987; Webb 1989; Flood 1989; Thorne in prep.). Rather than Wright's 'selection towards' argument, however, perhaps a 'persistence by selection' approach provides a better explanation for the continuing existence of rugged facial features and large dentitions among Murray people into the late Holocene. Thorne and others have long proposed that the robust morphology of the orofacial complex among Murray people has its foundations among heavily built Upper Pleistocene populations of Indonesia (Thorne 1975, 1977; Thorne and Wolpoff 1981, 1992). Recent metrical and non-metrical studies of Aboriginal craniofacial variation have suggested that the Murray Valley represents the least homogeneous region of an otherwise fairly homogeneous continent (Pardoe 1984, Pietruwsewsky 1990).

Studies of dentition alone show that while there is great continental variation in tooth size, the largest teeth occur in the central Murray (Townsend and Brown 1979; Brace 1980; Freedman and Lofgren 1981; Smith *et al.* 1981; Molnar *et al.* 1989). Similarly, while advanced dental attrition is common to many parts of Australia it is most common in central parts of the Murray river (Molnar *et al.* 1989). This implies stronger use-stress, in the form of mechanical forces acting on the jaws, teeth and associated facial structures, than are experienced among other groups. Ignoring for the moment what exactly these stresses are, the pattern of TMJ arthritis and tooth retention revealed in this study now join the attrition studies of others as further support for the inordinate stress that occurs among Murray people. These stresses, I suggest, have, over a very long period of time, consistently selected for the well recognised robust orofacial complex of the central Murray and have contributed also to the wide range of variation that is a hallmark of skeletal morphology from this region. Indeed, I would go further and say that the selection for large, hard-wearing teeth has served also for their retention in robust jaw structures. This is firmly established by the stark contrast in the frequency of tooth loss between Murray Valley and other Aboriginal groups from around the country. This trend is underpinned by the fact that tooth loss among central Murray people seems to predispose them to the breakdown of temporomandibular joint structures. The result would normally be a maladaptive and extremely deleterious process and one which could not stand up to the kind of stresses being imposed on orofacial structures. This is where 'persistence by selection' begins to operate.

Early Australians were heirs to an ancestral genetic complement that contained a suite of robust facial and dental characteristics. These were structurally adaptive on a number of behavioural and environmental levels commensurate with a hunting and gathering existence in Australia. But, I suggest, they were no more so than for those who lived along the Murray River. The persistence of some of the robust traits was maintained by selection processes acting particularly upon the orofacial complex. The later reduction in robustness of some of the dental and facial characteristics, rather than indicating a relief in stress and consequently the processes of selection, might be more easily and practically explained by gene flow through increasing frequency of contact with populations outside the Murray who possessed a less rugged orofacial morphology. They were brought to the region through migratory gene flow entering the continent and representing a less rugged morphology which gradually moved across Australia throughout the Holocene. So, the somewhat higher tooth loss in old people from Swanport over that of the upper Murray groups may well be an indication of dental size reduction through the introduction of 'lighter' genes which were moving inland and then upstream from surrounding coastal areas. Consequently, with continued and increased gene flow upriver these genes tended to reduce rugged facial complexes.

The difference between the adaptiveness of the central Murray dentition and that of other groups, typified in coastal and tropical areas, is exemplified by a greater propensity to lose teeth, smaller dentitions and generally less robust orofacial morphologies. This pattern may have been due to a combination of two factors. The first was 'swamping' of earlier and more rugged populations by extrinsic and intrinsic gene flow into and within Australia, respectively, facilitated by movement of people both around the coasts and, to some extent, across the continent. Differential flow rates meant an overall trend of robust genes being replaced by more gracile forms. These, in turn, became patchy centres of intrinsic flow which set up genetic clinal contouring of various shapes, sizes and rates depending on the socio-cultural relationships of neighbouring groups. Adaptation and local microevolutionary processes were then heaped on these different mixes over long periods of time. In some areas these variable mixes were fashioned further by behavioural patterns brought about by selective pressures which underpinned the morphology. Population growth then became as important to the resultant morphological pattern as any other process. The population of the Murray was steadily increasing throughout the Holocene and this too acted in a positive way together with the behavioural patterns of the region to add a further and important stimulatory force for selection (see Webb 1987b).

Wright's (1976) proposition that environmental pressure could have been the trigger for selection towards a robust morphology in the central Murray remains unproven, but I have to support the idea that selection pressures could have been strong enough to have *maintained* rather than *produced* a rugged morphology. I suggest, therefore, that the late Pleistocene–early Holocene inhabitants of the Murray Valley received a genetic endowment from their ancestors that enabled them to cope with extensive orofacial stresses. That endowment consisted of a rugged craniofacial buttressing and robust dental morphology that in combination provided them with the best orofacial complex to cope with the strong mechanical forces that were put on it. It is possible, indeed likely, that the familiar robust 'Murrayian' facial morphology was maintained because of its functional importance in combating the destructive potential of these stresses. Exactly what these stresses were remains obscure. Besides diet and chewing, it is worth considering, however, the net industry of these river people and the extensive work imposed on jaws, teeth and the TMJ during net manufacture. Nets for hunting and fishing were made from the chewed roots of the bulrush (*Typha* sp.) (Krefft 1862:361-362; Beveridge 1882:42; Gott 1982). Net sizes varied depending upon use: emu nets were 140 metres long with 15-centimetre mesh and those for catching ducks were 'usually 100 yards long, by 2 yards deep ... with a mesh of four inches' (Beveridge 1882:45). Fish nets were the same length but had an eight-centimetre mesh, while those used for crayfish were three metres by two metres with five-millimetre mesh. There were many other variations on these patterns. There was as well the production of a range of smaller baskets and carrying bags which employed the same processes of manufacture. Part of the preparation of the bulrush for twine involved 'everybody chewing the roots most vigorously' (Krefft 1862:361). Over a number of years, the enormous amount of mastication on this fibrous material must have produced massive repetitive mechanical stresses on all facial mechanisms, not least on the teeth and temporomandibular joint, in both men and women. Listen to Krefft's impression of this activity:

> If we take into consideration the large nets for catching water-fowl in use, it is indeed astonishing how great the perseverance of these people (and how sound their teeth) must have been, and it is not to be wondered at that the possession of one of these nets has always been considered to be a sort of fortune to its owner. (1862:361–362)

We have no idea how old this net industry is or how long such variation in manufacture has been employed. It seems likely, however, that the findings of this survey, with regard to male–female prevalence of TMJ arthritis and its early onset, may have their origins in the stress imposed by this sort of cultural activity. The retention of teeth is important in the continued integrity of dental structures, which includes the temporomandibular joint. The persistence of a robust craniofacial morphology surrounding and supporting these structures, which includes strong, heavily-muscled jaws and large teeth with broad grinding surfaces, firmly embedded in deep and well-constructed sockets, adds to this integrity. The facial robustness of Murray people is, therefore, a very important adaptive morphology for the inhabitants of the region to combat the stress encountered in their everyday life and it has persisted for a long period of time.

Chapter 8

Trauma

Life without injury can hardly be imagined.
(Wells 1964:45)

Introduction

Fractures of the limbs are almost a natural accompaniment to life. From Permian dinosaurs (Moodie 1923), to apes (Schultz 1939); from Australopithecines (Wells 1964), *Homo erectus* (Weidenreich 1939) to recent human populations (Steinbock 1976; Ortner and Putschar 1981), all have shown evidence of trauma. In this chapter I present the evidence for post-cranial and cranial trauma in Australian Aborigines, together with examples of surgical procedures which include amputation and trephination. My primary concern in this part of the survey is what the study of trauma can tell us about the behaviour and general lifestyle of Aboriginal groups from different parts of the continent. From analysis of fracture patterns it is hoped that we can learn something also of the social characteristics of different populations. Once again, the sample of post-cranial bones from the tropics was so small it had to be disregarded. Because the personal age of post-cranial material is unknown, I have avoided discussion of age-associated fractures or those resulting from pathological or metabolic causes (Aegerter and Kirkpatrick 1975; Mensforth *et al.* 1987). The only distinctive post-cranial fracture discussed as such is the 'parrying fracture'.

Post-cranial trauma

No overt sign of healed traumatic injury was found on any juvenile material surveyed. No classical Colles' or Pott's fractures were detected either, which corresponds to previous findings (MacKay 1938; Wells 1964). Aboriginal people suffered comparatively few post-cranial fractures but 75.9 per cent of those observed occurred on the upper limbs and on the left side of the body (Table 8–1). This is somewhat higher than the 69 per cent observed by MacKay (1938:3) but is close to the 77.6 per cent found among 2295 bones in the South Australian Museum (Dinning 1949:712). Desert people provide the only exception to this pattern with an almost even distribution of fractures between upper and lower limbs.

Table 8–1 *Distribution of fractures among the six major long bones.*

		LEFT			RIGHT			
		n	n̄	%	n	n̄	%	Bone
CM	Male	100	1	1.0	111	–	–	Humerus
	Female	54	1	1.9	55	–	–	Humerus
	Male	57	4(3)	12.3	60	4(2)	6.7	Ulna*
	Female	36	(2)	5.6	28	1(1)	7.8	Ulna*
	Male	49	–	–	55	1	1.8	Radius
R	Male	34	–	–	35	1	2.9	Humerus
	Female	21	–	–	23	1	4.3	Humerus
	Male	43	3(2)	7.0	46	(1)	2.2	Ulna*
	Female	22	(1)	4.5	23	(1)	4.3	Ulna*
	Male	64	1	1.6	62	–	–	Radius
	Female	30	1	3.3	32	–	–	Radius
	Female	26	1	3.8	25	–	–	Tibia
	Male	44	1	2.3	44	–	–	Fibula
	Female	31	1	3.2	29	–	–	Fibula
SC	Male	32	–	–	36	1	2.8	Humerus
	Male	21	(1)	4.8	28	3(1)	10.7	Ulna*
	Female	21	4(1)	19.1	19	1	5.3	Ulna*
	Female	21	2	9.6	20	–	–	Radius
	Male	34	–	–	33	1	3.0	Femur
DES	Male	23	2	8.7	21	–	–	Humerus
	Male	19	(2)	10.5	21	1	4.8	Ulna*
	Male	21	1	4.8	18	–	–	Radius
	Female	4	–	–	5	1	20.0	Femur
	Male	24	1	4.2	29	–	–	Tibia
	Male	18	2	11.1	16	1	6.3	Fibula
CTL	Male	56	1	1.8	63	–	–	Humerus
	Male	53	5(3)	9.5	60	2(1)	3.4	Ulna*
	Female	26	(5)	19.2	25	2(1)	4.0	Ulna*
	Male	59	1	1.7	56	1	1.8	Radius
	Female	20	–	–	22	2	9.1	Radius
	Female	25	1	4.0	27	–	–	Femur
	Male	49	1	2.0	69	–	–	Tibia
	Female	24	2	8.2	26	1	3.8	Tibia
	Male	49	2	4.1	41	1	2.4	Fibula
	Female	17	1	5.9	23	–	–	Fibula

Key:
*–This frequency is calculated minus parrying fractures
(n)–Number of parrying fractures
TRO (Tropics)–not used in this survey because of small sample size

Area Codes:
CM–Central Murray, R–Rufus River, SC–South Coast, DES–Desert, CTL–East Coast

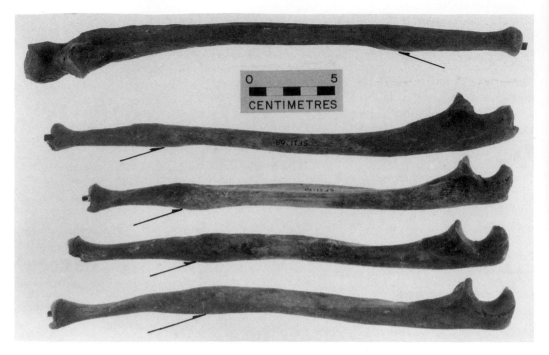

Plate 8–1
A series of parrying fractures (arrowed) are located in the distal one-third of the shafts of these ulnae.

Upper limb trauma consists predominantly of parrying fractures situated on the distal one third of the ulna diaphysis (Plate 8–1). They occur more often on the left than right arm and are caused by the upheld arm being used to parry or block a blow to the left side of the body, usually from a right-handed person. Parrying shields are often narrow and while taking much of the directed blow their slim design allows a club or similar weapon to glance from its edge and continue on to the wrist area. The ulna usually takes the brunt of the blow and fractures. In severe cases the blow may involve the radius producing a complete fracture of the lower arm just above the wrist. Double fractures occur in a number of cases but a large percentage of parrying fractures show exceptionally good healing, often with little or no misalignment of the diaphysis and minimal callus formation. The parrying fracture was experienced by men and women in most parts of the continent but the frequency is not large for any particular area. The only exception, again, is among desert men, and women living on the east coast, who have frequencies of 10.5 per cent and 19.2 per cent, respectively. Nearly 10 per cent of unsexed ulnae from the Murray River have parrying fractures but without further information this frequency means very little.

Discussion

Generally, parrying fractures heal very well but left arm fractures heal better than those occurring on the right which is probably a reflection of handedness and continued use of the right arm. A similar pattern in leg fractures is not as easily understood, however. The femur and humerus nearly always show a greater propensity for malunification but they are notorious for misalignment because of the massive muscle spasms which take place during and after a fracture and the need for sophisticated traction to circumvent deformation.

Fractures in Aboriginal skeletal material have been noted by a number of researchers (MacKay 1938; Dinning 1949; Macintosh 1967; Wood 1968, 1976; Sandison 1973a,b, 1980; Jurisich and Davies 1976; Prokopec 1979; Freedman 1985). Generally, healing and bone alignment are good with few examples of severe malformation. There are a number of similarities between the findings of this study and others from around the world; for example, there is a prevalence of upper limb over lower limb fractures (Wells 1964; Clabeaux 1976; Lovejoy and Heiple 1981). The ratio of upper to lower limb fractures in this survey varies with area, however.

Fractures of the lower limb

Among desert dwellers broken legs account for 45.5 per cent of all long bone fractures. This is the closest to an even upper/lower limb distribution found for any area and is similar to the 40.3 per cent found among North American hunter-gatherers (Lovejoy and Heiple 1981). Fractures are more likely to occur in people like desert nomads who move across large distances in search of food, water and suitable camp sites. Moreover, their hunting activities, which in Australia often entail scrambling over rocky terrain and running across open plain and savannah, would tend to cause more leg fractures than might be incurred by more sedentary people and those inhabiting rainforest areas. Leg fractures are comparatively common among women living along the Queensland coast. This is interesting in light of what has already been shown in the previous chapter with regard to their high incidence of knee arthritis. Nevertheless, it may be too premature to suggest that these two pathologies are connected in any way. It is reasonable to assume that 10–15 per cent of any population will sustain leg fractures merely by the vagaries of living and that, perhaps, the low frequencies of post-cranial trauma are, in themselves, the more interesting phenomena. The low frequency of leg fractures along the south coast contrasts strongly with the incidence at Rufus River, in the desert and on the eastern seaboard. It is a pattern which suggests that those living on the south coast led a less strenuous life, particularly with regard to activities that put the lower limb at risk. For example, this may have been the result of a greater degree of sedentism among south coast people. If this is a valid interpretation, the central Murray has an even greater propensity towards sedentism with its apparent lack of such fractures.

Trauma patterns are linked to the behavioural, social, economic and demographic disposition of a given society. Steinbock (1976:23) has shown that the overall frequency of fractures falls with increasing sedentism and the introduction of agriculture. Just the opposite seems to have occurred at the Dickson Mounds, however, where fractures increase from 20.5 per cent during the hunter-gatherer phase to 32.4 per cent when agriculture is in full swing, although the reverse is true among sub-adults (Goodman *et al.* 1983). There is twice the number of fractures in modern industrialised society as those incurred among more ancient cultures (Angel 1974:17), but with the mechanised world we live in there is obviously more opportunity for this to happen.

These contradictory findings suggest that there is no simple rule for interpreting what fracture patterns might represent in terms of a particular human activity or, if we want to be conservative, even basic behaviour. One way of tackling the interpretative uncertainties of extrapolating behaviour from bones is by knowing something about the activities and lifestyle of the particular group in the first place. This, however, is a partial defeat of the original aims of the study. Nevertheless, we cannot be completely isolated from what we already know about the lifestyle of tribal peoples and there is no disgrace in using this information to its fullest. For reasons of environment alone it is clear that Aboriginal people would have endured various types and weights of mechanical stress on their limbs; partial testimony to this is the arthritis that we have already seen in many. These stresses put some people at greater risk of, say, leg fractures than others. Take, for example, the strenuous activity of hunting in the desert. Tindale describes it:

> Sighting a kangaroo [a young man] would chase after it
> and relying on the curved course taken by such animals
> the second youth would take up the heavy running in
> the heat and over the heavy ground. (1981:1878)

His description provides us with good reason to suppose that leg fractures are to be expected among people in this area and reflect the behaviour of nomadic hunter-gatherers. Conversely, the sedentary life indicated by other palaeopathological data from the central Murray and presented in previous chapters provides us with some evidence to suggest why there are no leg fractures there. Clearly, these results do not mean that broken legs *never* occurred there, and I shall show later that they did, only that such accidents were far fewer than in other regions.

As I have said before, the central Murray sample consists of material collected from a number of known places in the Murray River Valley (Map 2–2). However, a number of fractured long bones were examined in a large unprovenanced sample from along this river. Although not used in the general survey a number of these were found to be fractured, among them a femur with a triple comminuted fracture of the proximal half of the diaphysis (Plates 8–2a and b). Although noted on a previous occasion (Sandison 1980), this trauma is the most severe of its type encountered in this study. As such this very spectacular and equally painful injury deserves further description as a particularly interesting and unique example of femoral fracture. The bone is robust and from the diameter of the femoral head (50 mm) it obviously belonged to a well-built adult male person. The injury is located in the proximal half of the bone where the shaft has been completely smashed and remodelled leaving it badly disfigured (Plate 8–2a). There are three fracture sites which have been substantially

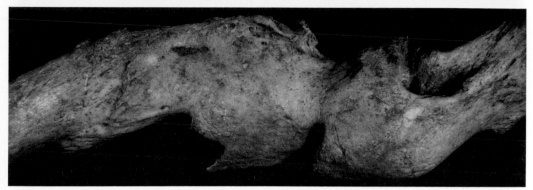

reinforced with an enormous amount of ensheathing callus bone of variable thickness. Some ossification of local tendinous insertions has followed and this has added an odd, spiked architecture to the uneven new bone formation (Plate 8–2b). The anterior spikes are placed at the position of the *vastus intermedius* and their inferior orientation conforms to the direction of action of this muscle, which indicates continued use of this limb while it was still in the process of mending. A similar spike on the posterior side is positioned close to the insertion of the *adductor brevis*. The shattering of the shaft and subsequent healing has caused severe diaphyseal distortion masking its original continuity and severely changing its morphology. The loss of support at the top of the shaft has allowed the lower half to lie more posteriorly than usual, reversing the natural anterior bow of the femur so that the shaft at this point is concave rather than convex. The lower part of the bone has rotated laterally so that the condyles face more outwardly than usual. The overall result would have made this individual a cripple, with a shortened left leg and a gait that threw the leg out to one side. Proper running would not have been possible and jogging would have been equally difficult, both severe disabilities for an active man.

The amazing thing about this bone is that it has healed *at all*, but this is only one of its surprising features. For example, I cannot suggest how it was caused in a traditional Aboriginal setting. Usually the femoral shaft fractures only as the result of 'severe violence such as may be caused by a road accident or an aeroplane crash' (Adams 1978: 218). Given that we can eliminate both of these causes there seem to be few activities that could produce this multiple fracture. It is possible that the victim may have fallen from the top of a tall tree. If the thigh had become caught in the crook of a large branch on the way down,

Plate 8–2a (top) *A triple comminuted fracture of a femur from the central Murray.*

Plate 8–2b (bottom) *A strong, well formed and very large callus has developed around the fracture shown in Plate 8–2a. There is no obvious sign of infection but substantial distortion of the shaft has taken place. The bony spikes have probably formed from ossification of tendonous insertions.*

the body's continued momentum may have applied forces on the bone severe enough to snap it. But one can imagine only a single, simple break resulting from this type of accident unless the leg was jammed in some very peculiar manner. On the other hand, it might have resulted from a fall from one of the 25–40 metre cliffs that occur along some parts of the Murray River. If the fall was sheer, however, the person is likely to have been killed outright or fallen in the river. Another possibility is that the leg may have been deliberately smashed, perhaps with an axe, as some sort of punishment or pay-back. Such treatment, however, is likely to have caused extensive and probably irreparable damage to muscle, tendon and other tissues covering the bone if not almost amputating the limb. Muscle, nerve and vascular tissues would have been damaged to such an extent that paralysis of the lower leg is likely to have resulted in later amputation or atrophy of the bone. Perhaps the most important factor to consider in this sort of trauma is the very real likelihood of fatal blood loss or shock. Infection would have been another danger almost impossible to avoid from such a large open wound and one of the surprising features of this bone is the lack of this. Unfortunately, we do not have the rest of the skeleton which hampers our pursuit of the origins of this particular injury.

As already noted, it is surprising that this fracture mended. Multiple, comminuted femoral fractures can take from six to nine months to heal, depending on the general health and age of the sufferer. Sophisticated traction is normally part of the initial nursing treatment and in the aged healing may take more than nine months or it may not take place at all without surgical intervention in the form of a plate or nail being inserted into the bone. For this bone to have mended in the way it has there must have been a considerable amount of medical knowledge applied to the treatment of this injury as well as long-term care for the patient. This included surgical skill which incorporated an ability to reduce the fracture, or at least position and possibly splint the leg in the best way possible. There is also a social factor that strongly indicates the provision of long-term care for the patient as well as the nutritional and other needs of this incapacitated man during the time the leg was mending. From the minimal size of the bone callus he must have been allowed to rest the limb extensively so that it could mend as well as it has. Such long-term immobility also implies a strong sedentary element in the group. It is doubtful whether this immobility lasted for months, however, because such inactivity would probably have resulted in atrophy of the bone to some extent which is not obvious here. After examining this femur Sandison (1980:46) commented that it 'must have required devoted attention over very prolonged periods'. I agree with him; this sort of injury is rare among tribally living peoples because long-term nursing is not normally possible for people constantly on the move. Once again, the sedentary nature of central Murray people is underpinned otherwise they would not have been able to take care of their sick and injured at this level.

Other fractures from the Murray Valley tell a similar story. Only two of six femoral fractures show fairly good unification which testifies to the well known difficulties with these fractures. Another type of fracture noted in a central Murray person is a femoral neck fracture (Plate 8–3). The causes of this injury must have been much less spectacular than the previous example and probably came from a fall or stumble, impacting the head into the neck and upwardly displacing the diaphyseal fragment. Hip displacement is common in these cases and the right leg of this person would have been shortened. A fracture of this kind 'needs rigid immobilisation if it is to have any chance of uniting' (Adams 1978:204). It did unite, the mend is excellent and callus is almost non-existent, all of which suggests that this patient received a similar sort of treatment as the previous case. The subcapital fracture in this individual is fairly common in those over 60 years, particularly females, because of age-associated osteoporosis (Adams 1978). As with the previous example, the rest of the skeleton is missing preventing an estimate of the age of this person. The stout

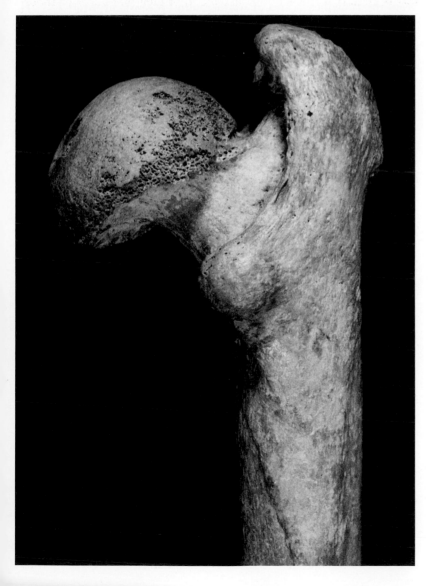

Plate 8–3
A femoral neck fracture with some upward displacement of the head and shortening of the neck.

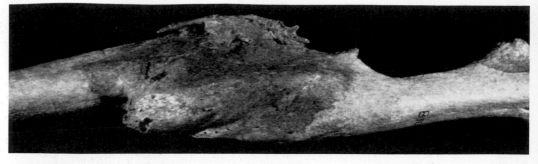

Plate 8–4

This fracture of the femoral shaft is from Broadbeach in southeastern Queensland. It has resulted in a large overlap of the broken ends which shortened the leg considerably.

condition of the bone, which includes thick cortices, suggests that osteoporosis was not a problem for this individual, however, and the diameter of the head indicates a male person.

Malunification is much more common among Aboriginal skeletal remains than united fractures. One particular example of this comes from the Broadbeach area of southeastern Queensland (Map 2–1, 1). This male individual suffered a mid-shaft fracture with overlap of the broken ends, probably due to muscular spasm following the accident pulling the broken ends past each other (Plate 8–4). In this case there seems little attempt (or lack of success) in reducing the fracture, which would have resulted in a shortened leg. The fact that the leg mended, however, is yet another example of Aboriginal people, living under what might be termed difficult conditions, nursing severe trauma and shows as well an innate capacity to heal.

I have tended to ignore fractures of the fibula in this study largely because they do not tell us very much. An unbroken tibia will always act as a natural splint for the broken fibula, enabling the smaller bone to mend without much difficulty. The reverse, however, is not possible.

> In fresh fractures of both bones of the leg attention should be concentrated solely on the fracture of the tibia. The fibula fracture may be disregarded because it always unites readily, and in any case the bone is of such secondary importance that the position of the fragments is immaterial. (Adams 1978:249)

Seven of the nine broken fibulae examined (77.8 per cent) displayed very good alignment which was no doubt due to tibial support.

Healed tibial fractures show a wide range of variation, with both very good and very poor examples of shaft alignment (Plate 8–5). The upper half of a partially fossilised bone from the Murray which could be late Pleistocene or early Holocene in age has a similar fracture (Plate 8–6). There is a complete lack of diaphyseal alignment in both the tibia and associated fibula which has resulted in an exaggerated anterior bow. A very large callus formation, which has fused both bones either side of the fracture, has produced a deformity of the lower leg which may have looked very like that in a photograph of an Aranda man, taken by Herbert Basedow near Henbury in the Northern Territory in the 1920s (Plate 8–7). There was either no attempt to reduce the fracture in either of these cases or continued activity prevented proper unification or both.

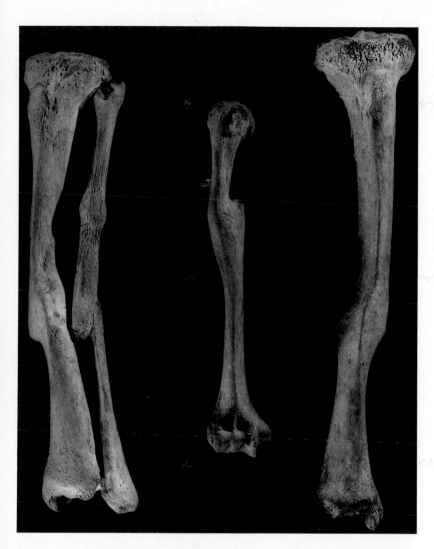

Plate 8–5
There is remarkably little callus formation around these fractures from the central Murray area. The humeral shaft (centre) has probably been shortened by muscle spasms pulling the broken ends past each other. The resultant shortening in these fractures is normal without the intervention of proper traction. Although the fractured tibiae are free from infection, an osteitic lesion lies in the proximal half of the fibula shaft (left).

Occasionally a fracture has resulted in non-unification of the shaft and the formation of a pseudo-arthrosis or pathological ball-and-socket joint. Basedow photographed an Aboriginal man from Denial Bay, South Australia, with an example of this in his left arm (Plate 8–8). The left arm suggests that it may have been a high parrying fracture, but the grotesque result obviously has its origins in the formation of pseudo-arthrosis in both the radius and ulna, similar to that shown in a left ulna from Swanport on the lower Murray (Plate 8–9).

When examining the Swanport skeletal remains uncovered at the beginning of this century, Stirling (1911:12) noted that the healed fractures among them 'would have done credit to a skilled surgeon'. Similarly, Dinning (1949:712) commented that many of the fractures he examined showed 'anatomical restoration that would be considered good even by modern orthopaedic standards'. Dinning showed surprise at his findings because he had read that Aborigines living in northwestern Western Australia were ignorant of splinting techniques and if this were so then probably all Aboriginal people lacked these skills (Love 1936:202). Both Basedow and Love's experiences appear

Plate 8–6
*This radiograph
shows a massive
bony callus around a
badly fractured tibia
and fibula resulting
in poor alignment of
the shaft. Some
remodelling of the
diaphyseal walls has
taken place and the
new trabecular bone
within the callus is
clearly visible. Note
also the hole in the
callus that has
formed to facilitate
the passage of a
large blood vessel.
The metal objects
are post-mortem
artifacts placed in
the bone.*

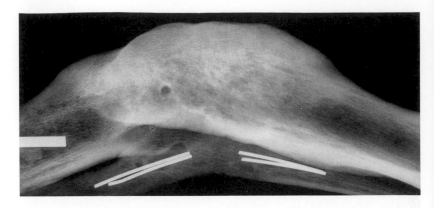

to be less than common, however. Besides the evidence presented in this study, ethnohistoric observations generally contradict those of Love. The practice of setting broken limbs has been noted in tribal groups from North America, Africa, parts of Pacific Oceania and New Zealand (Ackerknecht 1967).

Australian Aborigines living in many parts of the continent were fully cognisant of the techniques of reducing, setting and splinting limb fractures also. For example, MacKenzie, cited in Winterbotham (1951), says that Aborigines living in the northwest used human arm bones to splint arm fractures and leg bones for supporting a fractured lower limb. Bark, bound with vegetable string or sinew, was used for splinting in the Gulf country (Winterbotham 1951), north eastern New South Wales (Macpherson 1902) and the Gascoyne River district of Western Australia (Daisy Bates n.d.). Sticks tied tightly with possum or kangaroo skins formed an adequate splint in central

Plate 8–7
*This Aranda man
from the Northern
Territory was photo-
graphed by Herbert
Basedow around
1920. He has a
fracture of the lower
leg similar to that
illustrated in Plate
8–6. Although
causing considerable
inconvenience, the
deformity must have
been overcome to
enable this man to
continue leading a
traditional lifestyle.
(The Basedow Col-
lection, courtesy of
the National
Museum of
Australia)*

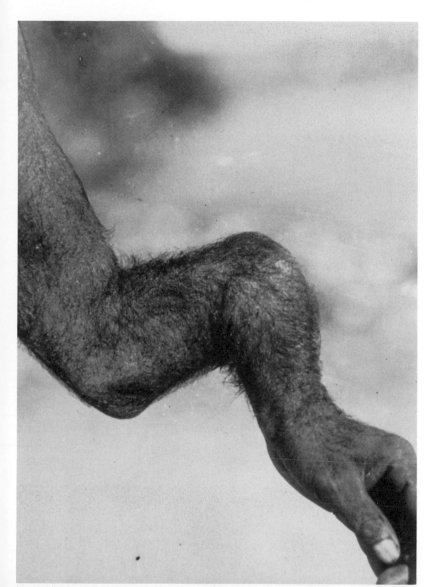

Plate 8–8
This extraordinary pseudoarthrosis developed following a complete break of both lower arm bones. No attempt was made to set the fracture so with the continued use the broken ends of the bones became rounded and covered with cartilage forming a ball and socket joint. This man had full use of his hand and fingers and the arm itself turned about the fracture point as if it were a second elbow. There is no sign of muscular atrophy and the arm looks strong and healthy. The photograph was taken by Herbert Basedow in 1920 and he reports that pseudoarthroses were not uncommon among Aboriginal groups living traditionally in central Australia. (The Basedow Collection, courtesy of the National Museum of Australia)

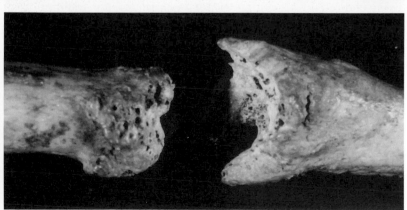

Plate 8–9
This pseudoarthrosis from Swanport shows changes typical of those which take place in unhealed long bone fractures. No doubt these are the sorts of change which took place in the arm of the man featured in Plate 8–8.

Queensland (Roth 1897), Victoria (Anon. 1861) and the Murray district of Western Australia (Daisy Bates n.d.). Grass, leaves and clay were applied in the form of a plaster cast in north central New South Wales (Parker 1905), central Australia (Giles 1882), on the Murray River (Hoets 1949) and in South Australia (Bartels 1893). In the Northern Territory bamboo was used (Foelsche 1882). Worsnop (1897, Plate 71) illustrates an arm sling for supporting a broken wrist used by Aborigines in southeastern South Australia. The explorer, Ernest Giles, recounts an incident when in central Australia he saw an Aboriginal child's broken upper arm bound with leaves and wrapped in bark (Giles 1889:132). There are many other reports of Aboriginal bone setting practices as well as various testaments to the adequate results obtained (Anon 1823; Eyre 1845 Vol.II:361; Black and Cleland 1938).

Fractures of the upper limb

It has been said that considering the warlike nature of people in the past, parrying fractures are surprisingly uncommon (Wells 1964). In some surveys, however, these have been the commonest type of fracture found (Angel 1974). It is difficult to know, therefore, whether a small frequency of parrying fractures is indicative of the degree of aggressive behaviour within a given group or society. Nevertheless, a high percentage must suggest that it is. These are the most common fractures among east coast females and desert males, which naturally leads to the conclusion that women on the east coast fought either with males or with each other and that fighting between desert men might be more common than it is in groups from elsewhere. Males in all areas do have more fractures of the left than right ulna but in most cases this difference is quite small.

The unification and alignment of broken upper limb bones is generally good, even though handedness probably adds a bias against this. For example, nearly 70 per cent of fractured lower arm bones displayed good unification without undue distortion. This is not a bad result considering that humeri, as mentioned above, are difficult to set correctly and often result in at least a shortened bone (Plate 8–5). Exact end-to-end apposition is not essential for the resumption of natural upper arm function, however. Only two of the 18 fractured humeri found during this survey showed reduction to a near-normal position. The situation is somewhat different for lower arm fractures, 'because even slight displacement may disturb the relationship between radius and ulna, with consequent impairment of the rotation' (Adams 1978:155).

The high percentage of well-mended limbs seen in this survey suggests a firm commitment to care and concern for the injured patient. Aboriginal people obviously set out to try and achieve the best results possible and these results are a testament to their ability to effect and maintain treatment to ensure this. If the distribution of well-healed fractures between the upper to lower arm is anything to go on, there seems to have been a particular emphasis on treating the former, perhaps to maintain mobility at all costs.

Cranial trauma

By far the most common cranial injury is the depressed fracture, usually in the form of an oval or circular dent in the outer cranial table (Plates 8–10a, b). Other forms of injury included in this category are split, linear and circular cranial fractures (Plate 8–11). For reasons of wider interpretation the position of each vault trauma was recorded. Any variation in patterning would then provide a better understanding of the behaviour of some groups as opposed to others.

Discounting pathological fractures, broken bones are a direct indication of accident or violence. In the case of post-cranial bones, only the parrying fracture can be directly attributed to aggressive behaviour.

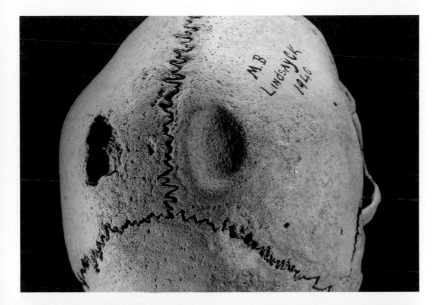

Plate 8–10a
The large, oval depressed fracture on the vault of this individual from Rufus River is a typical example of this type of cranial trauma common among Aboriginal people.

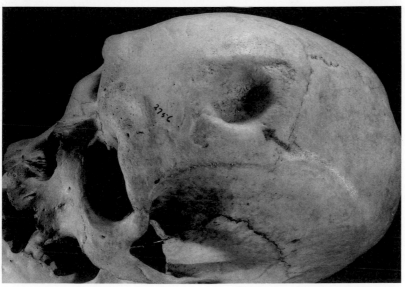

Plate 8–10b
Sometimes a depressed fracture can be very deep, pushing the outer cranial table well into the diploe, crushing the trabecular bone and flattening it. The depressed fracture on this individual is 7 mm deep.

Plate 8–11
This large split fracture takes the shape of a large V-shaped flap. The cranial wall has been pushed in by a blow (probably around the anterior margin of the fracture) which has forced the bone inward. The natural spring in the bone has popped it out again, catching the lower edge and forming a small overlap at this point. New bone formation has begun to close all the fractures, indicating that the victim did not die immediately from the injury. Death may have followed weeks later, perhaps from a cerebral haemorrhage which would not be unlikely following such a massive blow to the head.

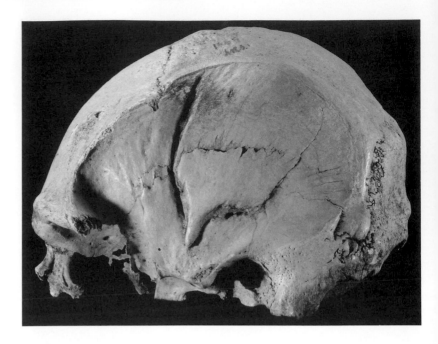

A circular injury to the cranium severe enough to cause a lasting depression on the skull can usually be regarded as the result of deliberate aggression, especially when it is positioned on the frontal or superior parts of the calvarium. An added complication of analysing the placement and origin of cranial trauma in Aboriginal people comes from the quite common practice of striking the head with stones and other objects, as a sign of grief during mourning (Krefft 1862:363; Meggitt 1962:125; Berndt and Berndt 1972:455; Tonkinson 1978: 84; Elkin 1979: 338-339). These blows can cause depressed fracturing as well as soft tissue injury, particularly to frontal areas of the head.

Not all cranial trauma is caused by direct aggression, but it is difficult to explain how depressed fracturing, severe enough to cause the split fracturing of the type seen in Plate 8–11 and denting of the zygomatic arch (Plate 8–12), was caused in any other way. For example, almost all depressed fractures were between one and three centimetres in diameter, round or oval and typical of that made by a blow from a blunt instrument with a small but symmetrical striking surface. Dented zygomatic arches can, of course, come from an accidental blow to the side of the face but this is much less likely to occur in a non-industrialised society. Moreover, although certain types of accidents and falls can produce serious cranial fracturing, these are normally associated with industrial societies (Miller and Jennett 1968). The average accidental 'bang on the head' derived from everyday living leaves very little, if any, trace on the bone, although the actual incidence of this type of injury is hard to assess because if no other clinical signs transpire there will be no formal report or record made. At the same time, the opportunity for a hunter-gatherer to accidentally bang his or her head severely enough to cause the sort of injury observed here is limited, even among those who occupy rock shelters.

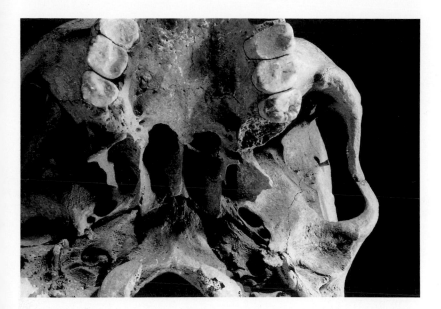

Plate 8–12
A dented zygomatic arch is almost certainly a sign of aggression rather than accident.

Results

The major finding of this survey is that, as a general rule, female crania from all parts of the continent display more head trauma than males (Table 8–2). Frequencies are variable and range from an almost even distribution between the sexes at Rufus River to a vast difference of 6.5 per cent and 24.2 per cent for men and women from the tropics, respectively. The female range is about 20–33 per cent as opposed to a range of 6.5–26 per cent for men. Contrary to the pattern of other pathologies, women from the central Murray area have less cranial trauma than those from any other and, with the

Table 8–2 *Multiple cranial trauma.*

	MALES					FEMALES				
	n	$\bar{n}$	T1	T2	T3	n	$\bar{n}$	T1	T2	T3
CM	247	33	13.4	3.6	–	151	30	19.9	4.0	1.3
R	122	32	26.2	7.4	0.8	83	23	27.7	8.4	2.4
SC	138	20	14.5	4.4	0.7	123	39	31.7	10.6	4.9
DES	132	22	16.7	3.8	1.5	51	17	33.3	11.8	5.9
TRO	92	6	6.5	–	–	62	15	24.2	9.7	4.8
CTL	133	31	23.3	6.8	1.5	86	28	32.6	10.5	3.5

Key:
$\bar{n}$ – Crania with one or more lesions
T1 – Percentage of crania with one lesion
T2 – Percentage of crania with two lesions
T3 – Percentage of crania with three lesions

Area Codes:
CM–Central Murray, R–Rufus River, SC–South Coast, DES–Desert, TRO–Tropics, CTL–East Coast

exception of men in the tropics, so do males. The highest frequencies of trauma are found in men from Rufus River and women living in the desert and on the east coast. If we look at the trends for multiple lesions a similar pattern emerges, with the central Murray registering the lowest frequencies and little differences between the individual coastal and desert groups.

The area of cranial vault most affected by trauma appears to be the parietals with a generally even distribution between right and left sides (Table 8–3). Almost all traumatised crania have some parietal involvement which shows a bias to the right in females and to the left in males. An exception to this pattern occurs in central Murray females who have more trauma on the left side. Surprisingly, no parietal trauma was recorded among men from the tropics although 92 crania were examined. Another rather unexpected finding is the low frequency of frontal trauma. While this bone is the second most affected, the incidence is not as high as one might expect, although the frequency range is rather wide with 5.9–35.7 per cent affected. The incidence of occipital trauma varies considerably between areas, most notably between Murray River groups, the south coast and the rest of the continent. Surprisingly, in the tropic sample, 83 per cent of men with cranial trauma have it on their occipitals. This is an unusual pattern compared to all other areas.

Table 8–3   *Distribution of cranial trauma between the frontal, parietal and occipital bones.*

		n	*n̄*	%	P%	PL%	PR%	F%	O%
CM	M	247	33	13.4	97.0	53.1	46.9	21.2	15.2
	F	151	30	19.9	100.0	53.3	46.7	23.3	10.0
R	M	122	32	26.2	96.9	58.1	41.9	28.1	–
	F	83	23	27.7	95.7	50.1	63.6	26.1	4.3
SC	M	138	20	14.5	90.0	72.2	27.8	35.0	10.0
	F	123	39	31.7	97.4	47.4	65.8	20.5	15.4
DES	M	132	22	16.7	86.4	52.6	47.4	31.8	27.3
	F	51	17	33.3	100.0	29.4	70.6	5.9	29.4
TRO	M	92	6	6.5	–	–	–	16.7	83.3
	F	62	15	24.2	100.0	46.7	53.3	33.3	13.3
CTL	M	133	31	23.3	96.8	50.0	50.0	22.6	22.6
	F	86	28	32.6	96.4	51.9	55.6	35.7	25.0

Key:
M   – Male
F   – Female
%   – Overall percentage of cranial trauma
P%   – Percentage of parietal trauma (combined left and right sides)
PL% – Percentage of left parietal trauma
PR% – Percentage of right parietal trauma
F%   – Percentage of frontal trauma
O%   – Percentage of occipital trauma

Area Codes:
CM–Central Murray, R–Rufus River, SC–South Coast, DES–Desert, TRO–Tropics, CTL–East Coast

Discussion

Cranial injury has not been a stranger to past human society (Moodie 1923; Wells 1964; Courville 1967; Jannsens 1970; Steinbock 1976; Ortner and Putschar 1981). It has also been noted before in Aboriginal skeletal remains (Morton 1845; Wood 1968; Prokopec 1979). Nevertheless, there are few studies of head injury patterns that tell us something about past behaviour and social construction and how cranial injury differs between groups and males and females (Angel 1974; Walker 1989). On the other hand, there are descriptions of weaponry used by various societies which could cause head injury (Courville 1942, 1951, 1952). The fact that clubs, maces, cudgels, axes, sling shots, boomerangs, digging sticks and other weapons can inflict trauma on the head is not surprising and, indeed, hardly needs illustrating. Rather than describe the weapon used to produce the injury it seems to be more appropriate to determine where the injury occurs on the head and from there the possible reasons for the variations which occur across the continent.

The obvious predisposition of Australian Aboriginal females to cranial injury is the reverse of results from studies of other peoples (Angel 1974; Walker 1989). Angel states, for example, that 'females have fewer fractures throughout, especially in the head and face' (1974:17). The great difference in the frequency of trauma among various Aboriginal groups is not unusual, however, and a similar pattern of variation is found among North American Indians (Walker 1989). The predominance of parietal injury in Aboriginal people is not unique either and has been recorded in other groups as diverse as Indians and Nubians (Brothwell 1961; Strouhal and Jungwirth 1980; Zimmerman et al. 1981). The predominance of frontal and parietal lesions in central Murray women suggests that blows were directed to the front and sides of the head. While the left parietal is involved more than the right, indicating a frontal assault by a right-handed person, the small difference in their frequencies suggests that some blows could have come from behind. Either way, the pattern suggests deliberate attack rather than unfortunate accident. These women may not have been the victims of male attackers either, they could have been involved in arguments among themselves. Self-inflicted injury may be another reason for injury to the frontal bone. As mentioned earlier, it was common practice for Aboriginal women in mourning to inflict wounds to the head by deliberately striking or beating their foreheads with waddies, stones or sharpened instruments.

Parietal injury around the continent forms a fascinating pattern from the point of view of its origin. With the exception of the east coast, where it is evenly distributed between males and females, men have a left bias as if involved in frontal attacks. It is tempting to suggest that blows directed upward from the parrying shield cause some of these, whereas blows directed down cause parrying fractures. With the exception of the central Murray, females have a right predominance, as though subjected to attacks from behind, perhaps during a domestic squabble. If this assumption is correct, the highest incidence of this type of attack is experienced by desert females who also have the highest amount of occipital injury. The even pattern of right and left parietal damage and the added high frequency of occipital involvement among desert men suggests attack from both front and back, but the overall degree of head trauma is less here than among Rufus River and east coast groups.

Women living on the south coast have a pattern of head injury similar to those in the desert, with twice as much as men and right side bias. Blows to the occipital are not as common as they are in the desert group. Among people in two individual component areas of the south coast sample, Swanport and Adelaide, the overall frequency of female trauma reaches a very high 39.6 per cent and 43.8 per cent, respectively, while males have 19.3 per cent and 9.1 per cent, respectively. This difference clearly points to common aggression towards or between females rather than the whole community being involved in warfare. Among south coast men, the combination of high left parietal and frontal involvement with a small amount of general head injury suggests that belligerent acts are restricted to individual rather than general bouts of hand-to-hand combat. Parrying fractures occur among these men as they do in groups from all over the continent but the frequency of these adds little to further interpretation of their head injury.

Further east, along the New South Wales coast, head injury is more evenly distributed. The bilateral pattern of parietal damage and substantial frontal and occipital involvement suggests that blows have come from all directions. The even distribution of trauma between males and females suggests, however, that both are involved in acts of aggression, perhaps towards neighbouring people. Such behaviour may have been a product of comparatively high population densities, and sedentism or competition for resources along this stretch of coast, or both. But the higher degree of social friction among these people compared to those inhabiting the central Murray is hard to explain in these terms. The reason for this is that the latter would seem to have been under a greater amount of social pressure with, perhaps, a more developed level of social and economic intensification. It is worth noting also that east coast females have, by far, the highest frequency of parrying fractures (19.2 per cent) found anywhere in Australia, including males.

Cranial fracture patterns at Rufus River are almost identical for men and women in all areas of the head. Men do not have occipital trauma, which is quite opposite to males in the tropics, but follow the general male trend of frontal and left parietal injury typical of face-to-face combat. Attacks from behind are rare and the rather even frequency of frontal trauma among both males and females may point to the involvement of both sexes in fights, internal or boundary warfare, or ritualised duelling. The incidence of cranial trauma in women from this area is greater than that found further upstream, but in men it is particularly significant because they have twice as much as those living upstream in the central Murray.

I have already referred to the unusual pattern of head trauma among men in the tropics and I cannot offer any good explanation for this. All that can be said is that with one frontal and five occipital injuries among 92 individuals, the pressure to fight must have been less and/ or ritualised. Mock battles to settle disputes, without direct hand-to-hand combat, must have been used more often in the north then they were in the south.

Other studies have shown some general correlation between sedentism in a particular population and head trauma, with less occurring as people settle down (see Walker 1989). It is difficult to assess whether this loose association is to be found among Australian Aborigines. Certainly there was no sedentism in Australia that matched Pueblo or Mississippian Indian farming communities, which display very small frequencies of head injury. Moreover, nowhere in Australia do we see those minimal frequencies of head injury, ignoring for the moment the 6.5 per cent among men in the north of the continent. Bearing in mind what I have already said concerning the central Murray, it is the only place where similar frequencies might be expected but these are very variable, ranging from 9.8 per cent to 25.0 per cent. Although the overall frequency is lower than elsewhere, it does not differ all that much from the general trend throughout the continent. Women are the major victims of aggression just about everywhere, but the reasons for this are different from area to area. Trauma in coastal areas may have its foundation in competition for resources; in that case the central Murray should show similar results to these areas, but it does not. The only answer I can give for this is that with larger and sedentary communities the opportunities for and avenues leading to aggression may have begun to change due to a greater necessity for co-operation in a geographically restricted area. Rather than direct conflict, disputes may have been settled by ritual argument and mock combat, perhaps acted out by a small group or even single combatants before a large audience, the highly involved ceremony taking over as a valve for release of social tensions.

Some ethnohistoric reports provide us with vivid accounts of how cranial as well as post-cranial injuries were acquired and treated by Aboriginal people. Often they contain fascinating accounts also of Aboriginal recuperative powers, such as that of 1838 given by Dr W. H. Leigh, a surgeon on the Australian Company's emigrant ship, *South Australian*. I will quote him at length, describing the traumatic results of a dispute between two Aboriginal men:

> They shook their waddies, [clubs] and rushed upon each
> other, when the battle began. It consisted in hitting
> alternate blows on the head … At length, a crack on the
> temple sprawled one of them … I went to the [man]
> and found a severe indentation of the temporal bone,
> extending across the brow three inches, and entirely
> dividing the temporal artery. I endeavoured to stop the
> hemorrhage, and elevated the bone, not doubting that he
> was soon to expire … Imagine my surprise, [the next

> morning] when in passing through the village I saw, not
> the corpse as I expected, but the very fellow himself,
> chattering and laying down the law as vociferously as the
> best of them ... he had by means of a bark fillet ...
> bound a piece of whale's entrail on the sore, and seemed
> to think nothing of it. I am sure, that if that blow and
> its fracture had been shared between two white men,
> they would have died instanter. (1982: 172–173)

He goes on to describe another incident and the miraculous recuperative powers of the injured, this time involving the lower arm.

> I saw a blackfellow at Adelaide ... who had fallen out of
> a tree, and in so doing, dislocated his wrist, the hand
> being forced back, so that the ulna bone was forced into
> the palm; the radius was broken, and the splinters
> pierced the hand. He refused to have it taken off; his
> arm swarmed with maggots: the bone remained exposed,
> and strange to say, he recovered, and I saw him before I
> left, rapping the denuded bone with his waddie, and
> laughing.

Surgery

This short section describes two forms of operations undertaken by traditional Aboriginal surgeons: trephination and amputation. I exclude circumcision and subincision because of their particular social and ritual purpose in the life of Aboriginal people that was not directly associated with health and the treatment of wounds.

Trephination

The first example of this ancient operation occurs in an adult female from the Northern Territory (Plate 8–13). The exact location is unknown but from the good condition of the bone it is likely that it originates from Arnhem Land or coastal regions. The trephined lesion is located in the roof of the vault approximately at bregma. A long, laterally-orientated groove has been scraped into the bone opening a hole measuring 10 by 8 mm that would have exposed the soft tissues of the cerebrum.

The other trephined cranium is also an adult female and comes from the south coast of New South Wales (Plate 8–14). In this case the surgery has taken place further back on the vault, where a large sagittally directed scrape has opened up a hole much larger than that in the first individual (27 by 17 mm). (For further details of these two examples see Webb 1988.)

Plate 8–13
A laterally placed trephined hole in the top of a female cranium from the Northern Territory.

The third individual is an adult female from the Tocumwal district of the upper Murray River (Plate 8–15a). The wound takes the form of a 53 mm-long by 38 mm C–shaped hole in the posterior half of the right parietal. The sides are very smooth, sloped and new bone growth has formed around all margins. Other evidence for post-operative healing takes the form of a small, blunt spike of bone which protrudes posteriorly from the inferior margin of the hole at its anterior end (Plate 8–15b). Forward of this a flake of compact bone is clearly out of place, its odd appearance suggests that it became detached from the inner table then reattached. Other trauma includes a 25 mm split fracture on the right of the external occipital crest and two depressed fractures; one 20 mm long in the centre of the left parietal, the other 33 mm long in the occipital at opisthocranion. There is no sign of associated infection or any other pathology on any part of the cranium.

Plate 8–14
This woman from the south coast of New South Wales has a large trephined opening at the back of the cranium. The operation formed a large hole in the middle of an even larger area of scraped bone that still bears some longitudinal scratches which may have resulted from several operations.

This wound is unique in my experience of Aboriginal skeletal remains and, I suggest, can only have been caused by a blow or trephination. Trauma severe enough to have made this extensive opening could normally be expected to cause the death of the individual. A weapon that produced a wound of this size would have entered the braincase, forcing bone splinters into and damaging cerebral tissues and causing widespread internal haemorrhaging. Evidence of such a blow would remain in the form of stellate fracturing, radiating from the edges of the wound, misplacement of the bone surface and no sign of healing. Instead, there is no evidence of such fracturing. The smooth and uniformly sloped edges suggest that they have been produced by being rubbed and, indeed, several scrape marks can be seen at either end of the hole around the margins. Resorption during healing may account for the eradication of many of these, however, and new bone growth is evident around the margins of the wound. Clearly, the presence of other trauma indicates that this person was the victim of aggression (the split fracture on the occipital may be a

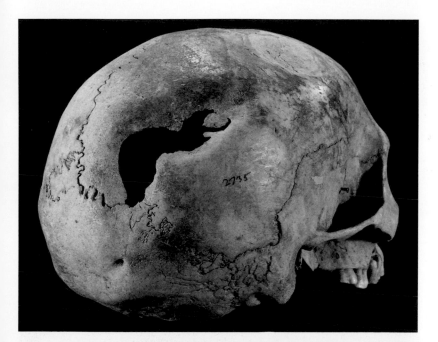

Plate 8–15a
The large S-shaped hole in this female cranium from Tocumwal either originated from one or more trephinations or similar surgical intervention following a primary trauma.

Plate 8–15b
A close-up of the large opening in Plate 8–15a shows the smooth, sloping edges of the wound with some new bone growth and a piece of reattached bone (upper).

post-mortem artifact, however). A similar example, also female, has been described from neolithic France (MacCurdy 1905).

From ethnographic observations we know that trephination was used for treating cranial wounds (Lisowski 1967; Ortner and Putschar 1981). These sources describe the Melanesian surgeon as a medicine man or wizard who was believed to have supernatural powers and able to perform sorcery. These powers added to his ability to carry out the surgery, which, in turn, usually increased the status of the surgeon before his people. Another reason for performing trephination was as a cure for epilepsy, insanity, vertigo, severe headache (migraine) and the release of the spirits, vapours or demons that might be causing these symptoms (Crump 1901; Parry 1931; Ford 1937; Piggott 1940). As in the case of most trephinations, we will never know what the precise reason was for Aboriginal people to carry out these operations. The nature of the head wound in the Tocumwal individual suggests either that surgery was used to tidy up a head wound or remedy the head pain that resulted from it. Crushed bone fragments may have been removed, for example, and the sharp, jagged edges of the wound tidied up using a sharpened stone implement. Several operations could have been performed over a period of months or even years. At least one anteriorly placed bone fragment was not removed, however, and this resulted in its later re-attachment. The main difference between this individual and the other two, therefore, is that there is a likelihood that this surgery was initiated by a primary trauma as it often was in Melanesia.

The absolute age of these individuals is not known but from their general appearance they are likely to be late Holocene. They are significant because until now there has been a total lack of evidence for this type of operation in Australia. It was generally assumed that trephination was not practised here and that the nearest use of this surgery was on the Melanesian islands of New Britain and New Ireland. To exemplify this I quote from Cleland (1953), who mentions that before the Second World War he saw a skull in the Wellcome Historical Medical Museum which had a trephine hole in it and a label indicating that it came from Australia. He goes on to say that: 'The label should have been "through" Australia, as I know of no trephining by our aboriginals [*sic*] (p. 410). I have not seen this example and have no idea whether it still exists. Aside from the crania described here being Aboriginal, there is little chance that they have any immediate connections, coming as they do from widely separated parts of the continent. These separate and rare examples of trephination are, therefore, interesting in terms of the seemingly spontaneous and unconnected manner of their appearance as a cultural phenomenon. Further, the fact that these individuals all survived surgery also says something for the skills of those administering aftercare.

Amputation

Today we associate the amputation of a limb with a very serious accident, as an attempt to prevent the spread of infection or with deliberate removal of a badly mutilated limb. The decision to remove even a part of an arm or leg by tribal socities would have been made with as much sobriety and careful consideration of alternatives as it would be now. Moreover, for the hunter-gatherer the loss of a limb must have been infinitely more of a handicap than it would be to people today with the availability of prosthetics. An active lifestyle, even among more sedentary groups, necessitated the full use of all limbs and the maintenance of their proper function. Yet, for a variety

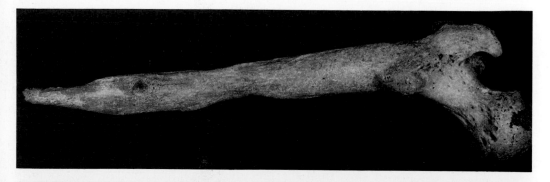

of reasons, limbs were lost in past societies and some of these were deliberately removed (Brothwell and Møller-Christensen 1963; Ackerknecht 1967; Steinbock 1976).

The two examples of amputation I want to describe here come from the central Murray region and involve the removal of the leg above the knee. The sex and age of these bones are not known although both are fully adult. The first example is a left femur which has the distal one third of its shaft missing (Plate 8–16a). Both bones are tapered to a pencil-like point at their distal ends, typical of well documented changes that take place following this type of operation (Gondos 1972). In the first example this pencilling extends up the shaft for about four centimetres until it attains a normal diameter. Some irregularity has occurred along the shaft to a point roughly halfway between the distal end and the lesser trochanter. It is difficult to know whether this can be attributed to disuse atrophy or not. The whole proximal end of this femur, however, seems to have retained a normal morphology and shows no sign of the limb not having been used. Minor osteophytosis has formed around the stump together with patches of periostitis and cortical swelling (osteitis) (Plate 8–16b, lower). An osteomyelitic lesion, surrounded by a collar of closely knitted woven bone, lies just beyond the pencilled portion of the shaft. The small cloaca in the bottom points to a chronic, low-grade secondary osteomyelitic infection.

Plate 8–16a (top)
This amputated femur from the central Murray has extensive remodelling of bone along most of the remaining shaft and infection near the amputated end.

Plate 8–16b (bottom) *Both these femora have sites of infection around their amputated stumps. These may have resulted from the operation itself or were the reason for the amputation. Bone resorption has caused the pointed morphology in both these examples which indicates also that the operations took place some considerable time before death.*

The second example involves a right femur. This bone has many of the features of the first except that the amputation took place closer to the knee. The tapered end is present, so too is osteophytosis in the form of a flange (Plate 8–16b, upper). One major difference between these bones, however, is the extent of infection in this second one. It has extensive osteomyelitic infection with a series of large, active and confluent cloacae around the stump. Another oval lesion surrounded by woven bone resides higher on the shaft which does not have the irregularity of the first.

There are two possible explanations for infection in these bones: one, it arose from the procedure itself, and two, it was a primary infection which was the reason for the amputation in the first place. The latter is probably the less likely reason but I draw the reader's attention again to the examples of chronic bone infection above the knee in Plates 6–1 and 6–4. The collapse of the tripod-like structure shown in Plate 6–4 would make the leg useless, extremely painful and a handicap. The only remedy would be amputation in order for the individual to lead any sort of active life in a tribal group, drastic though it sounds. Severe injury is another equally valid reason for this surgery but there is little evidence for this in either example discussed here.

Aboriginal people were not averse to amputation and ethnohistoric accounts suggest that at times they used quite drastic methods to do this. For example, the Reverend H. Wollaston, Assistant Colonial Surgeon in Western Australia, recorded several experiences of Aboriginal surgery. One of these is described by Worsnop and worth relating at length:

> At King George's Sound [Western Australia] Mr Wollaston had a native visitor with only one leg; he had travelled ninety-six miles in that maimed state. On examination, the limb had been severed just below the knee, and charred by fire, while about [5 cm] of calcined bone protruded through the flesh. This bone was removed at once by saw, and a presentable stump was made ... On enquiry the native told him that in a tribal fight a spear had struck his leg and penetrated the bone below the knee ... He and his companions made a fire and dug a hole in the earth sufficiently large to admit his leg, and deep enough to allow the wounded part to be on a level with the surface of the ground. The limb was then surrounded with the live coals or charcoal, and kept replenished until the leg was literally burnt off.
> (1897:143)

This account seems hardly believable but I have included it to illustrate to the reader the kind of reporting that comes down to us and from which we have to make our choices concerning their value in our work. If true, besides the pain and shock the victim suffered from this method of amputation, neither of which seems to have affected him, the method cauterised the wound and the man was, with the aid of a long stick, able to walk some distance two or three days following the operation. Cauterising by direct insertion into a small fire was also carried out on badly damaged fingers and toes (Worsnop 1897). Thomson (1975) documents an individual living in the Great Sandy Desert in 1957 who lost the lower half of his right leg following a severed nerve causing muscle atrophy and who used a crutch for support (Plate 8–17). This may have been the same individual described by others in his report as having lost his leg when it 'rotted off'. An anonymous contributor to the *British Medical Journal* of 1861 mentions the removal of the lower arm at the elbow but clay and leaves were used to staunch the bleeding rather than cauterisation. Other than these examples, I have found few references to amputation by Aboriginal people.

Plate 8–17
A photograph taken by Donald Thomson (1975) of a central Australian man with an amputated right leg who has taken to using a crutch. (Courtesy of Mrs D. M. Thomson)

I have no reason to doubt Wollaston's account and believe it may exemplify the amount of discomfort and pain that are often associated with Aboriginal people in their life in a traditional setting as well as the fortitude born out of necessity that they needed to cope with terrible injury. Cultural expectations concerning the bearing of pain without flinching or crying out by men may have been a hidden factor in this account, however, although this does not lessen the real pain of such surgery. It is, therefore, a cautionary tale for the palaeopathologist studying severe cases of trauma or infection in traditional societies. Our present cultural attitudes towards such injury, as well as our expectations of the 'normal' results of limb removal, may be quite inaccurate and cannot be readily extrapolated cross-culturally or into the past. Nor should we be too conservative when making predictions about survival among tribal or ancient victims of trauma. I have already mentioned the rapid healing of wounds and general recuperative powers of Aboriginal people and this is well documented (Army Medical Officer 1823; Smyth 1878; Spencer 1896; Worsnop 1897; Winterbotham 1951). Surviving amputation without the aid of anaesthetic may not, therefore, have been the problem for these patients that we think it was; nor, it seems, was their ability to move about following the loss of a leg. We must remember that similar operations have been carried out in war conditions for hundreds of years and graphic details of these are not rare in the literature. From the general paucity of information concerning traditional Aboriginal amputation, I would assume that while this type of surgery was undertaken from time to time it was something that was not practised regularly and only when there was little alternative.

Chapter 9

Neoplastic disease

Introduction

The mere mention of the word 'cancer' or 'tumour' causes even the sturdiest among us to shudder. Perhaps this is because the fear of developing these haunts us all. For most people that fear arises because cancer or neoplastic disease bears two very powerful connotations: extreme and unrelenting pain and, in its malignant forms, the inevitable death of its victim sooner or later. Abrams *et al.* (1950) adds a further chilling note: 'One of the most striking and disheartening qualities of cancer is the relentlessness of its spread throughout the organism'. Even with recent advances in surgical methods, drugs and chemotherapy the life of those suffering this condition can be often extremely uncomfortable and painful. The main differences between today's sufferers and those in the ancient past are our increased ability to alleviate pain as well as effect a cure in some instances by recent developments in drug therapy. Another significant difference is the kind of nursing care available to many of us.

Bony tumours derived from neoplastic disease are generally a rare phenomenon (Huvos 1979; Ortner and Putschar 1981). Naturally then, the incidence of these conditions in archaeologically-derived human remains is very low compared to other pathological conditions. Therefore, when one of these is discovered it takes on a greater importance than if it had been found among contemporary populations. One of the main reasons for the rarity of bony lesions is that with the exception of benign conditions, the death of the individual is usually brought about by the destruction of vital soft tissues long before the skeleton becomes affected. Another reason why neoplastic disease is rarer in past populations is that as a general rule it occurs in far greater frequencies in older age groups, particularly those over fifty years of age. With a shorter life expectancy in many ancient societies the incidence of neoplastic disease was naturally lower. The apparent increase in tumorous conditions among humans over the last 200 years or so has been blamed mainly on three factors: an increase in life expectancy, massive growth in population size and behavioural factors, which include widespread use and abuse of cancer-causing agents, for agricultural and industrial purposes, as well as smoking.

There are over forty types of bone tumour but poor preservation, including fragmentation, friability and incomplete skeletons reduce the palaeopathologist's ability to accurately identify many of these in archaeologically-recovered material (Steinbock 1976). It is for these reasons that the reporting of cancerous tumours in the palaeopathological literature is usually limited to individual cases rather than on population frequencies. The latter are difficult to assess when only one example might turn up in material spanning hundreds of years or in sample sizes involving thousands of bones, and so the history of this disease has been more difficult to understand. The palaeopathological treatment of cancerous conditions has by necessity become more one of recording the temporal and spatial presence of various types of neoplasm among human populations rather than using a particular frequency in a comparative manner to contrast interpopulational variations.

It is not known how long humans have suffered from neoplastic disease but evidence of benign tumours (osteoma and haemangioma) among reptiles living in the Cretaceous suggests that cancer has some very ancient beginnings (Moodie 1923; Steinbock 1976). The massive bony exostosis on the now famous *Homo erectus* femur from Trinil, Java, is probably our earliest evidence for a condition that comes close to a tumour (Manchester 1989). If we accept this large sprig of bone as a tumour rather than an exostosis (and I am not sure that I do) then it certainly predates the 'malignant tumour' on the Kanam mandible (Brothwell 1967). This mandible's age and pathological status are, like Trinil, controversial, however. Originally believed to be Lower Pleistocene in age, on recent evidence it now seems more likely that it dates from the Upper or even late Pleistocene (Tobias 1976; Wolpoff 1980). Lawrence (1935) first suggested that the swelling on the anterior surface of this mandible was caused by a tumour and this was taken up by others (Brothwell 1967). Because of the involvement of the jaw and its personal age, the possibility was raised that it might be a case of Burkitt's lymphoma (Stathopoulos 1975). But this diagnosis has not been accepted by all and it has even been proposed that the condition may not be malignant or neoplastic at all (Sandison 1975, 1981). This case adequately exemplifies the kind of controversy that surrounds palaeopathological diagnosis, even of prominent skeletal pathologies and by professional pathologists with years of experience to their credit. Evidence for neoplastic conditions among more recent peoples has been found in populations from both the New and Old Worlds (Urteaga and Pack 1966; Brothwell and Sandison 1967; Steinbock 1976; Strouhal 1976; Cassidy 1977).

Neoplasms in traditional Aboriginal people

The following descriptions are the first published evidence for neo-plastic disease in pre-contact Aboriginal people or prehistoric human skeletal remains from this region. In this survey of all the Aboriginal skeletal collections in Australia, I have not seen any evidence for giant cell tumours, haemangiomas, meningioma, ostcochondroma, chon-drosarcoma or osteosarcoma. The evidence for neoplastic disease described here includes multiple myeloma, metastatic carcinoma, naso-pharyngeal carcinoma as well as the benign osteomas and exostoses.

Multiple myeloma

Description

The first case involves a mature male Aboriginal person from the Shark Bay area of central Western Australia and who may have belonged to the Nanda tribal grouping of that region. As with the other individuals described in this chapter, there is no chronological age for these remains although their general condition suggests a late Holocene date. Personal age is not known but judging by pre-mortem tooth loss and cranial suture closure he was probably around 40 years old at the time of death. There is no post-cranial skeleton with the skull. The pathology appears as an obvious set of discrete perforations that affect most areas of the cranium and mandible (Plate 9–1). They vary in size and cluster in certain areas of the cranium. Multiple lesions appear on both parietal bones, the palate, left zygomatic arch and in a patch on the left side of the basi-cranium between and around the occipital condyle, carotid canal and foramen lacerum (Plate 9–2). The frontal bone and the mandible bear some of the largest lesions, with two large areas of destruction on the former and a wide hole on the right corpus of the latter (Plates 9–3 and 9–4). All the holes have jagged edges presenting the characteristic 'punched-out' appearance of multiple myeloma (Morse *et al.* 1974; Steinbock 1976). Both the inner and outer cranial tables are destroyed in this process together with the diploe or trabecular bone between. The lesions of multiple myeloma usually begin with metastasis from a primary site to areas where bone marrow can be found, such as the pelvis and the cranial vault. Once it reaches the diploe a gradual invasion of the compact bone of both cranial tables ensues at discrete locations. In the dry bone many of the larger holes display a 5 mm wide brown/yellow collar of discoloration around their periphery. Another distinguishing characteristic of these perforations is their sharp and quite irregular, scalloped margin.

Plate 9–1
A frontal view of 656 with multiple myeloma showing a series of large lesions on the frontal bone and mandible.

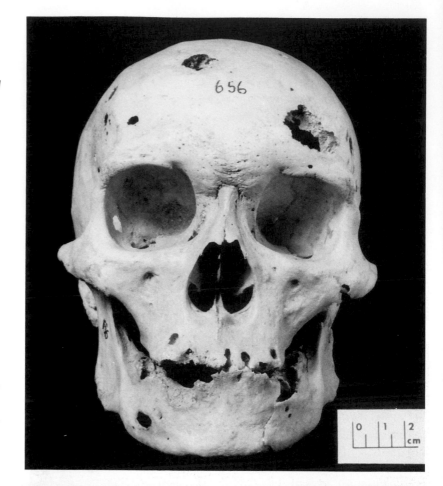

Plate 9–2
A left view of 656 in norma lateralis illustrating the scattered perforations of multiple myeloma across the bones of the vault.

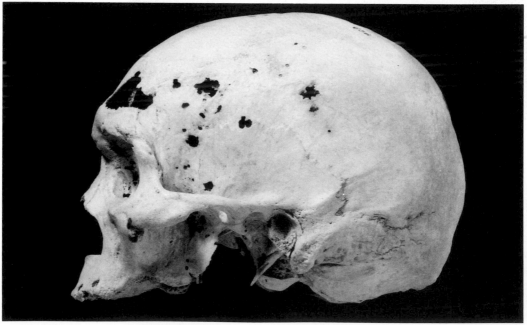

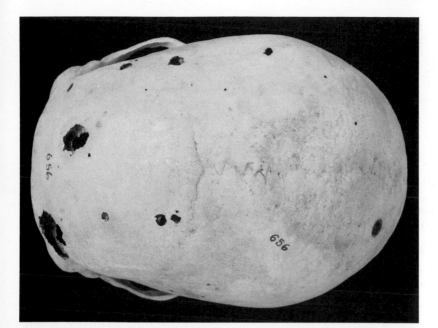

Plate 9–3
Number 656 in norma superioris.

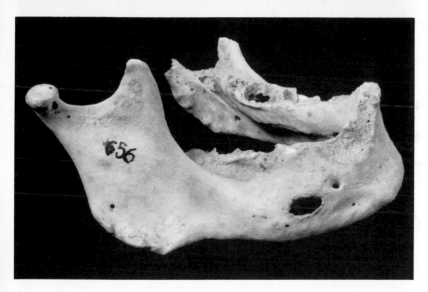

Plate 9–4
The mandible of 656, with a large lesion in the right body and extensive pre-mortem tooth loss.

The largest of the frontal lesions is situated on the left side of the cranium and measures 25 by 30 mm. Extensive and complete destruction of the bone has been caused in a 25 mm wide band from a point just behind the left superciliary ridge, laterally to and including the anterior portion of the temporal crest. A continuing inferior extension of the lesion has removed all the bone in the upper section of the wall of the left temporal fossa. Destruction of the orbital plate of the anterior frontal fossa has resulted in exposure of the orbit both superiorly and laterally. A second large circular lesion, measuring 12 mm in diameter, is situated on the right side of the frontal and somewhat higher up. The discoloration mentioned previously, surrounds this hole as it does the larger lesion and perforation is complete, with the inner table diameter slightly smaller than that of the outer. The lesions in other parts of the vault vary from a few millimetres to about one centimetre in diameter.

There is a pronounced lesion on the inferior border of the zygomatic bone at the position of the anterior attachments of the masseter muscle. Another lesion appears in the bony external wall of the maxilla, particularly the buccal portion of the alveoli housing the roots of all three molar teeth. It extends superiorly enough to have destroyed the entire area for the attachment of the buccinator muscle. On the opposite side of the mouth, three lesions appear in the lingual wall of the palate. A number of others occur on both the medial and lateral surfaces of the mandibular body. The largest of these appears on the right buccal surface just below the first molar. This individual suffered some pre-mortem tooth loss but it is difficult to assess how many teeth were lost as a direct result of lesions in the jaw.

Discussion

Multiple myeloma is the commonest of primary malignant bone tumours in adults, constituting up to 43 per cent of all cases (Steinbock 1976; Huvos 1979). As with many other neoplasms its incidence increases with age and in the United States appears to peak in the sixth and seventh decade of life with few cases reported in those below 30 years of age (Huvos 1979). A US National Cancer Survey found a case incidence of two to three in 100,000 in 1973 and that multiple myeloma seemed to be on the increase (Huvos 1979:413). Evidence for neoplastic disease affecting males more than females or vice versa is equivocal with different surveys showing each having more than the other. Although it is the most common neoplasm of bone among contemporary adult populations, reports of it in the palaeopathological literature are comparatively rare (Ritchie and Warren 1932; Brooks and Melbye 1967; Morse *et al.* 1974; Steinbock 1976). In his Table XV, Steinbock (1976:380) records only six from the New World and four from Europe, rejecting three of the four cases described by Morse *et al.* (1974) as well as another sub-adult from a previous study (Williams *et al.* 1941). Because the age of the latter is around ten years, it seems unlikely that this individual suffered from multiple myeloma, a disease mainly affecting the elderly (Porter 1963). In this case the lesions are probably the result of histiocytosis X, a disease causing skeletal lesions similar to those of myeloma but which occurs more often in the young.

Outside North America and Europe there seems to be a dearth of information regarding multiple myeloma among traditionally living indigenous people or prehistoric communities. In these circumstances the Australian evidence becomes extremely important. Having said that, I have to admit that I am not *absolutely* certain of this diagnosis. There is little doubt that it is a neoplastic condition but the band of discoloration around the lesions seems to fit more with that observed in the bony lesions of metastatic carcinoma (see below). Nevertheless, other characteristics, including the punched-out and scalloped appearance of the perforations, their size and the multiple foci in all parts of the cranium readily fit the description of multiple myeloma. The involvement of the mandible strengthens this diagnosis but the presence of the post-cranial skeleton may have contributed most to firming this conclusion. For example, further small lesions on the pelvis and scapulae would have been very helpful in this regard.

There are some other possible explanations for these lesions that we should consider. One is histiocytosis X, which has a similar appearance to multiple myeloma and affects the same parts of the human skeleton to the same degree (Steinbock 1976). The only difference is in the age of those affected, with histiocytosis X usually appearing in a much younger age group. Treponemal disease can be discounted as the lesions here are quite unlike those derived from this or non-specific infections (see Chapter 6). Besides this obvious lack of similarity, it is easy to see that their pathogenesis is quite different also (Hackett 1976).

Metastatic carcinoma is probably the only other condition that can be seriously considered as a cause of these lesions. More often than not, however, this secondary malignant tumour is marked by a single lesion which often achieves a larger diameter than those encountered in cases of multiple myeloma. Moreover, according to some researchers metastatic lesions do not normally occur over the complete cranial vault (Steinbock 1976). Others have reaffirmed the difficulty of unequivocally separating cases of multiple myeloma from metastatic carcinoma merely from the appearance of cranial lesions (Steinbock 1976). Brothwell, for example, has cautioned: 'I for one would prefer to see all … these multiple lesion cases considered as metastases until it can be proved otherwise …' (1967:337). Therefore, while leaving this individual from Western Australia as representing possibly the only case of prehistoric multiple myeloma yet discovered in this region, I would add a word of caution with respect to an absolute diagnosis to that effect.

Metastatic carcinoma

Description

The second individual with a neoplastic condition is female and comes from the Northern Territory. It was discovered with two others during the building of a casino in the capital city, Darwin. No proper archaeological study was undertaken at the time; the unearthing being part of the excavation for the foundations of the building. The manner of the discovery prevented dating of the crania. The soils in the tropical parts of Australia are not known for their bone-preserving qualities, so the generally good condition of these individuals suggests that they are probably very recent, dating to perhaps within the last two to

Plate 9–5
Metastatic carcinoma in an individual from Darwin in the Northern Territory.

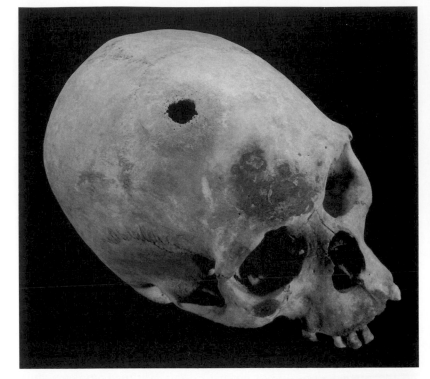

Plate 9–6
A close-up of the lesion in Plate 9–5 with peripheral discoloration around the lesion with scattered perforations.

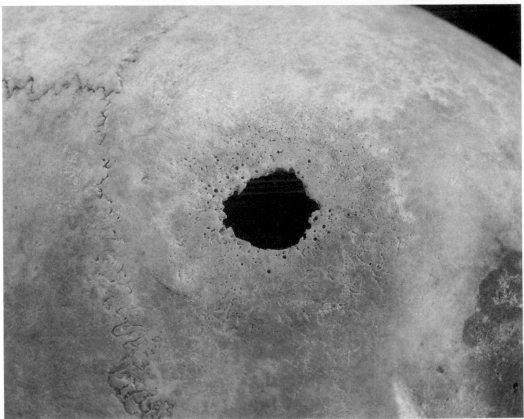

three hundred years. Cranial suture fusion, dental attrition and tooth loss on the pathological individual indicates a personal age of over 40 years. The pathology consists of a large opening on the top of the vault, situated posteriorly on the frontal bone, slightly to the right of the mid-line and close to the coronal suture (Plate 9–5). The hole is 21 mm in the antero-posterior direction and has completely perforated the cranial vault, destroying both the inner and outer cranial tables and the cancellous bone. The opening has the characteristic sharp, jagged or scalloped edge that is often encountered in malignant bone tumours (Plate 9–6). There is a zone of darker, discoloured bone around the opening similar to that observed in the multiple myeloma case and described above. Within this area there is an irregular pitting of the outer bone table by small foramina of various diameters. This occurs more commonly towards the edge of the pathology where the larger foramina are found.

Discussion

Both the appearance and position of this lesion points to it being of a neoplastic origin and particularly of the type encountered in metastatic carcinoma. The singular lesion with sharply-defined edges, discoloration and pitting is reminiscent of those in the previous case of multiple myeloma. Steinbock says that 'A differential diagnosis between metastatic carcinoma and multiple myeloma is difficult' (1976:388), but in this individual there is only the single lesion which tends to eliminate multiple myeloma as the cause. The bony lesions of metastatic carcinoma are normally a secondary effect of a metastasis in some other region of the body. Tumours of the breast, lung, kidney, prostate, ovaries as well as a range of other organs and tissues are primarily responsible for these (Møller and Møller-Christensen 1952; Brothwell 1967; Steinbock 1976; Møller-Christensen 1978). Between 12–76 per cent of malignant soft-tissue tumours metastasise to the skeleton, with breast and prostate cancers contributing 47.2 per cent and 42.4 per cent of these, respectively (Ortner and Putschar 1981). Of course, metastases can spread from a large range of affected soft-tissue areas, which include all the major organs (Manchester *et al.* 1983). Table 9–1 has been constructed from the work of Abrams and others (1950), who examined over 1000 autopsies of cancer victims. It shows some of the main areas of primary carcinoma from which secondary metastatic bone lesions are derived.

Although osteolytic metastatic carcinoma is said to be the most common form of malignant bone tumour found in palaeopathological specimens, there have been comparatively few cases reported in the literature (Steinbock 1976). Steinbock's Table XVI records ten from Europe and North America, while Ortner and Putschar (1981:395) describe another two: one from Switzerland and one from Alaska. Most of these specimens originate in the post-Christian era, the majority falling within the last millennium. The lesion on the Aboriginal person under discussion here is consistent with others diagnosed as

metastatic carcinoma and as such it is the first to be described from
the Australian continent. There is every likelihood that this woman
was suffering cancer of some primary organ or tissue elsewhere in her
body. The most likely of these is either breast or ovarian cancer.
Modern data indicates that breast cancer is the commonest cancer
among women by far (Robbins and Cotran 1974). It peaks around
the time of menopause (which might support the age assessment) but
there are striking geographic as well as racial differences in its frequency which varies also with the childbearing and pathological histories of individuals. Ovarian cancer is common also and accounts for
6 per cent of all cancers in females with malignant forms and breast
cancer occurring mostly in the 40–65 age group. Either of these could
have been primary causes of this metastatic lesion.

A second female individual displaying a similar lesion to the Darwin
individual, has also been noted. This cranium was recovered by
George Murray Black in the 1930s from an area near Lake Victoria
in southwestern New South Wales. It might be of interest to note
that it would lie within the Rufus River grouping mentioned in earlier
chapters. Unfortunately no photographic record of this individual or
detailed description of the lesion was made by me before it was reburied. The existence of this example from southeastern Australia
shows nevertheless that this particular neoplastic condition appeared
in widely separated groups.

Table 9–1 *Metastatic involvement of bone from cancerous soft tissue lesions
located elsewhere in the body (from Abrams et al. 1950; and Steinbock 1976).*

Overall	12.0–76.0%
Breast	20.5–73.1%
Lung	32.5%
Stomach	10.9%
Colon	9.3%
Rectum	13.0%
Ovary	9.0%
Kidney	19.0–40.0%
Pancreas	13.0–20.5%

Nasopharyngeal carcinoma

Case 1

Description

Two individuals are described in this section. The first is an undated
and unprovenanced adult male from Queensland, numbered 28 in the
Queensland Museum collection (Plate 9–7). Personal age is estimated
to be between 30–45 years but there is no accompanying mandible
or post-cranial skeleton. The pathology comprises a series of destructive lesions almost all of which have caused a reduction of bone due

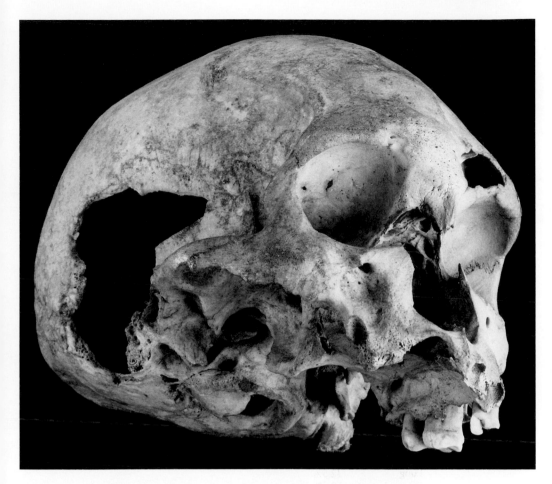

to osteolytic processes. The smooth edges of the bone are sharp and
rather jagged and there seems to be a complete absence of reactive or
new bone formation, typical of an infection of some kind. There is
massive destruction of bony structures forming the naso-palatine
region with extensive incursions into adjacent areas of the sphenoid
and ethmoid. Almost the whole right half of the palate has been
removed with the exception of a thin, transverse portion of the horizontal plate of the palatine and a small incomplete bar of bone that
almost bridges the palate at about mid-point on the right palatine
process (Plate 9–8). Laterally, the lesion has extended to the right
maxillary tooth row resulting in the removal of the whole alveolar
structure, including dental sockets, as well as other bone situated
latero-superiorly almost as far as the zygomatic process. As a consequence, all teeth from and including the second premolar back to the
third molar are missing on the right side. A large opening in the right
maxillo-alveolar region has destroyed the floor of the maxillary sinus
there, causing damage to internal structures of the nasal and sphenoid
areas and allowing the external wall of the maxilla to collapse inwards
at a point around the infra-orbital foramen (Plate 9–9). Further
damage has occurred around the incisor region and the sub-nasal area.

Plate 9–8
Most of the right side of the palate has been destroyed leaving a thin bar of bone in the subnasal region and part of the horizontal plate of palatine. The carcinoma has passed into the right maxilla and upward to the lacrimal area.

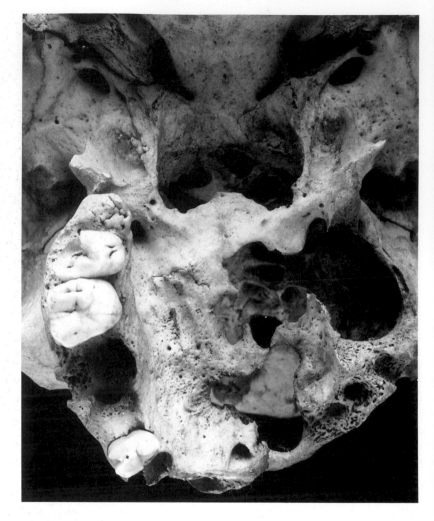

The incisors have been lost through bone atrophy to such an extent that the area separating the dental row from the nasal opening consists only of a thin bar of bone. Bone has also been removed from around the tooth sockets of the left second premolar and first molar. It is difficult to be sure whether this is directly connected to the major pathology or whether it is a separate dental pathology, although I would suggest that because of the extensive nature of the primary condition this is part of the same complex. The whole of the nasal opening has been expanded by the generalised resorption processes observed elsewhere (Plate 9–9). Inferiorly the anterior nasal spine has been resorbed together with parts of the superior margin so that the rim of the orifice is now rounded and lacks its usual sharp definition. Superiorly, both the shape and position of the nasal bones have been altered and their superior ends are atrophied in such a manner that they have become twisted. The osteolytic processes of this condition have also left them with a spiky 'melted wax' look at their inferior ends. Destruction in this region has continued to the medial side of both orbits as far as the lacrimo-maxillary sutures (Plate 9–10). The

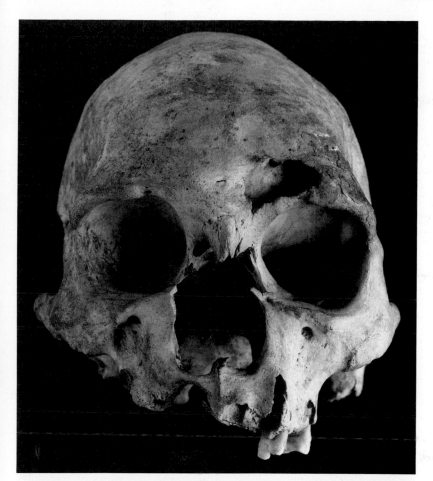

Plate 9–9
The extent of oro-facial destruction can be seen clearly in norma frontalis. All internal nasal structures have been destroyed together with the wall of the left frontal sinus into which the carcinoma has spread.

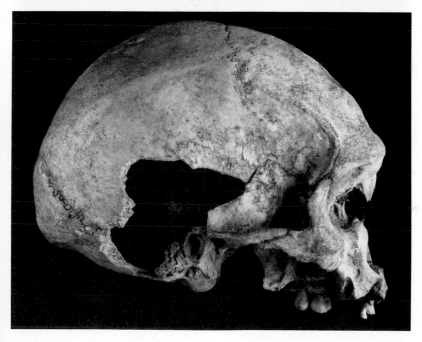

Plate 9–10
This view shows clearly the interorbital destruction that has accompanied the spread of the carcinoma.

surface of the bone in superior areas shows a disturbed, reactive surface due to the continuing destructive processes that have taken place beneath them.

Most of the internal structures of the nasal opening have been destroyed. These include the conchae, vomer, perpendicular plate of ethmoid and most of both perpendicular plates of palatine on either side. The process has expanded the whole of the nasal aperture and exposed both maxillary sinuses, the right one of which, has been 'hollowed out'. Superiorly, the pathology has extended through the roof of the nasal cavity so that both the ethmoid and sphenoid sinuses are exposed. From there the condition has spread upwards into the left frontal sinus where it has caused the formation of a large oval hole, 25 mm long by 13 mm wide, in the external bone table. The hole extends from the lateral section of the glabella and ends lateral to the supraorbital notch, removing the superciliary ridge completely. Exposure of internal sinus structures shows that the condition extended into superior portions of the air cells contained within.

Discussion

The total lack of reactive bone eliminates treponemal disease, non-specific infection and leprosy as possible causes of this pathology. The lesions conform more to the chronic, localised osteolytic destruction typical of nasopharyngeal carcinoma. A number of these cases have been reported and are described as being of a benign type (Brothwell 1967; Strouhal 1976; Ortner and Putschar 1981). The main diagnostic feature of this condition is the sharply demarcated area which has a smooth bone surface from supporting the tumour. The destructive morphology has been dictated by the gradual expansion of the slow-growing tumour, probably in a symmetrical fashion. Examples of this process are clearly shown in Fig. 590 of Ortner and Putschar (1981) and Figs. 9a and 9b of Brothwell (1967). Both the nature and degree of spread in this Aboriginal man, however, conform more to those shown in Brothwell's (1967) Fig. 9c and in Fig. 642 of Ortner and Putschar (1981). It is suggested that the nasopharyngeal region was the primary focus of this neoplasm, with its seat probably close to the wall of the right nasal fossa.

Besides the obvious inconvenience caused to the sufferer in this case, the constantly burrowing, fungating tumour must have been quite offensive to others. There must also have been a slow paralysis of much of the facial muscles, an increasingly severe speech impediment and enormous difficulties with eating and swallowing. Towards the end, quality of life for this man must have been very poor indeed.

Case 2

Introduction

The second case of nasopharyngeal carcinoma occurs in a robust male cranium from near Euston on the Murray River in southeastern

Australia. From the extent of dental attrition and the complete fusion of all cranial sutures the personal age for this individual has been put at over 50 years. The individual was part of the Murray Black collection assembled in the 1930s, which has now been reburied. As with almost all of the Murray Black collection, no chronological date is available for this individual but its partial mineralisation and the heavy blue-black manganese staining that completely covers all surfaces both suggest that it may be quite old, perhaps mid-Holocene or even earlier. There is no associated mandible or post-cranial skeleton.

Description

The pathology in this individual takes the form of a very large lesion in the right maxilla and centred on the molar area (Plate 9–11). Bone from around the tooth row has been destroyed so that all teeth from the third molar to the second premolar, inclusive, were lost pre-mortem. Deep scouring of the alveolar region at the first and second molars has passed through the roof of the socket, continued into the right maxillary sinus, penetrated the floor of the right orbit and perforated the orbital plate of the maxilla.

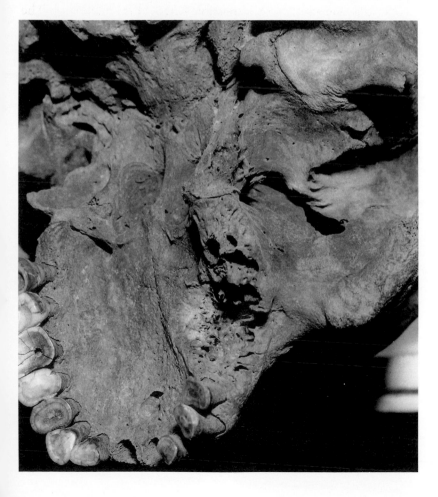

Plate 9–11
An oral carcinoma has destroyed a section of the right maxilla in a man from Euston in the central Murray.

Discussion

The sharp, spiky appearance of the bone at the margins of the lesion is typical of the osteolytic nature of this neoplasm. The bone surface conforms to a roughened appearance described elsewhere as an '... irritating osseous tissue to a medium osteoplastic reaction of honeycomb or excrescence appearance' (Stroughal 1976:615). Bone destruction is not as advanced or as widespread as in the previous case but it is reminiscent of what that individual might have looked like in the disease's formative phase.

A pathology in a prehistoric skull (No. 157) from Ancon in Peru, described by Moodie (1926:401, Fig. 6) displays a close similarity to the one in this individual. Moodie suggested that the erosion in the left maxilla of the Peruvian example was caused by pressure from a soft, unknown type of tumour. Presumably it was non-malignant, although following his examination of this same specimen, Brothwell proposed that 'malignancy can not be completely ruled out' (1967: 330). In the case of this Aboriginal person I would suggest that non-malignancy is very unlikely and that the destructive process was cut short by the death of this man before more extensive bone destruction could take place.

Osteomas

Osteomas (benign neoplasms) and exostoses are two of the terms used to describe bony outgrowths but each has a quite different appearance. (For a full explanation of the history and origin of terminology used to describe these tumours see Abbott and Courville 1943:20–21.) I excluded aural exostoses and mandibular, palatal or maxillary torii in this section as they are now more firmly recognised and used as non-metrical morphological characteristics.

Osteomas are usually small benign outgrowths of hard, dense lamellar or woven bone which occur on the outer table of the cranial vault. In archaeological specimens they appear as rounded, smooth and highly polished bumps that are often termed 'ivory' exostoses. They vary in both height and diameter from a few millimetres to several centimetres and their shape ranges from an elongated oval to an almost perfectly rounded knob. Very small 'button' osteomas are the most common form encountered by the palaeopathologist (Ortner and Putschar 1981). They appear in a male to female ratio of 3:1, affect any age group, particularly those from 16 to over 70 years, but most appear in the sixth decade of life (Huvos 1979). Although not uncommon in archaeological skeletal collections, in medical practice they are considered rare and are noted in only extremely small frequencies, usually of less than 1 per cent (Bullough 1965; Huvos 1979). This 'rarity' probably stems from the fact that they are normally painless and asymptomatic. Even those that slowly become larger are usually

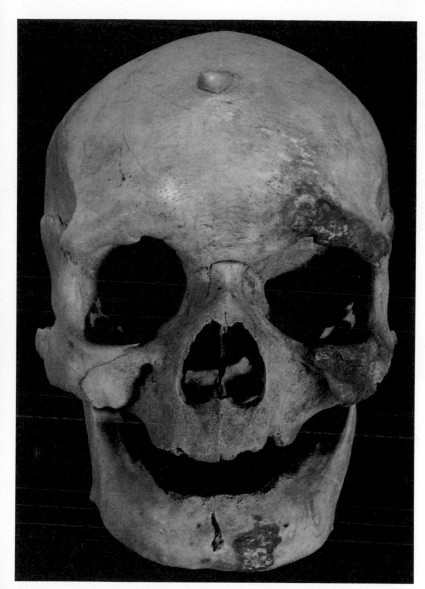

Plate 9–12
A button osteoma on a cranium from Darwin, Northern Territory.

monitored for perhaps two years or more by the 'sufferer' before he or she reports its presence. The growth only affects the person's general health if it is large or forms in the orbit, sinuses, or nasal and other areas where vital soft tissues can become displaced or damaged by it. Some prominent examples of this type are given in Abbott and Courville (1943).

The osteoma reported here acts only as an example of the type normally encountered on Australian Aboriginal crania. They usually present as a singular localised outgrowth in a similar fashion to the one shown in Plate 9–12. This male person is from Darwin and is the second of the three individuals mentioned earlier in this chapter that were discovered during building excavations. Edentulism suggests that he is of an advanced age, perhaps over sixty or even seventy years

Plate 9–13
The ivory-like appearance of the osteoma is typical of these outgrowths and this particular example shows also an undercut around its edge.

of age. The osteoma located high on the frontal area is a typical button type with some undercutting around its peripheral margin (Plate 9–13). Generally speaking, these small ivory osteomas are infrequent in Australian Aboriginal crania although when they do occur most are <5 mm in diameter. They may appear on all areas of the cranial vault, but I have not observed very large examples or those that present in sinuses, the nasal orifice or the orbits. Although my remarks stem largely from a casual series of observations, I would nevertheless suggest that the frequency of these benign tumours in Aboriginal Australia is much less than 1 per cent.

Chapter 10

Congenital malformations

Spina bifida
Meningocoele
Cleft palate
Scaphocephaly/craniosynostosis
Congenital malformations among
  Australian Aboriginal people

General introduction

About 2 per cent of children are born with some kind of congenital malformation or abnormality (Oldfield 1959). How far back this frequency goes or whether it has changed over time is impossible to tell. Congenital defects must have occurred among us from our earliest beginnings but we can only assume that many of these were terminated, either by natural spontaneous abortion or social sanction through abandonment or infanticide. If obvious skeletal defects have been with us for some time there is little solid evidence to support the idea. It is not until the late Pleistocene that firm evidence for such malformations becomes available (Ferembach 1963).

Spina bifida

The frequency of neural tube defects (NTDs), such as spina bifida, anencephaly and encephalocoeles, varies from 0.5–1.0 per cent (Jorde *et al.* 1983). Among modern societies spina bifida varies from around 0.1–0.25 per cent and rates of survival vary between 50–80 per cent depending on the severity of the defect (Schwidde 1952; Manchester 1983). In developed countries survival rates are much better than they used to be because of the intervention of modern medical care and improved surgical techniques. One can only assume that in the past, particularly the distant past, rates of survival were much lower. Certainly, those born with severe spina bifida with a myelomeningocoele (rachischisis) would quickly die, as they would today without medical care. Spina bifida occulta, on the other hand, manifests itself in a

number of ways and although a milder form, it may lead to maldevelopment of the feet or legs, scoliosis, incontinence or merely a
swelling at the base of the spine accompanied by localised hypertri-
chosis and scarring (Post 1966). Many of these symptoms, particularly
the latter, would still have been compatible with a tribal or hunter-
gatherer way of life, but much would depend on the severity of the
particular condition and the tolerance of the particular society.

The epidemiology of spina bifida is still largely unknown and sometimes symptoms are delayed to the second decade of life (Schwidde
1952). The defect has been variously ascribed to a number of causes,
such as mineral deficiencies and the ingestion of certain poisonous
minerals or salicylates, but the geographic, socioeconomic and
environmental disposition of the individual are important also (Post
1966). Genetic factors seem to play a prominent role where dominant
or recessive genes, polygenesis, cytoplasmic inheritance and certain
familial factors contribute in various ways (Post 1966; Bennett 1971;
Devore and Cordell 1981; Jorde *et al.* 1983; Dickel and Doran 1989).
Frequencies are always higher in industrialised than in non-industrialised societies. It is possible that a shift in mutation rates, stemming
from higher levels of environmental pollution since the industrial revolution, coupled with wider genetic assortment, due to enormous
growth in the world's population over the last two to three hundred
years, may have contributed to the general increase in the frequency
of congenital defects. Population increase may also go some way to
explaining why these defects are more prominent in recent populations
and rare in those existing before the late Pleistocene. Whatever the
reasons, the incidence that we see among us today may have little in
common with frequencies experienced by prehistoric or contemporary
tribal populations.

The Australian evidence

The evidence for spina bifida among pre-contact Australian Aboriginal
people comes from observations made on 18 sacra, comprising 15
males and three females (Table 10–1). Twelve have completely open
sacral canals and three have bridging at one sacral segment. None was
recovered from an archaeological context so all lack an accurate date.
As far as can be ascertained from other skeletal indicators, however,
they are from recent pre-contact populations.

Although I have examined sacra from all parts of Australia, my
observations were focussed on obtaining a general impression of neural
tube closure failure rather than establishing population frequencies.
Nevertheless, a marked variation in degrees of nonfusion and the position and length of both the superior and inferior sacral hiatus were
observed (Plates 10–1a and b). For reasons which I discuss below,
Table 10–1 lists those having complete dehiscence or bridging at one
segment only (Plate 10–2). In many collections sacra were separated
from their associated lumbar vertebrae so that associated lumbar bifurcation was checked only in number 1 and 2 and numbers 10–18.

Table 10–1   *Aboriginal sacra with severe neural tube defects (NTDs)*

	No.	Sex	Canal Defect	Origin
1.	17750	Male	Completely open	Cowes, VIC
2.	13003	Female	Completely open	Melbourne, VIC
3.	–	Female	Completely open	Nhill, VIC
4.	42.15	Male	Completely open	Murray River, SA
5.	47.82	Male	Closed at S2 only	Poon Boon, VIC
6.	47.119	Male	Completely open	Poon Boon, VIC
7.	X19	Male	Completely open	VIC
8.	–	Male	Completely open	VIC
9.	15268	Male	Completely open	Yeppoon, QLD
10.	B5	Male	Closed at S1 only	Broadbeach, QLD
11.	11966	Male	Thin bridge at S4	Cobar, NSW
12.	11434	Male	Completely open	Melville Is, NT
13.	14461	Male	Completely open	Pt Broughton, SA
14.	16503	Male	Completely open	Ceduna, SA
15.	42180	Female	Completely open	NT
16.	20723	Male	Completely open	SA
17.	25795	Male	Completely open	Goolwa, SA
18.	25335	Male	Completely open	Swanport, SA

Key:
NSW–New South Wales, NT–Northern Territory, QLD–Queensland,
SA–South Australia, VIC–Victoria

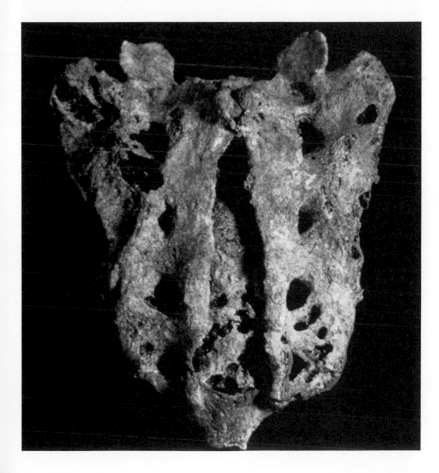

Plate 10–1a
A sacrum with partial bridging at the first segment only. This type of bridging occurs when bone extends from either wall but is divided by a thin opening or crack.

Plate 10–1b
This sacrum is fused across its third, fourth and fifth segments. Neither this specimen nor that shown in Plate 10–1a should be classed as examples of spina bifida but rather as examples of neural tube closure variant.

Plate 10–2
These sacra are from all parts of the continent and six are typical examples of complete neural tube defect. One (bottom, far right) has the defect in the form of a thin crack which divides the sacral walls between the third and fourth segments. The bone at the top (far right) is joined at the second sacral segment with a disturbed, partial join across the first.

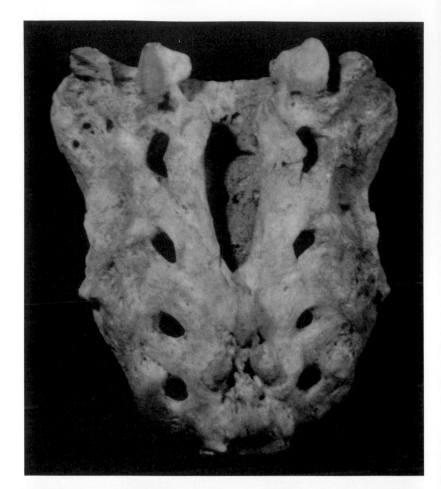

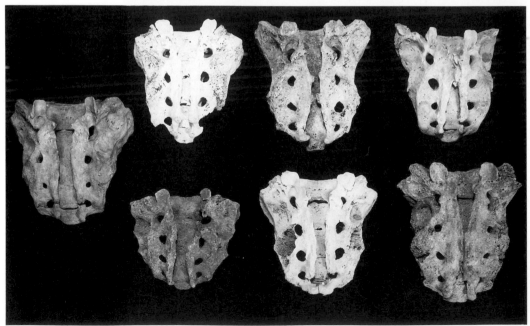

Previous reports of neural tube defect in Australian Aboriginal sacra include a single case of complete bifurcation (No. 61) from Roonka in South Australia (Prokopec 1979) and the results of a survey of 12 sacra held in the US National Museum (Post 1966). The American study found no evidence of total closure failure but in the meagre listing given in Table 10–1 there are fifteen such cases. These come from widely separated parts of the continent and show a clear bias towards males in a ratio of 5:1, which reflects the trend of 6.7:1 found by Trotter (1947) (see below). Population frequencies in such a diverse group mean absolutely nothing but the one defect from Swanport among 29 sacra surveyed indicates a frequency there of 3.5 per cent. If nothing else, the paucity of specimens among Australian collections suggests that the condition was not common and there is little doubt that those suffering severe impediments would have had a very limited chance of survival even in more sedentary groups.

A definition of spina bifida

Occasionally it is worth taking some time to reassess exactly what we mean by the definitions we use in palaeopathology. I want to do this here and look at what is meant when the palaeopathologist talks of 'spina bifida'.

The earliest evidence we have for spina bifida among skeletal remains comes from a 10–12,000 year old population found at Taforalt in Morocco (Ferembach 1963). This late Pleistocene sample suffered a much higher frequency (27 per cent) of the condition than we find in modern groups, but is this unusual? It is certainly not unique in the literature, because frequencies of between 10–90 per cent are regularly reported for such defects among various archaeological as well as more recent populations (Goldstein 1957; Post 1966; Brothwell and Powers 1968; Bennett 1971; Devore and Cordell 1981; Dickel and Doran 1989). These frequencies stem from the commonly held assumption that nonclosure of the sacral canal in these groups indicates spina bifida, particularly if more than one sacral segment is involved. As usual, the palaeopathologist has no case history, is divorced from the reality of fully examining the ancient patient and left to make an interpretation based on meagre evidence, laced with varying degrees of uncertainty. Clearly, it is difficult to believe that frequencies of 20–90 per cent are a true reflection of this serious and disabling congenital condition among ancient communities. From the genetic point of view, both social and natural factors would have surely eliminated the severely or even partially handicapped from the reproductive gene pool, thus selecting out and reducing the frequency of this defect.

In light of this I have to modify my original question. What, then, do we mean by 'spina bifida' in terms of nonfusion of the dorsal wall of the sacrum?

> Complete lack of closure of the neural canal shows the
> two halves of the spinous processes and neural arches

> pointing laterally (complete spina bifida). Incomplete
> bony fusion of one or several spinous processes (spina
> bifida occulta) is common, especially in the sacral area.
> (Ortner and Putschar 1981:355)

By this definition 'incomplete closure' of the sacral canal at one or more of the sacral segments is sufficient to indicate the presence of spina bifida. Others prefer a more cautious approach, however:

> The lack of uniform skeletal manifestation of neural-tube
> closure failure, which would lead to a more clear-cut
> definition of spina bifida, does call the link between
> these cases and modern clinical spina bifida into
> question. It is for this reason that we have opted for the
> more non-committal term 'neural-tube closure failure'.
> (Devore and Cordell 1981:67)

I would like to extend Devore and Cordell's caution even further on the following grounds. Trotter's (1947) survey of 1,227 white and Afro-American sacra clearly showed that 34 per cent had closure failure below the fourth segment; another 47 per cent displayed the apex of the inferior hiatus positioned at various points above the fourth segment, and 25 per cent presented apertures in various places along the dorsal wall of the canal. These results suggest that, at the very least, half of the sample suffered from spina bifida to some degree. Trotter makes no mention of a history of spina bifida in any of these cases, however, even for those with a completely open sacral canal, which she observed in 2.0 per cent of males and 0.3 per cent of females.

If the high frequencies reported above do indicate the real incidence of spina bifida in the past, then we can count ourselves fortunate indeed for the rather rapid decrease in the incidence of this disease in recent times. There is obviously great variation in both the position and shape of the superior and inferior sacral hiatuses and this has to be taken into consideration in any diagnosis. I support others, there-fore, in suggesting that 'spina bifida' is a more appropriate term only for those having a completely open sacral canal, preferably involving the lower lumbar vertebrae also (Dickel and Doran 1989). Moreover, with the wide range of morphological variation in the region of the sacral canal there is little need even to apply the more neutral term of 'neural-tube closure failure', because in itself it implies that such variation is a pathological defect and that cannot always be proven. Perhaps *neural tube closure variant* might be more appropriate. It is worth considering also that without involvement of the lumbar ver-tebrae the defect may have little effect on the life of the individual or even be noticeable. In such cases it is difficult to see it as pathological and, therefore, of little interest to the palaeopathologist.

Certainly, there is room for a widespread survey of the type and extent of vertebral malformations among various skeletal populations from different parts of the world. This should concentrate particularly in the lumbosacral region, in order to shed more light on both the

natural and pathological variations that occur there and their associations with clinical and sub-clinical spina bifida. A suitable comparative framework needs to be put in place so that future studies can
be put on a firmer footing in terms of these defects. Obviously, there
is an urgent need to define the extent and appearance of these sorts
of congenital conditions in order to understand the palaeoepidemiology of the disease in the past and in different parts of the world.

Meningocoele

Introduction

I want to include here the only case of cranial dysraphism (congenital
meningocoele) yet found among Australian Aboriginal skeletal
remains. The report is brief because it has been described more fully
elsewhere (Webb and Thorne 1985). I wanted to include it in this
volume, however, because of its importance as a very rare congenital
defect, as well as to ensure its place among the other congenital conditions included in this chapter.

Little is known about the history of this skull which was recovered
in the 1920s from the banks of the Darling River near Bourke in
northern New South Wales (Map 2–1, 14). It represents a young
female, probably in her mid-twenties, from the Kula tribal area. The
chronological age of the skull is not known but from bone coloration,
texture and adhering soil matrix it is thought to be late Holocene.

Description

The vault has a complete perforation of both the inner and outer
cranial tables just anterior to bregma (Plate 10–3). The hole is 12 mm
long by 10 mm wide and lies in the centre of a saucer-shaped depression 62 mm long and 47 mm wide. A rim of upward-projecting bone
rises above the normal cranial surface and defines the boundary of
this depression. Two horn-like projections lie on this rim, either side
of the hole and just anterior to the coronal suture (Plate 10–4).
Radiography shows that both the projections and the rim are composed of trabecular bone. There is no sign of infection, unusual pitting
or other irregularity on the bone surface. The only other features are
two openings, each about 6 mm in diameter, that lie posterior of the
rim and either side of the sagittal suture. They appear to be unrelated
to the main pathology and are believed to be enlarged parietal foramina. The only other sign of pathology on this individual is the presence
of multiple grooves conforming to dental hypoplasia on all incisor
teeth and the maxillary left canine.

Plate 10–3
A bregmatic menin-gocoele in a young woman from northern New South Wales. Note the large oval rim of bone encircling the central defect and the two large parietal foramina either side of the sagittal suture.

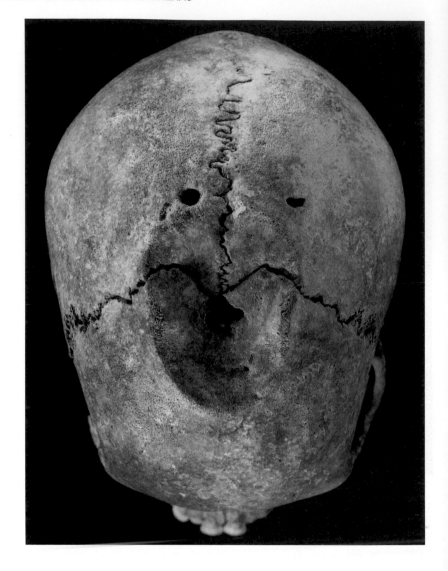

Discussion

When this individual was first examined the bregmatic defect was thought to be the result of trephination. This tentative diagnosis was soon dismissed, however, because of the complete absence of features usually associated with trephination, such as scratch marks and new bone formation from the processes of healing (Stewart 1958). Moreover, the presence of the encircling rim and horn-like bumps cannot be explained by trephination. No evidence for infection or other scarring normally associated with treponemal disease (yaws, syphilis) is present. A blow or a cut with a sharp weapon would have left a more asymmetrical scar and the likelihood of localised depressed and/or stellate fracturing. A downward-directed blow to the apex of the vault with enough force to penetrate the cranial walls would undoubtedly

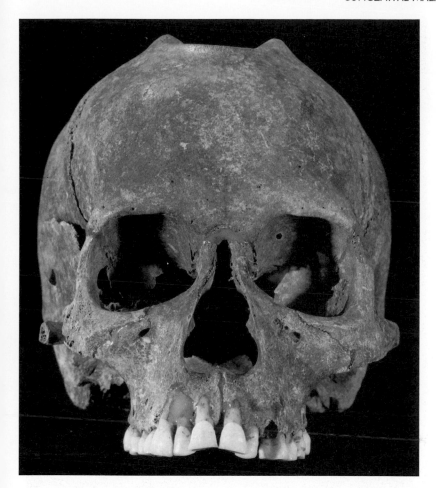

Plate 10–4
When viewed in norma frontalis the two protuberances lying posterior to the coronal suture are very prominent. They rise horn-like from each lateral edge of the bony rim surrounding the meningocoele.

have caused the woman's death. In this event, fresh crushing with little or no healing would be evident, particularly around the edges of the opening, and none of these features are present. The appearance of this pathology is not consistent with either neoplastic disease or cranial tuberculosis, neither of which could account for the raised rim and the bony bumps either.

The pathology on the vault of this woman is typical of that resulting from a congenital non-closure of the anterior fontanelle usually associated with a meningocoele. Examples of these are very rare in the archaeological record and I am aware of only four other reports, which record two cases from North America and two from Peru (Powell 1970; Gass 1971; Stewart 1975; Ortner and Putschar 1981). Bregmatic meningocoeles, such as this one, form when the anterior fontanelle is prevented from closing by pulsations transmitted upward through the infant cranium. Meningeal herniation usually forms before birth and is responsible for the 'bow-wave' morphology so prominent on the outer surface of the cranial vault. While the meningeal sac continues to protrude through the opening the anterior fontanelle is prevented from closing. The size of the sac varies from a small, almost inconspicuous herniation to one larger than the cranium itself. The diameter of the raised bony rim provides some idea of the size of the swelling, which in this case I can only assume must have been at least the size of an orange and would certainly have been very obvious. Meningocoeles are often associated with micro- or hydrocephaly but there is no sign of the alterations to the brain case consistent in these cases.

This meningocoele is significant for a couple of reasons. The first is that the individual reached adulthood. Normally, without surgical correction at an early age the chances of prolonged life depend heavily on the preservation intact of the meningeal membrane. Active protection of the delicate, membranous sac would be paramount and a constant worry to the sufferer (although whether this individual fully realised her precarious situation is not known, of course). In a tribal or hunter-gatherer society meningitis would automatically ensue if the membrane was damaged or punctured and death would be inevitable. A second reason for the significance of this meningocoele is that the woman was allowed to survive. In the light of this and other evidence presented later, the common belief that infanticide was automatically used by Australian Aborigines to dispose of every congenitally-deformed infant must be reassessed.

I am generally of the opinion that isolated palaeopathological phenomena are normally of limited value. If, however they are extremely rare or can be placed in demographic, environmental and cultural contexts they become much more valuable for interpreting the past. This meningocoele is a good example of both these. Its presence has increased our understanding of the geographical distribution of this sort of deformity; as well it has raised issues concerning cultural attitudes towards individuals who look different from others.

Cleft palate

Introduction

Cleft palate is used by the palaeopathologist as a blanket term to describe bony palatal defects resulting from a uni- or bilateral non-fusion of the embryonic maxillary and/or globular processes. The best known form of this defect is a U-shaped hole (partial cleft) of variable extent that is usually confined to the hard palate and which has a female to male ratio of 3:2 (Oldfield 1959). Another type is a more V-shaped defect which extends through the alveolar process in the region of the lateral incisor (complete cleft). This is more common in males with a ratio of about 7:3 (*ibid.*). Maldevelopment of the mandible can accompany cleft palate together with more moderate changes to the shape of the basicranium (Moss 1956).

Cleft palate has been documented in historic and prehistoric populations from many parts of the world (Alexandersen 1967b; Ortner and Putschar 1981). Today it occurs in about 1 per 600 live births in the United Kingdom and 1 in 750 in the United States, with 50 per cent having both hare lip and cleft palate and the rest divided evenly between the singular defect of hare lip or cleft palate (Oldfield 1959; Brooks and Hohenthal 1963). In this survey I describe three cases of partial cleft palate among Australian Aboriginal people.

Case 1

The first case is that of an undated female from Darwin. Minimal tooth wear indicates very little in terms of the individual's age, but partial fusion of the sagittal and bregmatic sutures suggest that she may have been in her thirties. There is a large, almost circular, hole 30 mm long in the palate which extends from a point just posterior of the incisive fossa back to and including the horizontal plate of the palate, a remnant spine of which still remains on the left side (Plate 10–5). The hole is 24 mm across at the level of the first molar and its margins follow the base of the lingual alveolar wall. There is no sign of an extension of this defect into the anterior portion of the alveolar process. The negligible tooth wear is in complete contrast to the usual pattern of attrition among traditional Aborigines, even young adults. There is little doubt that with such a large defect in the roof of the mouth chewing would have been very difficult. The almost total lack of a hard palate, essential for eating many foods, particularly those that need palatal leverage for mastication, must have restricted this person's diet to soft foods that needed little or no chewing and could be swallowed easily, thus minimising wear on the occlusal surface of the teeth.

Plate 10–5
A large cleft palate in a young woman from the Northern Territory.

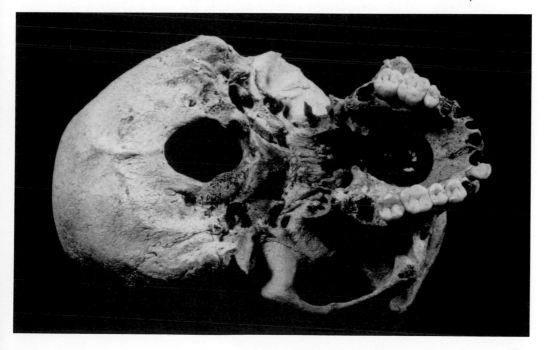

Plate 10–6
This picture was taken in partial shadow to emphasise the two circular markings on the forehead of the individual shown in Plate 10–5.

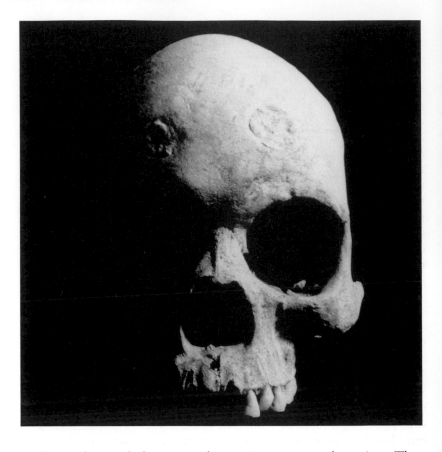

Two other pathologies on the cranium are worth noting. They appear as a pair of circular scars, 18 mm in diameter, on the frontal bone, 20 mm and 15 mm above the left and right orbits respectively (Plate 10–6). Most striking is their circular symmetry, outlined by a deep groove and positioned above each of the supraorbital notches. The circular grooving has not penetrated the outer cranial table, while in the centre of each circle the bone surface is roughened by uneven remodelling of the outer table typical of a reactive process of some kind. Both the symmetry and positioning of these scars do not conform to any familiar pathological process resulting from either an infection (yaws, syphilis, osteomyelitis, for example) or a neoplastic condition. After examining over 4500 crania in Australia I cannot recall seeing such marks before or a similar example in the literature. I suggest that they appear to be traumatic in origin and inflicted while this woman was alive. As horrific as it sounds, these may be the scars left from branding. Such cruel and inhumane treatment is ghastly to contemplate, perhaps even more so if it stemmed from the human failing to inflict cruelty on those who lack the normal mental or, in this case, physical attributes of others. The scars do give the appearance of being recent in the life of the woman and both were made by the same shaped weapon or instrument (branding iron?). I would like to add that while I cannot be absolutely sure that the lesions are the result of some deliberate act of torture, the fact this woman reached adulthood would suggest that she was probably cared for as a child by her own people and, therefore, it is difficult to believe that they were responsible for such treatment.

There is another scar over the left orbit. It extends medially across the brow from the frontozygomatic suture to a region below and including the superciliary ridge. Bone has been removed from the outer cranial table along the superior orbital margin as well as a narrow area running parallel to and above the margin. The lesion is most extensive medially where a slight excavation has formed in the area normally occupied by the superciliary ridge. The surface of the bone is roughened in this region which, in some respects, looks similar to that found in the centre of the circular scars described above. The pattern of this scarring would suggest that there has been some sort of reactive process, possibly an infection following a blow. Minor depressed fracturing has occurred on the nasal bones, particularly on the left side. Whether this trauma and the circular marks are connected in any way is not known, but all scars show complete healing.

Case 2

The second case of cleft palate is in an undated adult female from Victoria. The oval hole has eliminated the entire hard palate and is the largest defect of any of those described here (Plate 10–7). It stretches 40 mm from just posterior of the incisive fossa back to and including the horizontal plate of the palatine bone and out either side to the base of the lingual alveolar wall, where it is 28 mm across at the position of the first molar. Less of the horizontal plate of the palatine remains than in the first case described. Like that individual, there is no sign of osteoporosis or any other reaction that might be expected from an infection, the edge of the defect being quite smooth around its margin.

There is no obvious sign of a cleft lip but there is some irregularity in the right incisor area. The interproximal bone between the medial and lateral incisors has gone, nor is there any sign that it ever existed. The size of the resulting combined alveolar space is exacerbated by bone resorption on the labial and lingual margins. Lingually, the resorption has taken the alveolar margin back almost to a point where it meets the anterior edge of the cleft, only a thin bridge of smooth bone separates the two. This bridging is undermined by a hole in the posterior wall of the socket that opens into the cleft. On the labial surface of the maxilla the alveolar margin has been resorbed so that it has been brought close to the inferior margin of the right nasal aperture (Plate 10–8). It seems likely that the right central and lateral incisors were lost pre-mortem. I cannot be sure, however, whether this condition is related in any way to the cleft palate or is a quite separate pathology. A dental pathology of some sort cannot be ruled out but the lack of reactive bone and the normal appearance of infections, such as periapical abscess, make this possibility remote.

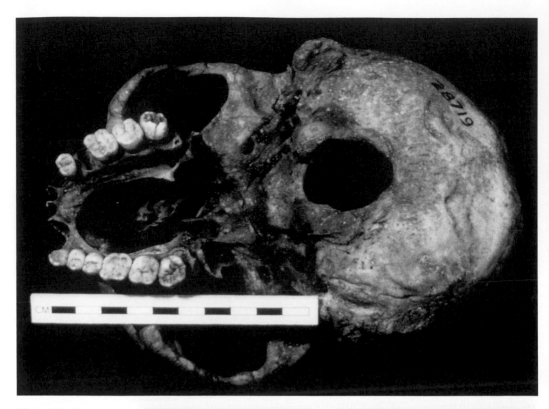

Plate 10–7

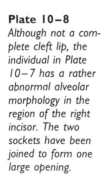

This example of cleft palate from Victoria is the most extensive defect of its type yet found in Australia. The straight appearance of the right tooth row, particularly distal of the molars, is no doubt associated with the cleft and/or the subnasal disfigurement (see Plate 10–8).

Plate 10–8

Although not a complete cleft lip, the individual in Plate 10–7 has a rather abnormal alveolar morphology in the region of the right incisor. The two sockets have been joined to form one large opening.

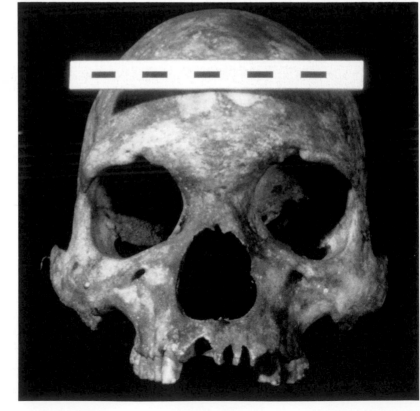

Even though this individual has a marginally larger defect than in the previous case the teeth have more wear on them. Most obvious is that all the cusps on the first and second molars have been worn down evenly. The third molars have almost no wear on them, however, suggesting that either food was not masticated this far back in the mouth or that they may not have been in occlusion very long prior to death. The cranial sutures have begun to close, suggesting this woman may have reached her late twenties or early thirties. If the third molars played no function in eating because of the defect, then their wear pattern may not tell us anything about her age and she may have been even older than is suggested.

Case 3

The third individual is an undated female also of about 40–50 years of age from the Balonne district of southern Queensland. The palatal cleft is not as extensive as in the two described above, measuring 19 mm across, at the second molar position, and 24 mm anteroposteriorly (Plate 10–9). The edge of the cleft is sharp, without any sign of osteoporosis, and its anterior margin stops well short of the base of the alveolar wall. Posteriorly, a vestigial part of the horizontal plate of the palate extends medially as a bar of bone into the gap from the right side. Anteriorly, the incisive fossa is elongated and just posterior to this there are signs of nonfusion along the intermaxillary suture. The right second molar and the left second premolar were lost premortem. The remaining teeth, including the right third molar, are

Plate 10–9

A cleft palate in an elderly male from southern Queensland. This is a smaller defect than in the previous case and there is no sign of a cleft or hare lip.

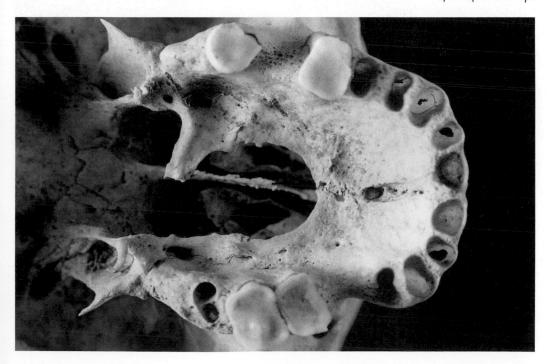

extensively worn. There is a minor periapical infection on the left lingual wall between the first and second molars.

Elsewhere, the vomer has obvious signs of atrophy around its anterior base and all conchae are reduced in size, probably by the same process. It is more than likely that these gross changes in the structures of the nasal region are associated with the more obvious congenital condition occurring in the palate. The asymmetrical nature of this defect could suggest a cause other than cleft palate. There is, however, no sign of any infectious or other pathological condition in the palate or elsewhere on the cranium from which this conclusion might be drawn. Therefore, while I am reluctant to suggest that anything other than a congenital condition is the cause of this palatal defect, my conclusion is more tentative than those I have made for the other cases described above.

Scaphocephaly/craniosynostosis

Scaphocephaly normally describes the elongated disfigurement of the cranium following craniostenosis, or premature suture closure (Ortner and Putschar 1981). The resulting head shape is determined by the amount of premature closure and what suture is involved. There have been a number of reports describing these alterations in a variety of human populations from different time periods and geographical settings (Eiseley and Asling 1944; Hohenthal and Brooks 1960; Comas 1965; Bennett 1967; Ortner and Putschar 1981; Susuki and Ikeda 1981). There are two nineteenth-century descriptions of Aboriginal scaphocephalic skulls although one of these written in 1883 does not recognise the morphology as pathological (Davies 1867; Miklouho-Maclay 1883). Five cases were described over fifty years ago by Fenner (1939), including the individual (B1) mentioned by Miklouho-Maclay. Another example, a five-year-old-child from the Roonka site, is mentioned very briefly by Prokopec (1979).

I have examined four of those described by Fenner (1939) and further descriptions of two of these are provided in Chapter 4. While I have little to add to Fenner's general description, his work contained only diopterographic drawings. In view of this I want to raise a few salient points concerning A248, which do not seem to have been discussed before, as well as provide some photographic record of this pathologically important individual.

A248

A248 is the cranium of a 6-year-old child and was last known to be in the collection of the South Australian Museum (Plate 10–10). No chronological age is available for this individual and except for the

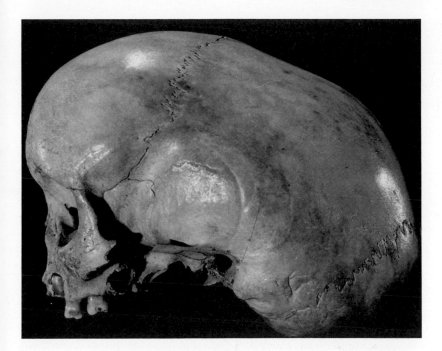

fact that it comes from the Wellington area of South Australia, the history of the find is not known. Its cranial morphology is typically scaphocephalic. It is long (maximum length 197 mm) but not partic- ularly high (basion-bregma 112 mm), with a downward projecting occipital and a bulging forehead. The shape has been formed by the complete premature fusion and obliteration of the sagittal suture and partial fusion of the temporal squamous sutures. Although both the coronal and lambdoid sutures remain open, their interdigitation dis- plays a wider than normal zigzag pattern as though drawn lengthwise by the anteroposterior expansion of the parietals (Plates 10–11 and 10–12). In *norma lateralis* there is a hint of two bulges, at bregma and in the mid-sagittal region, together with the post-bregmatic saddle, described in a more extreme form for 38586 in Chapter 4. Unlike 38586, however, the basi-occipital region of A248 curves downward behind the neck region, as though the lack of lateral expan- sion, due to the premature fusion of the sagittal suture, has directed growth towards the back of the head, resulting in its elongation. The most obvious difference between A248 and 38586 is the total lack of cranial thickening; in fact A248 has a rather thin and delicate bone construction (Plate 10–13).

The two scaphocephalic individuals described by Fenner came from Tea Tree, South Australia (A16520) and Rockhampton in Queensland (B1). Both have an extreme dolichocephalic morphology and oblit- erated sagittal sutures. The South Australian individual lacks the entire face and basi-cranium and the Queensland example has much of its face missing also (Plate 10–14). The cranial walls of both these adults are of a normal thickness and neither has any other pathology.

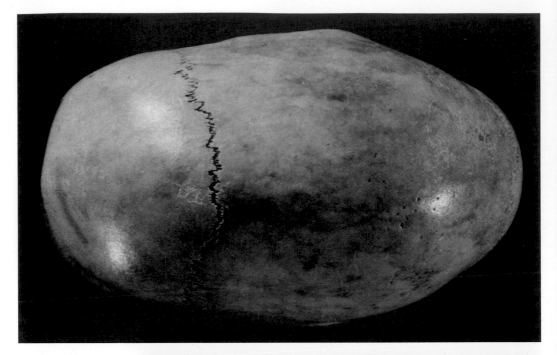

Plate 10–11
The long dolicho-cephalic shape of the cranium is plain in norma verticalis. There is no sign of the sagittal suture which has completely fused both externally and internally. The coronal suture has not fused which seems to have provided for some normal development in the area.

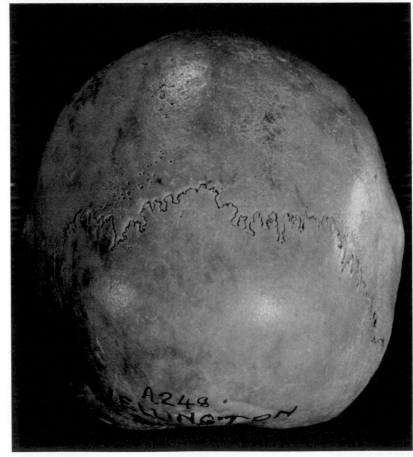

Plate 10–12
The scaphocephalic cranium in norma occipitalis. The lambdoid suture is fused endocranially and partially fused ectocranially. This, together with the sagittal fusion, is probably the reason for the posteriorly directed distortion at the back.

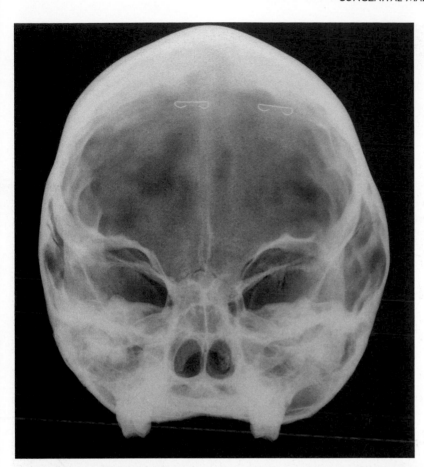

Plate 10–13
A radiograph in norma frontalis shows the thin cranial walls and delicate bone structure of this scaphocephalic cranium which contrasts strongly with that of the fossilised child (35856) described in Chapter 4. (The staples are contained in the support used for the radiograph.)

Plate 10–14
An adult scaphocephalic calvarium from South Australia with all sutures fused.

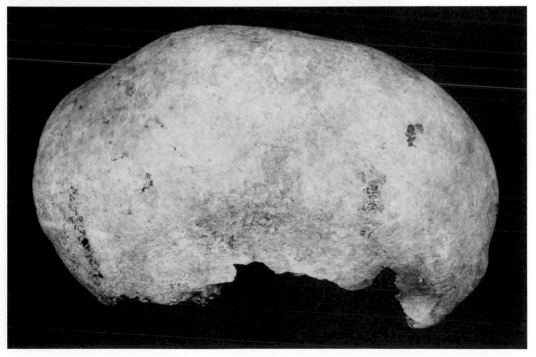

Plate 10–15
The number 77 individual from Roonka. Although all major sutures have closed prematurely, there has been no major distortion of the cranium as occurred in the other individuals described in this section. This is the only individual in Australia, apart from 38587, which has a 'clown's chaplet' at bregma (see Plate 4–27). Note also the patch of osteoporotic pitting on the parietal just anterior to the lambdoid suture. This occurs on both parietals at the same place, constituting the only known example of symmetrical osteoporosis from mainland Australia.

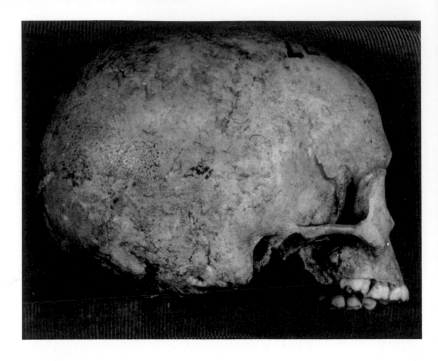

Roonka burial 77

This 6-year-old child comes from the Roonka Flat site on the lower Murray River in South Australia and is dated to 220 ± 80BP (ANU3262) (Pretty 1977; Prokopec 1979). The craniostenosis suffered by this individual has been described elsewhere (Prokopec 1984). There are, however, two patches of pitting, resembling symmetrical osteoporosis, are visible, one on either parietal, close to the lambdoid suture, but these are nowhere near as extensive as those on the individual from York Island, Torres Strait, and described in Chapter 5 (Plate 10–15). Symmetrical osteoporosis often affects the frontal base also but this is not the case for either individual. The association of this condition with anaemia has been well documented and, therefore, I can only assume that this individual was suffering some sort of severe anaemia at the time of death.

Congenital malformations among Australian Aboriginal people

No human population is free of congenital malformations. Like everyone else, Aboriginal Australians had their share and from the evidence presented above it seems as though there was a wide variety of these. We know also that traditional Aboriginal people suffered other congenital conditions that we are unable to detect from the skeleton alone, but many of these were minor or involved soft tissues (Crotty and Webb 1960). Others were more obvious, such as dwarfism, achondroplasia, supernumerary digits and so on, imposing varying degrees of hardship on the sufferer (Cleland and Maegraith 1930; Basedow 1932).

The presence of the conditions reported here, together with the evidence for severe trauma presented in Chapter 8, shows that there was a great tolerance in Aboriginal society of malformed and badly injured individuals as well as a willingness to look after their sick, deformed and maimed. On the one hand, that is not surprising, most societies share a compassion for the afflicted. In the case of Australia, however, there has been a widely held belief, particularly among non-Aboriginal Australians, that traditional Aboriginal people always dealt harshly with the afflicted, usually in the form of infanticide or abandonment (Blainey 1975). This is not to say that these means were not employed at certain times and for a variety of reasons, but the palaeopathological evidence presented so far shows that not all malformed individuals were treated in this manner, far from it, and in the case of some quite severe deformities the child may even have lived for as long as the particular defect allowed. Certainly many congenital conditions, such as cleft palate, were carried into old age. North American Indians believed that the mother of a child born with cleft palate had broken a food taboo, particularly associated with the rabbit. Hence the split lip of the animal was transferred to the infant (Manchester 1983). Similarly, some Australian Aborigines believed that malformations were brought about by the mother, under the influence of the stars, eating some kind of forbidden food during pregnancy (Eyre 1845). As with any human population in the past, explanation for the birth of innocent children in a deformed state has to have some sort of supernatural explanation. In some cases such malformation is taken as a sign that the sufferer is important in some way, with special powers and certainly someone that should be cared for.

Unfortunately we know nothing of how those described in this chapter were viewed by their people. The evidence presented here extends our knowledge of the variety and geographical spread of congenital defects among hunter-gatherer groups. It demonstrates also how people have coped with them as best they could without destroying individuals who might not function in quite the same way as the majority of the people in the group.

Chapter 11

Motupore: the palaeopathology of a prehistoric New Guinea island community

Introduction

At the beginning of this book I spoke of the divergence in the palaeo-epidemiological histories of Australia and Papua New Guinea following their separation by rising seas at the end of the last Ice Age. It is also interesting to see the stark differences that emerged in their respective epidemiologies by the intervention of what is a rather small shallow oceanic strait, rather than the pathological continuum that existed when they were part of the same continent. Prominent in my earlier remarks was the fact that we know almost nothing about the pre-contact history of human health in Papua New Guinea and, at this time, are not able to trace that history in quite the same way I have attempted for Australia. One of the main reasons for this is the difficulty of obtaining palaeopathological data from the region. I mentioned also that the major factors determining the particular health status of the inhabitants of Papua New Guinea have been the equatorial environment and the size and demographic organisation of its populace. It is because of these important contrasts between Australia and Papua New Guinea that I have included the following report. These data are vital in our story because they provide a unique opportunity to compare and contrast the Australian picture with our closest northern neighbour which, until about 7000 years ago, formed the northern end of our continent.

Motupore Island

Motupore Island lies half a kilometre from the southern coast of Papua New Guinea's Central Province and 16 km east of Port Moresby (Allen 1978). It is small, measuring only 800 m long and 100 m wide with a maximum elevation of 200 m; it is covered with eucalyptus, with mangroves along its northern protected shoreline. The prehistoric population of the island occupied a comparatively small section of the north end of the island. Twenty-two radiocarbon dates have bracketed this occupation from about 1200AD to the middle of the seventeenth century, with a date for transient occupation that began over 1000 years ago. Archaeological evidence suggests that the same cultural group, Austronesian-speaking Motu people, occupied the island throughout the main occupation period (Allen 1978). The Motu exploited local shell beds and analysis of shell size from midden deposits shows a gradual reduction in size and frequency over time: an indication of continuous occupation and, perhaps, a steady increase in the size of the population during the time that the island was occupied. Besides shellfish, other marine food consumed included fish, turtle and dugong (*Dugong dugong*). The people of Motupore also made pots for trading with the mainland people living across the bay as well as right along this section of the New Guinea coast. In return for the ceramics, the mainlanders exchanged Agile wallabies (*Macropus agilis*), yams and bananas which acted to supplement the islanders' diet (Allen 1977; Oram 1977).

The skeletal sample

The skeletal remains examined in this survey were recovered from a series of excavations on Motupore undertaken between 1970 and 1975 (Allen 1978). The work revealed a large cemetery population of which 42 individuals comprise the sample used in this survey. The sample is divided into two groups dated between 1200–1500AD (n=17) and between 1500–1700AD (n=25) which are only part of what is thought to be a much larger inhumed population. For this reason they cannot be used to give more than a rough indication of the health status of the people living on this island. Nevertheless, they do add some useful information to the developing picture of the antiquity and distribution of certain diseases in the region.

Pseudopathologies

As with any palaeopathological diagnosis, care has been taken to identify and eliminate specimens with post-mortem bone changes that can be mistaken for pathology. Such changes are perhaps more common in regions like Papua New Guinea because of the particular soil chemistry and insect communities that are common to humid tropical areas. These pseudopathologies can be caused by a variety of factors that usually stem from the environment in which the material has been interred. I make particular mention of these in this chapter because the soils of Motupore have caused severe leaching, friability and fragmentation of the bone, rendering much of it fragile so that it is difficult to reconstruct and analyse. On some specimens there is evidence of gnawing by rodents which gives the impression of a pathological process similar to periostitis. There is also some damage caused by the mud wasps (*Sphecidae* sp.) common to this region. These creatures burrow into the bone, producing neat, round holes which they then line with a 'paste' of chewed bone. The holes range from 0.5–1 cm in diameter and often look like cloacae typical of a chronic, suppurative condition. Alternatively, when they occur on the cranium they can give the appearance of a neoplastic condition such as multiple myeloma.

Groundwater action has produced an even erosion of the outer cranial table of some individuals which looks 'typically' treponemal, particularly the stage defined as serpiginous cavitation (Hackett 1976). Closer inspection, however, quickly dispels this conclusion. Periosteal erosion by soil acids and groundwater seepage often produces 'lesions' which occur more readily on the smaller and more fragile infant bones as well as on adult hands and feet. The absence of new or reactive bone formation around the periphery of these areas, however, normally confirms their post-mortem origin.

Because of the poor condition of these remains, reconstruction of many individuals has been difficult. Subsequently, ageing and sexing has been difficult also. Of the 42 skeletons recovered 22 (53.7 per cent) have some sort of pathology (Table 11–1). Of these, 11 are male and another seven are female with two infants and two of undetermined sex. One male and four females have been only tentatively sexed because of their poor condition. All skeletons are incomplete but mixing of the bones during interment has caused additional problems for interpretation. Site disturbance has been caused by later burials, reburial following local mortuary customs and by intrusive crab burrows which permeate the cemetery. The pathologies have been grouped into the following categories: trauma, non-specific infection, treponemal infection, tuberculosis, haemolytic disease, tumours and arthritis.

Trauma

A fracture of the left second rib of M33 has left a small callus just distal to the tubercle. Radiography does not show the type of break or whether it was complete or partial. Rib fractures can result in the piercing of the lung with serious or fatal results if left untreated. In this case the complete unification and good alignment of the bone seems to preclude such complications. This type of injury is usually the result of a violent blow to the chest or a fall onto a hard object.

Osteophytic spicules are evident on the superior border of the right patella of M15, M25 and M42. Such exostoses are indicative of strain on the patella from the quadriceps tendon, probably by repetitive extension of the knee from an acute flexed position, for example, the movement made in rising from a squatting position.

Table 11–1 *Pathological individuals from a cemetery population, on Motupore Island, Papua New Guinea.*

Serial Number	Sex	Date	TR	NI	TI	HD	AC	AT	AL	AO
M2	M	T			*		*			
M3	M	T					*			*
M4	M	T								*
M5	F	T								*
M7	F	T			*					
M8	M	T							*	
M10	F	T			*					
M12	SA	T			*					
M15	M	T	*		*					*
M17	M	T			*					*
M18	M	T				*				
M22	M	T			*	*	*		*	*
M23	M	K			*		*			
M24	?	K							*	*
M26	M	K					*		*	*
M27	SA	T				*I				
M29	M	K							*	
M32	F	K	*					*		
M33	?	K			*	*				
M37	F	T		*					*	
M39	F	T			*					*
M42	F	T			*					*

Key:
M – Male
F – Female
SA – Sub-adult
? – Sex unknown
K – Buried between 1100 and 1500AD
T – Buried between 1500 and 1700AD
*I – Thalassaemia sufferer

Pathology Key:
TR – Trauma, NI – Non-specific Infection, TI – Treponemal Infection, HD – Haematological Disease, AC – Arthritis on cervical vertebrae, AT – Arthritis on thoracic vertebrae, AL – Arthritis on lumbar vertebrae, AO – Arthritis on other joints

Non-specific infection

The only firm evidence for non-specific infection is found on the left humerus of M37 (Plates 11–1a and b). The whole diaphysis is moderately distorted with remodelled, sclerotic bone. Patches of periostitis appear over almost the whole surface together with striations and subperiosteal bone formation. Radiographic examination reveals a cortex comprised of mainly trabecular bone with a thin crust of hard, compact bone remodelled by irregular patches of periostitis (Plate 11–2). At the proximal end there are six large and one small cloacae; two of the larger ones have coalesced to form a single large opening (Plate 11–1b). Another large hole lies medial to the deltoid tuberosity and a smaller one lies inferior to the radial groove. Because the rest

Plate 11–1a
(*left*) *Non-specific infection in the left humerus from burial M37, anterior view.*

Plate 11–1b
(*middle*) *The humerus from burial M37, posterior view.*

Plate 11–2
(*right*) *A radiograph of the M37 humerus with multiple foci of infection.*

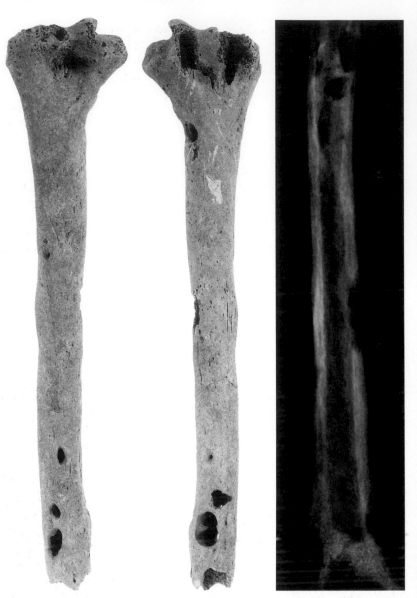

of the skeleton seems free of disease, it is thought that this is a localised, chronic bone infection resulting from an overlying soft tissue lesion. Further support for this diagnosis comes from the orientation of the cloacal margin. The smooth, new bone is directed towards the medullary cavity, suggesting an external to internal passage of infection.

Treponemal infection

Treponemal infection occurs in 11 individuals (26.2 per cent of the population) and is by far the commonest pathology found on Motupore. With so many individuals involved only a brief outline of the

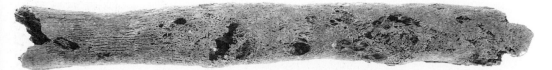

salient features will be given, together with a list of those affected. (For details of the diagnostic criteria used see Chapter 6.)

One of the most prominent features of osseous tertiary treponemal disease is osteomyelitis of the post-cranial skeleton and this, together with periostitis and osteitis, is the commonest pathological feature on the Motupore remains (Plate 11–3). The amount of antero-posterior bowing among tibia in this series is variable but distinct and easily discernible from normal tibia. Bowing, however, can often be a more apparent than real pathological phenomenon (see Chapter 6). Radiography reveals sub-periosteal apposition of bone both anteriorly and posteriorly on the tibia, thickening the bone along its middle one third (Plates 11–4a,b and c). The resulting shape gives the bone a bowed appearance when, in fact, little actual bowing has occurred. No extreme bowing, typical of the Australian 'boomerang tibia', is present among the prehistoric Motupore population.

Plate 11–3
Widespread osteo-myelitic infection in the left femur of M32 has destroyed large areas of compact bone, making it fragile and leaving it open to pathological fracturing.

Plate 11–4a
(bottom left)
There is marked anterior sub-periosteal bone apposition in the middle one-third of the shafts of these two bones which is typical in a bowed tibia. A uniform thickening occurs in the bone on the right, but in the bone on the left it is largely confined to the anterior wall. (The large mass in this bone is an artifact used to balance the specimen for the radiograph.) A crack in the lower end of the shaft of the bone on the right is post-mortem damage.

Plate 11–4b
(bottom right)
The obvious contrast between these two bowed tibiae is that the one on the left has no sign of infection and displays a typically uniform morphology, whereas the bone on the right is clearly suffering from an extensive, chronic infection with large areas of sclerotic sub-periosteal bone and associated cloacae.

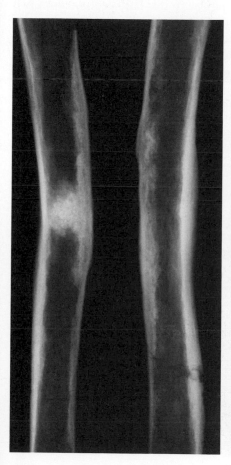

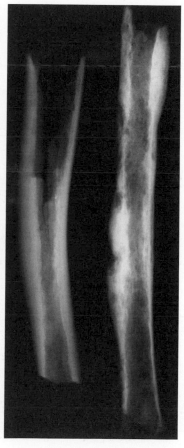

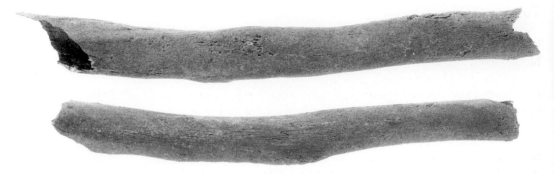

Plates 11–4c, d
The external view of the two tibiae shown in the previous plate.

Most long bone infection is probably derived from the treponemal disease which is patently obvious on one (M33) of five incomplete crania in this series. These lesions cover two-thirds of the frontal bone, some of the right parietal and present three stages in the pathogenesis of cranial treponemal infection (Plate 11-5). These include serpiginous cavitation, nodular cavitation and caries sicca (Hackett 1976).

An oval lesion 15 mm wide and 25 mm long lies on the inferior side of the left clavicle of M2 and the right clavicles of M22, M23 and M42. The eroded periosteum and cortex at the costo-clavicular articulation are suggestive of wear against the first rib during repetitive arm movement. A wear pattern similar to this has been noted on two clavicles recovered at Nebira, an archaeological site located 20 km to the northwest but 10 km inland from the coast (Pietrusewski 1976: 185). Handedness is reflected in the right clavicles, in that they are somewhat larger in diameter than the matching left ones.

Plate 11–5
Nodular and serpiginous cavitation with radial scars on the cranium of M33. These changes are typical of those found on the crania of individuals suffering tertiary stage treponematosis. This individual is the earliest known example of this particular disease from the region.

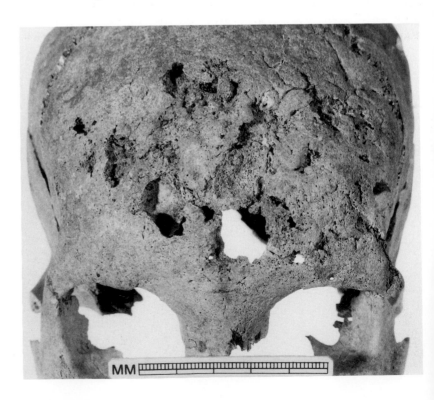

Tuberculosis

Pott's disease and other signs of tuberculosis have been found among burials from the contemporaneous site of Nebira, but no lesion that can be firmly identified as tuberculosis has been found among the Motupore population. Unfortunately, there has been no opportunity to compare the Motupore population with that from Nebira, but there is a great similarity between some forms of skeletal tuberculosis and natural bone erosion. It is possible, therefore, that given the fragmentary and eroded nature of the Motupore material, tuberculosis could be overlooked and interpreted as post-mortem damage. Skeletal tuberculosis mainly affects the spine and the hip region, two areas vulnerable to erosion and fragmentation, particularly in the Motupore remains. Besides the lack of evidence for tuberculosis, no overt signs of metabolic disease, congenital malformation or severe trauma were observed.

Anaemia and blood dyscrasias

I have already discussed cribra orbitalia and its association with anaemia at some length in Chapter 5. It is present in three of the Motupore crania, M22, M27 and M33. The most severe form lies in both orbits of M27, a 7–9 year-old-child dated to between 1500 and 1700AD (Plate 11–6). Symmetrical osteoporosis can be seen on the left side of the frontal bone as well as on the posterior portion of both parietals (Plates 11–7, 11–8). This distinctive condition is normally associated with genetically determined haemolytic blood disease, such

Plate 11–6
Although much of the orbital plate has been destroyed in burial M27, extensive cribra orbitalia indicative of severe anaemia is clearly visible.

Plate 11–7
The rough surface of the large frontal lesion on M27 is typical of symmetrical osteoporosis. The extensive nature of the condition suggests that this individual may have been a homozygous thalassaemia sufferer.

Plate 11–8
Symmetrical osteoporosis is clearly evident on the left parietal of M27, but only a fragment of this lesion remains on the right parietal (top, right).

as sickle cell anaemia and thalassaemia, as well as severe iron deficiency anaemia resulting from dietary deficiency or severe hookworm infestation (Cooley and Lee 1925; Britton *et al.* 1960; Shahidi and Diamond 1961; Aksoy *et al.* 1966; Steinbock 1976). The lesion on the frontal bone is 47 mm long by 46 mm across with a central thickness of 12 mm, compared to an average of 5 mm for other parts of the skull. An X-ray of this lesion clearly shows the typical 'hair-on-end' morphology of piled-up bony spicules caused by diploic hyperplasia which generally provides the best criterion for diagnosing a genetically determined blood disease (Plate 11–9). I have described in detail the pathogenesis of this condition in Chapter 3. Anaemia is much more prevalent in contemporary coastal groups than in Highland communities in Papua New Guinea, affecting up to 90 per cent of the population (Kariks 1969; Crane *et al.* 1971-72; Sinnett 1972).

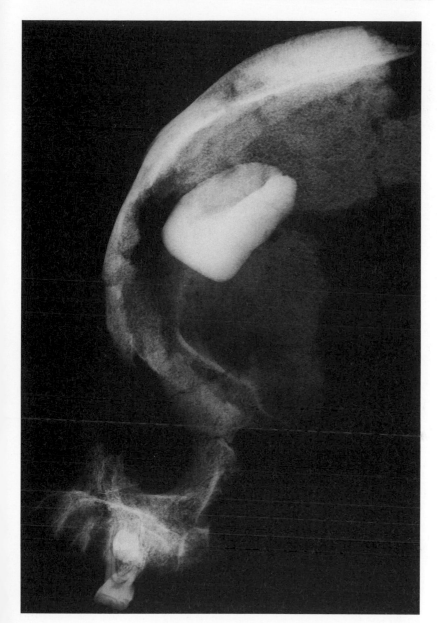

Plate 11–9
A radiograph of the frontal lesion of M27 in norma lateralis *which shows the typical 'hair-on-end' morphology associated with severe anaemia and genetic blood dyscrasias such as thalassaemia. (The large opaque object is an external artifact used for the radiograph.)*

Tumours

The only obvious tumour among these remains is that of a benign osteoma on the external occipital protuberance of M29. The origin of such an ivory-like projection may be a developmental abnormality, trauma or in some cases infection (Bullough 1965). They are often symptomless, particularly when they are small as in this case, and in this position on the head this one would have been of little consequence to the individual (see Chapter 9).

Arthritis

Of the 42 individuals in this survey 16 (38.1 per cent) were found to have some form of arthritis. Differential preservation of vertebral elements has rendered them largely unsuitable for detailed analysis, however. For example, more cervical and lumbar vertebrae have survived than thoracic, so even though arthritis occurs on the two former types, we cannot conclude that it affected these areas of the spine more than any other. Having said this, note should be taken of the prevalence of arthritic lipping on centra in the cervical and lumbar regions. Almost all individuals with these vertebrae preserved display some degree of osteophytosis on the superior and/or inferior margins of the vertebral body. Perhaps this is to be expected in the aged and those leading an active life which produces heavy stress demands on these vulnerable areas of the spine. Because accurate ageing is not generally possible for this population, I cannot be sure of the extent to which age has caused this condition among these people. If, as I suspect, they are living to a moderately old age and leading an active and rather arduous lifestyle, however, then osteophytic lipping should not be unexpected. The more debilitating forms of spinal arthritis, such as ankylosing spondylitis, severe vertebral osteophytosis or rheumatoid osteoarthritis, are not evident on Motupore.

Arthritis occurs on the associated articular heads of the right elbow joint of M5. Osteophytic exostosis has proliferated in the olecranon and coronoid fossae of the humerus and traces the line of attachment of the joint capsule. Further osteophytosis lies on the medial edge of the trochlear and around the capitulum, and eburnation is featured on the distal articular surface. There is osteophytic lipping around the border of the trochlear notch of the ulna and radial articulation. This also occurs around the head of the radius while the articular surface has erosion, pitting and slight eburnation. The reader may remember a similar pattern in the right elbow of WLH3 from Lake Mungo (see Chapter 4). M3 also displays slight osteophytic lipping around the glenoid fossa and a small cloaca in the olecranon fossa which is suggestive of a suppurative infection. The spread of a primary infection like this one causes pyogenic arthritis in 15 per cent of all cases (Steinbock 1976). This is thought to be the origin of the arthritis in M5.

'Cervical syndrome' is caused by reduction in the diameter of the transverse foramina of a cervical vertebra. It normally pinches a nerve of the cervical plexus which passes through these foramina causing various secondary effects. Such reduction is usually the result of osteoarthritic lipping which encroaches on the foraminal opening. It seems that this has occurred in M3. Here, the left transverse foramina that lies between C3 and C4 has been narrowed in this way, constricting the supraclavicular nerve. Pinching of the nerve could have caused numbing and partial paralysis of the levator scapulae, scalene, trapezius and sternomastoid muscles as well as interfering with diaphragm movement by trapping the phrenic nerve.

Treponemal disease

The evidence for treponemal disease among the Motu of Motupore Island has valuable implications for understanding its antiquity, origin and spread in the region. Although caries sicca on the cranium of M33 matches that caused by venereal syphilis, this individual was buried between the twelfth and sixteenth centuries, predating all known European contact in this part of Oceania. Identical lesions on human remains from the Bakong River, Sarawak, and dated to the early sixteenth century are believed to have been caused by yaws (Brothwell 1976:442). Further evidence of pre-contact yaws in Oceania has been found on Tinian Island in Micronesia and dated to the ninth century but caries sicca was not found on these remains (Stewart and Spoehr 1952). The Motupore date now joins those from Sarawak and Tinian to provide us with some idea of the earliest evidence for yaws found so far in this region. How long ago it first occurred or was brought into the area, and by what routes, remains a mystery but there lies a tantalising project for the enthusiastic palaeoepidemiologist. I would suggest that it was probably brought in by one of the many migrations into the area that took place throughout the Holocene. The dates for the evidence presented here firmly place treponematosis as an endemic disease in the region prior to European incursion.

When viewed with previous findings, these data clearly show also that yaws has some antiquity in the region and early European reports of syphilis among the people must now be reconsidered in the light of this. The age and geographical distribution of these sites also gives us some indication of the spatial and temporal movement of yaws into prehistoric Oceania, which probably originated from somewhere in southeast Asia. It has been suggested that the syphilitic form of treponematosis moved into Asia Minor and Europe from eastern Asia (Brothwell 1970). If so, then it is equally possible that the treponeme radiated into the island groups to the south and southeast of mainland southeast Asia. Perhaps on the way, the hardy treponeme adapted to a new ecology and even different forms of transmission, a process which eventually led to its manifestation as tropical yaws, while it retained some of its old identity in the type of bony lesion it produced, hence caries sicca is seen in those with yaws *and* syphilis.

What is important is that we are now sure that yaws was part of the pathological picture of southern Papua New Guinea, possibly by the twelfth century. It is only 550 km from Motupore Island southwest to the nearest Australian mainland across the Torres Strait. Therefore treponematosis could have been introduced into Australia's north through the well-established inter-island trade routes that existed between Australia and Papua New Guinea from at least that time. Once in Australia yaws was established in the tropical environment of the north. Continual transmission, perhaps through trading networks, took it further into the interior of Australia and eventually an endemic arid form emerged in areas further south.

Medical authorities have noted wide variation in the frequency of endemic yaws between different language groups and villages in Papua New Guinea (Garner and Hornabrook 1973). This variation seems to be greatest between mainland and island communities. Serological evidence of sub-clinical yaws showed nearly twice as many people were affected on Kar Kar Island (67.5 per cent) as on the nearby mainland (38.5 per cent) (Garner *et al.* 1972). If these hold true for prehistoric island communities, Motupore, with its 26.2 per cent, seems to fit the picture of high island prevalence for treponemal disease. This frequency is largely based on evidence of severe osteomyelitic destruction on long bones. The palaeopathologically invisible primary and secondary cases that would be picked up in modern medical surveys must be added to this, and, although it is hard to estimate the total number of sufferers at all stages, it is not fanciful to suggest that prehistoric Motupore may have had an overall frequency approaching that of Kar Kar. Tertiary stage ulcerations normally occur in only about 8 per cent of cases, which is far lower than the 26.2 per cent observed in this sample (Manson-Bahr 1961). We can speculate that such severity might be due to the reaction of a virgin soil population to the introduction of a new pathogen, but at the same time we must not forget the temporal spread of the sample. I believe, however, there is a better explanation. There is a difference in treponemal infection from 11.8 per cent to 36 per cent between the earlier (1200–1500AD) and later (1500–1700AD) samples, respectively. One reason for this increase may lie with an alteration in living conditions brought about, for example, by changes to the island's demographic structure. Population increase, due to a greater and more permanent use of the island as a trading centre, is one obvious possibility. A settled and subsequently burgeoning population may have emerged from an increasingly intensified economy based around closely-clustered dwellings in a village with gardens. The crowded conditions resulting from this would have made an ideal microenvironment for nurturing infectious diseases such as yaws. With an increasing population there is a greater likelihood of emerging genetic disease also.

Haemolytic disease

Earlier in this volume I discussed the balanced polymorphisms which have arisen among people living in endemic malarial areas and which confer heterozygote protection against malarial plasmodia (see Chapter 3). Until the late 1950s it was thought that none of these polymorphisms occurred in Papua New Guinea even though malaria was endemic there (Jonxis *et al.* 1958; Ryan 1961a). Then, in the next few years, a number of cases of thalassaemia from diverse areas of Papua New Guinea were reported by the medical authorities (Ryan 1961a,b,c). The symmetrical osteoporosis on the cranium of M27 suggests that this individual suffered from this disease also, but it is difficult to be absolutely sure whether this is due to thalassaemia or severe iron deficiency anaemia (Plates 11–7, 11–8). Differential diagnosis between these two conditions is possible but only if the whole skeleton is available for examination and in good condition. Thalassaemia retards pneumatisation of the facial sinuses but the fragmentary nature of this area of the face of M27 prevents this being checked. However, the much rarer occurrence of cranial lesions in severe iron deficiency anaemia tends to suggest that an aetiology of thalassaemia might well be cautiously proposed here (Ryan 1962: Angel 1964). Pietrusewski (1976) found that one-third of the Nebira crania had thickened frontal bones to a depth of 6–9 mm, but there is no mention of symmetrical osteoporosis or other cranial lesions among these. Iron deficiency anaemia was obviously common at Nebira but whether thalassaemia was present is not known. The young child from Motupore with severe osteoporotic lesions of the outer cranial table does, however, suggest to me that it was present among coastal Papua New Guinea people in the sixteenth or seventeenth centuries. Moreover, this evidence represents the first of its kind from this part of the world showing a human genetic adaptation to a pathological stress.

Arthritis

The pattern of arthritis on Motupore is commensurate with the usual type and severity found in an active population (Jurmain 1977a, b). There seems to be far more vertebral involvement in Motupore than among the Nebira people which may point to a more arduous work regime among islanders than mainland people. Men have more arthritis, both in the major joint areas and vertebrae, than women, although it is worth remembering that there are more men than women represented in the sample. The reason for the pattern of arthritis probably lies in Motupore's intensified economy, which was the result of the need to feed a growing population living in a limited space with finite resources.

Conclusion

The complex, large-scale trading systems that existed along the south coast of Papua New Guinea must have played an important part in the palaeoepidemiology of the region. The scale of the trading is exemplified by the fact that these people:

> ... engaged extensively in a variety of year round
> exchange, including an annual long-distance trading
> voyage to the Gulf of Papua [300km away] ... where as
> many as 30,000 pots might be exchanged for up to 600
> tons of sago. (Allen 1978:54–55)

Not only is the size of the trading system an important clue to the demographic structure of this region, but what was traded is important also. The movement of hundreds of tons of carbohydrate (sago) suggests that the population was comparatively large, as bulk carbohydrate (sago) is infinitely easier to obtain to fill empty bellies than protein is. The teeth of Motupore people reflect this consumption of sago in that they are characterised by a high incidence of caries where the Nebira population had less than 9 per cent. Moreover, an analysis of calculus samples taken from Motupore teeth links the caries quite firmly to the ingestion of large amounts of sago (Hope *et al.* 1983; Schamschula *et al.* 1978).

Motupore Island played an important part in the trading networks of southern Papua New Guinea. Its demographic character also strongly reflects the type of village community organisation along this coast that is well described ethnographically. The people lived in very close proximity to one another in a typical coastal village setting. Houses were constructed on raised posts and positioned close to the shore, often extending out over the water which also facilitated waste disposal. Ceremony was important and ceremonial platforms were a vital part of village planning. Communal living was concentrated around the raised dwellings and probably involved more than one family, each of which was of an extended family structure. Because of this they suffered from a substantial amount of infectious disease and no doubt high frequencies of anaemia and parasitism. Island environments naturally limit space both for people and their building activities and enforce close physical association between individuals. This provides the perfect setting for transmission of infectious diseases like yaws through a much greater proportion of the population than might occur in a mainland community with greater access to space. Such a situation depends also on the size of the island's population: the larger the population the greater the crowding and with limited chances for spreading out there is an increased likelihood of infection.

The major difference between the health of Australian Aborigines and Motupore Papua New Guineans is the prevalence of infectious disease among the latter. Their different economic and demographic profiles are strongly reflected in the distribution and frequency of infectious disease in each community. The crowding of village life and the use of closely-clustered, permanent dwellings by many people encourages infections. The general lack of such tight demographic structures among Australia's Aboriginal people kept them comparatively free from this type of disease when compared to their northern neighbours. Although treponemal disease was endemic to many parts of the Australian continent, its prevalence was limited by the generally more open demographic structure of Aboriginal society. Nevertheless, Murray River people as well as some other groups were beginning to experience growing infection as they became more sedentary (see also Chapter 12).

It is interesting to see that thalassaemia did not cross Torres Strait even though it would have conferred no particular advantage on Aboriginal people in malaria-free Australia. Nevertheless, with trade links running from Papua New Guinea across the island-dotted strait and deep into Cape York, it is almost impossible to believe that the genes for this condition did not move south along with linguistic, cultural and other genetic baggage that Melanesians and Torres Strait Aborigines exchanged for many centuries. The individual with symmetrical osteoporosis from York Island in Torres Strait lacks the distinctive frontal lesion that might suggest thalassaemia and so lacks the hard evidence needed to implicate a polymorphism (Plate 5–3). At the present time, therefore, the marked demarcation of this disease between Papua New Guinea and Australia joins other mysteries of non-shared biological and cultural markers between the two countries even after close physical and social contact which has been going on for thousands of years.

Chapter 12

The old and the new: Australia's changing patterns of health

Introduction

The main purpose of this volume is to provide empirical data concerning the health of Australia's original inhabitants over the last 50,000 years. The trouble with such a task is that the palaeopathological evidence on which it is based is comparatively slight, because of its limited disease spectrum, and incomplete in terms of the skeletal material that is available. Unfortunately, we have no data for thousands of years at a time and when it is available it almost always covers only a minute part of the continent. Nevertheless, one must remain undaunted by these constraints as well as being slightly buoyed by the fact that this is the nature of this type of study for any area of the globe. Therefore, in the first part of this chapter I will try and gather together the meagre evidence for the health of people living in the Australian late Pleistocene. The second part puts together a more complete picture of Aboriginal health in the Holocene. It compares and contrasts different parts of the continent and interprets health in terms of the wider lifestyle of Aboriginal people and how they lived.

No doubt some people will disagree with certain diagnoses, that is normal in palaeopathology; others will reject the social and demographic conclusions and implications that I have made based on these. In the end it is my hope that the presentation of the data in itself will improve our understanding of Aboriginal health, demography, ecology, epidemiology, palaeobiology and the adaptive capabilities of the people that lived here before European colonisation. From this we may also develop a wider appreciation of the complex social and biological diversity that existed in Australia for over 50,000 years.

The late Pleistocene

The earliest detectable pathology in Australia consists of trauma, arthritis, minor infection, anaemia as well as some congenital disorders. Bone infections are rare, but examples may include the possible infectious arthritis in the right elbow of WLH3 from Lake Mungo and periostitis in one or two other late Pleistocene individuals from the same area. I have mentioned on several occasions the likelihood of infectious wounds developing either from spears tipped with natural poisons or, in the time honoured way, from dirt entering the lesion. There is no evidence of osteomyelitis in the late Pleistocene although secondary infections following trauma may have occurred from time to time. The question of the age and origin of treponemal infection remains open. So far we have no late Pleistocene evidence for this disease in Australia as there is in North America, but I would not be surprised if it had not entered Melanesia by at least the early Holocene, coming down from southeast Asia with human migrations. More research will need to be carried out into the origin, geographical distribution and age of this disease in Australia. Other late Pleistocene infection includes periodontal disease, although this has not been included in this survey. Eye infection in the form of trachoma seems to have been present in the terminal Pleistocene and its origins may go back some considerable time. Certainly, the very dry, dusty and wind-blown marginal areas of inland Australia that were occupied between 10–25,000 years ago would have provided an excellent environment for the transmission of this disease.

Trauma is so common among humans it is not surprising that we see it in Australia from the earliest times. Limb fractures and cranial injuries are quite common from the late Pleistocene onwards. Prominent examples have been found in many areas including the Willandra Lakes, Kow Swamp and Murrabit on the Murray River, Roonka in South Australia, Green Gully in southern Victoria and Mossgiel in central New South Wales (Map 2–1) (Macintosh 1967; Freedman 1985; Pretty and Kricun 1989). The main difference between these fractures and those that appear in late Holocene populations is the degree of surgical skill and care that seems to emerge in the latter.

Congenital disease occurred in late Pleistocene Australian populations. Anomalies include premature synostosis, neural tube defects and, perhaps, a very rare case of leontiasis ossea. In most individuals these defects seemed to have been compatible with life and the social context of that time or they were tolerated for other reasons. Perhaps those born with strange cranial deformations that made them look so different, were thought to be special, possessing magical or unique talents or powers or thought to be visitors from the spirit world. Although I have found no evidence of dwarfism or achondroplasia among the skeletal collections, it is not unknown among later Aboriginal groups in which these individuals were often given authority or were believed to possess supernatural powers.

I have little doubt that a genetically controlled precursor for the later balanced polymorphisms that provide partial immunity against malaria were developing or existed in this region as far back as 40–50,000 years ago. As with any mutation of this type, the initial frequency may have been very low indeed and it could have remained that way for millennia. Frequencies probably increased as human populations grew during the Holocene, a process which may have given rise also to the different types we are familiar with today. So, the full protection of such a mechanism in endemic malarial areas came into its own. The exaggerated cranial thickening of MLH50 is, I believe, an early generalised indication of this adaptation and is also the earliest evidence for such pathology in the Australasian region found so far.

Anaemia, as indicated by cribra orbitalia, is by no means as prevalent among late Pleistocene remains as it is in later populations. The best example of this trend is found in a sample of 41 individuals from the Kow Swamp and Coobool Crossing areas of the Murray Valley. In this late Pleistocene/early Holocene group 15.4 per cent of men and 13.3 per cent of women are affected, none, I might add, having the worst (category 3) form of lesion. There is an obvious difference between these frequencies and the 29.7 per cent and 40.3 per cent for late Holocene males and females, respectively. One explanation for this difference, and one I particularly favour, lies in certain changes in the economy and demography of the people living in the area. I will outline these ideas in more detail when I discuss the central Murray below.

Besides lower frequencies of anaemia, the late Pleistocene sample also has lower frequencies of DEH. The 26.4 per cent of affected males in the toddler category is lower than that observed among other samples from the Murray region, except Rufus River, and well below the modern frequency for males in other parts of Australia. Whether this can be interpreted as an increase in the amount of stress over the last 8–10,000 years is, however, open to speculation. Nevertheless, it is significant that this group has no molar hypoplasia, perhaps adding some support to a general interpretation as follows. Weaning has always been a physiologically stressful time for hunter-gatherer children in this part of the Murray, as it has elsewhere on the continent. As environmental and demographic pressures increased during the mid-to-late Holocene, other causes of hypoplasia began to appear which prolonged stress into later childhood and became reflected in the third molar DEH frequencies which we find among people living there in late pre-contact times.

The Holocene

The previous chapters describe the continental pattern of pathology by discussing individual categories. They present trends and try to provide an explanation for those trends across the continent. I want now to essentially reverse this approach and discuss the cumulative pathology for each area, bringing together the data distributed throughout the preceding chapters. By doing this I hope to reveal more about people occupying various environmental settings and different demographic and socio-economic contexts. While this provides a cumulative view of health in a particular area it will also help us understand more fully the varied regional lifestyles of Australia's first people.

The desert

There is little that is surprising about the health of people inhabiting arid parts of Australia. They have the lowest incidence of anaemia in both children and adults, which strongly suggests that the main causes of this condition, such as starvation, population aggregation and parasitism, are minimal. Although young children are affected to some degree it decreases rapidly with age. The DEH survey confirms the overall reduction in stress as children grow. Those under six years living in all parts of Australia display this to some degree, but those living in desert areas are generally the least affected. Relief from the stresses of infancy arrives early, thus, the frequency of DEH on teeth formed after six years is much lower than it is in other groups. Evidence to support this view comes from the Harris lines survey which shows that fewer lines are formed as children grow. The DEH and Harris line evidence can, therefore, be used to suggest that stress is reduced as the child grows. The formation of Harris lines in desert people probably reflects periods of famine, poor nutrition or some other acute stress rather than a more chronic stress of the type that causes cribra and DEH. Life in an arid environment may not have been as hazardous for the very young as might be expected and probably no worse overall than for infants in other regions, it may even have been better. The susceptibility of the very young to stress of any kind makes it difficult to make too much of these results, however. The notable reduction of stress from early to late childhood might be expected as the older child is naturally more able to withstand stress than younger children. Nevertheless, it is not an easy life for these children as they have to withstand episodes of acute stress probably from short term or the seasonal episodes of food shortage that are not unknown in central Australia and which affect everyone to some degree (Peterson 1978; Tindale 1981; Long, cited in Nathan and Jabanangka 1983:73).

Even though desert people have learned to utilise a wide range of food resources to offset such a precarious situation, shortages still occur (Sweeney 1947; Lawrence 1969; Cane 1984). At one end of the environmental spectrum scarce water in the landscape confines people to places where permanent water is available in the form of springs and/or ephemeral or permanent wells. But many of these may dry up during prolonged drought that may last years. During 'the dry' hunting away from permanent water becomes difficult, game dies, vegetable food becomes scarce and the need to stay near a water source often causes the hunting-out of the surrounding area. Moreover, high temperatures force people into inactivity in an effort to conserve body fluids and energy. Even with the first rain there may be no real relief: 'The first rains bring starvation as birds and mammals disperse' (Tindale 1981:1878). Water is a rare but crucial element in desert life but, at the other end of the spectrum, hardship can come also from too much of it.

Tropical depressions that move into central Australia from the northwest can turn it into the fabled inland sea that the first European explorers searched for (Kotwicki 1986). Areas with a 100–150mm annual rainfall can receive as much as 360 mm in a couple of days. Flooding has occurred regularly every ten years or so at which time large areas become inundated. For traditional communities these events would have isolated people and drowned thousands of square kilometres of vegetable foods as well as game. Of course, good times follow these rather widely-spaced events when the desert blooms with grains, fruits, nuts and tubers as well as other vegetation that attracts animals. Large ephemeral lakes may remain for several years, becoming regular roosts for a great variety of bird life that comes from the coast, thousands of kilometres away, to congregate in flocks numbering tens or even hundreds of thousands. It is precisely a short-lived stress, like a drought or extended dry, or the even rarer flood, followed by the relief of a bountiful season that could produce the pattern of Harris lines recorded here. The fact that over 70 per cent of individuals have these lines indicates that the majority of sub-adults experience at least one stress episode at some time during their life, but the absence of the 'step-ladder' pattern of lines might mean a physiological adaptation to or the lack of regular seasonal stress.

Desert people display the highest frequency of bony infection found anywhere. Its origin probably lies with the endemic treponematosis that occurred widely in central Australia. The evidence strongly suggests that this disease was unequivocally part of the health problems faced by people in this area, possibly for centuries (Nathan and Jabanangka 1983). For such a high frequency of truly 'non-specific' infection to be present, certain epidemiological factors, such as population aggregation and sedentism, would need to exist. We know this not to be the case and, indeed, if it were so it would have shown up in higher frequencies of anaemia (cribra), in adults as well as children, and DEH in the older age group. Therefore, a case for widespread non-specific infectious disease cannot be supported and treponematosis is the most likely culprit, not needing the demographic aggregation that non-specific infection requires to thrive. I would suggest further that this condition was not confined to northern, northwestern and central Australia, but extended to many other parts of the inland not normally considered to be part of central Australia. These include northern Victoria, northern South Australia as well as western New South Wales and southwestern Queensland.

Osteoarthritis is common in people leading a nomadic existence involving extensive physical activity, so its frequent occurrence in the elbow and knees of desert men should not be regarded as particularly unusual. It is possible also that because more men reach old adult status in this group than in any other, the incidence of arthritis may be due to age as much as anything else. The pattern of fractures is similar in that they occur with equal regularity in arms as well as legs. These also can be explained by the active lifestyle of a nomadic hunter. I have to say, however, that the small sample of female long bones used in this survey does not allow me to make too much of the results from this section of the community and so trends for women must remain largely unknown.

The pattern of cranial trauma in both sexes and the frequency of parrying fractures in men highlights aggressive behaviour, perhaps duels used for the settlement of disputes. There is more trauma among females in this group than in women from other areas, but it seems to have little association with high mortality which is the second lowest for any area for young adult females. The cause of early death among young desert women probably has a different origin than that of men from that area and for females living elsewhere. Moreover, when we consider the results from the stress indicators, they point to much less metabolic and physiological stress among females than for those living in the central Murray, for example. So it is difficult to explain the early deaths among young women from this area on the palaeopathological evidence alone. On the other hand, we cannot expect every pathological trend that emerges from a study like this one to have a simple or straightforward explanation. For example, to directly link the pattern of female cranial trauma to their untimely death is probably misleading, although it is tempting given the pre-dominance of attacks from behind previously noted in Chapter 8. What palaeopathology can never tell us is whether the victims suffered a cerebral haemorrhage days or even weeks later as a result of these blows. The evidence for violence in the desert group does suggest, however, that the delicate socio-economic balances needed to survive in this harsh environment could create social stresses within and between groups that might lead to situations usually resolved by violent action.

The desert sample is too small to show any of the intraregional differences that may have existed across this very big area. All the crania from this region were put together to make an adequate sample. Nevertheless, the health of this group does reflect a pattern of high mobility and low population density. There must have been some variation in the degree of nomadism as well as in social and demo-graphic construction among various groups. Unfortunately, we are able to see only the very coarse picture of health which may have varied considerably across an area which measures over three and a half-million square kilometres. Very little palaeopathological data exist for desert-dwelling hunter-gatherers from other parts of the world so direct comparisons of these results are not easy to make. I must assume, therefore, that these Australian data reflect the way of life of the desert hunter-gatherer and that we now have a basic palaeopath-ological template for people who live and thrive in these very special but equally harsh arid environments. In the past, anthropologists and others have often regarded Australian desert people as sort of quintessential Aborigines, representing all other Aboriginal people on this continent and their way of life. This has been taken even further and, together with the African Bushman, the Australian desert dweller has become a model for hunter-gatherers world-wide. It is interesting, therefore, that these people appear to be the healthiest of Australia's original inhabitants.

The central Murray

There are, of course, vast differences in Aboriginal culture across the continent and in moving from the desert to the central Murray we arrive at what is clearly the other end of the palaeopathological spectrum in Australia. There is obviously some positive bias towards this area because it constitutes the largest skeletal sample in the survey and in those terms provides the most accurate picture of the health of Aboriginal people for any area.

I have to confess that the level of stress in this sample was patently obvious to me while undertaking the survey and before any results had been properly collated. The primary indicator was the common occurrence of cribra among these people who lived along a 350 km stretch of Australia's largest river. Even more extraordinary was that their level of anaemia is higher than for almost all other hunter-gatherer groups from around the world for which there are comparable data. Children have only marginally lower levels of anaemia than those living downstream at Rufus River, a difference which, at this order of frequency, I regard as inconsequential. The concomitant high frequency of third molar DEH emphasises the persistence of stress in central Murray boys and girls to about 11 years. Anaemia continues in this age group also although this gradually eases as children reach their teens. While the stress causing DEH may not be the same as that precipitating the anaemia, the pattern that these two pathological markers provides does give us a measure of the stressful conditions existing for the young. It is, therefore, valid to use both as mutually supportive on that general level. The level of anaemia is not alleviated on reaching adulthood in the same way that it is for other Aboriginal groups and similar populations from around the world. The remaining high frequencies adequately demonstrate that while adults have the physical and constitutional ability to combat the effects of a continuing stress more readily, these may be persistent enough to maintain rather high levels of anaemia among them. To emphasise this the combined adult frequency for this group is 33.7 per cent, over four times that in desert people, an enormous and very obvious difference. What this means is that the stresses which cause this condition are found right across the age spectrum and must, therefore, be closely related to the particular socio-demographic factors existing in central Murray society.

We might justifiably expect that high frequencies of both cribra and DEH would be reflected in a similar pattern for Harris lines. Instead, we find that while the central Murray index of morbidity is the second highest in the survey, it is far below that of the south coast and much closer to that found in the other areas. We know there was seasonal variation in food resources along the Murray and these often brought hardship and nutritional insufficiency for many, particularly during winter months (Allen 1972). The 'feast and famine' step ladder pattern of Harris line formation that is associated with this regime is, however, not present in the central Murray. The most likely explanation for this is that the stressful conditions which existed more or less constantly in the area produced a suppression of line formation. The recovery phase needed to produce lines was either infrequent or non-existent for long periods, although bone growth may have continued at a reduced rate to compensate for this. The latter suggests that people may have adapted to the constant stress in such a way as to enjoy a continuous but slower pattern of bone growth without interruption in the face of the stress. This may have resulted in a comparatively shorter stature, although not exaggeratedly so. For the population as a whole the constancy of broad-spectrum stress probably acted to eliminate regular line formation. Thus, while the IM of the central Murray sample is similar to that for the desert population, the individual reasons for their respective indices are quite different.

More adults die before their mid-thirties in the central Murray than they do elsewhere, which suggests that age is not necessarily a causal factor in the high incidence of arthritis in the area. Its pathogenesis, therefore, lies more likely with physically hard and repetitive activity for both men and women, with the upper limbs bearing the brunt of the work. Such activity may have come from the regular gathering of large amounts of vegetable foods in order to maintain adequate levels of nutrition. Various plant species were used by these people, root vegetables including *Triglochin* sp. and *Scirpus* sp., but *Typha* sp. seems to be a dietary mainstay throughout the Murray River corridor (Gott 1982). Gathering the rhizomes, bulbs, corms and tubers of these plants requires enormous physical activity using a digging stick the stress of which is almost all centred on *both* upper limbs. There is little doubt that the Murray has always been an area of plenty but it is likely that in the late Holocene there were increasingly more people sharing it. Under such circumstances it seems that the diet of the central Murrayian was fast becoming one biased more towards a high carbohydrate than a high protein intake. This type of diet would certainly increase the chances of nutritional stress, thus contributing to the high levels of anaemia observed there. It is worth remembering that while bulk vegetable food fills bellies and is largely always available, its quality and food value is not necessarily high. Further evidence for the ingestion of large amounts of sticky carbohydrates comes from the presence of thick calculus build-up around the marginal or free gingivae of molars and premolar teeth of these people. This is similar to the dental deposit on the teeth of New Guinean sago traders discussed in Chapter 11. Calculus is far more common on the teeth of central Murray people than it is on teeth of those living elsewhere. It forms a thick deposit and is probably due to the widespread use of the cooked *Typha* root as a staple food.

I have discussed how societies with different economic structures have concomitant differences in their patterns of arthritis and trauma. For example, those with an economy based on subsistence farming usually suffer from high upper limb stress loads while the lower limb is much less affected. These same groups normally have very low frequencies of lower limb trauma, compared to hunter-gatherers, because of lower levels of activity. Central Murray people reflect this pattern with high frequencies of upper limb arthritis and a low frequency of leg fractures. Evidence for aggression, in the form of head trauma and parrying fractures, indicates that social tensions must have been of a low order and that serious hand-to-hand combat often used to settle disputes was not common either. Patterns of female head trauma suggest they fought among themselves, but patterns of domestic violence are comparatively less obvious here than elsewhere. It is not likely, therefore, that trauma is the reason for high mortality among young adults. Both the pattern of arthritis and trauma indicate a more sedentary society than can be argued for any other part of Australia. We must not forget also the cases of fracture repair and amputation that have been described from this region. These procedures together with the degree of nursing and rest required for proper healing of lower limb fractures, seem to underpin the conclusion that the central Murray represents a very settled community indeed. But what other evidence is there to support this?

In Chapter 6 I spoke of the central Murray having an 'infectious environment', brought about by the particular structure of its population. Some pertinent demographic factors to consider are: the size of the family, the size of the area it occupies, how many families are clustered together, the space occupied by the cluster, how many clusters there are, cluster densities, the level of sedentism (length of occupation), how large the overall population is, its rate of increase, the efficiency of community hygiene and so on. The highest frequency of non-specific infection in Australia is found in the central Murray, although some may, in fact, be due to treponemal disease. There is little doubt that treponematosis was present, as the many distinctive cranial lesions testify. The health of central Murray people, in terms of stress indicators, infectious disease and, to a certain extent, arthritis, is not the result of episodic nutritional deprivation, seasonal hardship or even the effects of group or family isolation on small portions of high ground during flooding, although all these probably contributed at one time or another to the general level of stress that was suffered. Instead, it is the health of a large, sedentary population intensifying its economy to feed itself.

The large, distinctive oven mounds found in the region have another importance in that they are the only firm evidence we have of population structure in this area. Large concentrations consisting of over 95 per square kilometre were built and these can still be found in some places, even after 150 years of extensive and intensive European ploughing, irrigation and agriculture. In fact, the highly productive fruit and vegetable farming of the Murray Valley and Murrumbidgee Irrigation Area today is testament to the nutrient-rich soils of the area. The potential of these soils to produce large amounts of carbohydrates testifies to their ability to produce high yields in the pre-European period also. Unfortunately, intensive agricultural practices during the last century have caused vast environmental problems in the inter-riverine corridors of the Murray–Murrumbidgee and Murrumbidgee–Lachlan which include land degradation and salination. The Aboriginal mounds, however, cover an area of nearly 20,000 square kilometres in this region but, as far as we know, they are only in dense concentrations in the central Murray. Few dates are available for these structures, although none seem to be older than 3000BP and the further away from the central Murray area they are, the younger they seem to be. Size varies from eight to 48 m in diameter, with 85 per cent averaging around 18 m, and they rise from 0.5 m to 1.5 m above the ground. Spatial analysis of their distribution shows that they were built with a planned regularity, as though personal space was consciously sought (Berryman pers. comm.). The most logical reason for such a strategy would be that delineation between families was necessary in an area where space was at a premium. Thus, a demarcation of one living area from another was the social norm. In other words, the concept of family ownership and rights over a prescribed section of land may have been common. Some mounds are believed to be communal cooking ovens owned by a group of families, where up to one ton of *Typha* sp. was cooked at a time. It is hard to believe that such large amounts of carbohydrate were needed for a few hunter-gatherers. Observations by early settlers recount that fish traps located near a mound were owned by the group or family who occupied the mound. Constant or regular mound occupation with random defecation by children and dogs in the confined space would create ideal conditions for parasitism as well as infection. If I may repeat what I said earlier about plenty of food but many sharing it, even the best of diets can be thwarted by parasite loads which cause malabsorption of nutrients and infection that adversely affects general health.

Further investigation of the origin and use of mounds by Aboriginal people, therefore, holds the key to establishing at least a basic understanding of central Murray demography, population size and the human ecology of this region. The pattern of young adult mortality, persistent physiological stress and infection is more likely explained by an infectious environment than anything else. That environment probably arose from the effects of a large and increasing population together with high levels of sedentism and social clustering.

Coastal people

Both adults and children living on the east coast suffered far less anaemia than those living in the central Murray. Persistent stress, in the form of third molar DEH, is more prevalent on the east than the south coast which shows a wide stress variation along the coastal fringe. Nowhere are frequencies near the magnitude of central Murray trends. Overall, then, much less stress is experienced by coastal people who also have a greater recuperative potential, although this is not of an order found among desert people.

East coast people have the smallest number of Harris lines per person as well as the fewest people with them. The main sufferers are boys under six years in whom at least one line might be caused by weaning, a physiologically traumatic time to which male toddlers are particularly susceptible. Multiple lines are almost non-existent and the 'step ladder' pattern of the south coast does not appear at all. Either seasonal nutritional stress did not bother these people to any extent, or if it did economic strategies along this coast overcame it. Nevertheless, anaemia should not be as prevalent as it is with the high levels of iron freely available in all the regular dietary components such as birds, fish and particularly shellfish. It is possible that while the thousands of shell middens scattered along this coast might suggest a plentiful and regular diet of shellfish, an increasing population would have meant a reduced amount available for each person. In these circumstances people might have begun to rely more and more on smaller specimens while large aggregations of people in sedentary situations meant that parasitism and, thus, anaemia increased.

The pattern of anaemia among people living along the coast between Adelaide and the New South Wales border, is basically a continuation of that seen on the east coast, with very similar adult male and female frequencies. There is, however, less persistent stress among south coast children in the form of third molar DEH with only one-third of that recorded in the east coast group. Coastal people suffered childhood stress but nowhere near as badly as those living in the central Murray, neither was it of an order that prevented the recuperative phase of line formation, as occurred along the Murray. While there is less persistent stress there is a vast difference in acute or seasonal stress patterns between the two sections of coastline. The 0.8 IM of the east coast and nearly 3.2 for the south lie at either end of Australia's Harris line spectrum. Seasonal stress might be expected on the south coast and that seems to be confirmed with over 80 per cent of individuals having lines, nearly twice as many as on the east coast. The presence of repetitive seasonal stress on the south coast is further supported by the presence of multiple line formation whereas not a single individual from coastal New South Wales has this. These quite different patterns from adjacent coastlines are significant and the reasons for them must lie in their respective environmental settings.

Anaemia is not as prevalent among adult Queensland coastal Aborigines as it is farther south but persistent stress is. The pattern of female arthritis is interesting because it shows that these women are subjecting their lower limbs, particularly the knee region, to vigorous mechanical activity in a way that contrasts strongly with the total absence of this condition among women further south. Biomechanical stress is not pronounced among males in any sample but right arm predominance is probably a bias typical of handedness. The rapid, repetitive movement used for spear fishing from rocks could have been one of the contributory activities producing this pattern among coastal men as much as any other hunting activity (Lampert 1966; Lawrence 1969; Bowdler 1975). Arthritis in only one arm of coastal men is in complete contrast to the bilateral pattern and much higher frequencies in Murray men. Unfortunately, specific work activities and their degree of difficulty cannot be deduced from this evidence alone. Noting the negative evidence, one might, nevertheless, presume that whatever these activities were, the task of resource procurement on the coast involved less work than it did in the central Murray, where tasks imposed high degrees of bilateral rather than unilateral stress.

While the level of domestic aggression on the coast is high, there is less fighting among men in the south than on the eastern margins, although there is far more in both these areas than in the central Murray. It could be argued that this situation would make more sense if it were reversed. It is much easier to explain aggression between and within groups under substantial and constant stress because such an environment should produce the most antagonism. I can suggest only that some communities may have developed social mechanisms principally designed to take the heat out of arguments and disputes arising from socio-economic and demographic intensification. Outright war and fighting have even worse consequences for those living in close proximity to one another and it would advantage no one to have these potentially devastating situations flare up regularly. One example of such a social safety valve is mock battles and fights before a large crowd. Disputes between groups or individuals are often settled by two chosen men hurling nothing more than insults at each other and brandishing spears. Such ceremonies are known to have taken place along the Murray but they were not so common along coastal New South Wales.

The major differences between riverine and coastal food resources is that while the variety is similar for both, a coastal larder remains relatively plentiful and varied all year round. Moreover, it is not subject to quite the same drastic shortages from droughts and floods that riverine environments face (Bickford 1966; Lawrence 1969). Nevertheless, it has been argued that people on the east coast would still have experienced some degree of hardship during winter, when many species of shellfish, fish and plants disappear (Poiner 1976:191). Even with resources halved, this situation does not force people to rely on one or two carbohydrate staples as central Murray people probably had to during hard times. Nevertheless, I suggest that the cause of stress in these two areas had a common origin: demography.

Aborigines living on the east coast, particularly along the New South Wales section, may not have experienced population growth and the need for sedentism that Murray people did. It is likely also that their population was smaller for the area they occupied. Our understanding of Aboriginal subsistence patterns and demography in southeastern Australia has depended heavily on nineteenth century ethnohistoric observations. In his investigation of pre-1788 Aboriginal economy and demography, the economic historian Noel Butlin proposed that smallpox outbreaks in 1789 and 1828 caused large-scale Aboriginal depopulation in southeastern Australia (Butlin 1983). Important for our discussion is that these epidemics brought about vast changes in both numbers and distribution of people before they could be observed by the new colonists. If Butlin's proposition is correct, and there is no reason why it should not be, it leaves a large question mark over the accuracy of early ethnohistoric accounts of Aboriginal society in southeastern Australia.

How much can we rely on ethnohistoric information concerning population size, among other things? It is possible, for example, that smallpox epidemics not only changed Aboriginal society before it could be recorded but they could have wrought all kinds of changes the results of which did not reflect pre-epidemic patterns of Aboriginal behaviour and lifestyle. Take, for example, the seasonal movement of coastal New South Wales people inland and along the coastal fringe. This is the seasonal behaviour that has been reported ethnohistorically but these movements are not obvious in the archaeological record (Poiner 1976; Sullivan 1982). It has been proposed that on the south coast of New South Wales life revolved around 'semi-nomadism' in spring, summer and autumn and 'full nomadism' by smaller groups in winter (Poiner 1976:201). Mobility was one response to the seasonal variability of resources but it is easier to move about if there are fewer people. Others have argued that south coast people would be inclined to stay closer to the more reliable littoral environment, of which they had specialised knowledge, and perhaps take advantage of the variety of micro-environments around their coastal camp sites (Lampert 1971b:130). Presumably this would mean a more sedentary lifestyle than that proposed by the previous model. Sedentism is thought to have arisen from a littoral-based economy on the north coast of New South Wales and extended at least as far as Moreton Bay in southern Queensland (Hall 1982; Sullivan 1982). Support for sedentism comes from historical evidence which describes large, solidly-built, permanent dwellings centred around extensive fish traps which were constructed right along the northern New South Wales coast (Coleman 1982). But there is no ethnohistoric evidence for a sedentary lifestyle among south coast people as there is for the north coast. Could it be that, as Butlin has suggested, the smallpox outbreak at Sydney Cove in 1789 went south rather than north, causing massive depopulation and widespread social collapse among a people unfamiliar with this disease 30–40 years before European settlement of the area? Even if it did, could it have changed society to such an extent that when 30 years later European explorers began to describe the culture and population distribution in the region, they saw a society much changed from that which existed before? One of these changes may have been in the degree of sedentary behaviour which was partly or completely abandoned in the face of a much reduced and totally disrupted population suffering high rates of mortality.

At this point some may want to take up the question of the impact of smallpox and the degree of mortality it inflicted on Aboriginal society, so perhaps I should. One obvious question is: could smallpox have caused such social upheaval? This has become an important issue for those dealing with the prehistory of southeastern Australia and it exemplifies, once again, the part that disease has played in the history of humans. Moreover, it would not be the first time that smallpox has almost brought about the demise of an indigenous people. So, before moving on, I want to recall the impact this disease had on Aboriginal people who had no previous experience of it.

It is difficult to determine how far inland or along the coastline the 1789 epidemic spread or by how much the population of Australia was reduced by its effects. Accounts of smallpox in the centre of Australia (Giles 1889; Schultze 1891), as well as in other remote areas (Green 1981; Campbell 1983), suggest that no region was safe from its ravages. But there must have been some variation in the number of people who succumbed depending on population densities and the degree of contact between groups. Butlin's work dealt largely with the killing power of smallpox, or, more correctly, the previous *under-estimation* of its killing power. A similar reappraisal of the effects of smallpox, as well as other introduced diseases, on American Indian people has prompted reassessment of the size of pre-contact Indian populations with estimates ranging from as low as 1,152,960 (Mooney 1911, cited in Dobyns 1976) to as high as 90–112 million for the whole hemisphere in 1492 (Dobyns 1966). It is the principle these figures represent rather than their absolute accuracy that is important here. A more recent and moderate estimate puts the Indian nation at around eighteen million. Whatever it was, Indian numbers were drastically reduced by the effects of diseases such as smallpox and measles (Dobyns 1983). In Mexico the number of Indian deaths from small-pox alone has been estimated at 1.5 million (Molnar 1983). Other estimates of certain groups and tribes put mortality around 60 per cent on the northern plains and upper Great Lakes (Joralemon 1982), at 75 per cent among the Hopi and Californian peoples (Dobyns 1966, 1983), 85–90 per cent in Texas (Aten 1983) and as high as 98 per cent among the Ontario Cree (Young 1979). Even if the latter figure is an exaggeration, eyewitness accounts like those of the Hudson's Bay Company trader, Edward Umfreville, suggest they are not too far from the truth:

> That epidemical and raging disorder [smallpox] has spread an almost universal mortality throughout the country in the interior parts of Hudson's Bay, extending its destructive effect through every tribe and nation, sparing neither age nor sex ... and by the fall of the year 1782, it had diffused to every known part of the country. The distress of the Indians by this visitation have [sic] been truly deplorable ... As the smallpox had never before been among them ... Numbers began to die on every side: the infection spread rapidly; and hundreds lay expiring together without assistance. (Cited in Young 1979:197)

Henschen also reminds us of the inadvertent aid that disease has provided to the conquests of European colonisers:

> ... smallpox and other epidemic diseases from Europe contributed far more than weapons to the swift conquest of America. One might say that it was a kind of unintentional bacteriological warfare. The English Puritans thanked their God for the wonderful support He gave them when they took possession of their new country ... (1966:53)

We now know that in some cases this was not as 'inadvertent' as has been suggested.

There has never been any suggestion that Aboriginal mortality rates from smallpox were anywhere near those reported from North America. There is no real reason why they should not have been, however, and arguments proposing that Aboriginal Australians may have had some sort of resistance to this disease are completely without foundation and blatantly contradict the evidence we have. Unlike America, Australia generally lacks the many eyewitness accounts of the passing of this disease, but we do have that of Collins, who we heard from in Chapter 6 describing syphilis among Aborigines at Sydney Cove. He graphically relates how the smallpox outbreak of 1789 affected the Aboriginal population of Sydney:

> The number that [smallpox] swept off, by [Aboriginal] accounts, was incredible ... in the different coves we visited; not a vestige on the sand was to be found of human foot; the excavations in the rocks were filled with putrid bodies of those who had fallen victims to the disorder; not a living person was any where to be met with. It seemed as if, flying from the contagion, they had left the dead to bury the dead ... On visiting Broken Bay, we found that [smallpox] had not confined its effects to Port Jackson, for in many places our path was covered with skeletons, and the same spectacles were to be met with in the hollows of most of the rocks of that harbour ... a North American Indian, a sailor belonging to Captain Ball's vessel, the *Supply*, sickened of it and died ... To this disorder [Aborigines] also gave the name Gal-gal-la; and that it was the small-pox [*sic*] there was scarcely a doubt; for the person seized with it was affected exactly as Europeans are ... As proof of the numbers ... who were carried off ... Bennillong told us, that his friend Col-be's tribe being reduced by its effects to three persons, Col-be, the boy Nan-bar-ray, and some one else, they found themselves compelled to unite with some other tribe ... (Collins 1798:496–7)

The order of depopulation, the social impact and cultural devastation that is implied in Collins' account is enormous. Whether this is the sort of scenario that can be offered for all areas of southeastern Australia affected by the 1789 and 1829 outbreaks is anyone's guess.

If it is there are ample grounds to believe that these changes took place well before later ethnohistoric reports were compiled. Take the North American experience once again: 'Entire populations in the southwest died from epidemics even before they were visited by Europeans; the disease was transmitted from village to village by infected Indian travellers' (Molnar 1983:225). For some areas of Australia, therefore, ethnohistoric accounts may describe a radically changed Aboriginal society, particularly in its demographic and social appearance.

The old, the young and pregnant women are the most likely to die from smallpox. Culturally, this means the loss of the teachers who know the lore, the ceremonies, the stories, who possess the skills and have the knowledge of the secret places that are so important in Aboriginal society. With their loss, the very foundations of meaning and social construct are suddenly lost also. The unique oral pegs on which the social fabric is so elegantly draped no longer function and the culture is not passed on to future generations in the way it has been for thousands of years. Demographically, it means a much reduced population for several generations because of the loss of fertile females as well as the children who would have been the next generation of parents. Fewer adults means fewer people to defend territory and the group becomes vulnerable to replacement by others, including colonists. Moreover, the terror stemming from the unknown nature of an invisible weapon which kills great numbers, so quickly and effectively, probably compelled people to abandon their traditional places and the sick as well forcing them to leave the many dead unburied. Perhaps the most terrifying aspect of this process was the fact that in their haste to move away they took with them this highly infectious disease, only to pass it on to others with a fission effect almost as deadly as any nuclear weapon. Smallpox, therefore, meant more than death, it meant one of the most effective ways by which a society without written records could be devastated or come close to being completely eradicated.

The southwestern districts of Victoria have, in recent years, been the centre of a number of archaeological studies (Coutts *et al.* 1976, 1978, 1979; Lourandos 1976, 1977, 1980, 1983; McBryde and Harrison 1981; Williams 1985, 1988). Subsequent hypotheses concerning Aboriginal economic intensification, sedentism, and social complexity have emerged from these. Some suggest that while seasonal stress was experienced in this region, it was never serious (Coutts *et al.* 1978; Lourandos 1980). It depends what is meant by 'serious' because the Harris line evidence renders this view very much open to question. Sporadic events did not cause the line patterns observed here, rather they were caused by regular annual episodes of stress. I doubt whether these were ever life-threatening although malnutrition may not have been unheard of in some years. What is difficult to know is whether this was due to a genuine reduction in food availability or whether the population had become too large to do moderately well during hard times. It has been pointed out quite rightly that in order to make estimations of population size there is a need for ' ... access to biological data that do not exist at the present time' (Coutts 1978:37). For example, the biology of archaeological populations often tells us something about resource over-exploitation and, thereby, something about population size (Hayden 1975). My interpretation of the palaeopathological data supports the sedentism claimed by others from the archaeology as well as the large population implicit in the notion of late Holocene Aboriginal economic intensification. The construction of extensive drainage systems in western Victoria featuring extensive canals and fish and eel traps was probably part of this intensification, which emerged from a necessity to reach beyond normal hunting and gathering strategies in order to feed a growing population. This in itself suggests that the people in the area were living close to the ceiling of existing food-carrying capacities and that there was a need to go beyond it. The construction of permanent villages accompanied these economic changes, the one at Lake Condah comprised 146 permanent dwellings each constructed with stone walls and a thatched roof (Flood 1989). Each house was probably occupied by a family, which would mean that this village contained about 700 people. Seasonal nutritional stress, indicated by Harris lines, must have provided a pointed impetus for people living in this manner to intensify their economy. Food supplies may have become more or less reliable but health, in terms of infectious and other types of crowd disease, would have begun to deteriorate sooner or later as it did for other people around the world who experienced similar socio-economic change.

At the same time, further west on the eastern Coorong in South Australia, people were also becoming more sedentary with group clustering (Luebbers 1978). In turn, demographic changes would have brought about increasing use of marginal resources in order to '... intensify exploitation of all available resources in the swamps and on the coast' (*ibid.* 1978:307). Luebbers goes on to say that:

> With downturns occurring in food supply and Aboriginal populations being forced to exploit a comparatively limited set of resources, the need to equalize energy flow throughout the year became stronger. This is not only because of the seasonal flux in supply but because access to foods in times of stress was being denied by neighbours and friends alike.

The biological data, particularly the Harris lines, support this view. Certainly the nutritional stress being experienced by one group will not be avoided by its neighbour with whom it will be in competition. If it is possible to use these data as a measure of the magnitude of population size, however coarse this might be, it could be suggested that the population of the Victorian coast was probably smaller than that living along the New South Wales coast and both were certainly smaller than that of the central Murray, but larger than those in the centre and north of the continent.

In summary, it is reasonable to conclude that the eastern seaboard imposes a regime of persistent stress which varies depending on the part of the coast. What we can say is that it is not of the order of that found in the central Murray. The environmental circumstances of the coast afford stress relief that presents a better palaeopathological picture overall. Death rates among young women living along the Queensland and New South Wales coasts are similar and high, but they are very high for coastal Victoria, the second highest anywhere. Judging by the pattern of trauma, it could be that violence, domestic or otherwise, is one reason for the early demise of women living along the east coast. On the other hand, deaths among young women from Adelaide and Swanport are low even though multiple cranial trauma is prominent among them. Early deaths among young females from coastal Victoria may be exacerbated by the accumulated effects of seasonal stress, which probably reflect dietary insufficiencies. This may be contrary to the belief that: '... it is unlikely that Aboriginals in any part of Victoria died from malnutrition or starvation ...' (Coutts *et al.* 1978:39), but is worth more than passing consideration in the light of these results. Consider also, that any food taboos for women added to such dietary insufficiencies would only make matters worse for them.

Rufus River

The level of anaemic stress among children at Rufus River is almost the same as that found in the central Murray further upstream. Among older girls and boys, this condition decreases in a more pronounced manner than in the same group from the central Murray and follows a similar trend to that observed among east coast children. In addition, there is far greater relief from anaemia on reaching adulthood than for central Murray adults. One reason for this relief among women could come from the lifestyle at Rufus River. If, for example, they followed a more nomadic existence than the central Murray people it could have resulted in irregular or infrequent menstruation, as it does among desert women, thus providing additional relief from anaemia caused by other factors (Elphinstone 1971).

There is a significant difference between male and female canine DEH, with young boys showing their usual susceptibility over young girls. Relief among older boys is enormous, however, indicating that persistent stress is not a problem for them, but this is not the case for girls in the same age group. They are the only group in this survey that registers no relief of persistent stress with age, in fact the frequency rises slightly. I can only suggest that this pattern suggests a bias towards this age group, perhaps involving food taboos or food distribution priorities, rather than widespread primary health problems among young girls. It is well to keep in mind that female frequencies are still only 60 per cent of those in the central Murray for this age group.

The pattern of Harris line development in the Rufus River area actually tells us very little about seasonal or continual stress. Both can be invoked, depending upon the interpretation placed on the index of morbidity. With some of the highest frequencies of sub-adult anaemia and persistent stress levels among young females, it could be argued that because metabolic and/or nutritional stress is high and constant, Harris line development will be suppressed, an argument proposed for the central Murray above. We have seen that persistent stress is not great, like coastal patterns, and is nothing like the picture that has emerged from the nearby central Murray. So, there should be no barrier to the formation of Harris lines. Less than 46 per cent of individuals are affected, however, which is similar to the east coast but contrasts with the figure of over 70 per cent in the desert. This might indicate that seasonal stress is not as prominent at Rufus River as it may have been in the desert, although it was along the south coast. Harris lines at Rufus River seem only to imply some stress of an intermittent nature occurring perhaps during either a major flood or river failure such as can occur once or twice in a generation.

The population at Rufus River was probably larger than might be expected in a generally arid, low rainfall region. At times large aggregations of people gathered around riverine and lacustrine resources. Water resources included large sections of the Murray and lower Darling Rivers, smaller tributaries and creeks like the Lindsay and Rufus Rivers and scattered ephemeral lakes of various sizes. A dependence on these, of which the Murray was probably the most reliable, was fraught with times of stress when river and lake levels were low and food scarce. It has been argued that during drought people would have used the hinterland more intensively (Kefous 1983). While this may have been visited occasionally, movement into the hinterland was probably a last resort because of the lack of a regular water supply and if it was dry along the major rivers it would have been much worse inland. Moreover, places with limited water supply would entice people into them because they would have attracted and concentrated game. At times of drought it becomes necessary for people to take up permanent residency around dwindling water holes, soaks and springs as a natural response to the contraction of water supplies (Cane 1984). It is well known that at permanent water 'tribes congregate in dry times. It is to these that the Pintubi retreat in dry periods … when the waters further East fail' (Long, cited in Nathan and Jabanangka 1983:72). The clustering of large groups of people along water courses during dry times, together with that reduced level of nutrition at these times, could cause the frequencies of anaemia seen in the region. Extended periods of this would also explain the lack of Harris lines which seem to indicate more acute stress events. Population dispersal following rains would help prevent chronic and widespread parasite infections, but children would still be susceptible. The way of life of the people in this area would, by necessity, have included a large component of continuous competition for resources, either to protect those which they already had or to relieve others of them. This situation would have sparked animosity resulting in inter- and intragroup belligerence. Such behaviour might explain why Rufus River men are second only to those from coastal New South Wales for multiple head trauma and why deaths among young men are the highest for any area. It nevertheless remains a puzzle why in an area where cranial injury is prominent, parrying fractures are rather rare.

The incidence of arthritis points to high activity levels, especially among men. Like those for most inland groups, these are far higher than coastal patterns but are commensurate with the kind of lifestyle outlined above. Women, on the other hand, have less arthritis overall than their coastal sisters and far less in the elbow than central Murray women. This may be linked to early death and lighter work loads or both, a picture quite opposite to the central Murray, however, where even young women develop arthritic degeneration in the major joints.

The tropics

It is unfortunate that the post-cranial sample size for this area is so small that it precludes investigation of trends in arthritis, limb trauma, non-specific infection and Harris lines. This situation severely limits what can be said about traditional Aboriginal health in the area and, of course, restricts comparisons with other regions. Nevertheless, the cranial sample shows that toddlers have a rather high order of anaemic stress which lies between the levels for the coastal and Murray people. This probably stems from a combination of helminthiasis, including hookworm infection which is endemic to the north of the continent, and the semi-sedentary nature of some Cape York and coastal Northern Territory groups, particularly during extended wet seasons (Thomson 1939; Chase and Sutton 1981; Hynes and Chase 1982; Meehan 1982). The obvious relief from this condition among adults is demonstrated by the dramatic drop in frequency among them which is the second lowest on the continent. In the DEH survey there is a stark difference between male and female frequencies in the youngest age group. Almost half of the boys suffer stress whereas only 20 per cent of girls are involved, a trend that occurs in all areas of the continent and yet another indication of the inherent susceptibility of young males to stressful events which register as canine DEH. This sexual division of susceptibility continues into the next age group, but relief among both sexes is marked, with females registering the same frequency as desert females in the 7–14 age group; the two together have the lowest incidence anywhere on the continent. I can only assume that both the trend in anaemia reduction and the DEH figures point to little persistent stress in the region and good general health among adults. The composition of the 'tropics' sample does not allow me to make too much of the results from this region, however, as it represents the whole of northern Australia. It combines communities which may, for example, have had very different lifestyles, nutritional intakes and demographic patterns. To make more than a very general interpretative statement concerning these results using such a comparatively small sample would be foolish.

Treponemal disease was endemic to the tropics but as far as I can tell this was largely confined to the Northern Territory and northwest Western Australia as well as large areas of the arid inland. No evidence of it has emerged from Cape York but I have no doubt that sporadic introductions did occur from time to time through the Torres Strait corridor. The only observation I feel justified in making about the tropical sample used here is that people of the north are, generally, healthier with respect to environmental stress than those in the south. Deaths among young males and females are almost equal, and may reflect that survival chances for both sexes are more equal than they are in the south, where they are particularly biased against females. On the other hand, there are mortality factors independent of gender which balance the population. Only more representative samples from different locations across tropical Australia will provide better data and more precise interpretations from this diverse and fascinating area that has been Australia's front door for human migrations for tens of thousands of years.

Concluding remarks

This survey has revealed a diverse pattern of stress as well as other pathological conditions among Aboriginal populations across the continent. These are the first to be documented and interpreted in this way. While the survey has not been as all-encompassing as I would like, it is probably the last time such an assemblage of data will be gathered together.

Inter-regional variations in both stress and trauma emphasise radical differences in lifestyle and behaviour between groups which are so different that I believe there is a need for a radical reappraisal of the concept of prehistoric Aboriginal society in terms of its palaeodemography, nutritional standards and intake, socio-economic status and some aspects of its adaptive biology. I have, throughout this work, consistently argued that the results point strongly to permanent pathological pressures on some Aboriginal populations, particularly those living in southeastern Australia, that are inconsistent with the comparatively stress-free lifestyle often associated with the hunter-gatherer and which has been demonstrated in this study among desert dwellers (cf. Sahlins 1972). I have suggested that population pressures probably played a significant role in the frequency of stress found particularly in the southeast and, indeed, these findings prompted me to explain further how sedentism, aggregation and large populations in this area may have arisen. The model that I proposed concentrated on the central Murray region and used palaeopathological, physiological and reproductive data to demonstrate how substantial population growth could have occurred during the last two to three thousand years (Webb 1987b).

A number of alternative explanations for the central Murray and, to a lesser extent, coastal New South Wales patterns of stress are possible. Perhaps Aboriginal society was maladapted to a hunter-gatherer lifestyle or the Murray River and the coasts were not as resource-rich as we have tended to believe. Perhaps populations were not as high or as sedentary as I have proposed. Perhaps the Murray River corridor was just an extremely poor area in which to live in terms of nutritional and metabolic stress. Any one or a combination of these explanations is possible, but in my view highly unlikely. Knowing what we do about the richness of soils and natural resources in the Murray Valley and along the eastern coasts of Australia as well as the adaptive qualities of Aboriginal society, I cannot seriously accept that the enormous frequencies of stress found here reflect anything but a society undergoing change which, at the very least, involves sedentary behaviour inconsistent with hunting and gathering in the way normally associated with Aboriginal people. These findings, therefore, have no adequate explanation outside increasing populations, sedentism and economic intensification, particularly in the central Murray. Further archaeological and biological study will undoubtedly help refine our understanding of this possibility one way or another.

In the course of writing this book I have been asked innumerable times, 'Well, what was Aboriginal health like before Europeans arrived?' From the results I have presented here I can only say that the general health of Aborigines was very good anywhere on the continent. I feel I can hear some say: but we knew that. Wrong. We did *not* know that, we only assumed we did, using pure guesswork; there was little empirical data on which to base such a belief. Moreover, the diversity of health standards among Aboriginal communities across this vast continent is enormous and blanket statements are not good enough. The health of Aboriginal people was different in different regions—vastly different in some cases. Western health standards are very good, generally speaking, but 'generally speaking' does not provide an accurate picture of the range and frequency of our modern diseases and how these change over time and in response to all sorts of environmental, behavioural and social factors. So too Aboriginal health varied right across this Europe-sized continent. It is not the general health of a continent that matters, what matters is that it was not a 'general' health but a very varied one and one that, I suggest, we cannot even roughly understand just yet.

As usual, some places were healthier to live in than others. These differences were largely due to socio-economic and demographic circumstances. What we can say is that Aboriginal health was nowhere near as poor as it was among those who came to colonise this continent just over 200 years ago, nor did their diseases include the highly infectious ones carried by the new settlers and which led to the devastation of numerous Aboriginal communities in many parts of Australia. The vast Aboriginal pharmacopoeia that arose over thousands of years today looks inadequate and antiquated, but we should not look at that vast body of knowledge in the light of the range of diseases that we suffer at present nor with a Eurocentric mind. For Aboriginal people it was sufficient to cope with the limited range of conditions from which they suffered and it was obtained purely from an environment of which they had an intimate knowledge. That knowledge in itself constituted a good enough reason to trust the potency of bush medicine. Naturally, if an Aboriginal person developed appendicitis they almost surely would have died, but then so would most Europeans in 1788. Surgery was no less hazardous in a London hospital of that time than it was for an Aboriginal person lying on the desert sand or beside the Murray River. Certainly the ability to set and repair fractures was not lacking, nor to amputate, to do cranial surgery and provide long-term care. Trachoma was found in all parts of the continent but this was common outside Australia also, with Moorfields Eye Hospital in London founded especially to deal with the thousands of cases of trachoma in people returning from the Napoleonic Wars. Endemic treponemal disease was probably widespread also but this did not kill and cause sterility in the same way that introduced syphilis did. Cancer has no doubt been with humans since the beginning of time and the healthy hunter-gatherer lifestyle, the loss of which is mourned by many today, offered no defence against this terrible disease.

Palaeopathology can tell us only so much. I somehow feel that what I have done here is not good enough, but it is all that can be done at this time. I concede that the picture I have presented is incomplete and relies heavily on a bony legacy that stretches back thousands of years. Naturally, it is limited in what it can tell us but without it we are the poorer in our knowledge of us as humans and how we have lived, adapted and survived, sometimes against great odds. I can't help feeling that if we do not try and understand and fully appreciate that common heritage and pay more attention to where we have come from we cannot properly understand our contemporary situation and will be increasingly poorer for it in the future.

GOOD HEALTH.

References

Anon 1823 On the Aborigines of New Holland and Van Diemen's Land, *Medical and Physical Journal* (London) 50:180–191

—— 1861 Aboriginal surgeons and surgery, *British Medical Journal* 2:518

Abbie, A.A. 1950 Closure of cranial articulations in the skull of the Australian Aborigine, *Journal of Anatomy* 84:1–12

—— 1960 Physical changes in Australian Aborigines consequent upon European contact, *Oceania* 31:140–144

—— 1966 Physical characteristics. In *Aboriginal Man in South and Central Australia*, Cotton, B.C. (ed.), Government Printer, Adelaide, pp.9–45

—— 1969 *The Original Australians*, A.H. and A.W. Reed, Sydney

Abbott, K.H. and C.B. Courville 1943-45 Notes on the pathology of Cranial Tumors: 1. Osteomas of the skull with incidental mention of their occurrence in the Ancient Incas, *Bulletin of the Los Angeles Neurological Society* 8–10:19–34

Abrams, H.L., R. Spiro and N. Goldstein 1950 Metastases in carcinoma, *Cancer* 3:74–85

Acheson, R.M. 1959 Effects of starvation, septicaemia and chronic illness on the growth cartilage plate and metaphysis of the immature rat, *Journal of Anatomy* 93:123–130

—— 1960 Effects of nutrition and disease on human growth. In *Human Growth*, Tanner, J.M. (ed.), Pergamon Press, New York pp.73–92

Ackerknecht, E.H. 1953 Palaeopathology. In *Anthropology Today*, Kroeber, A.L. (ed.). University of Chicago Press, Chicago pp.120–126

—— 1967 Primitive surgery. In *Diseases in Antiquity*, Brothwell, D.R. and A.T. Sandison (eds). Charles C. Thomas: Springfield, Ill. pp.635–650

Acsadi, G.Y. and J. Nemeskeri 1970 *History of Human Life Span and Mortality*, Ackademiai Kiado, Budapest

Adachi, B. 1904 Die Orbitae und die Hauptmasse des Schadels der Japaner, *Z. Morphol. Anthropol.* 7:379

Adam, W. 1943 The Keilor fossil skull: palate and upper dental arch, *Memoirs of the National Museum of Victoria* 13:71–77

Adams, J.C. 1976 *Outline of Orthopaedics*, Churchill Livingstone, London, New York

—— 1978 *Outline of Fractures*, Churchill Livingstone, London, New York

Adeloyde, A., K.R. Kattan and F.N. Silverman 1975 Thickness of the normal skull in the American blacks and whites, *American Journal of Physical Anthropology* 43:23–30

Aegerter, E. and J.A. Kirkpatrick 1975 *Orthopedic Diseases*, W.B. Saunders Company, Philadelphia

Aksoy, M., N. Camli and S. Erdem 1966 Roentgenographic bone changes in chronic iron deficiency anemia. A study of twelve patients, *Blood* 27(5):677–686

Alexandersen, V. 1967a The evidence for injuries to the jaws. In *Diseases in Antiquity*, Brothwell D.R. and A.T. Sandison (eds), Charles C. Thomas, Springfield, Ill., pp.623–629

—— 1967b The pathology of the jaws and temporomandibular joint. In *Diseases in Antiquity*, Brothwell D.R. and A.T. Sandison (eds), Charles C. Thomas, Springfield, Ill. pp.551–595

Allen, F.J. 1969, 'Archaeology and the history of Port Essington'. Unpublished PhD thesis, Australian National University, Canberra

—— 1977 Fishing for wallabies: Trade as a mechanism for social interaction, integration and elaboration on the central Papuan coast. In *The Evolution of Social Systems*, Friedman, J. and M.J. Rowlands (eds), Duckworth, London pp.419–455

—— 1978 The physical and cultural setting of Motupore Island, Central Province, Papua New Guinea, *Bulletin of the Indo-Pacific Prehistory Association* 1:47–55

Allen, H.R. 1972 'Where the crow flies backwards'. Unpublished PhD thesis, Australian National University, Canberra

Allison, M.J., D. Mendoza and A. Pezzie 1974 A radiographic approach to childhood illness in precolumbian inhabitants of southern Peru, *American Journal of Physical Anthropology* 40:409–416

Alpagut, B. 1979 Some palaeopathological cases of the ancient Anatolian mandibles, *Journal of Human Evolution* 8:571–574

Anderson, J.A.D., J.J.R. Duthie and B.P. Moody 1962 Social and economic effects of rheumatic diseases in a mining population, *Annals of Rheumatic Diseases* 21:342–352

Anderson, R.M. and R.M. May 1979 Population biology of infectious disease, part I *Nature* 280: 361–367; part II *Nature* 280:455–461

Angel, J.L. 1964 Osteoporosis: Thalassemia? *American Journal of Physical Anthropology* 22:369–371

—— 1966 Early skeletons from Tranquillity, California, *Smithsonian Contributions to Anthropology* 2:1–15

—— 1967 Porotic hyperostosis or osteoporosis symmetrica. In *Disease in Antiquity*, Brothwell, D.R. and A.T. Sandison (eds), Charles C. Thomas, Springfield, Ill. pp.378–389

—— 1974 Patterns of fractures from Neolithic to modern times, *Anthropologiai Kozlemenyek* 18:9–18

—— 1979 Osteoarthritis in prehistoric Turkey and medieval Byzantium, *Henry Ford Hospital Medical Journal* 27(1):38–43

Archer, M., I.M. Crawford and D. Merrilees 1980 Incisions, breakages and charring, probably man-made, in fossil bones from Mammoth Cave, Western Australia, *Alcheringa* 4:115–31

Armelagos, G.J., J.H. Mielke, and J. Winter 1971 *Bibliography of Human Paleopathology*. Research Reports, Department of Anthropology, University of Massachusetts, Amherst. Number 8

Army Medical Officer 1823 On the Aborigines of New Holland and Van Diemen's Land, *Medical and Physical Journal (London)* 50:180–191

Arundel, J.H., I.K. Barker and I. Beveridge 1977 Disease of marsupials. In *Biology of Marsupials*, B. Stonehouse and D. Gilmore (eds), University Park Press, Baltimore pp.141–154

Asada, T. 1924 Uber die Entstehung und pathologische Bedentung der im Röntgenbild des Röhrenknochers am Diaphysenende zum Vorschein kommenden 'parallelen Querbinienbildung', *Mitt. Med. Fak. Univ. Kyushee Inknoka*, 9:43–95

Aten, L.E. 1983 *Indians of the Upper Texas Coast*, Academic Press, New York

Attenbrow, V. 1982 The archaeology of Upper Mangrove Creek catchment: research in progress. In *Coastal Archaeology in Eastern Australia*, Bowdler, S. (ed.), Proceedings of the 1980 Valla Conference on Australian Prehistory pp.67–78

Aufdermaur, M. 1957 The morbid anatomy of ankylosing spondylitis, *Documenta Rheumatologica*, January

Bahr, P. 1914 Notes on yaws in Ceylon, with special references to its distribution in that island and its tertiary manifestations, *Annals of Tropical Medical Parasitology* VIII:675–680

Baker, B.J. and G.J. Armelagos 1988 The origin and antiquity of syphilis: Paleopathological diagnosis and interpretation, *Current Anthropology* 29:703–737

Barker, S., J.H. Calaby and G.B. Sharman 1963 Diseases of Australian laboratory marsupials, *Veterinary Bulletin* 33:539–544

Barrett, M.J. 1957 Dental observations on Australian Aborigines: tooth eruption sequence, *Australian Dental Journal* 2:217–227

—— 1969 Functioning occlusion, *Annals of the Australian College of Dental Surgeons* 2:68

—— 1977 Masticatory and non-masticatory uses of teeth. In *Stone Tools as Cultural Markers*, R.V.S. Wright (ed.), Prehistory and Material Culture Series No.12, Australian Institute of Aboriginal Studies, Canberra. pp.18–23

Barrett, M.J. and T. Brown 1966 Eruption of deciduous teeth in Australian Aborigines, *Australian Dental Journal* 11(1):43–50

Barwick, D.E. 1971 Changes in the Aboriginal population of Victoria, 1863–1966. In *Aboriginal Man and Environment in Australia*, Mulvaney, D.J. and J. Golson (eds), Australian National University Press, Canberra pp.218–315

Basedow, H. 1904 Anthropological notes made on the South Australian Government north-west prospecting expedition, 1903, *Transactions of the Royal Society of South Australia*, 28:12–51

—— 1932 Diseases of the Australian Aborigines. *Journal of Tropical Medicine and Hygiene* 35:1–32

Bass, W.M., J.B. Gregg and P.E. Provost 1974 Ankylosing spondylitis (Marie Strumpel disease) in historic and prehistoric Northern Plains Indians, *Plains Anthropologist* 18:303–305

Bates, D.M. n.d. *Diseases, remedies, death and burial and disease remedies.* Typescript copy of manuscript Section 10, 2a, 2a(1), 2a, (a) entitled: Diseases of natives before white contact, idiocy, deformities, and names for diseases, Australian National Library, Canberra

Beaton, J.M. 1982 Fire and water: aspects of Australian Aboriginal management of cycads, *Archaeology in Oceania* 17:59–67

Benenson, A.S. 1975 *Control of communicable diseases in Man.* An Official Report of the American Public Health Association, Washington. 12th edn.

Bennett, G.G. 1834 *Wanderings in New South Wales,* 2 vols., London. (Facsimile edn., Adelaide 1967)

Bennett, K.A. 1967 Craniostenosis: A review of the etiology and report of new cases, *American Journal of Physical Anthropology* 27:1–10

—— 1971 Lumbo-sacral malformations and spina bifida occulta in a group of proto-historic Modoc Indians, *American Journal of Physical Anthropology* 36:435–440

Bennett, M.M. 1927 Notes on the Dalleburra tribe of northern Queensland, *Journal of the Anthropological Institute* 57:399–415

Berndt, R.M. and C.H. 1981 *The World of the First Australians,* rev. 4th ed., Aboriginal Studies Press, Canberra

Beute, G.H. 1979 Arthritis: a radiologic overview, *Henry Ford Hospital Medical Journal* 27(1):24–31

Beveridge, I. 1986 Parasitic diseases of monotremes and marsupials. In *Zoo and Wild Animal Medicine,* Murray, E.F. (ed.), 2nd edn., W.B. Saunders, London pp.577–588

Beveridge, P. 1883 Of the Aborigines inhabiting the great lacustrine and riverine depression of the lower Murray, lower Murrumbidgee, lower Lachlan and lower Darling, *Journal of Proceedings of Royal Society of New South Wales* 17:19–68

Beyron, H. 1964 Occlusal relations and mastication in Australian Aborigines, *Acta Odontologica Scandinavica* 22:597–678

Bibliography of Anthropology and Genetics 1991 Department of Dentistry, University of Adelaide

Bickford, A. 1966 'Traditional economy of the Aborigines of the Murray Valley'. Unpublished BA (hons) thesis, University of Sydney

Billington, B.P. 1960 The health and nutritional status of the Aborigines. In *Records of the American-Australian Scientific Expedition to Arnhem Land.* Vol.II. *Anthropology and Nutrition* pp.27–59

Binns, R.T. 1945 A study of diseases of Australian natives in the Northern Territory, *Medical Journal of Australia* (1):421–426

Birdsell, J.B. 1957 Some population problems involving Pleistocene man, *Cold Spring Harbor Symposia on Quantitative Biology* 27:47–69

Black, E.C. and J.B. Cleland 1938 Pathological lesions in Australian Aborigines, central Australia (Granites) and Flinders Range, *Journal of Tropical Medicine and Hygiene.* 1 March 1938:1–15

Black, F.D. 1975 Infectious diseases in primitive society, *Science* 187:515–518

Blackwood, H.J.J. 1963 Arthritis of the mandibular joint, *British Dental Journal* 115:317–326

Blackwood, Sir R. and K.N.G. Simpson 1973 Attitudes of Aboriginal skeletons excavated in the Murray Valley region between Mildura and Renmark, Australia, *Victorian National Museum Memoirs* 34:99–150

Blakely R.L. 1971 Comparison of the mortality profiles of Archaic, Middle Woodlands, and Middle Mississippian skeletal populations, *American Journal of Physical Anthropology* 34:43–54

—— 1980 Sociocultural implications of pathology between the village area and mound C skeletal remains from Etowa, Georgia, *Tennessee Anthropological Association* 5:28–38

Bluhm, G.B. 1979 Gout and pseudogout, *Henry Ford Hospital Medical Journal* 27(1):14–17

Blumberg, B.S. (ed.) 1961 *Proceedings of the conference on genetic polymorphisms and geographic variations in disease.* Grune and Stratton, New York

Blumberg, B.S., K.J. Bloch, R.L. Black and C. Dotier 1961 A study of prevalence of arthritis in Alaskan Eskimos, *Arthritis and Rheumatism* 4(4):325–41

Blumberg, J.M. and E.R. Kerley 1966 A critical consideration of roentgenology and microscopy in palaeopathology. In *Human Paleopathology*, Jarcho, S. (ed.). Yale University Press, New Haven and London pp.64–87

Bodmer, W.F. and L.L. Cavalli-Sforza 1976 *Genetics, Evolution, and Man*. W.H. Freeman, San Francisco

Borah, W. 1964 America as a model: the demographic impact of European expansion upon the non-European world. *Actas y Memorias del XXXV Congreso Internacional de Americanistas* 3:173–205

Boserup, E. 1965 *The Conditions of Agricultural Growth*, Aldine Press, Chicago

Boule, M. 1911-13 L'homme fossile de La Chapelle-aux-Saints, *Annales de Paléontologie* 6:109–172

—— 1923 *Fossil Men*, Oliver and Boyd, Edinburgh

Bourke, J.B. 1967 A review of the palaeopathology of the arthritic diseases. In *Diseases of Antiquity*, Brothwell D.R. and A.T. Sandison (eds). Charles C. Thomas, Springfield, Ill. pp.352–370

—— 1971 The palaeopathology of the vertebral column in ancient Egypt and Nubia, *Medical History* 15:363–375

Bowdler, S. 1975 Hook, line and dilly bag: an interpetation of an Australian coastal shell midden, *Mankind* 10:248–58

—— 1977 Coastal colonisation of Australia. In *Sunda and Sahul*, Allen, J., Golson, J. and R. Jones (eds), Academic Press, Sydney pp.205–246

——1981 Hunters in the highlands: Aboriginal adaptations in the eastern Australian uplands, *Archaeology in Oceania* 16:99–111

—— 1983 *Archaeological Investigation of a Threatened Aboriginal Burial Site*. Unpublished report to the Victorian Archaeological Survey

Bowers, W.F. 1966 Pathological and functional changes found in 864 pre-Captain Cook contact Polynesian burials from the sand dunes at Mokapu, Oahu, Hawaii, *International Surgery* 45:206–217

Bowler, J.M. and A.G. Thorne 1976 Human remains from Lake Mungo. In *Origin of the Australians*, Kirk, R.L. and A.G. Thorne (eds), Australian Institute of Aboriginal Studies Publications, Canberra pp.127–138

Brace, C.L. 1980 Australian tooth-size clines and the death of a stereotype, *Current Anthropology* 21(2):141–146

Breinl, A. 1912 Report on the health and disease in the Northern Territory, *Bulletin of the Northern Territory*, No. 1

—— 1915 Gangosa in New Guinea and its etiology, *Annals of Tropical Medicine and Parasitology* 9:213–233

—— 1915 On the occurrence and prevalence of diseases in British New Guinea, *Annals of Tropical Medicine and Parasitology* 9:285–335

Breinl, A. and M.J. Holmes 1915 Medical report on data collected during a journey through some districts of the Northern Territory, *Bulletin of the Northern Territory*, No. 15

Breinl, A. and H. Priestley 1915 Boomerang leg, *Journal of Tropical and Medical Hygiene* XVIII:217

Bridges, P.S., 1989 Spondylosis and its relationship to degenerative joint disease in the prehistoric southeastern United States, *American Journal of Physical Anthropology* 79:321–329

Britton, C.J.C. 1963 *Disorders of the Blood*, J. and A. Churchill, London

Britton, H.A., J.P. Canby and C.M. Kohler 1960 Iron deficiency anemia producing evidence of marrow hyperplasia in the calvarium, *Pediatrics* April 1960, pp.621–628

Brodelius, A. 1961 Osteoarthritis of the talar joints in footballers and ballet dancers, *Acta Orthopedica Scandinavica* 30:309–314

Brooks, S.T. and W.D. Hohenthal 1963 Archeological defective palate crania from California, *American Journal of Physical Anthropology* 21:25–32

Brooks, S.T. and J. Melbye 1967 Skeletal lesions suggestive of pre-Columbian multiple myeloma in a burial from the Kane Mounds, near St Louis, Missouri. In *Miscellaneous Papers in Paleopathology: 1*, Wade, W.D. (ed.), Museum of Northern Arizona, Flagstaff, Arizona pp.23–29

Brothwell, D.R. 1961 The palaeopathology of early British man: An essay on the problems of diagnosis and analysis, *Journal of the Royal Anthropological Institute of Great Britain and Ireland* 91:318–344

—— 1963a The macroscopic dental pathology of some earlier human populations. In *Dental Anthropology*, D.R. Brothwell (ed.), Pergamon Press, Oxford pp.271–288

—— 1963b *Digging Up Bones*, British Museum, London

—— 1967 The Evidence for Neoplasms. In *Diseases in Antiquity*, Brothwell, D.R. and A.T. Sanderson (eds), Charles C. Thomas, Springfield, Ill. pp.320–345

—— 1970 The real history of syphilis, *Science Journal* 6–7(1):27–32

—— 1976 Further evidence of treponematosis in pre-European population from Oceania. *Bulletin of Historical Medicine* 50:435–442

—— 1977 Human population history, from Afro-Asia to the New World, and its possible relationship to economic change. In *Hunters, Gatherers and First Farmers Beyond Europe*, J.V.S. Megaw (ed.), Leicester University Press, Leicester pp.15–23

—— 1978 Possible evidence of the parasitisation of early Mexican communities by the micro-organism treponema, *Bulletin of the Institute of Archaeology* 15:113–130

Brothwell, D.R. and R. Powers 1968 Congenital malformations of the skeleton in earlier man. In *The Skeletal Biology of Earlier Human Populations, Vol. VIII*, Brothwell, D. (ed.), Pergamon Press, Oxford pp.173–203

Brothwell, D.R. and A.T. Sandison (eds) 1967 *Diseases in Antiquity*, Charles C. Thomas, Springfield, Ill.

Brown, A.R. 1930 Former numbers and distribution of the Australian Aborigines, *Official Year Book of the Commonwealth of Australia* 23:687–696

Brown, P. 1981 Artificial cranial deformation: a component in the variation in Pleistocene Australian Aboriginal crania, *Archaeology in Oceania* 16: 156–167

—— 1989 Coobool Creek. A morphological and metrical analysis of the crania, mandibles and dentition of a prehistoric Australian human population, *Terra Australis* 13, Department of Prehistory, Research School of Pacific Studies, Australian National University, Canberra

Brown, T. and S. Molnar 1990 Interproximal grooving and task activity in Australia, *American Journal of Physical Anthropology* 81:545–553

Brown, T., G.C. Townsend, L.C. Richards, and V.B. Burgess 1990 Concepts of occlusion: Australian evidence, *American Journal of Physical Anthropology* 82:247–256

Bruce-Chwatt, L.J. 1965 Paleogenesis and paleo-epidemiology of primate malaria, *Bulletin of the World Health Organisation* 32:363–387

Bullough, P.G. 1965 Ivory exostosis of the skull, *Postgraduate Medical Journal* 41:277–281

Butler, C.S. 1928 Presidential address, *American Journal of Tropical Medicine* 7:363–370

Butler, R. 1986 Bacterial diseases of monotremes and marsupials. In *Zoo and Wild Animal Medicine*, Murray, E.F. (ed.), 2nd ed., W.B. Saunders, London pp.572–576

Butlin, N.G. 1983 *Our Original Aggression*, George Allen and Unwin, Sydney and Boston.

Caddie, D.A., D.S. Hunter, P.J. Pomery and H.J. Hall 1987 The ageing chemist–can electron spin resonance (ESR) help? In *Archaeometry: Further Australian Studies*, Ambrose, W.R. and J.M.J. Mummery (eds). Department of Prehistory, ANU, Canberra pp.167–176

Cadell, F. 1868 Report of an exploring expedition to the Northern Territory. *South Australian Parliamentary Papers*, 31 March

Caffey, J. 1931 Clinical and experimental lead poisoning: some roentgenologic and anatomic changes in growing bones, *Radiology* 17:957–983

Campbell, J. 1983 Smallpox in Australia, *Historical Studies* 20:536–556

Campbell, T.D. 1925 *Dentition and Palate of the Australian Aboriginal*, University of Adelaide Publications 1:72–81

—— 1937 Observations on the teeth of Australian Aborigines, Hermannsberg, central Australia, *Australian Journal of Dentistry* 41:1–6

—— 1939 Food, food values and food habits of the Australian Aborigines in relation to their dental condition, *Australian Journal of Dentistry* 43(1):1–198

Campbell, T.D. and M.J. Barrett 1953 Dental observations on Australian Aborigines: a changing environment and food pattern, *Australian Journal of Dentistry* 57:1–6

Cane, S.B. 1984 'Desert Camps'. Unpublished PhD thesis, Australian National University, Canberra

Cannefax, G.R., L.C. Norrins and E.J. Gillespie 1967 Immunology of syphilis, *Annual Review of Medicine* 18:471–482

Carlson, D.S., G.J. Armelagos and D.P. van Gerven 1974 Factors influencing the etiology of cribra orbitalia in prehistoric Nubia, *Journal of Human Evolution* 3:405–410

Cassidy, C.M. 1977 Probable malignancy in a Sadlermiut Eskimo mandible, *American Journal of Physical Anthropology* 46:291–296

—— 1979 Arthritis in dry bones: diagnostic problems, *Henry Ford Hospital Medical Journal* 27(1):68–69

Chaplin, R.E. 1971 *The Study of Animal Bones from Archaeological Sites*, Academic Press, London

Chapman, F.H. 1962 Incidence of arthritis in a prehistoric middle Mississippian Indian population, *Proceedings of the Indiana Academy of Science* 72:59–62

—— 1968 Comparison of osteoarthritis in three Aboriginal populations, *Proceedings of the Indiana Academy of Science* 74:84–86

Chase, A. and P. Sutton 1981 Hunter-gatherers in a rich environment: Aboriginal coastal exploitation in Cape York Peninsula. In *Ecological Biogeography of Australia*, Keast, A. (ed.), Junk, The Hague pp.1819–1851

Chesterman, C.C. 1927 The relation of yaws and goundou, *Transactions of the Royal Society of Tropical Medicine and Hygiene* 20:554

Cilento, R. 1942 *Tropical Diseases in Australia*, Smith and Paterson, Brisbane

Clabeaux, M.S. 1976 Health and disease in the population of an Iroquois ossuary, *Yearbook of Physical Anthropology* 19:359–370

Clark, G.A. and J.A. Delmond 1979 Vertebral osteophytosis in Dickson mound populations: a biomechanical interpretation, *Henry Ford Hospital Medical Journal* 27(1):54–58

Clarke, S.K. 1980 Early childhood morbidity trends in prehistoric populations, *Human Biology* 52(1):79–85

—— 1982 The association of early childhood enamel hypoplasias and radiopaque transverse lines in a culturally diverse prehistoric skeletal sample, *Human Biology* 53(1):77–84

Cleland, J.B. 1924 Injuries and diseases in Australia attributable to animals (except insects), *Medical Journal of Australia* 2:339–345

—— 1928 Disease amongst the Australian Aborigines, *Journal of Tropical Medicine and Hygiene* 31:125–130

—— 1932 Injuries and diseases in Australia attributable to animals (other than insects), series IV, *Medical Journal of Australia* 1:157–166

—— 1942 Injuries and diseases in Australia attributable to animals (insects excepted), *Medical Journal of Australia* 2:313–320

—— 1953 The healing art in primitive society, *Mankind* 4:395–411

—— 1958 Aborigines: diseases and medicines. *Australian Encyclopaedia* 1:82–87

—— 1962 Disease in the Australian native, *Journal of Tropical Medicine and Hygiene* 65:95–105

—— 1966 The ecology of the Aboriginal in South and Central Australia. In *Aboriginal Man in South and Central Australia, Part 1*, Cotton, B.C. (ed.), Government Printer, Adelaide, South Australia pp.111–158

Cleland, J.B. and B.G. Macgraith 1930 Notes on the pathological lesions and vital statistics of Australian natives in central Australia, *Medical Journal of Australia* 2:80–83

Clement, A.J. 1963 Variations in the microstructure and biochemistry of human teeth. In *Dental Anthropology*, D.R. Brothwell (ed.), Pergamon Press, Oxford pp.254–264

Cockburn, E. (ed.) 1977 Porotic hyperostosis: an enquiry. *Paleopathology Association Monograph No.2*. Detroit, Michigan

Cockburn, T.A. 1967 (ed.) *Infectious Diseases: Their Evolution and Eradication*, Charles C. Thomas, Springfield, Ill.

—— 1971 Infectious diseases in ancient populations, *Current Anthropology* 12:45–62

Cockburn, T.A., H. Duncan and J.M. Riddle 1979 Arthritis ancient and modern: guidelines for field workers, *Henry Ford Hospital Medical Journal* 27(1):74–79

Cockram, F.A. and A.R.B. Jackson 1974 Isolation of a chlamydia from cases of kerato-conjunctivitis in koalas, *Australian Veterinary Journal* 50:82–83

Cohen, H.J. and H. Diner 1970 The significance of developmental dental enamel defects in neurological diagnosis, *Pediatrics* 46(5):737–747

Coleman, J. 1982 A new look at the north coast: fish traps and 'villages'. In *Coastal Archaeology in Eastern Australia*, S. Bowdler (ed.), Proceedings of the 1980 Valla Conference on Australian Prehistory pp.1–10

Collins, D. 1798 *An account of the English colony in New South Wales*. A Royal Australian Historical Society facsimile edition (1975). A.H. and A.W. Reed, Sydney, London

Comas, J. 1965 Crânes Mexicains scaphocephales, *L'Anthropologie* (Paris). 69 (3-4):273–302

Cook, C.E. 1970 Notable changes in the incidence of disease in Northern Territory Aborigines. In *Diprotodon to Detribalization*, Pilling A.R. and R.A. Waterman (eds), Michigan State University Press, Detroit

Cook, D.C. and J.E. Buikstra 1979 Health and differential survival in prehistoric populations: prenatal dental defects, *American Journal of Physical Anthropology* 51:649–664

Cook, S.F. 1976 *The Population of the California Indians 1769-1970*. University of California Press, Berkeley, Calif.

Cooley, T.B. and P. Lee 1925 Series of cases of splenomegaly in children with anemia and peculiar bone changes, *Journal of the American Pediatric Society* 37:29

Copeman, W.S.C. 1955 *Textbook of the Rheumatic Diseases*, E.S. Livingstone, Edinburgh and London

Courville, C.B. 1942 Cranial injuries of the pre-Columbian Incas, *Los Angeles Neurological Society* 7:107–142

—— 1951 Injuries to the skull and brain in Oceania, *Los Angeles Neurological Society* 16:14–70

—— 1952 Cranial injuries among the early Indians of California, *Los Angeles Neurological Society* 17:137–162

—— 1967 Cranial injuries in prehistoric man. In *Disease in Antiquity*, Brothwell D.R. and A.T. Sandison (eds), Charles C. Thomas, Springfield, Ill. pp.606–622

Coutts, P.J.F., R.K. Frank and P. Hughes 1978 Aboriginal engineers of the western district, Victoria, *Records of the Victoria Archaeological Survey* No. 7 June

Coutts, P.J.F., P. Henderson and R.L.K. Fullagar 1979 A preliminary investigation of Aboriginal mounds in northwestern Victoria, *Records of the Victoria Archaeological Survey*, No. 9

Coutts, P.J.F., D.C. Witter, M. McIlwraith and R. Frank 1976 The mound people of western Victoria: a preliminary statement, *Records of the Victoria Archaeological Survey* No. 1:1–54

Cowlishaw, G. 1981 The determinants of fertility among Australian Aborigines, *Mankind* 13:37–55

Cran, J.A. 1955 Notes on the teeth and gingivae of central Australian Aborigines, *Australian Journal of Dentistry* 59:356–361

Crane, G.G., R.W. Hornabrook, and A. Kelly 1971-2 Anemia on the coast and highlands of New Guinea, *Human Biology in Oceania* 1:235–241

Crosby, A.W. Jr. 1969 The early history of syphilis: A reappraisal. *American Anthropologist* 71:218–227

Crotty, J.M. and R.C. Webb 1960 Mortality in Northern Territory Aborigines, *Medical Journal of Australia* 1:184–186

Crump. J.A. 1901 Trephining in the South Seas, *Journal of the Royal Anthropological Institute* 31:167–172

Cunningham, P. 1827 *Two years in New South Wales*, Henry Colburn, London

Curr, E.M. 1886 *The Australian race*, John Ferris, Government Printer, Melbourne

Cybulski, J.S. 1977 Cribra orbitalia, a possible sign of anemia in early historic native populations of the British Columbia coast, *American Journal of Physical Anthropology* 47:31–40

—— 1980 Skeletal remains from Lillooet, British Columbia, with observations for a possible diagnosis of skull trephination, *Syesis* 13:53–59

Danenberg, P.J., R.S. Hirsch, N.G. Clarke, P.I. Leppard and L.C. Richards 1991 Continuous tooth eruption in Australian Aboriginal skulls, *American Journal of Physical Anthropology* 85:305–312

Darling, A.I. 1956 Some observations on amelogenesis imperfecta and calcification of the dental enamel, *Proceedings of the Royal Society of Medicine* 49:759–765

Dastugue, J. 1980 Possibilities, limits and prospects in paleopathology of the human skeleton, *Journal of Human Evolution* 9:3–8

Davivongs, V. 1963a The femur of the Australian Aborigine, *American Journal of Physical Anthropology* 21:457–467

—— 1963b The pelvic girdle of the Australian Aborigine; sex difference and sex determination, *American Journal of Physical Anthropology* 21:443–456

Dawson, J. 1881 *Australian Aborigines: the languages and customs of several tribes in the western district of Victoria*, George Robertson, Melbourne and Sydney

Day, M.H. and T.I. Molleson 1973 The Trinil femora. In *Human Evolution*, Day, M.H. (ed.), Symposia of the Society for the Study of Human Biology, Taylor and Francis, London pp.127–154

Dedekind, A. 1896 A novel use for the rontgen rays, *British Journal of Photography* 43:131

Dennie, C.C. 1962 *A History of Syphilis*, Charles C. Thomas. Springfield, Ill.

Devor, E.J. and L.S. Cordell 1981 Neural-tube defects in a prehistoric south-western Indian population, *Annals of Human Biology* 8:65–75

Dickel, D.N. and G.H. Doran 1989 Severe neural tube defect syndrome from the Early Archaic of Florida, *American Journal of Physical Anthropology* 80:325–334

Dinning, T.A.R. 1949 A study of healed fractures in the Australian Aboriginal, *Medical Journal of Australia* (2):712–713

Dobyns, H.F. 1966 Estimating the Aboriginal American population: an appraisal of techniques with a new hemispheric estimate, *Current Anthropology* 7:395–416

—— 1976 Brief perspective on a scholarly transformation: widowing the 'virgin' land, *Ethnohistory* 23:95–104

—— 1983 *Their Number Became Thinned*, University of Tennessee Press

Dodson, J.R. 1989 Late Pleistocene vegetation and environmental shifts in Australia and their bearing on faunal extinctions, *Journal of Archaeological Science* 16:207–217

Dongen, R. van 1963 The shoulder girdle and humerus of the Australian Aborigine, *American Journal of Physical Anthropology* 21:469–488

Dreizen, S., C.N. Spirakis and R.E. Stone 1964 The influence of age and nutritional status on 'bone scar' formation in the distal end of the growing radius, *American Journal of Physical Anthropology* 22:295–306

Duke-Elder, Sir Stewart *et al.* 1961 *The Anatomy of the Visual System*, Vol.II. Henry Kimpton, London

Duncan, H. 1979 Osteoarthritis, *Henry Ford Hospital Medical Journal* 27(1):6–9

Dunn, F.L. 1968 Epidemiological factors: health and disease in hunter-gatherers. In *Man the Hunter*, Lee, R.B. and I. De Vore (eds), Aldine Press, Chicago pp.221–228

Duray, S.M. 1990 Deciduous enamel defects and caries susceptibility in a prehistoric Ohio population, *American Journal of Physical Anthropology* 81:27–34

Edynak, G.J. 1976 Life-styles from skeletal material: a medieval Yugoslav example. In *The Measures of Man*, Giles, E. and J.S. Friedlaender (eds), Peabody Museum Press, Cambridge, Mass. pp.408–432

Eiseley, L.C. and C.W. Asling 1944 An extreme case of scaphocephaly from a mound burial near Troy, Kansas, *Transactions Kansas Academy of Science* 47:241–255

Elkin, A.P. 1979 *The Australian Aborigines*, Rev. ed. Angus and Robertson, Sydney and London.

Elkington, J.S.C. 1912 Report on an inspection of the Torres Straits Islands and vaccination of the islanders, *Annual Report of the Commonwealth Department Public Health, Queensland* pp.21–27

El-Najjar, M. 1976 Maize, malaria and the anemias in the pre-Columbian new world, *Yearbook of Physical Anthropology* 20:329–337

—— 1979 Human treponematosis and tuberculosis: evidence from the new world, *American Journal of Physical Anthropology* 51:599–618

El-Najjar, M.Y., M.V. DeSanti and L. Ozebek 1978 Prevalence and possible etiology of dental enamel hypoplasia, *American Journal of Physical Anthropology* 48:185–192

El-Najjar, M.Y., D.J. Ryan, C.G. Turner and B. Lozoff 1976 The etiology of porotic hyperostosis among the prehistoric and historic Anasazi Indians of southwestern United States, *American Journal of Physical Anthropology* 44:477–488

Elphinstone, J.J. 1971 The health of Australian Aborigines with no previous association with Europeans, *Medical Journal of Australia* (2):293–301

Enwonwu, C.O. 1973 Influence of socio-economic conditions on dental development in Nigerian children, *Archives of Oral Biology* 18:95–107

Esper, E.J.C. 1774 *Ausfurliche Nachrichten von neuentdeckten Zoolithen unbekannter vierfussiger Thiere*, Nürnberg

Eylmann, E. 1908 *Die Engeborenen der Kolonie Sudaustralien*, Dietrich Riemer, Berlin

Eyre, E.J. 1845 *Journals of Expeditions of Discovery into Central Australia*, Australiana Facsimile edition no. 7 (1964), Libraries Board of South Australia, Adelaide

Falin, L.I. 1961 Histological and histochemical studies of human teeth of the Bronze and Stone Ages, *Archives of Oral Biology* 5:5–13

Fenner, F.J. 1938 Some Australian Aboriginal scaphocephalic skulls. *Records of South Australian Museum* 6(2):144–157

Ferembach, D. 1963 Frequency of spina bifida occulta in prehistoric human skeletons, *Nature* 199:100–101

Fiennes N. T-W-. 1978 *Zoonoses and the Ecology and Origin of Human Disease*, Academic Press, New York

Finnie, E.P. 1986 Viral diseases of monotremes and marsupials. In *Zoo and Wild Animal Medicine*, Murray E.F. (ed.), 2nd ed. W.B. Saunders, London pp.577–578

Flannery, T.F. 1990 Pleistocene faunal loss: implications of the aftershock for Australia's past and future, *Archaeology in Oceania* 25:45–67

Flood, J. 1980 *The Moth Hunters*, Australian Institute of Aboriginal Studies: Canberra

—— 1989 *Archaeology of the Dreamtime*. Collins, Australia, rev. ed.

Foelsche, P. 1882 Notes on the Aborigines of north Australia, *Transactions and Proceedings of the Royal Society of South Australia* 5:1–18

—— 1886 Port Darwin: the Larrakia tribe. In *The Australian Race*, E.M. Curr (ed.), Vol.1 pp.250–259

Follis, R.H. and E.A. Park 1952 Some observations on bone growth with particular reference to zones and transverse lines of increased density in the metaphysis, *American Journal of Roentgenology* 68:709–724

Ford, E. 1937 Trephining in Melanesia, *Medical Journal of Australia*, 18 September pp.471–477

Franzen, J.L. 1985 What is '*Pithecanthropus dubius* Koeningswald, 1950'? In *Ancestors: The Hard Evidence*, Delson, E. (ed.), Alan R. Liss, New York pp.221–226

Freedman, L. 1985 Human skeletal remains from Mossgiel, NSW, *Archaeology in Oceania* 20:21–31

Freedman, L. and M. Lofgren 1981 Odontometrics of Western Australian Aborigines, *Archaeology in Oceania* 16:87–93

Garn, S.M. and R.S. Baby 1969 Bilateral symmetry in finer lines of increased density, *American Journal of Physical Anthropology* 31:89–92

Garn, S.M. and P.M. Schwager 1967 Age dynamics of persistent transverse lines in the tibia, *American Journal of Physical Anthropology* 27:375–378

Garn, S.M., F.N. Silverman, K.P. Hertzog and C.G. Rohmann 1968 Lines and bands of increased density, *Medical Radiography and Photography* 44(3):58–89

Garner, M.F. and R.W. Hornabrook 1968 Treponematosis in the Eastern Highlands of New Guinea, *Bulletin of the World Health Organisation* 38:189–195

—— 1970 Treponematosis in New Guinea, *Papua New Guinea Medical Journal* 13:53–55

—— 1973 Treponematosis in Papua New Guinea–a review of surveys undertaken between 1964 and 1972, *Papua New Guinea Medical Journal* 16:189–193

Garner, M.F., R.W. Hornabrook and J.L. Backhouse 1972 Treponematosis along the Highlands Highway, *Papua New Guinea Medical Journal* 15:139–141

Garner, M.F., J.L. Backhouse, and G.J. Tibbs 1973 Yaws in an isolated Australian Aboriginal population, *Bulletin of the World Health Organisation* 43:603–606

Garner, M.F., J.L. Backhouse, P.M. Moodie and G.J. Tibbs 1972 Treponemal infection in the Australian Northern Territory Aborigines, *Bulletin of World Health Organisation* 42:285–293

Gass, H.H. 1971 Skull from Spruce Swamp: Case of cranial dystraphism, *Science* 171:1268

Gejvall, N-G. and F. Henschen 1971 Anatomical evidence of Pre-Columbian syphilis in the West Indian Islands, *Beitrag Pathologie Bd.* 144:138–157

Giles, E. 1889 *Australia Twice Traversed.* Sampson Low, Marston, Searle and Rivington, London

Gill, E. 1968 Examination of Harris' lines in recent and fossil Aboriginal bones, *Current Anthropology* 9(2–3):215

Gillespie, R., D.R. Horton, P. Ladd, P.G. Macumber, T.H. Rich, A.G. Thorne, and R.V.S. Right 1978 Lancefield Swamp and the extinction of the Australian megafauna, *Science* 200: 1044–1048

Gindhart, P.S. 1969 The frequency of appearance of transverse lines in the tibia in relation to childhood illnesses. *American Journal of Physical Anthropology* 31:17–22

Giro, C.M. 1947 Enamel hypoplasia in human teeth: an examination of its causes, *Journal of the American Dental Association* 34:309–317

Gladykowska-Rzeczycka, J. and M. Urbanowicz 1970 Multiple osseous exostoses of the skeleton from a prehistoric cemetery of a former population of Pruszcz Gdanski, *Folia Morphologica* 29: 284–296

Goff, C.W. 1967 Syphilis. In *Diseases in Antiquity,* Brothwell D.R. and A.T. Sandison (eds), Charles C. Thomas, Springfield, Ill. pp.279–294

Goldfuss, G.A. 1810 *Die Umgebringen von Muggendorf,* Erlangen

Goldstein, M.S. 1957 Skeletal pathology of early Indians in Texas, *American Journal of Physical Anthropology* 15:299–307

—— 1969 Human paleopathology and some diseases in living primitive socities: A review of the recent literature, *American Journal of Physical Anthropology* 31:285–294

Goldstein, M.S., B. Arensberg and H. Nathan 1976 Pathology of Bedouin skeletal remains from two sites in Israel, *American Journal of Physical Anthropology* 45:621–640

Gondos, B. 1972 The Pointed Tubular Bone, *Radiology* 105:541–545

Goodman, A.H., G.J. Armelagos and J.C. Rose 1980 Enamel hypoplasia as indicators of stress in three prehistoric populations from Illinois, *Human Biology* 52(3):515–528

Goodman, A.H., J. Lallo, G.J. Armelagos and J.C. Rose 1983 Health changes at Dickson Mounds, Illinois (AD950–1300). In *Paleopathology and the Origins of Agriculture,* Cohen M.N. and G.J. Armelagos (eds), Academic Press, New York pp.271–304

Goodman, A.H., J. Lallo, G.J. Armelagos and J.C. Rose 1984 The Chronological distribution of enamel hypoplasias from prehistoric Dickson Mounds population, *American Journal of Physical Anthropology* 65:259–266

Gott, B. 1982 Ecology and root use by the Aborigines of southern Australia, *Archaeology in Oceania* 17:59–67

Green, M.K. 1982 'A Review of Enamel Hypoplasia and its Application to Australian Prehistory'. Unpublished BA (hons) thesis, Australian National University, Canberra

Green, N. 1981 Aborigines and white settlers in the nineteenth century. In *A New History of Western Australia,* C.T. Stannage (ed.), University of Western Australia Press Perth pp.51–88

Grin, E.I. 1953 Endemic syphilis in Bosnia: clinical and epidemiological observations on a successful mass-treatment campaign, *Bulletin of the World Health Organisation* 7:1–74

Hackett, C.J. 1936a *Boomerang Leg and Yaws in Australian Aborigines* Monograph I, September 1936, Royal Society of Tropical Medicine and Hygiene. London

—— 1936b Boomerang legs and yaws in Australian Aborigines, *Transactions Royal Society of Tropical Medicine and Hygiene* 30:137–150

—— 1936c A critical survey of some references to syphilis and yaws among the Australian Aborigines, *Medical Journal of Australia* 1:773

—— 1947 Incidence of yaws and of venereal diseases in Lango (Uganda), *British Medical Journal* 18 January: 88–90

—— 1951 *Bone Lesions of Yaws in Uganda,* Blackwell, Oxford

—— 1963 On the origin of human treponematoses, *Bulletin of the World Health Organisation* 29: 1–41

—— 1968 Some aspects of treponematoses in past populations, *Journal of the Anthropological Society of South Australia* 6(9):5–14 (Minutes of 1967 Annual General Meeting)

—— 1974 Possible treponemal changes in a Tasmanian skull, *Man* 9:436–443

—— 1975 An introduction to diagnostic criteria of syphilis, treponarid and yaws (treponematoses) in dry bones, and some implications, *Virchows Archives of Pathology, Anatomy and Histology* 368:229–241

—— 1976 *Diagnostic Criteria of Syphilis, Yaws and Treponarid (Treponematoses) and of some other Diseases in Dry Bones*, Springer-Verlag, Berlin, Heidelberg and New York

Haddon, A.C. 1935 *Reports of the Anthropological Expedition to Torres Strait, Vol.1 General Ethnography*, Cambridge University Press, Cambridge

Haglund-Calley, L. 1968a The Aboriginal burial ground at Broadbeach, Queensland: excavation report. *Mankind* 6:676–680

—— 1968b 'The Relation Between the Broadbeach Burials and the Cultures of Eastern Australia'. Unpublished MA thesis, University of Queensland, Brisbane

Haglund, L. 1976 *The Broadbeach Aboriginal Burial Ground*, University of Queensland Press, Brisbane

Hall, J. 1982 Sitting on the crop of the bay: an historical and archaeological sketch of Aboriginal settlement and subsistence in Moreton Bay, *In Coastal Archaeology in Eastern Australia*, Bowdler, S. (ed.), Proceedings of the 1980 Valla Conference on Australian Prehistory pp.79–95

Hamdy, R.C. 1981 *Pagets Disease of Bone*, Armour Pharmaceutical Co., England

Hamilton, A. 1981 *Nature and Nurture: Aboriginal Child-Rearing in North-Central Arnhem Land*, Australian Institute of Aboriginal Studies, Canberra

Hare, R. 1967 The Antiquity of Diseases Caused by Bacteria and Viruses, A Review of the Problem from the Bacteriologist's Point of View. In *Disease in Antiquity*, Brothwell D.R. and A.T. Sandison (eds), Charles C. Thomas, Springfield, Ill. pp.115–131

Harpending, H.C. 1974 Demographic changes accompanying sedentarization in !Kung hunter-gatherers, *American Journal of Physical Anthropology* 40:139

Harris, H.A. 1926 The growth of the long bones in childhood, with special reference to certain bony striations of the metaphysis and to the role of vitamins, *Archives of Internal Medicine* 38: 785–806

—— 1931 Lines of arrested growth in the long bones in childhood. Correlation of histological and radiographic appearances in clinical and experimental conditions, *British Journal of Radiology* 4:561–588

—— 1933 *Bone Growth in Health and Disease*. Oxford University Press, London

Harrison, G.A., J.S. Weiner, J.M. Tanner and N.A. Barnicot 1977 *Human Biology*, Oxford University Press, 2nd ed.

Hartney, P.C. 1978 'Palaeopathology of Archaeological Aboriginal Populations from Southern Ontario and Adjacent Region'. Unpublished PhD thesis, Department of Anthropology, University of Toronto

Head, L. 1983 Environment as artefact: a geographic perspective on the Holocene occupation of southwestern Victoria, *Archaeology in Oceania* 18:73–80

Helms, R. 1896 Anthropology reports of the Elder scientific expedition 1891. *Royal Society of South Australia Transactions* 16(3):237–332

Hennessy, W.B. 1979 *Lay Course in Tropical Medicine*. School of Public Health and Tropical Medicine, Service Publication No. 14, 2nd ed., University of Sydney

Hengen, O.P. 1971 Cribra orbitalia: pathogenesis and probable etiology, *Homo* XXII(2):57–75

Henschen, F. 1961 Cribra cranii, a skull condition said to be of racial or geographical nature. Seventh Conference, International Society of Geographical Pathology, London 1960, *Pathology and Microbiology* 24:734–729

—— 1966 *The History of Diseases*, Longmans, London

Hochberg, M.C., D.G. Borenstein and F. Arnett 1978 The absence of back pain in classical ankylosing spondylitis, *Johns Hopkins Medical Journal* 143:181-183

Hoets, J. 1949 A study of healed fractures in the Australian Aboriginals, *Medical Journal of Australia* (Correspondence) November 26 (2):794

Hoffbrand, A.V. and J.E. Pettit 1984 *Essential Haematology*, 2nd ed., Blackwell Scientific Publications, Oxford

Hogan, M.J. and L.E. Zimmerman 1862 *Ophthalmic Pathology*, 2nd edn., Saunders, Philadelphia

Hohenthal, W.D. and S.T. Brooks 1960 An archaeological scaphocephal from California. *American Journal of Physical Anthropology* 18:59–67

Hollander, J.L. 1962 *Arthritis and Allied Conditions*. 7th ed., Lea and Febiger, Philadelphia

Holmes, M.J. 1913 Report of the medical officer for the year ending 31 December 1912, *Bulletin of the Northern Territory* No. 6

Hooton, E.A. 1930 *Indians of Pecos Pueblo*, Yale University Press, New Haven pp.306–333

Hope, G., J. Golson and J. Allen 1983 3. Palaeoecology and prehistory in New Guinea, *Journal of Human Evolution* 12:37–60

Horsfall, W.R. and H. Lehmann 1953 Absence of the sickle cell trait in 72 Australian Aborigines, *Nature* 172:638

Horton, D.R. 1979 The great megafaunal extinction debate 1879–1979, *Artefact* 4:11–25

—— 1980 A review of the extinction question: man, climate and megafauna, *Archaeology and Physical Anthropology in Oceania* 15:86–97

—— 1984 Red kangaroos: last of the Australian megafauna. In *Quaternary Extinctions: A Prehistoric Revolution* Martin P.S. and Klein R.E. (eds) University of Arizona Press, Tucson

Horton, D. and J. Samuel 1978 The palaeopathology of a fossil macropod population, *Australian Journal of Zoology* 26:279–292

Houghton, P. 1980 *The First New Zealanders*, Hodder and Stoughton, Auckland and London

Howells, N. 1976 The population of the Dobe area !Kung. In *Kalahari Hunter-Gatherers*, Lee R.B. and I. De Vore (eds), Harvard University Press, Cambridge, Mass. pp.138–151

Hoyme, E. St 1969 On the origins of new world paleopathology, *American Journal of Physical Anthropology* 31:295–302

Hrdlicka, A. 1914 Anthropological work in Peru in 1913 with notes on pathology of the ancient Peruvians, *Smithsonian Miscellaneous Collection* 61:57–59

—— Trepanation among prehistoric people, especially in America, *Ciba Symposia* 1:170–177

Hudson, C., R. Butler and D. Sikes 1975 Arthritis in the prehistoric southeastern United States: biological and cultural variables. *American Journal of Physical Anthropology* 43:57–62

Hudson, E.H. 1958a *Non-venereal syphilis: a sociological and medical study of Bejel*, Livingstone, London

—— 1958b The treponematoses–or treponematosis? *British Journal of Venereal Diseases* 34:22–23

—— 1961 Endemic syphilis–heir of the syphiloids, *Archives of Internal Medicine* 108:1–4

—— 1963 Treponematosis and anthropology, *Annals of Internal Medicine* 58:1037–1048

—— 1965 Treponematosis in perspective, *Bulletin of the World Health Organisation* 32:735–748

Hughes, P.J. and R.J. Lampert 1982 Prehistoric population changes in southern coastal New South Wales. In *Coastal Archaeology in Eastern Australia*, Bowdler, S. (ed.), Proceedings of the 1980 Valla conference on Australian prehistory pp.16–28

Hummert, J.R. and D.P. van Gerven 1985 Observations on the formation and persistence of radiopaque transverse lines, *American Journal of Physical Anthropology* 66:297–306

Hunt, E.E. Jr. and J.W. Hatch 1981 The estimation of age at death and ages of formation of transverse lines from measurements of human long bones, *American Journal of Physical Anthropology* 54:461–469

Huss-Ashmore, R., A.H. Goodman and G.J. Armelagos 1982 Nutritional inference from paleopathology, *Advances in Archaeological Method and Theory* 5:395–474

Huvos, A.G. 1979 *Bone Tumors, Diagnosis, Treatment and Prognosis*, W.B. Saunders, Philadelphia

Hynes, R.A. and A.K. Chase 1982 Plants, sites and domiculture: Aboriginal influence upon plant communities in Cape York Peninsula, *Archaeology in Oceania* 17:38–50

Infante, P.F. 1974 Enamel hypoplasia in Apache Indian children, *Ecology of Food and Nutrition* 2: 155–164

Infante, P.F. and G.M. Gillespie 1974 An epidemiologic study of linear enamel hydroplasia of deciduous anterior teeth in Guatemalan children, *Archives of Oral Biology* 19:1055–1061

Infante, P.F. and G.M. Gillespie 1977 Enamel hypoplasia in relation to caries in Guatemalan children, *Journal of Dental Research* 56:493–498

Jacobs, D.S. 1978 Syphilis in Australian Aborigines in the Northern Territory, *Medical Journal of Australia* (1):10–12

Jaffe, H.L. 1975 *Metabolic, Degenerative and Inflammatory Diseases of Bones and Joints*, Lea and Febiger, Philadelphia

Jannsens, P.A. 1970 *Palaeopathology*, John Baker, London

Jarcho, S. (ed.) 1966 *Human Paleopathology*, Yale University Press, New Haven

Jelliffe, D.B. and E.F.P. Jelliffe 1971 Linear hypoplasia of deciduous incisor teeth in malnourished children, *American Journal of Clinical Nutrition* 24:893

Johnston, T.H. and J.B. Cleland 1937 A survey of the literature relating to the occurrence in Australia of helminth parasites of man, *Transactions and proceedings of the Royal Society of South Australia* 61:250–277

Jones, P.R.M. and R.F.A. Dean 1959 The effects of kwashiorkor on the development of the bones of the knee, *Journal of Pediatrics* 54:176–184

Joralemon, D. 1982 New World depopulation and the case of disease, *Journal of Anthropological Research* 38:108–127

Jorde, L.B., R.M. Fineman and R.A. Martin 1983 Epidemiology and genetics of neural tube defects: an application of the Utah Genealogical Data Base, *American Journal of Physical Anthropology* 62:23–31

Jose, D.G. and J.S. Welch 1970 Growth retardation, anaemia and infection, with malabsorption and infestation of the bowel. The syndrome of PCM in Australian Aboriginal children, *Medical Journal of Australia* (1):349–356

Jurisich, M. and D. Davies 1976 The palaeopathology of prehistoric Aboriginal skeletal remains excavated by the Victoria Archaeological Survey, *The Artefact* 1(4):194–218

Jurmain, R.D. 1977a Paleoepidemiology of degenerative knee disease, *Medical Anthropology* 1:1–23

—— 1977b Stress and the etiology of osteoarthritis, *American Journal of Physical Anthropology* 46:353–366

—— 1990 Paleoepidemiology of a Central California prehistoric population from CA-ALA-329: II. Degenerative Disease, *American Journal of Physical Anthropology* 83:83–94

Kariks, J. 1969 Iron deficiency–A widespread cause of anaemia in coastal areas of New Guinea, *Medical Journal of Australia* (2):1289–1295

Karsh, R.S. and J.D. McCarthy 1960 Archaeology and arthritis, *Archives of Internal Medicine* 105:640–644

Kefous, K. 1983 'Riveraine'. Unpublished MA thesis, Australian National University, Canberra

Kelley, M.A. 1979 A survey of joint disease at the Libben site, Ottawa County, Ohio, *Henry Ford Hospital Medical Journal* 27(1):64–67

Kellgren, J.H. and J.S. Lawrence 1958 Osteoarthritis and disc degeneration in an urban population, *Annals of Rheumatic Disease* 17:388–397

King, A.J. and R.D. Catterall 1959 Syphilis of bones. *British Journal of Venereal Disease* 35:116–128

Kirk, R.L. 1981 *Aboriginal Man Adapting*. Research Monographs on Human Population Biology, Clarendon Press, Oxford

Klepinger L.L. 1979 Paleopathologic evidence for the evolution of rheumatoid arthritis, *American Journal of Physical Anthropology* 50:119–122

—— 1983 Differential diagnosis in palaeopathology and the concept of disease evolution, *Medical Anthropology* 7:73–77

Knaggs, R.L. 1923-24 Leontiasis Ossea, *British Journal of Surgery* 11:347–379

Koganei, Y. 1912 Cribra cranii and cribra orbitalia, *Mitt. med. Falk.* University of Tokyo 10:113

Kotwicki, V. 1986 *The Floods of Lake Eyre*, Government Printer, Adelaide, South Australia

Krefft, G. 1862 On the manners and customs of the aborigines of the Lower Murray and Darling, *Transactions of the Philosophical Society of New South Wales* 1862–65:357–374

Krogman, W.M. 1962 *The Human Skeleton in Forensic Medicine*, Charles C. Thomas, Springfield, Ill.

Krzywicki, L. 1934 *Primitive Society and its Vital Statistics*, Macmillan, London

Kuhl, I. 1980 Harris's lines and their occurrence also in bones of prehistoric cremations, *Ossa* 7:129–171

Kuttmer, R.E. 1978 Prehistoric spina bifida, *Journal of the American Medical Association* 240:26–31

Kuzell, W.C. and G.P. Gaudin 1956 Gout, *Documenta Rheumatologica* September 1956

Ladurie, E. LeRoy 1975 Famine amenorrhoea (seventeenth–twentieth centuries). In *Biology of Man in History*, Forster, R. and O. Ranum (eds) Johns Hopkins University Press, Baltimore and London

Lallo, J.W. and J.C. Rose 1979 Patterns of stress, disease and mortality in two prehistoric populations from North America, *Journal of Human Evolution* 8:323–335

Lallo, J.W., G.J. Armelagos and R.P. Mensforth 1977 The role of diet, disease and physiology in the origin of porotic hyperostosis, *Human Biology* 49(3):471–483

Lampert, R.J. 1966 An excavation at Durras North, New South Wales, *Archaeology and Physical Anthropology in Oceania* 1(2):83–118

—— 1971a Burrill Lake and Currarong: Coastal sites in southern New South Wales, *Terra Australis No.1* Department of Prehistory, Australian National University, Canberra

—— 1971b Coastal Aborigines of Southeastern Australia. In *Aboriginal Man and Environment in Australia*, Mulvaney, D.J. and J. Golson (eds), Australian National University Press, Canberra pp.114–132

Lampert, R.J. and P.J. Hughes, 1974 Sea level changes and Aboriginal coastal adaptations in southern New South Wales, *Archaeology and Physical Anthropology in Oceania* 9:226–235

Lane, L. 1980 Aboriginal earthen mounds along the Little Murray River in northern Victoria, *Records of the Victorian Archaeological Survey* 10:98–108

Larnach, S.L. and L. Freedman 1963 Sex determination of Aboriginal crania from coastal New South Wales, Australia, *Records of the Australian Museum* 26(11):295–308

Larnach, S.L. and N.W.G. Macintosh 1966 The craniology of the Aborigines of New South Wales, *Oceania Monographs No. 13*. University of Sydney

Larnach, S.L. and N.W.G. Macintosh 1970 The craniology of the Aborigines of Queensland, *Oceania Monographs No. 15*. University of Sydney

Larsen, C.S. 1981 Skeletal and dental adaptations to the shift to agriculture on the Georgia Coast, *Current Anthropology* 22(4):422–423

—— 1982 The anthropology of St Catherines Island 3. Prehistoric human biological adaptation, *Anthropological Papers American Museum of Natural History* 57:197–270

Lawrence, J.S. 1955 Rheumatism in coalminers. Part III: Occupational factors, *British Journal of Industrial Medicine* 12:249–261

Lawrence, J.W.P. 1935 A Note on the Pathology of the Kanam mandible. In *Stone Age Races of Kenya*, Leakey, L.S.B. (ed.), Oxford University Press, London. App. A

Lawrence, R. 1967 *Aboriginal Habitat and Economy*. Occasional Paper No. 6, Department of Geography, Australian National University, Canberra

Leigh, R.W. 1925 Dental pathology of Indian tribes of varied environmental and food conditions, *American Journal of Physical Anthropology* 8:179–199

—— 1929 Dental pathology of Aboriginal California. *Dental Cosmos* 71:756–767

Leigh, W.H. 1982 *Travels and Adventures in South Australia: 1836-1838*, facsimile edition, Currawong Press, Singapore

Leisen, J.C. and H. Duncan 1979 The impact of rheumatic disease on society, *Henry Ford Hospital Medical Journal* 27(1):70–72

Lisowsky, F.P. 1967 Prehistoric and early historic trepanation. In *Diseases in Antiquity*, Brothwell, D. and A.T. Sandison (eds), Charles C. Thomas, Springfield, Ill. pp.651–672

Lourandos, H. 1976 Aboriginal settlement and land use in south western Victoria: a report on current fieldwork, *The Artefact* 1:174–193

—— 1977 Aboriginal spatial organization and population: South Western Victoria reconsidered, *Archaeology and Physical Anthropology in Oceania* 12:202–225

—— 1980 Change of stability? Hydraulics, hunter-gatherers and population in temperate Australia, *World Archaeology* 11:245–264

—— 1983 Intensification: a Late Pleistocene-Holocene archaeological sequence from Southwestern Victoria, *Archaeology in Oceania* 18:81–94

Love, J.R.B. 1936 *Stone-Age Bushman of Today*, Blackie and Son, London and Glasgow

Lovejoy, C.O. and K.G. Heiple 1981 The analysis of fractures in skeletal populations with an example from the Libben site, Ottawa County, Ohio, *American Journal of Physical Anthropology* 55:529–541

Lovejoy, C.O., Mensforth, R.P. and G.J. Armelagos 1982 Five decades of skeletal biology as reflected in the *American Journal of Anthropology*. In *A History of American Physical Anthropology 1930-1980*, Spencer, F. (ed.), Academic Press, San Francisco pp.329–336

Luebbers, R.A. 1978 'Meals and Menus?: A study of Change in Prehistoric Coastal settlements in South Australia.' Unpublished PhD thesis, Australian National University, Canberra

Maat, G.J.R. 1984 Dating and rating of Harris lines, *American Journal of Physical Anthropology* 83:291–299

McBryde, I. and G. Harrison 1981 Valued good or valuable stone? Consideration of some aspects of the distribution of greenstone artefacts in south-eastern Australia. In *Archaeological Studies of Pacific Stone Resources*, Leach F. and J. Davidson (eds), Oxford BAR International Series 104, pp.183–208

McDevitt, H.O. and E.G. Engleman 1976 Association between genes in the major histocompatibility complex and disease susceptibility. In *Arthritis: a quarter century of research*. Proceedings of the Conference Commemorating the 25th Anniversary of the Arthritis Foundation Research Fellowship Program. Proceedings editors E.M. Tan and M. Ziff

McHenry, H.M. 1968 Transverse lines in long bones of prehistoric California Indians, *American Journal of Physical Anthropology* 29:1–18

McHenry, H.M. and P.D. Schulz 1976 The association between Harris lines and enamel hypoplasia in prehistoric Californian Indians, *American Journal of Physical Anthropology* 44:507–512

MacConaill, M.A. 1969 On the Harris lines in bone, *Current Anthropology* 10(2-3):224

MacCurdy, G.G. 1905 Prehistoric surgery–a Neolithic survival, *American Anthropologist* 7:7–23

Macintosh, N.W.G. 1949 Crania in the MacLeay Museum. *Proceedings of the Linnean Society of New South Wales* 3-4:188–191

—— 1952a The Cohuna cranium: teeth and palate, *Oceania* 23(2):95–105

—— 1952b The Cohuna cranium: history and commentary from November, 1925, to November, 1951, *Mankind* 4(8):307–329

—— 1953 The Cohuna cranium: physiography and chemical analysis, *Oceania* 23(4):277–296

—— 1965 The physical aspect of man in Australia. In *Aboriginal Man in Australia*, R.M. and C.H. Berndt (eds), Angus and Robertson, Sydney pp.29–70

—— 1967 Fossil man in Australia, *Australian Journal of Science* 30(3):86–98

Macintosh, N.W.G. and S.L. Larnach 1976 Aboriginal affinities looked at in a world context. In *The Origin of the Australians*, Kirk, R.L. and A.G. Thorne (eds). Human Biology Series No.6, Australian Institute of Aboriginal Studies, Canberra pp.113–126

Macintosh, N.W.G., K.N. Smith and A.B. Bailey 1970 Lake Nitchie skeleton–unique Aboriginal burial, *Archaeology and Physical Anthropology in Oceania* 5:85–101

MacKay, C.V. 1938 Some pathological changes in Australian Aboriginal bones, *Medical Journal of Australia* 14(2):537–555

Mackerras, I.M., M.J. Mackerras and D.F. Sandars 1953 Parasites of the bandicoot, *Proceedings of the Royal Society of Queensland* 63:61–63

Mackerras, M.J. 1958 Catalogue of Australian mammals and their recorded internal parasites. Parts I-IV, *Proceedings of the Linnean Society of New South Wales* Vol.83 Part 2

Mackillop, D. 1893 Anthropological notes on the aboriginal tribes of the Daly River, North Australia, *Transactions of the Royal Society of South Australia* 17:254–264 and 27:637–647

Macpherson, J. 1902 'Ngarrabul' and other aboriginal tribes. Part I: Medical and Surgical Practices, *Proceedings of the Linnean Society of New South Wales* 27:637–647

Macumber, P.G. and R. Thorne 1975 The Cohuna cranium Site–a re-appraisal, *Archaeology and Physical Anthropology in Oceania* 10(1):67–72

Maddocks, I. 1973 History of disease in Papua New Guinea. In *The Diseases and Health Service of P.N.G.*, Bell, C.O. (ed.), Department of Public Health, Papua New Guinea, Port Moresby pp.70–81

Mahoney, D.J. 1943a The problem of antiquity of man in Australia, *Memoirs of the National Museum of Victoria* 13:7–56

—— 1943b The Keilor Skull: geological evidence of antiquity, *Memoirs of the National Museum of Victoria* 13:79–82

Manchester, K. 1983 *The Archaeology of Disease*, University of Bradford Press

Manson-Bahr, Sir P.H. 1960 *Manson's Tropical Diseases*, 15th ed., Cassell, London

Markell, E.K. and M. Voge 1976 *Medical Parasitology*, W.B. Saunders, Philadelphia

Martin, D.L., G.J. Armelagos and J.R. King 1979 Degenerative joint disease of the long bones in Dickson mounds, *Henry Ford Hospital Medical Journal* 27(1):60–63

Masters, G. 1877 Exhibition of, and remarks upon, the skull of an Aboriginal female, *Proceedings of the Linnean Society of New South Wales* 2

Meehan, B. 1982 *Shell Bed to Shell Midden*, Australian Institute of Aboriginal Studies, Canberra

Meggitt, M.J. 1962 *Desert People*, Angus and Robertson, Sydney

Menken, J., J. Trusswell, and S. Watkins 1981 The nutrition fertility link: an evaluation of the evidence, *Journal of Interdisciplinary History* 11:425–441

Mensforth, R.P., C.O. Lovejoy, J.W. Lallo and G.J. Armelagos 1978 The role of constitutional factors, diet, and infectious disease in the etiology of porotic hyperostosis and periosteal reactions in prehistoric infants and children, *Medical Anthropology* 2(1):1–59

Mensforth, R.P., S.A. Surovec and J.R. Cunkle 1987 Distal radius and proximal femur fracture patterns in the Hamann-Todd skeletal collection, *Kirtlandia, Journal of the Cleveland Museum of Natural History* 42:3–24

Merrilees, D. 1968 Man the destroyer: later Quaternary changes in the Australian marsupial fauna, *Journal of the Royal Society of Western Australia* 51:1–24

—— 1984 Comings and goings of late Quaternary mammals in extreme southwestern Australia. In *Quaternary Extinctions*, Martin, P.S. and R.G. Klein (eds), University of Arizona Press, Tucson pp.629–638

Merrill, E.M. 1875 'One-eyed Billy–the Aboriginal', *Wagga Wagga Advertiser*, August 7

Meston, A. 1895 *Geographic History of Queensland*, Government Printer, Brisbane

Middelton, M.R. and S.H. Francis 1967 *Yuendumu and its Children*, Australian Government Publishing Service, Canberra

Miklouho-Maclay, N. 1975 *New Guinea Diaries 1871–1883* trans. C.L. Sentinella, Kristen Press, Madang

Miller, J.D. and W.B. Jennett 1968 Complications of depressed skull fracture, *The Lancet* (2):991–995

Milne, N., L.H. Schmitt and L. Freedman 1983 Discrete trait variation in Western Australia Aboriginal skulls, *Journal of Human Evolution* 12:157–158

Mims, C.A. 1977 *The Pathogenesis of Infectious Disease*, Academic Press, New York

Møller, P. and V. Moller-Christensen, 1952 A mediaeval female skull showing evidence of metastases from a malignant growth, *Acta Pathologica Microbiologica Scandinavica* 30:336

Møller-Christensen, V. 1961 *Bone Changes in Leprosy*, Munksgaard, Copenhagen

—— 1978 *Leprosy Changes of the Skull*, Odense University Press, Denmark

Møller-Christensen, V. and R.G. Inkster 1965 Cases of leprosy and syphilis in the osteological collection of the Department of Anatomy, University of Edinburgh, *Danish Medical Bulletin* 12:11–18

Molnar, S. 1972 Tooth wear and culture: a survey of tooth functions among some prehistoric populations, *Current Anthropology* 13:511–526

—— 1983 *Human Variation*, Prentice-Hall, New Jersey

Molnar, S. and I. Molnar 1985 Observations of dental diseases among prehistoric populations of Hungary, *American Journal of Physical Anthropology* 67:51–63

Molnar, S. and S.C. Ward 1975 Mineral metabolism and microstructural defects in primate teeth, *American Journal of Physical Anthropology* 43:3–18

Moodie, P.M. 1971 *The health of Australian Aborigines: an annotated bibliography*, Australian Government Publishing Service, Canberra

Moodie, R.L. 1923 *Paleopathology: an introduction to the study of ancient evidences of disease*, Urbana, University of Illinois Press

—— 1926 Studies in paleopathology XVIII: tumours of the head among Pre-Columbian Peruvians, *Annals of the History of Medicine* 8:394–412

Moody, J.E.H. 1960 The dental and periodontal conditions of Aborigines at settlements in Arnhem Land and adjacent areas. In *Records of the American-Australian Scientific Expedition to*

Arnhem Land: Anthropology and Nutrition, Vol. 2, Mountford, C.R. (ed.), Melbourne University Press pp.60–71

Moorrees, C.F.A., E.A. Fanning and E.E. Hunt Jr. 1963 Age variation of formation stages for ten permanent teeth, *Journal of Dental Research* 42:1490–1502

Morse, D., Gailey, R.C. and J. Bunn 1974 Prehistoric multiple myeloma, *Bulletin of the New York Academy of Medicine* 50:447–458

Morton, R.S. 1967 The Sibbens of Scotland, *Medical History* 11:374–380

Morton, S.G. 1845 Remarks on the skulls of two natives of New Holland, *Proceedings of the Academy of Natural Science* 2:292–293

Moseley, J.E. 1966 Radiographic studies in hematologic bone disease: implications for palaeopathology. In *Human Paleopathology*, Jarcho, S. (ed.), Yale University Press, New Haven and London pp.121–130

Moskowitz, R.W. 1974 Clinical and laboratory findings in osteoarthritis. In *Arthritis and Allied Conditions*, Hollander J.L. and D.J. McCarthy Jr. (eds), 8th ed. Lea and Febiger, Philadelphia

Moss, M.L. 1953 Malformations of the skull base associated with cleft palate deformity, *Plastic and Reconstructive Surgery* 17(3):226–231

Mulvaney, D.J. 1960 Archaeological excavations at Fromm's Landing on the Lower Murray River, South Australia, *Proceedings of the Royal Society of Victoria* 72:53–85

—— 1975 *The Prehistory of Australia*, Penguin, Melbourne

—— 1989 Reflections on the Murray Black Collection, *Australian Natural History* 23(1):66–73

Murray, P. 1984 Extinctions down under: a bestiary of extinct Australian late Pleistocene monotremes and marsupials. In *Quaternary Extinctions*, Martin, P.S. and R.G. Klein (eds), University of Arizona Press, Tucson pp.600–628

Murray, R.O. and H.G. Jacobson 1972 *Radiology of Skeletal Disorders*. Vol. 1, Churchill Livingstone, London

Muul, I. 1970 Mammalian ecology and epidemiology of zoonoses, *Science* 170:1275–1279

Nathan, H. 1962 Osteophytes of the vertebral column, *Journal of Bone and Joint Surgery* 44(A): 243–268

Nathan, H. and N. Haas 1966 Cribra orbitalia. A bone condition of the orbit of unknown nature, *Israel Journal of Medical Science* 2:171–191

Nathan, P. and D.L. Japanangka 1983 *Settle Down Country*, Kibble Books, Central Australian Aboriginal Congress, Alice Springs

Newland, S. 1926 *Memoirs*, F.W. Preece, Adelaide

Newman, M.T. 1976 Aboriginal New World epidemiology and medical care, and the impact of Old World disease imports, *American Journal of Physical Anthropology* 45:667–672

Neiburger, E.J. 1990 Enamel hypoplasias: poor indicators of dietary stress, *American Journal of Physical Anthropology* 82:231–232

Oberg, T., G.E. Carlsson and C-M. Fajers 1971 The temporomandibular joint. A morphologic study on human autopsy material, *Acta Odontologica Scandinavica* 29:349–384

Oetteking, B. 1909 Kraniologische Studien an Altaegypten, *Archaeological Anthropology* 8:1–90

Ogilvie, M.D., B.K. Curran and E. Trinkaus 1989 Incidence and patterning of dental hypoplasia among the Neanderthals, *American Journal of Physical Anthropology* 79:25–41

Oldfield, M.C. 1959 Some observations on the cause and treatment of hare-lip and cleft palate, based on the treatment of 1041 patients, *British Journal of Surgery* 46(198):311–321

Oram, N. 1977 Environment, migration and site selection in the Port Moresby coastal area. In *The Melanesian Environment*, Winslow, J.H. (ed.), Australian National University Press, Canberra pp.74–99

Ortner, D.J. 1968 Description and classification of degenerative bone changes in the distal joint surfaces of the humerus, *American Journal of Physical Anthropology* 28:139–156

Ortner, D.J. and W.G.J. Putschar 1981 Identification of pathological conditions in human skeletal remains, *Smithsonian Contributions to Anthropology No. 28*. Smithsonian Institution Press, Washington

Owen, W.J. 1934 *Trypanosoma in the Monotreme*. Publications of the Australian Institute of Anatomy, Canberra

Pales, L. 1930 *Paléopathologie et Pathologie comparative*, Masson, Paris

Pardoe, C. 1984 'Prehistoric Human Morphological Variation in Australia'. PhD thesis, Australian National University, Canberra

Park, E.A. 1954 Bone growth in health and disease, *Archives of Disease in Children* 29:269–281

—— 1964 The imprinting of nutritional disturbances on the growing bone, *Pediatrics* 33:815–862

Park, E.A. and C.P. Richter 1953 Transverse lines in bone: the mechanism of their development, *Bulletin of Johns Hopkins Medical School* 93:234–248

Park, E.A., D. Jackson, T.C. Goodwin and L. Kajdi 1933 Shadows in growing bones produced by lead: their characteristics, cause, anatomical counterpart in bone and differentiation, *Journal of Pediatrics* 3:265–298

Parker, K.L. 1905 *The Euahlayi Tribe*, Archibald Constable, London

Parry, T.W. 1914 Prehistoric man and his early efforts to combat disease, *The Lancet* 1:1699–1702

—— 1931 Neolithic man and penetration of living human skulls, *The Lancet* 2:1388–1390

Perizonius W.R.K. 1984 Closing and non-closing sutures in 256 crania of known age and sex from Amsterdam (A.D.1883–1909), *Journal of Human Evolution* 13:201–216

Peterson, N. 1972 Totemism yesterday: sentiment and local organisation and the Australian Aborigines, *Man* 7:12–32

Pickering, R.B. 1979 Hunter-gatherer/agriculturalist arthritic patterns: a preliminary investigation, *Henry Ford Hospital Medical Journal* 27(1):50–53

Pietrusewsky, M. 1969 An osteological study of cranial and infracranial remains from Tonga, *Records of the Auckland Institute Museum* 6(4-6):287–402

—— Prehistoric human skeletal remains from Papua New Guinea and the Marquesas, *Asian and Pacific Archaeology Series*, No. 7, Sciences and Linguistics Institute, University of Hawaii

—— 1979 Craniometric variation in Pleistocene Australian and more recent Australian and New Guinea populations studied by multivariate procedures. *Occasional Papers in Human Biology*, No.2, Australian Institute of Aboriginal Studies, Canberra

—— 1990 Craniofacial variation in Australasian and Pacific populations, *American Journal of Physical Anthropology* 82:319–340

Piggott, S. 1940 A trepanned skull of the Beaker period from Dorset and the practice of trepanning in prehistoric Europe, *Proceedings of the Prehistoric Society* 6:112–132

Pindborg, J.J. 1970 *Pathology of the Dental Hard Tissue*, W.B. Saunders, Philadelphia

Platt, B.S. and R.J.C. Stewart 1962 Transverse trabeculae and osteoporosis in bones in experimental protein-calorie deficiency, *British Journal of Nutrition* 16(4):483–495

Poiner, G. 1976 The process of the year among Aborigines of the central and south coast of New South Wales, *Archaeology and Physical Anthropology in Oceania* 11(3):186–206

Polgar, S. 1975 *Population, Ecology, and Social Evolution*, Mouton, The Hague

Porter, F.S. 1963 Multiple myeloma in a child, *Journal of Pediatrics* 62:602–606

Post, R.H. 1966 Pilot study: Population differences in the frequency of spina-bifida occulta, *Eugenics Quarterly* 13:341–352

Powell, D.W. 1970 Aboriginal trephination: case from southern New England, *Science* 170:732–734

Powers, R. 1962 The disparity between known age and age as estimated by cranial suture closure, *Man* 62:52–54

Presland, G. 1977a Journals of George Augustus Robinson: January–March 1840, *Records of the Victoria Archaeological Survey No.5*

—— 1977b Journals of George Augustus Robinson: March–May 1841, *Records of the Victoria Archaeological Survey No.6*

—— 1980 Journals of G.A. Robinson: May to August 1841, *Records of the Victoria Archaeological Survey No.11*

Pretty, G.L. 1977 The cultural chronology of the Roonka Flat. In *Stone Tools as Cultural Markers*, Wright, R.V.S. (ed.), Australian Institute of Aboriginal Studies, Canberra pp.288–331

Pretty, G.L. and M.E. Kricun 1989 Prehistoric health status of the Roonka population, *World Archaeology* 21:198–224

Prokopec, M. 1975 'Analysis of Human Remains from Roonka'. Doc.No. 76/2021. Ms 669 in Australian Institute of Aboriginal Studies Library. (Records of the South Australian Museum 1976), June 1976

—— 1979 Demographical and morphological aspects of the Roonka population, *Archaeology and Physical Anthropology in Oceania* 14:11–26

Prokopec, M., Simpson, D., Morris, L. and G. Pretty 1984 Craniosynostosis in a prehistoric Aboriginal skull: A case report, *OSSA* 9–11 and 111–118

Rabkin, S. 1942 Dental conditions among prehistoric Indians of northern Alabama, *Journal of Dental Research* 21:211–222

—— 1943 Dental conditions among prehistoric Indians of Kentucky. The Indian Knoll Collection, *Journal of Dental Research* 22:355–366

Reinhard, K.J. 1990 Archaeoparasitology in North America. *American Journal of Physical Anthropology* 82:145–163

Reyman, T.A. 1979 The search for 'Arthritis' in antiquity: paleoarthritis workshop, *Henry Ford Hospital Medical Journal* 27(1):32–37

Richards, L.C. and T. Brown 1981 Dental attrition and degenerative arthritis of the temporomandibular joint, *Journal of Oral Rehabilitation* 8:293–307

Richards, L.C. and S.L.J. Miller 1991 Relationships between age and dental attrition in Australian Aboriginals, *American Journal of Physical Anthropology* 84:159–164

Riddle J.M. 1979 Rheumatoid arthritis, *Henry Ford Hospital Medical Journal* 27(1):18–23

Riley, I.D. 1983 Population change and distribution in Papua New Guinea: an epidemiological approach, *Journal of Human Evolution* 12:125–132

Ritchie, W.A. and S.L. Warren 1932 The occurrence of multiple bony lesions suggesting myeloma in the skeleton of a pre-Columbian Indian, *American Journal of Roentgenology* 28:622

Robbins, S.L. and R.S. Cotran 1979 *Pathologic Basis of Disease*, W.B. Saunders, London and Toronto

Roberts, R.G., R. Jones and M.A. Smith 1990 Thermoluminescence dating of a 50,000-year-old human occupation site in northern Australia, *Nature* 345:153–156

Robinson, J.T. 1956 The dentition of the Australopithecinae, *Transvaal Museum Memoirs No.9*

Rogers, J., T. Waldron, P. Dieppe and I. Watt 1987 Arthropathies in palaeopathology: the basis of classification according to most probable cause, *Journal of Archaeological Science* 14:179–193

Rogers, S. 1964 The healing of trephined wounds from pre-Columbian America, *American Journal of Physical Anthropology* 23:321

Roheim, G. 1933 Women and their life in Central Australia, *Journal of the Royal Anthropological Institute* 63:207-265

Roney, J.G. 1959 Palaeopathology of a California archaeological site, *Bulletin of the History of Medicine* 33(2):97–109

—— 1966 Palaeoepidemiology: an example from California. In *Human Paleopathology*, Jarcho, S. (ed.), Yale University Press, London pp.99–120

Rose, J.C. 1977 Defective enamel histology of prehistoric teeth from Illinois, *American Journal of Physical Anthropology* 46:439–446

Rose, J.C., G.J. Armelagos and J.W. Lallo 1978 Histological enamel indicator of childhood stress in prehistoric skeletal samples, *American Journal of Physical Anthropology* 49:511–516

Ross, A. 1981 Holocene environments and prehistoric site patterning in the Victorian Mallee, *Archaeology in Oceania* 16:145–154

Roth, W.E. 1897 *Ethnological studies amongst the North-west Central Queensland Aborigines*, E. Gregory, Government Printer, Brisbane

—— 1903 Superstitition, magic and medicine. In *North Queensland Ethnography Bulletin No. 5.* E. Gregory, Government Printer, Brisbane

Rothschild, B.M. and W. Turnbull 1987 Treponemal infection in a Pleistocene cave bear, *Nature* 329:59–62

Roydhouse, R.H. and B.O. Simonsen 1975 Attrition of teeth, *Syesis* 8:263–273

Ruffer, M.A. 1909 Preliminary note on the histology of Egyptian mummies, *British Medical Journal* 1:1005

Ruffer, M.A. and A. Rietti 1912 On osseous lesions in ancient Egyptians, *Journal of Pathology and Bacteriology* 16:439–466

Rushton, M.A. 1964 Hereditary enamel defects, *Proceedings of the Royal Society of Medicine* 57:53–58

Ryan, B. 1961a Thalassaemia: report of a case in Papua, *Medical Journal of Australia* (1):128–129

—— 1961b Thalassaemia in Melanesia, *Nature* 4797:75–76

—— 1961c Thalassaemia Major in New Guinea, *Medical Journal of Australia* (2):753–757

—— 1962 Skull changes associated with chronic anaemias in Papuan children, *Medical Journal of Australia* 1:844–847

Sahlins, M. 1972 *Stone Age Economics*, Aldine, Chicago

Sandford, M.K., D.P. van Gerven and R.R. Meglan 1983 Elemental hair analysis: new evidence on the etiology of cribra orbitalia in Sudanese Nubia, *Human Biology* 55:831–844

Sandison, A.T. 1967 Parasitic diseases. In *Disease in Antiquity*, Brothwell D.R. and A.T. Sandison (eds), Charles C. Thomas, Springfield, Ill. pp.178–183

—— 1968 Pathological changes in the skeletons of earlier populations due to acquired disease, and difficulties in their interpretation. In *The Skeletal Biology of Earlier Human Populations*, Brothwell, D. (ed.), Pergamon Press, Oxford pp.205–243

—— 1972 Evidence of infective disease, *Journal of Human Evolution* 1:213–224

—— 1973a Disease changes in Australian Aboriginal skeletons, *Australian Institute of Aboriginal Studies Newsletter* 1970–73(3):20–23

—— 1973b Palaeopathology of human bones from Murray River Region between Mildura and Renmark, Australia, *Memoirs of National Museum of Victoria* 34:173–174

—— 1975 Kanam mandible's tumour, *The Lancet* No. 7901 p.279

—— 1980 Notes on some skeletal changes in pre-European contact Australian Aborigines, *Journal of Human Evolution* 9:45–47

—— 1981 Diseases in the Ancient World. In *Recent Advances in Histopathology*, Anthony, P.P. and R.N.M. Macsween (eds), Churchill Livingstone, London pp.1–18

Sandison, A.T. and C. Wells 1967 Endocrine diseases. In *Disease in Antiquity*, Brothwell D.R. and A.T. Sandison (eds), Charles C. Thomas, Springfield, Ill. pp.521–531

Sarnat, B.G. and I. Schour 1941 Enamel hypoplasia (chronologic enamel aplasia) in relation to systemic disease: a chronologic, morphologic and etiologic classification, *Journal of American Dental Association* 28:1989–2000

—— 1942 Enamel Hypoplasia (Chronologic Enamel Aplasia) in relation to systemic disease: a chronologic, morphologic and etiologic classification, *Journal of American Dental Association* 29:67–75

Saul, F.P. 1972 The human skeletal remains of Altar de Sacrificios, *Papers of the Peabody Museum*, Harvard 63(2):34–75

Schamschula, R.G., B.L. Adkins, D.E. Barmes, G. Charleton and B.G. Davey 1978 *WHO study of dental caries etiology in Papua New Guinea*, World Health Organisation Offset Publication No. 40

Schamschula, R.G., M.H. Cooper, B.L. Adkins, D.E. Barmes and W.M. Agus 1980 Oral conditions in Australian children of Aboriginal and caucasian descent, *Community Dentistry and Oral Epidemiology* 8:365–369

Schmerling, P.C. 1835 Description des ossemens fossiles, à l'état pathologique provenant des cavernes de la province de Liège, *Bulletin de la Société Géologique de France* 7:51–61

Schrire, C. 1982 The Alligator Rivers: prehistory and ecology in western Arnhem Land, *Terra Australis No. 7*, Department of Prehistory, Research School of Pacific Studies, Australian National University, Canberra

Schultz, A.H. 1939 Notes on diseases and healed fractures of wild apes, *Bulletin of the History of Medicine* 7:571–582

Schulz, P.D. and H.M. McHenry 1975 Age distribution of enamel hypoplasia in prehistoric California Indians, *Journal of Dental Research* 54:913

Schulze, L. 1891 The aborigines of the Upper and Middle Finke River: their habits and customs, with introductory notes on the physical and natural-history features of the country, *Royal Society of South Australia, Transactions* 14:210–246

Schuman, E.L. and R.F. Sognnaes 1956 Developmental microscopic defects in the teeth of subhuman primates, *American Journal of Physical Anthropology* 14:193–198

Schwidde, J.T. 1952 Spina bifida: survey of two hundred and twenty-five encephaloceles, meningoceles, and myelomeningoceles, *American Journal of Diseases of Children* 84:35–51

Sciulli, P.W. 1977 A descriptive and comparative study of the deciduous dentition of prehistoric Ohio Valley Amerindians, *American Journal of Physical Anthropology* 47:71–80

—— 1978 Developmental abnormalities of the permanent dentition in prehistoric Ohio Valley Amerindians, *American Journal of Physical Anthropology* 48:193–198

Scott, E.C. and B.R. DeWalt 1980 Subsistence and dental pathology etiologies from prehistoric coastal Peru, *Medical Anthropology* 4:263–290

Scott, J.H. and N.B.B. Symonds 1977 *Introduction to Dental Anatomy*, 8th ed. Churchill Livingstone, Edinburgh, London

Scrimshaw, N.S. 1964 Ecological factors in nutritional disease, *American Journal of Clinical Nutrition* 14:112–122

Scrimshaw, N.S., C.E. Taylor and J.E. Gordon 1968 Interactions of Nutrition and Infection, *World Health Organisation (W.H.O.) Monograph Series*, No. 57

Seward, F.S. 1976 Tooth attrition and the temporomandibular joint, *Angle Orthodontics* 46(2): 162–170

Shahidi, N.T. and L.K. Diamond 1961 Medical intelligence: skull changes in infants with chronic iron-deficiency anaemia, *New England Journal of Medicine* 3:137

Shermis, S. 1975 Common types of paleopathological lesions and some cultural inferences, *Pacific Coast Archeological Society Quarterly* 11(3):33–58

Shipman, P., A. Walker and D. Bichell 1985 *The Human Skeleton*, Harvard University Press, Cambridge (Mass.)

Short, C.L. 1974 The antiquity of rheumatoid arthritis, *Arthritis and Rheumatism* 17(3):193–205

Siegel, J. 1976 Animal palaeopathology: possibilities and problems, *Journal of Archaeological Science* 3:349–384

Sigerist, H.E. 1955 *A History of Medicine* Vol.I., Oxford, 2nd ed.

Sinnet, P. 1972 Nutrition in a New Guinea Highland community, *Human Biology in Oceania* 1: 299–305

Skinner, M.F. and J.T.W. Hung 1989 Social and biological correlates of localized enamel hypoplasia of the human deciduous canine tooth, *American Journal of Physical Anthropology* 79: 159–175

Smith, A. 1976 *The Body*, Penguin, England

Smith, G.E. and W.R. Dawson 1924 *Egyptian Mummies*, Allen and Unwin, London

Smith, L.R. 1980 *The Aboriginal Population of Australia*, Australian National University Press, Canberra

Smith, Moya 1982 Late Pleistocene zamia exploitation in southern Western Australia, *Archaeology in Oceania* 17:117–121

Smith, M.B. 1989 The case for a resident human population in the Central Australian ranges during full glacial aridity, *Archaeology in Oceania* 24:93–105

Smith, P., T. Brown and W.B. Wood 1981 Tooth size and morphology in a recent Australian Aboriginal population from Broadbeach, south east Queensland, *American Journal of Physical Anthropology* 55:423–432

Smyth, R.B. 1878 *Aborigines of Victoria*, 2 vols, John Ferres, Government Printer, Melbourne and London

Sognnaes, R.F. 1956 Histological evidence of developmental lesions in teeth originating from Paleolithic, prehistoric, and ancient man, *American Journal of Pathology* 32(1):547–577

Sokoloff, L. 1974 The pathology and pathogenesis of osteoarthritis. In *Arthritis and Allied Conditions*, Hollander J.L. and D.J. McCarthy Jr (eds), 8th ed. Lea and Febiger, Philadelphia

Solonen, K.A. 1966 The joints of the lower extremities of football players, *Ann. Chir. Gyrnaec. Fenn.* 55:176–180

Soriano, M. 1970 The fluoric origin of the bone lesion in the *Pithecanthropus erectus* femur, *American Journal of Physical Anthropology* 32:49–58

Spencer, B. (ed.) 1896 *Report on the Work of the Horn Scientific Expedition to Central Australia*, Dulau and Co., London

Spencer, B. 1928 *Wanderings in Wild Australia*, Macmillan, London

Spencer, B. and F.J. Gillen 1969 (1899) *The Native Tribes of Central Australia*, Anthropological Publ., Oostenhout, Netherlands

Sprent, J.F.A. 1967 'Helminth zoonoses': an analysis. *Helminthological Abstracts* Vol. 38, Part 3 pp.333–351

Stansfield, W.D. 1981 *Serology and Immunology,* Macmillan, New York

Stathopoulos, G. 1975 Kanam mandible's tumour, *The Lancet* No. 7899, p.165

Steinbock, R.T. 1976 *Paleopathological Diagnosis and Interpretation,* Charles C. Thomas, Springfield, Ill.

Stewart, R.J.C. and B.S. Platt 1958 Arrested growth lines in the bones of pigs on low-protein diets, *Proceedings of the Nutrition Society* 17:v

Stewart, T.D. 1958 Stone Age skull surgery: a general review, with emphasis on the New World, *Annual Report of the Smithsonian Institute* pp.469–491

—— 1960 A physical anthropologist's view of the peopling of the New World, *Southwestern Journal of Anthropology* 16:259–273

—— 1966 Some problems in human palaeopathology. In *Human Palaeopathology,* Jarcho, S. (ed.), Yale University Press, New Haven and London pp.43–55

—— 1974 Nonunion of fractures in antiquity, with descriptions of five cases from the New World involving the forearm, *Bulletin of the New York Academy of Medicine* 50:875–891

Stewart, T.D. and A. Spoehr 1952 Evidence on the paleopathology of yaws, *Bulletin of the History of Medicine* 26:538–553

Stini, W.A. 1971 Evolutionary implications of changing nutritional patterns in human populations, *American Anthropologist* 73:1019–1030

Stirling, E.C. 1894 Notes from Central Australia, *Intercolonial Quarterly Journal of Medicine and Surgery* 1:221

—— 1911 Preliminary report on the discovery of native remains at Swanport, River Murray; with an inquiry into the alleged occurrence of a pandemic among the Australian Aborigines, *Transactions of the Royal Society of South Australia* 35:4–46

Stone, A.C. 1911 The Aborigines of Lake Boga, Victoria. *Proceedings of the Royal Society of Victoria* 23(2):433–468

Straus, W.L. and A.J.E. Cave 1957 Pathology and the posture of Neanderthal man, *Quarterly Review of Biology* 32:348–363

Stringer, C.B. 1979 A re-evaluation of the fossil human calvaria from Singa, Sudan, *Bulletin of the British Museum of Natural History (Geol)* 32:77–83

Stringer, C.B., L. Cornish and P. Stuart-Macadam 1985 Preparation and further study of the Singa skull from Sudan. *Bulletin of the British Museum of Natural History (Geol)* 38:347–358

Strouhal, E. 1976 Tumours in the remains of ancient Egyptians. *American Journal of Physical Anthropology* 45:613–620

Strouhal, E. and J. Jungwirth 1980 Paleopathology of the Late Roman-Early Byzantine cemeteries at Sayala, Egyptian Nubia. *Journal of Human Evolution* 9:61–70

Stuart-Macadam, P. 1989 Porotic Hyperostosis: Representative of a Childhood Condition. *American Journal of Physical Anthropology* 66:391–398

Sturt, C. 1833 *Two Expeditions into the Interior of Southern Australia. 2 vols.* Libraries Board of South Australia, Facsimile edition (1963), Adelaide

—— 1849 *Narrative of an Expedition into Central Australia,* 2 vols., T. and W. Boone, London

Sullivan, M.E. 1982 'Aboriginal Shell Middens in the Coastal Landscape of New South Wales'. Unpublished PhD thesis, Australian National University, Canberra

Sullivan, M.E. and R.A. Buchan 1980 Distinguishing between Aboriginal natural mounds in the Murray Valley, *Records of the Victoria Archaeological Survey* 10:87–97

Sunderland, S. and L.J. Ray 1959 A note on the Murray Black collection of Australian Aboriginal skeletons, *Royal Society of Victoria Proceedings* 71:45–48

Sutton, D.G. 1979 The prehistoric people of Eastern Palliser Bay, *National Museum Bulletin* 21: 185–203

Suzuki, T. and J. Ikeda 1981 A palaeopathological study of the craniosynostoses, *Journal of the Anthropological Society of Nippon* 89:479–492

Sweeney, E.A., A.J. Saffir and R. de Leon 1971 Linear hypoplasia of deciduous incisor teeth in malnourished children, *American Journal of Clinical Nutrition* 24:29–31

Sweeney, E.A., J. Cabrera, J. Urrutia and L. Mata 1969 Factors associated with linear hypoplasia of human deciduous incisors, *Journal of Dental Research* 48:1275–1279

Sweeney, G. 1947 Food supplies of a desert tribe, *Oceania* 187(3):289–99

Sweet, W.C. 1924 The intestinal parasites of man in Australia and its dependencies as found by the Australian Hookworm Campaign, *Medical Journal of Australia* (1):405–407

Taplin, G. 1879 The Narrinyeri. In *The Native Tribes of South Australia*, Woods, J.D. (ed.). Adelaide pp.1–156

Tempelaar, H.C.G. and J. van Breeman 1932 Rheumatism and occupation, *Acta Rheumatology* 4: 36–38

Thomson, D.F. 1939 The seasonal factor in human culture, *Proceedings of the Prehistory Society* 5(2):209–221

—— 1975 *Bindibu Country*, Thomas Nelson, Melbourne

Thorne, A.G. 1969 Preliminary comments on the Kow Swamp skeleton, *Australian Institute of Aboriginal Studies Newsletter* 2:6–7

—— 1971a The racial affinities and origins of the Australian Aborigines. In *Aboriginal Man and Environment in Australia*, Mulvaney D.J. and J. Golson (eds), Australian University Press, Canberra pp.316–325

—— 1971b Mungo and Kow Swamp: morphological variations in Pleistocene Australians, *Mankind* 8:85–89

—— 1972 Recent discoveries of fossil man in Australia, *Australian Natural History*, June pp.191–196

—— 1975 'Kow Swamp and Lake Mungo: towards an osteology of early man in Australia'. Unpublished PhD thesis, University of Sydney

—— 1976 Morphological contrasts in Pleistocene Australians. In *Origin of the Australians*, Kirk R.L. and A.G. Thorne (eds), Human Biology Series No. 6, Australian Institute of Aboriginal Studies, Canberra

Thorne, A.G. and P.G. Macumber 1972 Discoveries of late Pleistocene man at Kow Swamp, Australia, *Nature* 238:316–319

Thorne, A.G. and M.H. Wolpoff 1981 Regional continuity in Australian Pleistocene hominid evolution, *American Journal of Physical Anthropology* 55:337–349

Tindale, N.B. 1955 Archaeological site at Lake Menindee, New South Wales, *Records of the South Australian Museum* 11:269–298

—— 1974 *Aboriginal Tribes of Australia*, University of California Press, Los Angeles

—— 1981 Desert Aborigines and the southern coastal peoples: some comparisons. In *Ecological Biogeography of Australia*, Keast, A. (ed.). Junk, The Hague pp.1855–1884

Tobias, P.V. 1967 *The cranium and maxillary dentition of Australopithecus (Zinjanthropus) boisei, Olduvai Gorge, Volume II*, Cambridge University Press

—— 1976 White African: an appreciation and some personal memories of Louis Leakey. In *Human Origins: Louis Leakey and the East African Evidence*, Isaac, G.L. and E.R. McCown (eds), W.A. Benjamin, California pp.55–74

Toft, J.D. 1986 The pathoparasitology of non-human primates: a review. In *Primates: The Road to Self-Sustaining Populations*, Benirschke, K. (ed.), Springer-Verlag, New York pp.571–680

Toldt, C. 1886 Uber Welckers Cribra Orbitalia, *Mitt. der Anthropol. Gessell Wien* 16:20–24

Tonkinson, R. 1978 *The Mardudjara Aborigines*, Holt, Rinehart and Winston, New York

Topinard, P. 1894 *Anthropology*, Chapman and Hall, London

Townsend, G.C. and T. Brown 1980 Dental asymmetry in Australian Aboriginals, *Human Biology* 52:661–673

Townsend, G.C., H. Yamada and P. Smith 1990 Expression of the entoconulid (sixth cusp) on mandibular molar teeth of an Australian Aboriginal population, *American Journal of Physical Anthropology* 82:267–274

Trinkaus, E. 1977 The Alto Salaverry child: a case of anemia from the Peruvian preceramic, *American Journal of Physical Anthropology* 46:25–28

—— 1983 *The Shanidar Neanderthals*, Academic Press, New York

—— 1984 Western Asia. In *The Origins of Modern Humans*, Smith F.H. and F. Spencer (eds), Alan R. Liss, New York pp.251–293

—— 1985 Pathology and the posture of the La Chapelle-aux-Saints Neanderthal, *American Journal of Physical Anthropology* 67:19–41

Trinkaus, E. and M.R. Zimmerman 1982 Trauma among the Shanidar Neanderthals, *American Journal of Physical Anthropology* 57:61–76

Trotter, M. 1947 Variations of the sacral canal: their significance in the administration of caudal analgesia, *Anesthesia and Analgesia* September-October, pp.192–202

Ubelaker, D.H. 1980 Human skeletal remains from site OGSE-80, a preceramic site on the Sta. Elena Peninsula, coastal Ecuador, *Journal of the Washington Academy of Science* 70:3–24

Ubelaker, D.H. 1982 The development of American paleopathology. In *A History of American Physical Anthropology*, Spencer, F. (ed.), Academic Press, San Francisco pp.337–356

Urteaga, O.B. and G.T. Pack 1966 On the antiquity of melanoma, *Cancer* 19:607–610

Vanderwal, R. 1982 *The Aboriginal photographs of Baldwin Spencer*, John Currey O'Neil, National Museum of Victoria

Wadsworth, G.R. 1975 Nutritional factors in anaemia, *World Review of Nutrition and Dietetics* 21:75–150

Walker, A.C. and S.P. Bellmaine 1975 Severe alimentary bleeding associated with hookworm infestation in Aboriginal infants, *Medical Journal of Australia* 1:751–752

Walker, E.G. 1978 The paleopathology of certain skeletal remains from Saskatchewan, *Na'pao: a Saskatchewan Anthropology Journal* 8:30–47

Walker, P.L. 1989 Cranial injuries as evidence of violence in prehistoric southern California, *American Journal of Physical Anthropology* 80:313–323

Watson, P. 1983 This precious foliage, *Oceania Monograph No. 26*, University of Sydney

Webb, L.J. 1973 'Eat, Die, and Learn'–The Botany of the Australian Aborigines, *Australian Natural History* 17(9):290–295

Webb, S.G. 1981 'Palaeopathology and its Future Use in Australian Prehistory'. Unpublished BA (hons) thesis, Australian National University, Canberra

—— 1982 Cribra Orbitalia: a possible sign of anaemia in pre- and post-contact crania from Australia and Papua New Guinea, *Archaeology in Oceania* 17(3):148–156

—— 1984 'Prehistoric Stress in Australian Aborigines'. Unpublished PhD thesis, Australian National University, Canberra

—— 1987a Reburying Australian skeletons, *Antiquity* 61:292–296

—— 1987b A palaeodemographic model of late Holocene Central Murray Aboriginal society, Australia, *Human Evolution* 2(5):385–406

—— 1988 Two possible cases of trephination from Australia, *American Journal of Physical Anthropology* 75:541–548

—— 1989 *The Willandra Lakes Hominids*, Prehistory Department, Research School of Pacific Studies, Australian National University, Canberra

—— 1990a Prehistoric eye disease (trachoma?) in Australian Aborigines, *American Journal of Physical Anthropology* 81:91–100

—— 1990b Cranial thickening in an Australian hominid as a possible palaeoepidemiological indicator, *American Journal of Physical Anthropology* 82:403–411

Webb, S.G. and A.G. Thorne 1985 A congenital meningocoele in prehistoric Australia, *American Journal of Physical Anthropology* 68:525–533

Webb, T.T. 1933 Aboriginal medical practice in East Arnhem Land, *Oceania* 4:91–98

Wegner, G. 1874 Ueber das normale und pathologische Wachsthum der Rohrenknochen. Eine knitische Untersuchung auf experimenteller und casiustischer Grindlage, *Archives of Pathological Anatomy* 61:44–76

Weidenreich, F. 1939a The duration of life of fossil man in China and the pathological lesions found in his skeleton, *Chinese Medical Journal* 55:34–44

—— 1939b Recent researches on early man in China, *Nature* 1; 44:1054–1056 Pt.I; 144:1097–1098 Pt.II

—— 1943 The skull of sinanthropus Pekinensis; a comparative study on a primitive hominid skull, *Palaeontologia Sinica*, New Series No. 10

—— 1945 The Keilor skull: a Wadjak type from southeast Australia, *American Journal of Physical Anthropology* 3:21–32

—— 1951 Morphology of Solo Man, *Anthropological Papers of the American Museum of Natural History* 43:205–290

Weinmann, J.P., J.F. Svoboda and K.W. Woods 1945 Hereditary disturbances of enamel formation and calcification, *Journal of the American Dental Association* 32:397–418

Welcker, H. 1885–7 Die Abstammung der Bevolkerung von Scotia, *Mitthellung im Geographentage zu Hamburg, Sitzung vom 11 April 1885. Verhandlungen des fünften deutschen Geographentages*, Berlin pp.92–94

—— 1888 Cribra Orbitalia, ein ethnologisches diagnostisches Merkmal am Schadel mehrerer Menschrassen, *Archives of Anthropology* 17:1–18

Wells, C. 1961 A new approach to ancient disease. *Discovery* 22:526–531

—— 1963 The radiological examination of human remains. In *Science and Archaeology*, Brothwell, D. and E. Higgs (eds), Thames and Hudson, London pp.401–412

—— 1964 *Bones and Bodies and Disease*, Thames and Hudson, London

—— 1965 Diseases of the knee in Anglo-Saxons. *Medical Biological Illustrations* 15:100–107

—— 1967 A new approach to palaeopathology: Harris's lines. In *Diseases in Antiquity*, Brothwell, D. and A.T. Sandison (eds), Charles C. Thomas, Springfield, Ill. pp.390–404

—— 1973 The palaeopathology of bone disease, *Practitioner* 210:384–391

Wells, C. and P. Lawrance 1976 A pathological dolphin, *Medical and Biological Illustration* 26:35–37

—— 1977 A pathological cannon bone of a giant deer cf. *Praemegaceros verticornis* (Dawkins), *Ossa* 3:3–9

Westgarth, W. 1848 *Australia Felix*, London

White, J.P. and J.F. O'Connell 1982 *A Prehistory of Australia, New Guinea and Sahul*, Academic Press, New York

White, T.D. 1978 Early hominid enamel hypoplasia, *American Journal of Physical Anthropology* 49:79–84

Williams, E. 1985 'Wet Underfoot? Earth Mound Sites and the Recent Prehistory of Southwestern Victoria'. Unpublished PhD thesis, Australian National University, Canberra

—— 1988 *Complex Hunter-Gatherers*, BAR International Series 423, Oxford

Williams, H.U. 1929 Human paleo-pathology with some observations on symmetrical osteoporosis, *Archives of Pathology* 7:839–902

—— 1932 The origin and antiquity of syphilis: the evidence from diseased bones, *Archives of Pathology* 13:779–814 and 931–981

Williams, O.B. 1979 Ecosystems of Australia. In *Arid-land ecosystems: structure, functioning and management Vol. 1.*, Goodall, D.W., R.A. Perry and K.M.W. Howes (eds), Cambridge University Press, pp.145–212

Wilson, P.W. and M.S. Mathis 1930 Epidemiology and pathology of yaws. A report based on a study of 1,423 consecutive cases in Haiti, *Journal of the American Medical Association* 94:1289

Wing, E. and A.B. Brown 1980 *Paleonutrition*, Academic Press, New York

Winterbotham, L.P. 1951 Primitive medical art and primitive medicine-men of Australia, *Medical Journal of Australia* 1(13):461–468

Wolff, E. 1954 *The Anatomy of the Eye and Orbit. Including the Central Connections, Development and Comparative Anatomy of the Visual Apparatus*, 4th ed., H.K. Lewis, London

Wolpoff, M.H. 1980 *Paleoanthropology*, A.A. Knopf, New York

Wood, W.B. 1968 An Aboriginal burial ground at Broadbeach Queensland. Skeletal material, *Mankind* 6(12):681–686

—— 1976 The skeletal material from the Brooloo Range and Rocky Hole Creek burial sites, *Archaeology and Physical Anthropology in Oceania* 11(3):175–185

Wood, W.Q. 1920 The tibia of the Australian Aborigine, *Journal of Anatomy* 54:232–257

Woodall, J.N. 1968 Growth arrest lines in long bones of the Casas Grandes population, *Plains Anthropologist* 13:152–160

Worsnop, T. 1897 *The Prehistoric Arts, Manufactures, Works, Weapons etc. of the Aborigines of Australia*, Bristow, Adelaide

Wright, R.V.S. 1976 Evolutionary process and semantics: Australian prehistoric tooth size as a local adjustment. In *The Origin of the Australians*, Kirk, R.L. and A.G. Thorne (eds), Australian Institute of Aboriginal Studies, Canberra pp.265–274

Wunderly, J. 1943 The Keilor skull: anatomical description, *Memoirs of the National Museum of Victoria* 13:57–70

Yamada, H. and T. Brown 1990 Shape components of the maxillary molars in Australian Aboriginals, *American Journal of Physical Anthropology* 82:275–282

Young, T.K. 1979 Changing patterns of health and sickness among the Cree-Ojibwa of northwestern Ontario, *Medical Anthropology* 3:191–224

Zaino, D.E. and E.C. Zaino 1975 Cribra orbitalia in the Aborigines of Hawaii and Australia, *American Journal of Physical Anthropology* 42:91–94

Zimmerman, L.J., Emerson, T., Willey, P., Swegle, M., Gregg, J.B., Gregg, P., White, E., Smith, C., Haberman, T. and M.P. Bumstead 1981 *The Crow Creek Site (29BF11) Massacre*, US Army Corps of Engineers, Omaha District

Zivanovic, S. 1982 *Ancient Diseases*, Methuen, London

Zorab, P.A. 1961 The historical and prehistorical background to ankylosing spondylitis, *Proceedings of the Royal Society of Medicine* 54:415

Index